X-FILES CONFIDENTIAL
The Unauthorized X-Philes
Compendium

TED EDWARDS

X-FILES CONFIDENTIAL

The Unauthorized X-Philes Compendium

LITTLE, BROWN AND COMPANY

Boston   New York   Toronto   London

Library of Congress Cataloging-in-Publication Data
Edwards, Ted.
     X-files confidential : the unauthorized X-philes
compendium / by / Ted Edwards. — 1st ed.
          p.   cm.
     ISBN 0-316-21252-0
     1. X-files (Television program) I. Title.
PN1992.77.X22E38   1996
791.45'72 — dc20   (96-28561)

10 9 8 7 6 5 4 3 2 1

MV-NY

Designed by Barbara Werden and Caroline Hagen

Published simultaneously in Canada by Little, Brown & Company (Canada) Limited

Printed in the United States of America

To Chris Carter and the crew of The X-Files,
*for bringing equal doses of quality
and terror to the tube*

The X-Files

Contents

Foreword
BY JEFF RICE

I'd had it in mind, back when I was a copyboy for the *Las Vegas Sun,* even before I became a reporter for that paper, to write a modern-day vampire novel that would do away with most of the clichés associated with such stories, eliminating the conventions such as people living in dread of the night; the fog that usually appears as "atmosphere"; the instant acceptance by a populace that there *is* a vampire stalking them, and the corresponding response of massed action in knowing just where to look for the vampire and what to do when the vampire is found — a story without the customary isolated settings, torchlit prowlings, and eerie castles.

By the time I was a reporter, I'd also had it in mind to write a novel about Las Vegas, but not about gambling or gamblers per se; one in which the city wasn't just the background setting but an integral part of the tale, a character in itself.

In addition to being a reporter in Las Vegas, I'd also had jobs in advertising and public relations there, and even some private investigative work from time to time.

By the time I started to write the novel, I'd also been a columnist and editorialist for a magazine in Las Vegas, done a few stints as a wire editor, field reporter, and fill-in news-caster for a radio station, and was doing more of the same in Los Angeles. While holding down a job as the copy director for an advertising agency, I also did some work as a reporter and critic for a small newspaper and some part-time investigative work as well.

Somewhere along the line, as I struggled to decide which of the novels to write, it occurred to me that I could combine both into a genre or subgenre of fiction that I didn't think had been tried: a thriller combining the vampire story with a police and political cover-up, all based on what I knew would be the logical bureaucratic response to the situation I could create: a threat not only to life but also to the all-important tourist trade of a city that existed on the strength of it.

In writing *The Kolchak Papers* (which chronicles an adventure in the life of reporter Carl Kolchak), and later rewriting it into *The Night Stalker,* I felt I'd succeeded fairly well at not only entertaining the reader but also showing some things about Las Vegas that didn't make it into the publicity generated by the hotels and casinos and into the feature stories greased by the Chamber of Commerce. Others must have felt that way, too, because it was very quickly picked up as a property to be adapted into a script for a 1971 TV movie, which became the highest-rated TV movie aired to that date and the fourth-highest-rated movie ever broadcast. Certain elements of my approach to the novel, such as the idea of keeping the news of the vampire from the public because it was bad for business, would crop up in later films like *Jaws,* and many of the elements of both the book and movie were so widely imitated following the success of the

"Many of the elements of *The Kolchak Papers* and *The Night Stalker* were so widely imitated . . . that they became and have remained a kind of formulaic approach."

movie that they became and have remained a kind of formulaic approach to such thrillers.

The Night Stalker, its book and TV movie sequel *The Night Strangler,* and the subsequent weekly series came out at a time when the American public was beginning to shake off the relative innocence of the 1950s (and I mean "relative") and the hopes of the brief Camelot era of the 1960s, and settle into the slowly dawning realization that the war in Vietnam and other matters the government said were in the national interest were not quite what they appeared to be. The release of what came to be known as the Pentagon Papers only served to fuel this growing awareness that our government, like any other government, had a double set of books, one for the insiders and one for the people, and their bottom lines didn't jibe.

Reporters were enjoying a period of increased appreciation that would peak for a few years with the near-canonization of Woodward and Bernstein, who nailed the story of the Watergate break-in and what Richard Nixon had really been up to in his near paranoid bid to gain re-election when, in his blindered insecurity, he ordered or allowed things to be done that were totally unnecessary in regard to a campaign he could not possibly have lost.

Kolchak, dealing with "monsters" every week, dealing with various forms of official denials and cover-ups, gave people a chance to root for someone who was, essentially, one of them, an ordinary guy who just kept on digging to get at the facts, to get at the truth, and to lay it out for his readers. Covert government activities — which have been going on since the dawn of governments — and their exposure had made people feel increasingly powerless and cynical, and Kolchak came along at just the right time to give them someone to identify with.

People often talk about the *X-Files* protagonists, Mulder and Scully, picking up the baton of Kolchak, in battling to get at the facts about the matter at hand — whether it be extraterrestrial contact and government involvement or other side issues. And with decades now of periodic revelations of other government cover-ups (most notably Iran-Contra), once again the ordinary citizen can focus on something fictitious yet see all the intense behind-the-scenes workings of agencies and departments and bureaucrats who work to serve their own ends. It's not only entertaining, of course, but it serves as a kind of safety valve for people's emotions, confirming their worst fears about malfeasance and misfeasance in matters more esoteric than skimming a little money from budgets or taking payoffs from lobbyists.

I don't think anyone has done more to foster the idea of picking up where Kolchak left off, at least in a general thematic way, than *X-Files* creator Chris Carter, who has repeatedly credited Kolchak, in his various incarnations from the novels to the TV series, as his inspiration. And his acknowledgments of me and my work are very gratifying.

It has become something of a popular pastime for hardcore genre fans to compare and contrast the series *Kolchak: The Night Stalker* with *The X-Files*, and, to a degree, these efforts are valid. Certainly, they are fun. Kolchak and Mulder and Scully all have to deal with eerie situations and constantly find themselves up against officials at various levels who wish, at the least, that they'd just go away, and who will act, at the most and worst, to discredit or even destroy them. All three protagonists are after the truth.

But Kolchak operates *outside* the system, seeking to dig out facts and expose them to the American public. He rather oddly combines the skepticism and even cynicism of a reporter with the curious open-mindedness of a child who can accept what most adults refute, pro forma; that there are "more things in heaven and earth," as Shakespeare put it, "than are dreamt of in [our] philosophy." He is driven by a reporter's zeal to get the *story*, whatever it is, and lay it out for the public.

Mulder and Scully operate *within* the system, seemingly as an afterthought of some

"Kolchak gave people a chance to root for someone who was, essentially, one of them, an ordinary guy who just kept digging to get at the facts."

department head, trying to tie up loose ends — or dig them out and tie them up — and trying to make their part of the system work *for* the people, rather than against them. But, if one may push their analogous relationship to Kolchak a bit, they bifurcate many of the conflicting aspects of his character. Mulder is the open-minded one, the one who accepts the "infinite possibilities," as Gene Roddenberry characterized them; is fascinated with them, and approaches them eagerly, as a child would. Scully is the skeptic — not a cynic like Kolchak, but very, *very* solidly grounded in the world of hard facts, or science, and in what is known rather than suspected or dreamt-of. They work very well together (and with relatively little and generally productive friction), with Mulder inspiring Scully to take that "one step beyond," while Scully acts as a kind of grounding wire, a check and balance to Mulder's enthusiastic pursuits.

All of them — Kolchak, Mulder, and Scully — are constantly frustrated by official interference in just about every conceivable form, but none of them really ever quit trying to do what they see as their jobs: to get at the truth, whatever it may be.

If *The X-Files* has succeeded in terms of ratings and longevity, where Kolchak did not (at least in its single 1974–75 season as a series), it must be due in part to superior writing, in part to a willingness by Fox to stick by it, and in part due to a much more diverse and fragmented TV marketplace. There were only three networks when *Kolchak: The Night Stalker* was on the air, and very little original dramatic programming being syndicated for "local" TV stations. Today, thanks to the advent of cable broadcasting, there are so many TV venues that it is possible with much lower ratings — relative to all the shows extant—for a series to survive and even to

thrive and become not only a cult classic but a genuine phenomenon. Thus it is with *The X-Files,* and if *Kolchak* is due any credit at all, it may be because it first tapped in to a segment of the viewing audience that was, perhaps, undervalued in its day.

For the most part, *The X-Files'* writing quality has stayed very high, and though some purists (and I am not really quite in that category) may have become slightly disenchanted by the second season, and some of the stories in the third season have appeared to stray a bit from the main plotline of the show, *The X-Files* maintains its overall quality very well. The writers appear to work hard at not becoming too formulaic or predictable within the show's own necessary formula and style, but the bulk of the credit for its continued quality and ongoing success must go to Chris Carter, who is its creator and has kept up a grueling hands-on control since its inception.

Since its inception, I have greatly enjoyed *The X-Files* and consider myself a very definite fan. I try to never miss an episode, because I feel somehow cheated of one of the better things in life when I do, and await the next episode with eager anticipation. (Okay. I need my regular *X-Files* "fix.")

From what I've heard, *The X-Files* has continued to gather to it new viewers, and most viewers of *The X-Files* have (possibly because they have been inspired by the show) sampled, and become regular watchers of, the Sci-Fi Channel's offerings, which, I'm told, have included reruns of episodes of *Kolchak: The Night Stalker*. This brings my series to the attention of a new generation of viewers, which is always gratifying, and gives some of those in my own generation a chance for a second look at it. In regard to other venues, I've heard that *The X-Files* has done well in comic book form for Topps and as novels for HarperCollins.

I think it's become clear, certainly from Chris, that my Kolchak work, to some degree, inspired him to create *The X-Files* and, for my own part, I'm very pleased that he did and very pleased with the ongoing result.

If I may be allowed to express an overall opinion as to the success of *The X-Files*, I'd put it this way: Chris Carter has become, in his own right, the Robert Ludlum of series television. And, thanks to him, the genre of paranoia and conspiracy is alive and well. More power to him.

October 1996

The X-Files

Acknowledgments

This book has its origin in the vast research done by a variety of people who have come together to present an all-encompassing view of *The X-Files*. For their invaluable assistance, I would like to thank Joseph Rugg, Thomas Sanders, Edward Gross, Dexter Frank, Bill Planer, and John Raymond. Special thanks to Albert Ortega for use of his photographic materials. Thanks also to my agent, Laurie Fox, and my editor, Geoff Kloske.

I would also like to offer a very special thanks to Douglas Perry for his vast editorial skills.

the X-Files

An Introduction

Write what you know — that's been the mantra of creative-writing instructors for at least half an eon, and if it's a truism of all good writing, then *X-Files* creator Chris Carter has had a terribly traumatic life. "Good doesn't necessarily win," says Carter, who worked in sitcoms before devising the concept for his Fox network hit. "In fact, it wins a surprisingly paltry amount of the time — and we often try to live in denial of that."

Not anymore. *The X-Files* revels in the power of our darkest impulses; it gets down in the mud and rolls around with them. And we can't stop watching: Carter's stories of evil and violence, using black magic, demons, and aliens to represent very real fears, have turned *The X-Files* from an episodic curio into a cultural phenomenon. Of course, Carter and his writers probably have little firsthand knowledge of toxic monsters from Chernobyl, circus freaks with their siblings growing out of their chests, or rampaging manitous. But they understand that what's important in fantastic stories is the emotional validity of the charac-

ters who are facing those horrors. Then it becomes what writer Joe Haldeman calls "invented truth." And so Carter uses FBI agents Fox Mulder and Dana Scully to ground his show in reality: we see through their eyes, and experience their fear, their confusion, their desperation. Typically, *The X-Files* is described as science fiction, but a more accurate description might be "social-science fiction." It is, after all, fueled by the realities — and internal anxieties — of its time: the era of diminished expectations.

It is that grounding in the psychology of the 1990s that differentiates *The X-Files* from its closet relative, the noir film, which has had a resurgence recently but which, in most cases, is little more than the sum of its double crosses and knifing shadows. *The X-Files,* on the other hand, doesn't merely show us the symptoms of societal disintegration — corruption, hypocrisy, violence, fear — it attacks the cause. It concerns itself with the dark side of technology, competition, politics, ambition, and selfishness; it warns against the risks of abandoning an interior life or one's community. To be sure, it reinforces the notion that our attempts to combat evil are usually an exercise in futility. But Mulder and Scully also give us hope — however Sisyphean — that the effort alone is significant.

PART ONE

The X-Files

Given the skepticism — even condescension — their findings receive within the FBI hierarchy, special agents Fox Mulder and Dana Scully would be justified in feeling that they were blazing new ground with every alien encounter, vampire battle, and monster sighting. But _The X-Files'_ investigators actually are relative latecomers to the paranormal beat, appearing on the scene twenty years after a boozing, burned-out journalist named Carl Kolchak first saw the netherworld where others just saw bizarre crimes in _The Night Stalker_ — a direct progenitor of the later series.

The X-Files, winner of the 1994 Golden Globe Award for best television drama, is a phenomenon so large that it has generated spin-off products, on-line services, and serious talk of a feature film version within the next few years. "It was just one of those ideas that seemed to work on a number of levels," says series creator Chris Carter, recalling his initial concept. "Also, it just seemed like a TV series to me. Lots of stories to tell without having to be self-referencing, without having to rely on going into the lives of the characters. But, basically, I just wanted to do something as scary as I remember _The Night Stalker_ being when I was in my teens."

The Night Stalker is the 1971 TV movie that introduced the character Kolchak (Darren McGavin), a newspaper reporter whose investigation of a series of murders in Las Vegas leads him to a vampire. Due to the popularity of both the film and the character, created by author Jeff Rice, Kolchak returned the following year for another TV movie, _The Night Strangler,_ and then again in 1974 for a short-lived weekly series. In the series, Kolchak relocated to Chicago, where he took on werewolves, mummies, zombies, Indian demons, sewer-roaming creatures, and, of course, aliens.

As inspiration for the character, Rice cites old-time journalists such as Ben Hecht and Charles MacArthur, who wrote the play _The Front Page_ and who, Rice points out, had been hard-nosed reporters themselves in the 1920s, when newspapers were practically the only source of information. But Rice didn't draw solely from the legends of the profession. "Part of the inspiration came from my chief mentor at the _Las Vegas Sun,_ Alan Jarlson," the former journalist recalls. "He was probably one of the last of the generation of those reporters trained in a time when TV had not yet become the be-all, end-all of 'news,' which creates news as often as it reports it. [Kolchak was based in part on] what I saw of him and how he worked—how he reacted not only to news as it developed and he reported and edited it, but also how he handled the sneakier aspects of censorship when he encountered it. And, certainly, part of the inspiration was the projecting I did in my own mind of what I'd be like when I reached the age I am now, if I chose to remain a reporter."

As Rice points out, his effort, originally titled *The Kolchak Papers*, was the first and

"Mulder and Scully are equal parts of my nature," muses Carter.

only one to blend the newsroom and horror-fiction genres. "That wasn't my main consideration when I started the actual drafting," he says. "All I wanted to do was create a 'good read' of the type that I thought I would find entertaining; something for people to use to kill time in airports, on planes, or in hotels when stuck overnight in a strange town. Of course, I also felt I could use the book as a vehicle to say a few serious things about my town — to use it as an intrinsic part of the story rather than as a mere background setting — and to make a few pithy comments about the misuse of power, the latter being an underlying theme in the novel."

An interesting parallel between *The X-Files* and *Kolchak: The Night Stalker* is the employment of opposing emotional and intellectual perspectives about the bizarre things occurring in the story. In short, both shows counterbalance the believer and the skeptic to ground the story in a realistic milieu. On *The Night Stalker*, skeptics surrounded Kolchak

on all sides — except when the monsters had him cornered. On *The X-Files*, the conflict is more personal and less accusatory. Mulder is the believer and Scully is the skeptic.

"Mulder and Scully are equal parts of my nature, I guess," Chris Carter muses. "I'm a natural skeptic, so I have much of the Scully character in me, yet I'm willing to take leaps of faith, to go out on a limb. I love writing both those characters, because their voices are very clear in my head." He does admit, however, that as the series has progressed, Scully's skepticism has been somewhat eroded. "But she is a scientist first and foremost," he says. "What she sees, what is unexplainable, what seems fantastic to her, she believes, truly, can be ultimately explained scientifically. She is a scientist and will always be one, so she maintains a scientific distance from things, whereas Mulder leaps in and wants to believe."

In *The Night Stalker*, Kolchak is the sole believer against a world of skeptics, and it's his battle to get the truth out despite the odds that makes viewers root for him. But while audiences always cheer those who endure ridicule and worse in their fight against conventional wisdom — be it Galileo or the 1969 Mets — that isn't the only source of the show's enduring popularity.

"Maybe its appeal remains because it was

then, and remains now, a very different kind of show," Rice says. "Maybe people see, in the monsters and the way public knowledge and discussion are stopped, symbols for all those things various government entities wish the people not to know about. Maybe people — fans — admire Kolchak because he just keeps on trying to do what he sees as work that has value: trying to keep the public informed about what is going on."

Indeed, it sounds like Rice could be talking about *The X-Files*. But as much as he's a fan of *The Night Stalker*, Carter identified some fundamental misjudgments in the '70s series that he wanted to avoid when creating his own show.

"I saw what the limitations were," he says. "I think having a 'monster of the week' reduced the longevity of the storytelling capabilities. I thought there was a wide world of weird science, paranormal phenomena, and other kinds of stories to tell that were best explored by people who had a reason to explore them, and who actually could effect some outcome. Rather than being limited, as Kolchak was, to just writing about something and trying to convince people what the truth is, it seemed to me it was stronger using FBI agents. There

David Duchovny and Gillian Anderson at the 1994 Golden Globe Awards, where *The X-Files* won for best television drama.

must be somebody out there who responds to all the weird things we read about or hear about, even though the FBI says it doesn't have a so-called X-Files division. But one has to wonder."

In an attempt to expand the narrative format of *The X-Files*, Carter occasionally throws in episodes that have no supernatural threat whatsoever. In season two's "Irresistible," for example, the antagonist is a mortuary worker who likes to cuddle with the clientele, the rigor mortis the better. Looking for new thrills, he begins seeking breathing victims to kill, one intended cadaver being Scully.

"I think it's one of our scarier shows, and I think I was able to explore the character of Scully in a way I wouldn't have been able to with a supernatural theme," Carter says. "Sometimes even more scary than the things we can imagine are the things that are unimaginable, which is that the man standing next to you could be this kind of guy. Sometimes the face of evil can become frighteningly real and distorted through a prism of your own unconscious fears. That's what we were playing with. I thought it worked in its own way. You'll see more stuff like that. I think *The X-Files* works the best when it's closest to being real, and that allows us to go and cast our lines out farther into the supernatural at other times. I think, if anything, we have to keep the show fresh and keep reinventing it, or else it's going to become stale and fall into a 'ghost of the week' format."

Jeff Rice concurs with many of Carter's criticisms of the old *Night Stalker* series, particularly the monster-of-the-week tack.

"What I proposed to ABC lo these many years ago," he says, "was that Kolchak deal with more realistic issues of misfeasance and malfeasance in high office; I wanted to deal with people in power covering things up, things they didn't want made public, things they were dealing with badly or couldn't deal with at all because they didn't understand them. Now, Kolchak was only a reporter. It gave him a certain freedom of thought and mind-set, though it limited his access to everything. Carter has put his protagonists into a position that gives them some access to information and allows them to operate in ways Kolchak never could. And they do manage to have some effect on the outcome of situations, despite interference from those far more powerful, in ways Kolchak never could. Part of the appeal is that they care enough to try, and they do — over and over — and take their lumps for their efforts. My impression is that people like to think somebody gives a damn about the truth and is willing to risk all to get at it."

Mulder and Scully's Kolchak-like search for truth at almost any cost — along with the show's paranormal creepiness and gritty narrative realism — has given *The X-Files* the kind of broad-based popularity Kolchak never quite achieved.

"I feel we've been doing good work all along," Carter says. "Now, with the success, everybody is going to look at us closely. But I don't want the standard to change. I don't want people to expect *T2* [*Terminator 2*] or something like that. We're going to be doing the same good shows we've always done; we're not going to pump them up. I don't feel any reason to try and outperform myself. At the same time, what happens when the spotlight goes on you is that you are considered mainstream. I still think of this as being cultish in its feel, subversive. It worries me that all of a sudden the perception will change. I can guarantee you that the show won't."

One thing that has changed is the silence coming from Kolchak's typewriter, which has begun clacking to life again in a new novel and a forthcoming comic book line from Topps. Additionally, producer–director Dan Curtis (known to older genre fans for the '60s gothic soap opera *Dark Shadows)* is talking about resurrecting the character for either the big screen or TV. The common thread linking all these efforts is that Kolchak will be transplanted from the '70s to the '90s unaged, and he will continue to deal — in his own cynical way — with our fast-changing society.

"His reaction to the present-day situation won't be markedly different from what it was to the 1970s," Rice predicts. "He'll still be cynical (his best armor against the slings and arrows of outrageous fortune), sarcastic (his manifestation of that cynicism), and he'll still

be idealistic enough to keep plugging away at doing what he feels is his job, his calling: protecting the public's right to know what the hell is going on around them, whether or not they even want to know.

"Despite all the tremendous societal changes that occur within each decade," he

> **"When I was sitting in my office in my surf trunks, barefoot . . . writing the pilot for *The X-Files*, I never imagined that they would be making *X-Files* underwear."**

elaborates, "there are still constants: greed, the lust for power, prejudice, and so on. The late H. L. Mencken, a man of incredibly sharp eye and tongue and pen (and not without some damned ugly prejudices of his own), skewered all forms of pretense in his heyday, the 1920s and 1930s. Kolchak will have to be our Mencken for the nineties."

As *The X-Files* continues to see its audience swell, Carter occasionally pauses — awed by what his creation has become. "When I was sitting in my office in my surf trunks, barefoot, playing ball with the dog every twenty minutes, writing the pilot for *The X-Files,* I never imagined that they would be making *X-Files* underwear," he says with a laugh, "and that ten thousand people a week would be logging on to the Internet to talk about the show. You can't imagine that kind of growth or success. It's unreal.

"But the show itself and the stories have grown in ways that have been surprising," Carter says. "You set out to do something, and it's like Lewis and Clark in that you don't know what you're going to encounter. The surprise is in the discovery of where the show has gone and how the people I've hired have brought amazing things to it. Oftentimes, things can never be as good as you imagined them, [but] oftentimes on this show, things are better."

CHAPTER TWO
It's Alive! Creating
The X-Files

The Walt Disney Company bills itself as the happiest place on Earth, where the sun is always shining and smiles are handed out like Chiclets. Not the kind of place you'd expect Fox Mulder to cut his teeth. Or, for that matter, Mulder's alter ego.

"If you look at my résumé," says *X-Files* creator Chris Carter, "you won't find any clear connection between my previous work and *The X-Files*."

Until he became the Fox network's master of creepiness, Carter was a veritable poster boy for Mom, apple pie, and Chevrolet. Born and raised in the blue-collar Southern California town of Bellflower, Carter had what he terms a "fairly normal" childhood made up of Little League baseball and surfing. After graduating from Cal State Long Beach with a degree in journalism, he weighed the pros and cons of his two greatest ambitions — being a beach bum and being a writer — and decided to split the difference.

"I went to work for *Surfing* magazine, which is a big deal — an international magazine," Carter says. "It was really to postpone my growing up, and those were the best years of my life. I ended up working for them for thirteen years and was listed as senior editor when I was twenty-eight. So I went around

the world, surfing, and I got to write. I wrote constantly. I learned how to run a business. It was a wonderful, adventurous time. I did many other things, too. I was a potter during those times."

A what?

"Yes," he says with a laugh, "I did all those California cliché things. I actually made hundreds of thousands of pieces of pottery. I sat and made dinnerware. I threw most of it away because I got tired of looking at it, but I hope to do that again someday. It was wonderful, repetitious. There's a certain Zen thing that goes on when you make something with your hands, over and over."

Carter attributes his "settling down" to his wife, Dori Pierson, whom he met in 1983. It was Pierson who encouraged him to find something to be passionate about besides surfing, and suggested screenwriting. His first efforts were strong enough to attract the attention of then–Disney executive Jeffrey Katzenberg, who signed him to a multipicture deal. As a result, he wrote the TV movies *B.R.A.T. Patrol* and *Meet the Munceys*.

"When I went to Disney," Carter explains, "I actually became known as a comedy writer. So that was what people thought of me as: a person who had a certain handle on the voice of contemporary youth and the comedic voice. That's what people kept wanting me to write. I like that type of writing very much, and I think I can do it. But *The X-Files* really is more where my heart is: in scary, dramatic, thriller writing."

But it would take several years before he had the opportunity to prove it. While at Disney, Carter met with then–NBC president Brandon Tartikoff, who brought him to the network. There he wrote and produced a number of pilots, including *Cameo by Night*, a detective show starring *Sisters'* Sela Ward, and a sitcom called *A Brand New Life*, which was supposed to have been a modern take on *The Brady Bunch*. Carter followed that by producing the musical comedy series *Rags to*

"Sometimes the *Night Stalker* influence is overstated," explains Carter.

Riches, which starred veteran actor Joseph Bologna. "Basically, I took the job on *Rags to Riches* to learn how to produce television," he admits. "It was a terrific opportunity to do that. And I got to learn physical production."

Carter wrote and produced a Disney Channel pilot called *The Nanny* before drawing the attention of Stephen J. Cannell Productions president Peter Roth, who read and enjoyed Carter's script for *Cool Culture*, based on the writer's experiences working for *Surfing* magazine. Although the script was never purchased, Roth planned on utilizing Carter for the CBS series *Palace Guard*. But

when the executive shifted over to Fox as head of TV production in 1993, he hired Carter, along with several other producers, to develop programming. At that point, Carter began to nurture his idea for a series that would tap in to his childhood memories of *The Night Stalker* and *The Twilight Zone*.

"Sometimes the *Night Stalker* influence is overstated," Carter explains. "Somebody asked me in what way it inspired me and I said, 'I think I remember two scenes from the old show. One where Darren McGavin is confronted by a vampire and is able to drive a stake into his heart, and the other is in an alleyway.' I just remember being scared out of my wits by that show as a kid, and I realized that there just wasn't anything scary now on television. The inspiration is general rather than specific."

He also points out a distinction between *The X-Files* and Rod Serling's *Twilight Zone* that he feels is too often overlooked. "Rod Serling was telling fables, almost allegorically. You see a lot of that in *The X-Files*, too, but each of the episodes of *The Twilight Zone* had a bigger message, a bigger purpose, and that was to illuminate something about the human comedy. We don't set out to do that; we don't set out to be instructive — there's no message behind each *X-Files* episode. Although there is something you can take from it, we're not teaching."

Beyond the influence of *The Night Stalker* and *The Twilight Zone*, *The X-Files* began to take solid form in Carter's mind thanks to an old friend who was familiar with the work of Dr. John Mack of Harvard. "Mack, who has become famous in UFO circles, surveyed a big cross-section of American citizens and found that three percent of Americans believe they've actually been abducted by UFOs," Carter says. "That means if there are one hundred people in a room, three of them have actually been abducted, or believe they have. And this psychologist friend of mine, whose specialization is schizophrenia, told me that — and this is a sane, credible, believable person —he's looked into people's eyes and he's seen, whether it be multiple personalities or the schizophrenic himself, what he feels is not human. So he believes in the alien abduction syndrome, or in alien abduction. I thought that was a great leaping-off point for the series."

But this was going to be somewhat different from the typical alien premise. Carter decided to ground the show in reality by offering a counterpoint to the mysterious paranor-

The surfer dude is actually Chris Carter, creator and executive producer of television's most frightening series, *The X-Files*.

mal happenings: that is, Scully's scientific skepticism. Mulder, who believes his sister was abducted by extraterrestrials, is obsessed with proving the existence of ETs. But Scully, originally assigned to partner with Mulder to

The X-Hoax

Like many a television series, *The X-Files* went through some changes between conception and hitting the airwaves. When the show was first presented to the press, series creator Chris Carter announced an idea that in fact never came to pass

"One character is a skeptic and one is a believer," he said. "The skeptic is going to be right as much as the believer is. They'll uncover hoaxes. There will be, indeed, more traditional FBI cases that involve what seem to be paranormal phenomena and we'll have evidence and MOs that seem otherworldly, if you will. But they won't always be alien abduction. Or it may turn out to be someone, as I say, perpetrating a hoax. I'd say about half the time these are going to play out as either hoaxes or traditional cases that appear to have paranormal aspects to them. Oftentimes you'll end up with a crook in handcuffs."

In the series's first three seasons, there was only one episode ("Jose Chung's *From Outer Space*") that could possibly be interpreted as a hoax.

debunk his theories, finds more prosaic explanations for the cases they encounter.

❊ ❊ ❊

As originally conceived, the show wasn't so much *The Night Stalker* as, uh, *The Avengers*.

"I loved that show," Carter says of the classic '60s series starring Patrick Macnee and Diana Rigg. "I loved that relationship between Steed and Emma Peel, the intensity of the stories. It's the way I sort of instinctively write, so that has also fed in to my ultimate concept of the show. The character of Mulder came first, because he was the key to the series in that he was the person who wanted to believe. You need that before you can move ahead. Then Scully as his opposite. It's the nature of any interesting relationship. When someone forces you to justify what you believe in, you take that person more seriously and, in turn, that person really turns you into a better, clearer thinker, which is what Scully does for Mulder. I always felt that the show was from Scully's point of view. We would cut to her reaction to what Mulder was saying. She was the one who would pull Mulder back and say, 'Look what you're doing; look what you're saying.'"

And from the very beginning Carter has been adamant about one thing: Mulder and Scully — despite a tantalizing bedroom pictorial in *Rolling Stone* — will *not* be sweating up the sheets together. "I think a little sexual tension goes a long way," he says, "and I think the thing that makes this show unconventional in that way is that we're not going to have the characters jump into the sack for sweeps. The fact that their relationship is a cerebral one, first and foremost, actually is more interesting for me to write. I also think it'll carry us a long way, and it makes the show an interesting one because it is a suspense–mystery genre show. It's allowed us to play the stories rather than these characters' love lives. So it will never be *Moonlighting.* But with men and women, there is, whether by society's projection or by our natural biological projections on these things, a sexual tension between the two. I've always said that the best kind of sexual tension for me is when you put a smart man and a smart woman in a room. You've got immediate sexual tension, no matter if it's romantic."

❋ ❋ ❋

Creating credibility was the chief mandate from the start. "To make the show convincing, you do have to make it believable. I felt that the characters and the investigative process had to be really believable, so I set out to do just that. Credible, believable characters and credible, believable situations dealing with

incredible and unexplainable phenomena. I did as much research as I could through the FBI, and they were rather reluctant then. It was a limited resource. But I did research on all the things that I was writing about —

Carter decided to ground the show in reality by offering a counterpoint to the mysterious paranormal happenings: that is, Scully's scientific skepticism.

aliens, UFOs, and the FBI — just by reading about it."

Producer–director Daniel Sackheim, who took home the 1994 Best Directing Emmy for his work on *NYPD Blue* and who also produced the *X-Files* pilot, worked closely with Carter throughout the development of the series. "Chris wanted to do something that was scary and that felt real, and that's what attracted me to the project," Sackheim says. "In the initial stages, we had talked about two projects as stylistic sources, one of which was *The Thin Blue Line,* a documentary about a cop-killing in Texas back in 1976. The result of the documentary was that the case was reopened and the man convicted of the crime was found innocent by virtue of the material and evidence presented in the documentary, and the man who had identified him as the killer turned out to have actually committed the crime. It was an unusual film because it was the first of its kind to ever be presented in an intensely stylized fashion, with much emphasis being on the evidence produced: the letters being typed on a report or a piece of evidence being dropped on the street.

"To be fair," Sackheim continues, "Chris came up with the concept of the show, he wrote it, he really deserves all the credit for it, but I guess he was looking for someone to help him execute it — and that's where sources like *The Thin Blue Line* came in. We had also talked about the realism of something like *Prime Suspect,* which was the miniseries on PBS with Helen Mirren. There was much discussion of sort of mining the style for the show, but the reality is that *The X-Files* has sort of found its own style in that it doesn't have a confined style to it. Everybody who comes on the show attempts to make a little scary movie. I think it's a testament to the uniqueness of the show, unlike something like *NYPD Blue,* which is more rigid in its format. The *X-Files* style is distinctive and yet it is also fluid."

Sackheim admits he doubted the show could prosper for long, considering the inherent limitations of the character arcs of Scully as a doubting Thomas and Mulder as the believer, because every week Scully is exposed to situations that in all likelihood would make her a believer.

"Yet they manage to offer the appropriate point of view," he adds. "I think Chris is really smart in that he had a well-thought-out plan. He had a game plan going into the pilot and he knew where he would be halfway through year one, at the end of year one, halfway through year two, the end of year two, and the beginning of year three. He had a plan in his mind as to how it would develop and how the characters would develop. There was sort of an internal bible worked out. He said it to me when we were doing the pilot: 'The reason most series fail is that nobody has a long view of where the show is going to go,' and he felt that he did."

Carter himself believes humbly that the show's success has as much to do with viewers' fascination with UFOs as it does with the creativity of the show itself.

"The idea that there are visitors to the planet, that they are not only visiting now but have been visiting since prehistory, and how it affects us is a very interesting idea," he muses. "I suppose just looking up into the night sky at all those millions of stars up there, you wonder if it's possible. I have a pet theory that everyone wants to have that experience where they're driving through the desert at night, and they see something and can't explain what it is. I think it's all about religion. Not necessarily Christian religion, but it's about beliefs — and meaning and truth and why are we here and why are they here and who's lying to us. It's religion with a lowercase 'r.'

Encountering a UFO would be like witnessing a miracle."

The true miracle was that the show got on the air at all. The Fox executives were, to say the least, nervous about a show that explored the paranormal and UFOs, a premise that had a spotty track record on TV. They also wondered whether such a show — which Carter was selling to them as inspired (however minimally) by real-life events — could compete with such network stalwarts as *Unsolved Mysteries* and *Cops*. As Carter noted in the pages of the show's official companion, "Everyone thought this has got to be as real as possible. No one could understand why someone would want to watch a show if it weren't true."

The pilot script was delivered around Christmas 1992, and Carter was given the go-ahead for production. Robert Mandel, who had helmed the cult favorite *F/X* among other films, was hired to direct, with Sackheim serving as producer. The premiere episode had Mulder and Scully investigating a series of supposed abductions which, despite her best efforts, Scully cannot completely explain away scientifically.

Fox was willing to give this upstart Carter a chance to justify the kudos Roth was heaping

on him, but it really had little faith in the *X-Files* concept. The network was convinced that another quasi-fantastic series, the Sam Raimi–produced *Adventures of Brisco County, Jr.*, would be their fall hit, and that *The X-Files* would last maybe half a season. But when the 1993–94 season began, it quickly became obvious that there was little audience interest in *Brisco*, while the core demographics, if not the initial ratings, for *The X-Files* were exceptionally promising. Vindication was Carter's, and he shares it enthusiastically with the crew that brings the show to life each week.

"People feel very invested in the show and they're proud to work on it," Carter enthuses. "My feeling is that most things fail in this business, and the powers that be always proceed as if what you're going to do is going to fail; they're always hedging. So we went boldly forward and showed them we knew what we were doing, what kind of stories we were telling, that we could tell them well. I think that boldness translated into a winning team. I'm sounding like a coach now, but in many ways it is like putting together a good team of people. And this is the best team you could hope for."

The X-Files

CHAPTER THREE
Two of a Kind: David Duchovny and Gillian Anderson

"It's weird," muses David Duchovny, who plays FBI agent Fox Mulder. "To me, *The X-Files* is like a wave and I'm on top of it looking down. And right now it's a *biiiiig* wave, so sometimes it's scary. I feel I've got ten more years of playing the guy. When I'm forty-five, I'll start thinking about what else I want to do."

Duchovny sometimes wishes he wasn't involved at all.

The ambitious Duchovny, who's starring in the feature *Playing God,* wasn't always so enthusiastic about an extended run as the obsessive G-man who warily sports the nickname "Spooky." "When you're trying to envision the career that you want to have — especially before your [career] has really taken a turn into reality and you're just living in possibility — you have everybody's career," he says. "You do all the parts. So there's a certain disappointment when your life becomes just one part."

That disappointment has been alleviated recently not only by the opportunity to pursue other roles during *The X-Files'* summer break but also by a whopping $100,000 paycheck for each episode and greater creative involvement in the show. "Being offered the chance to submit storylines and to direct — it reminds me of playing with my dog," Duchovny says. "I'll give him a choice between a tennis ball and a Frisbee: whatever it takes to keep him involved."

And yet, Duchovny sometimes wishes he wasn't involved at all. Though the Ivy League–educated actor understood at the beginning of his career that fame was the price of success in the performing arts, he still wasn't prepared when his star went supernova.

"Privacy is something I have come to respect," he says. "And ultimately, you also come to realize that you're being appreciated for something that doesn't have that much to do with you. So it's not satisfying. It's perfume. Nothing goes inside. [The fame] doesn't give you anything deep or meaningful. You get Knicks tickets — that's about it. Being on TV and having so many people see you makes you self-conscious enough as it is. So there are two things I don't want to do in my spare time: One is talk about *The X-Files* and the other is to think about how people are perceiving me."

Gillian Anderson, who plays Mulder's partner Dana Scully, echoes her co-star.

"I think that with any success, there is a bittersweet quality to it," she offers. "In order to produce the quality of show that we're producing, everybody who's involved has to do an incredible amount of work. Especially with all the attention we've received, the Golden Globe award, and the snowball effect that's going on. It [creates] a lot of pressure to keep doing more and to keep doing better. At the same time, we're working and we're on a quality show, and it can be incredibly enjoyable sometimes. It depends on the day, and the hour, and the mood. I wouldn't wish it on anybody, but it's also the most wonderful thing to have the opportunity."

Viewing the *X-Files* phenomenon from the inside, Anderson has developed her own ideas about the show's success.

"The series deals with many aspects of the paranormal, and one of the aspects is the spiritual one," she says. "That's very appealing to people. I'm less sure about what intrigues people about the horror side of it, because that never appealed to me. But on a spiritual level, some of the episodes deal with the possibility of coming back to life or some sort of spiritual awakening. And that offers hope, some way out of the fear and the pain of everyday life on this planet."

Duchovny concurs, adding: "I think *The X-Files* is very nineties, because everything is left in doubt. There's no closure, no answers. Most of the credit goes to Chris Carter. . . . Obviously, it's tapping in to something the nation wants. I think it has to do with religious

David Duchovny in an uncharacteristically giddy mood, which fans of the X-*Files* aren't used to seeing.

stirrings — a sort of New Age yearning for an alternate reality and the search for some kind of extrasensory god. Couple that with a cynical, jaded, dispossessed feeling of having been lied to by the government, and you've got a pretty powerful combination for a TV show.

Gillian Anderson, probably not used to the attention, smiles nervously for the paparazzi.

and excellent production values offered by Carter's behind-the-scenes pros, *The X-Files* probably wouldn't be the monumental success it is today if the lead roles had gone to, say, Patrick Duffy and Heather Locklear.

"At first, I cast the roles separately," says Carter. "We cast David and then we cast Gillian. So they did have a chance to go into a room together and act together. And I saw the chemistry immediately, which is unusual. I said, 'These are our two people.' Honestly, I think you just get lucky with the chemistry. And I'm lucky to work with them, too, because they're both smart and good people. Both personally and professionally, we lucked out in getting the chemistry we did."

✿ ✿ ✿

Either that, or the Fox network has an *amazing* marketing department."

Fox's amazing marketing execs were no doubt aided in their task by Carter's casting of Duchovny and Anderson, who immediately clicked as a team. Screen chemistry is a nebulous, hard-to-predict quality, and the two leads of a weekly series must have it for the show to work. Even with the top-notch writing

Born and raised in Manhattan, Duchovny attended a boys' prep school in the city, where he excelled both in the classroom and on the playing field. After finishing up his secondary education with honors, he enrolled at Princeton University, where he played on the baseball and basketball teams. Next came Yale University, where he earned a master's degree in English literature while serving as a teaching assistant. But his march toward a life of rigorous academic study and tenured ease came abruptly to a halt in the mid-1980s, when an actor friend convinced him to try out for a Löwenbräu beer commercial. He landed the part and found his passion. In his case, the acting bug turned out to be a leech — he soon abandoned his PhD program and moved back to New York City, where he scored a few Off Broadway roles and bit parts in such films as *Working Girl, New Year's Day,* and *Beethoven.* Then came his breakthrough: playing a transvestite FBI agent in the David Lynch series *Twin Peaks.* For Duchovny, it was a significant experience beyond the career repercussions. People on the crew, he says dolefully, actually laughed at him. "The interesting thing is it hurt my feelings," he admits. "I have been lucky — or unlucky — enough to be an accepted human being. I'm white, I'm male, I'm straight. But now I know the constraints women feel when they dress, and what it's like to be ridiculed for being gay by unfeeling men. And on top of all that, my vanity kicked in. I felt so unattractive."

With *Twin Peaks* providing something meaty to put on his curriculum vitae, his career really started to move. He starred in Zalman King's sexy anthology series *The Red Shoe Diaries* on Showtime, and landed roles in the feature films *The Rapture, Julia Has Two Lovers,* and *Chaplin.* Then Chris Carter came into his life, though Duchovny didn't think he'd get much of a chance to become acquainted. "I thought I could go to Vancouver for a month and get paid, and then go on and do my next movie. After all, a show about extraterrestrials — no matter how well made — how many can you do? I didn't see the show opening up to be about *anything* that's unexplained, which is limitless."

Carter, for his part, had greater faith in Duchovny than the actor had in Carter's show. "David read for the part and was perfect," the

"*The X-Files* is very nineties, because everything is left in doubt. There's no closure, no answers."

X-Files creator says. "We were obligated to give the network a choice of at least two actors, but we knew David was it from the start. He was just very, very right for the role."

Daniel Sackheim, who produced the pilot and directed three episodes, reflects: "I remember the first time we screened the pilot. Everybody thought David was a movie star. I think he offered a certain sense of vulnerability. He was handsome, but he was sort of like the boy next door. He was the brother that you wanted to comfort. That was the quality David brought that we were excited about."

✻ ✻ ✻

David Duchovny and Gillian Anderson attend an X-Files event at the Museum of Television and Radio.

School in Chicago and impressed the school's admissions committee with her raw talent. Her stage work at the university attracted the attention of the William Morris talent agency, which took her on as a client with the provision that she relocate to New York City. She did so, and while working as a waitress she landed the lead in the Off Broadway show *Absent Friends*, which won her a Theater World award. Roles in a production of *The Philanthropist* in New Haven, Connecticut, and in the feature film *The Turning* quickly followed. Then, in 1993, the then-twenty-five-year-old read the pilot script for *The X-Files* and auditioned the next day.

"It's very interesting," Anderson says, "because I remember exactly where I was when I read the script. I was enthralled by it. It was very different from anything I'd read, and certainly the character of Dana Scully was incredibly appealing to me. I had a very distinct feeling that the show would be a part of my life when I read it, even though in the process of going to the auditions, which took about a week and a half, there was certainly nervousness, fear, and questioning of my ability to land the role. I nonetheless still had a very strong feeling that it was going to be a part of my life."

She wasn't the only one. "When she came into the room, I just knew that she was Scully," says Carter. "She had an intensity

The road to fame for Gillian Anderson was more direct. An indifferent student in high school and given to punk-rock dress and attitudes, the rebellious, spiky-haired teen found the theater to be a sanctuary of sorts. After graduating from public school in Grand Rapids, Michigan, she auditioned for DePaul University's prestigious Goodman Theater

about her, the kind of intensity that translates well across the screen."

The network's execs, however, still had some trouble with the interpretation. After viewing Anderson's filmed audition, Fox's honchos were nonplussed. She wasn't the bouncy, former-model type that typically fit into the second lead, they told Carter. Of course, they were right.

"Gillian is an attractive woman," says Daniel Sackheim, "but she is not what one would call a sex queen. She's not the classic sex symbol type — tall, blonde, big-breasted — you know, the kind of woman networks love to put in those kinds of roles. What appealed to me was Chris's desire to cast the role real, as opposed to casting it in the traditional way networks cast, which is to skew it to a certain level of sex appeal. Chris didn't want to do that, and that's one of the things that drew me into the project."

"When she came into the room, I just knew that she was Scully."

In the end, the network relented, and Carter got his Scully.

"I sort of staked my pilot and my career at the time on Gillian." Carter smiles. "I feel vindicated every day now."

PART TWO

The X-Files

CHAPTER FOUR
The Beginning: A
Season in Hell

The only thing we have to fear, said Franklin Roosevelt, is fear itself.

Our thirty-second president must not have gone to the movies very often. If he had, he would have known that there were horrors far darker than self-doubt and pessimism. There were vampires and giant gorillas and zombies and swamp creatures. And they all wanted to kill you in the most gruesome fashion imaginable.

From the medium's beginnings at the turn of the century, filmmakers have exploited our fascination with fear, using horrific creatures to represent everyday terrors. In 1910, when film was still just a hobby for geek tinkerers, Thomas Edison created a silent short of Mary Shelley's *Frankenstein*. And the manipulation of our fears has steadily gained in variety and sophistication since. In the 1930s and '40s, audiences were introduced to a multitude of monsters, most notably Bela Lugosi's Dracula, who flitted through a long series of successful films — even an Abbott and Costello comedy. In the '50s, the studios put Dracula on hold to make way for alien invaders, a threat more applicable to the Cold War era.

In the traditional horror film of the Red Scare years, the supernatural threat ultimately becomes known to the community at large, which rallies together — and around the flag — to put a stop to it. But as the Soviet menace receded (psychologically, if not tangibly), we became more concerned about the momentum of our own society, a technological behemoth that we feared alienated, or simply disposed of, individuals. Its antennae tuned to this shift, the horror genre became more internalized, examining the dark side of the soul and the consequences of moral decay. The result, at its best, was films like *Rosemary's Baby*, *The Omen*, and *The Exorcist*. And it's here, beginning with *The Invaders* and *The Night Stalker* in the late '60s and early '70s, that television began to outpace its big-screen parent.

Considerable influences on films and TV shows of this bent were the Vietnam War and the Watergate scandal. Trafficking in the public's loss of confidence in its representatives, films like *Three Days of the Condor* obliterat-

> **Most television fare is just eye candy, whereas *The X-Files* is "an intellectual exercise."**

Shooting in Vancouver

Throughout its production history, *The X-Files* has appeared to be taking place in various locations throughout the world, but in fact all of it has been shot in Vancouver.

"The drawback is that I'm sitting in Los Angeles right now while they're shooting up there and I can't walk over to the stage to make changes and tweaks," Chris Carter explains. "The quality control suffers, so you hope you get what I have right now, which is Bob Goodwin, who has similar sensibilities to me. He does a great job up there. But there's a communication problem, first of all, by the very nature of the distance between us. There is a problem with weather — you get a lot of rain up there. If you want to shoot a day-for-day scene outside, chances are you're going to be doing it in the rain, and chances are you've got between the hours of nine and three to do it. The sun never gets too high in the sky. The opposite is true in the summer. You don't get much darkness. It gets dark like eleven at night and gets light at about four in the morning. Those are the hours you have to work if you want to get night scenes. Those are some of the drawbacks.

"On the positive side," he adds, "there are financial benefits. Obviously the exchange rate is something that works to our benefit, saving us twenty percent on the dollar. You can't argue the economics of going to Canada with a show like this, a two-lead show. More importantly, Vancouver turned out to be a very multipurpose city. It can double as almost anywhere in the U.S. There are only a few limitations. You can't do big desert scenes. So as far as the location, it's ideal and is a pretty negotiable city. Plus, there aren't any traffic jams to deal with."

ed the line between horror and realism. As public cynicism only grew in the following years, *The X-Files* almost seems inevitable.

Which is not to say it was easy to get the show on the air. Chris Carter brought a fresh, even radical, approach to supernatural horror, and TV executives embrace change with about as much enthusiasm as Russian pensioners do. But for the creative talent, it was a dream come true.

"Working on *The X-Files* was a relief," says writer Glen Morgan. "Jim Wong [Morgan's longtime writing collaborator] and I worked at Cannell Productions for so long on shows such as *21 Jump Street* and *The Commish,* and we were looking to move on. But then we sat down and watched the pilot for *The X-Files* and said, 'Wow.'"

Adds Wong, "In some ways, Glen and I have always liked suspense and the darker side of life. When we watched the pilot we said, 'You know, there are so many ideas that come to mind when you think about *The X-Files* versus anything else out there.' That's what appealed to us."

Once he had Morgan and Wong in the fold, Carter recruited Howard Gordon and Alex Gansa, best known to genre fans for their work on *Beauty and the Beast.* "I loved *Star Trek,* but I was not a hardcore SF fan," Gordon admits. "Except for films like *The Exorcist,* I wasn't a horror film fan. I didn't dislike it, but it certainly wasn't something that I'd ever given much thought to. Alex and

I found ourselves baffled and, frankly, a little bit out of our depth at first. We were more inclined towards straight-ahead dramas. We struggled mightily with our first script for the show. I didn't think the show was a perfect fit, but I was glad for the opportunity. I've often described it as feeling like I'm a miler being asked to do sprints. It's not really my event, but I've developed certain muscles that have enabled me to survive and thrive."

Filling out the core staff for the series's launch were co–executive producer Robert Goodwin, who was given the assignment of overseeing the physical production of every episode; director of photography John Bartley; special-effects pro Mat Beck; composer Mark Snow; co-producer Paul Rabwin; production designer Graeme Murray, a veteran of TV's *Wiseguy* and the feature films *Never Cry Wolf* and John Carpenter's remake of *The Thing;* and makeup artist Toby Lindala. Together, they crafted a new style of television storytelling.

"There are a lot of people involved in the production of the episodes," Carter says. "It's music, it's lighting, it's photography, it's production design and scripts, and, of course, the actors. My relationship with each of those people is very tight, and we work very closely

together. This is a rare case, I think, where when you give them the scripts, they come up with ideas to make them better. Everyone's stock rises with success, and so what usually happens is people want to take their stock and trade it up, and everybody wants to do something different or better, or maybe even a feature. Everybody thinks that features are the big thing. But I think we're doing feature-quality work on the TV show, week in and week out, and that's the reason that these people have stayed: it's an opportunity to consistently do good work.

"One-hour episodic drama is the hardest show in town," he continues. "Beyond that, when you have shows that succeed in the format — *Hill Street Blues, L.A. Law, Picket Fences* — they're usually ensembles, so you've got a lot of people to carry the workload. They're done as interiors on standing sets inside buildings. We are really doing a little movie each week. We are out usually about five or six of the eight days we're shooting; we can't go back to standing sets. This all takes a lot of intensive production attention. We have two characters who have to carry most of the workload. And we're all laboring to make it real for the audience."

That commitment to realism within a supernatural premise is what attracted director David Nutter to the series. "The key to the drama is making everything as real as possible," says Nutter, who directed the pilot episode of Carter's new series, *Millennium*. "To do this, you really have to get the characters' emotions and the environment of the story just right. You also have to get into the hearts and minds of people — not only those who are putting the show together, but the people who are at home, watching. I looked at the show as a strong, realistic drama. If the audience believed it and could relate to it, you could then turn it on its head and do the things that make the show what it is. That's

the key: to get the audience to go along for the ride. It's like locking them in to a seat of the roller coaster. Once you've done that, you've got them."

Michael Lange, who directed a pair of episodes during the first season, offers the opinion that most television fare is just eye candy, whereas *The X-Files* is "an intellectual exercise."

"I remember when I first started watching the show, which was before I even got an assignment to direct one, my first impression was that these were true stories taken from the deep files of the FBI," he says. "And I'm a fairly sophisticated viewer. And with the subjects it deals with, you can, for the most part, accept that maybe this *could happen.* One of my favorite Hitchcockisms is his saying that he didn't believe films had to be believable, merely plausible. That's the same thing with *The X-Files.*"

And the two people most responsible for making it plausible aren't the writers or directors, but David Duchovny and Gillian Anderson. The give-and-take between their characters provides the series with its analytical and moral code. Duchovny's Fox Mulder is the primary champion of the FBI's X-Files; he's obsessed with paranormal investigations. Anderson's Scully, a doctor and forensics expert, is assigned to the X-Files to temper Mulder's enthusiasms. It is the emotional reality of their characters that lets the audience accept the bizarre happenings. No other

Attracting Opposites

On *The X-Files*, Fox Mulder (David Duchovny) believes in UFOs and the paranormal, while his FBI partner, Dana Scully (Gillian Anderson), is a skeptic. But the actors who play Mulder and Scully see things differently from the way their characters do.

"Personally," Duchovny says, "I'm the kind of person who needs to be shown something before I can believe it, and I haven't had any personal experiences with UFOs. But, on the other hand, it's hard for me to believe that we're the only sentient life in this universe. I think there's got to be something else out there. I just don't know why they always seem to choose people in North Dakota. So I'm waiting.

"I guess I believe in the abstract, but not in the specific," he continues. "You know, if you ask me if I believe that the things we do on the show are possible, I say yes. But if you ask me if I believe that they actually have happened, I say no. *The X-Files* aims at a point where physics and metaphysics meet; where science and poetry come together. We take the real world and put imagined things in it. We're not science fiction and we're not cops and robbers. We have one foot in each."

Unlike Duchovny, Anderson is something of a believer. "I think the more I get comfortable with this character, the more she's becoming like me in some of her mannerisms," the actress says of Dana Scully. "But I am not that much of a skeptic. I do believe in UFOs, I do believe in certain paranormal phenomena like ESP and psychokinesis. In that respect, I think I'm different from Scully. I think I have a tendency to get as single-minded and obsessed with my work as Scully does, but in a different way. She's a medical doctor and an FBI agent, and I'm an actress. But the paranormal is something that I've always been fascinated with, and I think on a certain level, I've always just known or assumed it to be a reality."

One of the most hotly debated questions on the Internet these days is whether or not Fox Mulder and Dana Scully should — to quote Maddie and David in *Moonlighting* — "get horizontal." Despite the cover of *Rolling Stone*, which seems to say the opposite, Chris Carter emphasizes that it will never happen. "That's David and Gillian in bed, *not* Mulder and Scully," says Carter, regarding the *RS* cover.

series traffics so subversively in the unexpected, but Mulder and Scully make it all seem like just another day at the office.

Considering that the *X-Files* budget is significantly lower than that for such genre fare as *Lois & Clark* and the now defunct *seaQuest,* Robert Goodwin is amazed that the show is able to achieve all that it does. "I feel, with some pride, that what we're delivering is the best-quality television you can get. We don't skimp; we just find a way to do what we want within our budget. The first year, I almost had a nervous collapse every time I got a new script: 'Okay,' I would say to myself, 'here's a good one: This guy can relocate all the bones in his body and slither through tiny air vents and suck people's livers out of their bodies. Great. How do we do that?' Every episode there's something that's really amazingly challenging to create. From great fires to worms wriggling under the skin of people."

After an episode is shot, co-producer Paul Rabwin steps in and supervises all aspects of postproduction. "Many things that I do have to be done during the preproduction stage when, for example, there are television screens that have to be photographed. The film that is being projected on the TV screen has got to be processed so that it can be rephotographed by a camera. In one episode we have our guys watching film supposedly from the 1950s showing DDT being sprayed over kids in a swimming pool. I have to find and obtain the material, have it transferred in

In Praise of The Night Stalker

Not to belabor the point, but at this juncture it's pretty obvious that Chris Carter was inspired by night-stalking reporter Carl Kolchak to create *The X-Files*. The love affair doesn't stop at the top, however.

Although *The X-Files* is quite different from *The Night Stalker*, there are undeniable similarities between the experiences of agents Mulder and Scully and those of the journalist Kolchak.

"I recently saw *The Night Stalker* for the first time since the early seventies," says Glen Morgan, who has co-written many *X-Files* episodes, "and I was surprised how much we are similar to it. In the TV movie, they find a girl in a river of sand. Everyone else is stumped, and Kolchak is saying, 'There are no footprints. And all her blood is gone.' He's raising all these weird questions. That's what Mulder would do. I guess that type of show was long overdue. There was a hole in TV that needed to be filled."

Adds Morgan's writing partner James Wong, "I just remember watching *The Night Stalker* as a kid and being so scared. So it's great to be doing *The X-Files* as an adult, and to really be conscious of what we're doing: trying to scare a new generation."

such a way that it can be rephotographed, and have it sent back up there in time for them to shoot the scene. So there are certain areas that are considered postproduction which actually happen prior to the filming taking place."

The bulk of Rabwin's work involves editing, music, sound effects, and special optical effects. Terming himself a "general overseer" of these areas, he notes that specific experts work in each of those departments.

"We have three editors who work in rotation," he explains. ""One would get all of the film on one episode and will spend three or four weeks working on it, then he finishes that and starts working on another. The three of them rotate. The editor works in conjunction with the director and the producers of the series, all of whom have a say in what will make the show better. Sometimes a show will be several minutes longer than network requirements, and we have to edit material out. On a rare occasion we have a show that actually comes in a little on the short side and we have to come up with creative ways to lengthen it.

"Generally, the main focus during the editing process is to get the show to work well, to make it interesting, to make it flow, to make it entertaining, and to drop a bombshell at the magic moment at the end of the act so that people will come back after the commercials."

One particularly difficult aspect of each episode of *The X-Files* is the use of special optical effects, supplied by Mat Beck during postproduction. "Those require a certain amount of time, and very often we need to have the film edited before we can start making the effects," Rabwin notes, "because with special effects very often you're paying for the amount of time spent in a particular kind of edit bay, where each frame has to be artistically rendered. You want to be as specific as possible as to where the special effects have to be. You can't just say, 'Let's just treat the entire scene and we'll just cut it.' You have to say, 'There are exactly three and a half seconds of this particular scene that needs to have this special effect.' If you made it four seconds, it could cost you another thousand dollars for that extra half second. So you need to have the show edited fairly substantially before you can begin many of the special effects.

"On a television schedule," he elaborates, "they're shooting eight working days, which is ten calendar days, but we're on the air every seven days. Eventually the law of averages catches up with you. As you get deeper into the season, you get closer and closer to the airdates from the time you finish shooting. The show is on the air Fridays. We've had some very madcap schedules where we have finished shooting a show on a Thursday, we look at all of our film on Friday, work all weekend, and then on Monday we finalize the show. We give it to the sound effects people on Tuesday and we deliver it a week later. That's the kind of a schedule we've had on occasion.

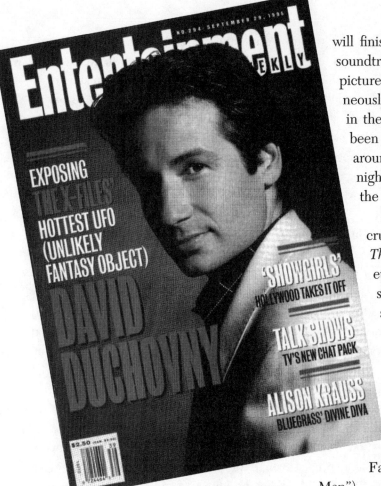

will finish on Wednesday night, take that soundtrack and put it onto the completed picture that has been worked on simultaneously with color correction and putting in the opticals and special effects we've been talking about. It all comes together around three in the morning Thursday night–Friday morning. We deliver it to the network and they air it that night."

Despite this kind of seemingly crushing schedule, in its first season *The X-Files* managed to offer a variety of supernatural or paranormal stories, ranging from liver-eating serial killers ("Squeeze" and "Tooms"), technology run amok ("Ghost in the Machine"), possession ("Ice," "Space," "Lazarus," "Born Again"), genetic experimentation ("Eve"), ghosts ("Shadows," "Beyond the Sea"), deadly insects ("Darkness Falls"), and faith healers ("Miracle Man").

But there is one theme above all others that everyone on the crew can count on regularly: space aliens and government conspiracies, the show's bread-and-butter subject.

Aliens arrived in the pilot episode, which brought Mulder and Scully together and launched them on their first case: the mysterious disappearance of several teenagers in Oregon. Upon investigation, evidence of possible extraterrestrial involvement is discov-

"The composer will generally spend a week creating the score, the sound effects supervisor and his staff will spend a week collecting all of the sound effects and putting them into a package that will, in essence, have them all in sync with each other. Generally on the Tuesday and Wednesday of the week the show is airing, we will mix together all of the music and sound effects. It's a two-day process. We generally

ered. But such a traditional treatment of ET visitation was not indicative of the course of the series. Whereas the pilot dealt with standard UFO premises, the next episode, "Deep Throat," took a further step into the fantastic. Mulder sneaks onto a U.S. Air Force base, where he discovers that the military is conducting experiments with alien technology it has stumbled upon, hoping to develop an advanced aircraft.

In the character-driven "Conduit," Mulder and Scully investigate the disappearance of a young girl, which taps in to Mulder's memories of the abduction of his sister. "Fallen Angel" turns up the heat on the aliens-among-us premise. In this episode, an alien creature survives the crash of its ship and flees authorities, using its ability to become invisible to human eyes. Mulder and Scully, naturally, want to find it before the military does.

"E.B.E." begins with Mulder and Scully hearing that an alien craft has been downed, and that an extraterrestrial body has been found by the government. This time — thanks to Deep Throat's manipulations — Mulder *just* misses alien contact, probably by a moment or two. It all culminates with "The Erlenmeyer Flask," and its tale of experimentation with alien DNA, an alien embryo, the death of Deep Throat, and the closing of the

X-Files, all of which was designed to lead in to the show's second season. Together, these episodes bring Mulder and Scully, as well as the audience, ever closer to actual contact with extraterrestrials.

"I think it was a very conscious thing with

> **"It's easy to scare people,"
> says Carter simply, "but it's
> hard to scare them in a way
> that has some resonance; that
> really makes them double-lock
> their doors at night."**

us," Chris Carter says. "We realize you can't keep playing with the audience; you have to bring them closer. Actually, my feeling is that even by the end of season one we *had* had contact of a sort. We came closer than I had anticipated coming in the first twenty-four episodes."

Also accomplished during that first season was the establishing of some of the series's parameters on what would and would not work within the format.

"We're charting uncharted waters; we're figuring it out and telling the best stories that we can with our wonderful characters," Carter says. "I don't want it to be each week that we

The Death of Deep Throat

Guiding Fox Mulder through the treacherous waters of government intrigue during the debut season of *The X-Files* was Deep Throat, the shadowy inside informant who was dramatically knocked off in the first-year finale, "The Erlenmeyer Flask."

"The mystery of a character who has unlimited sources of information, but also has enemies, makes for interesting acting work," says Jerry Hardin, who played the enigmatic informant. "Since he wasn't clearly defined by the writers, I had a chance to pursue the role freely. That's interesting to do, because he could be a bad guy just as easily as a good guy. In TV, you're often dealing only with characters who are black or white, and the actor must make a big effort to somehow get a few specks of the other colors."

Deep Throat, who appeared in seven episodes of the first season, acquired a surprisingly strong cult following during his run. The character's death at the end of the season caught a lot of viewers off guard.

"When you kill a character like Deep Throat, it's almost like killing off Janet Leigh in *Psycho*," says co–executive producer and "Erlenmeyer Flask" director Robert Goodwin. "It affects people."

Although he enjoyed Hardin and his portrayal, series creator Chris Carter says, "The character had provided information in a very systematic and predictable way, and I was interested in exploring new ways of Mulder getting his information."

But Hardin blames himself for aiding his character's demise. "I was pushing to make the character a regular," he notes. "I think they felt they needed to accede to my desires or get rid of me. So they decided to get rid of me."

go for the expected. We'll take detours. I think we've got so many strong episodes that we can take chances. It's what I always try to do, and I think it's what makes a series fresh — you bear off in different directions and check them out."

His favorite catchphrase for the series is that every story has to take place within the realm of extreme possibility. "I just think it's a much more interesting show if it's believable. I think it's much more frightening. You know, if you look at Michael Crichton's *Terminal Man* or *Jurassic Park* or *The Andromeda Strain,* the most frightening part is that you actually believe that it *could* happen. The tricky part each week is taking these stories and rooting them in reality; making it believable that they could really be happening, therefore heightening the scare.

"It's easy to scare people," says Carter simply, "but it's hard to scare them in a way that has some resonance; that really makes them double-lock their doors at night."

SEASON ONE
Episode Guide

Episode 1.1
"The X-Files" (pilot)
Original airdate: September 10, 1993
Written by Chris Carter
Directed by Robert Mandel
Guest starring: Doug Abrams (Patrolman),
Zachary Ansley (Billy Miles), Alexandra Berlin
(Orderly), J. B. Bivens (Truck Driver), Ken
Camroux (Third Man), Charles Cioffi (Section
Chief Scott Blevins), William B. Davis
(Cigarette-Smoking Man), Cliff DeYoung (Dr.
Jay Nemman), Lesley Ewen (Receptionist),
Katya Gardener (Peggy O'Dell), Jim Jansen
(Dr. Heitz Werber), Sarah Koskoff (Theresa),
Stephen E. Miller (Truitt), Ric Reid
(Astronomer), Leon Russom (Det. Miles),
Malcolm Stewart (Dr. Glass)

*FBI agent Dana Scully is assigned to be the
partner of Fox Mulder, the agency's leading
expert on the so-called X-Files: cases involving
the unexplainable, from reported UFO abductions to the paranormal. Essentially given the
task of debunking Mulder's discoveries by
applying a scientific approach, Scully nevertheless finds it impossible to completely skew-
er her new partner's efforts through scientific
reasoning.*

Their first assignment brings them to
*Oregon, where the death of a teenage girl and
the disappearance of several other teens indicate that they have been abducted by aliens.
At episode's end, the one piece of evidence
obtained — a tiny metallic cylinder that had
been inserted in a victim's nose — is given to
the enigmatic Cigarette-Smoking Man, who
places it in a storage house within the
Pentagon.*

✿   ✿   ✿

A justifiably proud Chris Carter states, "I
think the pilot worked great, and I'm helped
to that opinion by the response I've gotten to
it. Also, when we tested it with test audiences,

it was the kind of response that you only dream about. In fact, I remember when I first screened the pilot for Rupert Murdoch and the Fox executives, I'd finished the pilot at five in the morning and they saw it at eight in the morning. That's how close we were to deadline. But after the screening, there was spontaneous applause from the audience. These are people who usually watch to see how the boss responds, but it was an overwhelmingly positive response to the show. I think it succeeds on many levels.

"I was helped on the pilot by a very collaborative group consisting of director Bob Mandel and Daniel Sackheim, the producer. Dan also directed 'Deep Throat,' 'Conduit,' and 'The Host.' The two of them were instrumental in giving the pilot the quality and standard for what has become the series."

"What impressed me," notes former scriptwriter and co–executive producer Glen Morgan, who went on to co-create *Space: Above and Beyond* with James Wong, "was the merging of *Silence of the Lambs* and *Close Encounters of the Third Kind*. It got Jim and me aboard, and I liked the open ending. It was scary, and there's nothing scary on TV."

Howard Gordon, who along with partner Alex Gansa had produced the fantasy series *Beauty and the Beast*, was also impressed with the pilot and irresistibly drawn to the series itself. "The pilot set the tone of the show really successfully," he says. "It established Mulder and Scully's characters, as well as the aspect of Mulder's sister supposedly being

abducted. There was also a good solid murder investigation. Pilots are a strange breed, because you have to tell a story while simultaneously introducing the characters the audience is going to love, and you have to do it all in forty-eight minutes. Although I think the series has improved on it, the pilot was a tremendous synthesis of all the parts."

Rating/Audience Share: 7.9/15

Episode 1.2
"Deep Throat"
Original airdate: September 17, 1993
Written by Chris Carter
Directed by Daniel Sackheim
Guest starring: Charles Cioffi (Section Chief Scott Blevins), John Cuthbert (Commanding Officer), Michael Bryan French (Paul Mossinger), Brian Furlong (Lead Officer), Seth Green (Emil), Jerry Hardin (Deep Throat), Doc Harris (Mr. McLennen), Andrew Johnston (Col. Budahas), Lalainia Lindejerg (Zoe), Vince Metcalfe (Kissell), Sheila Moore (Verla McLennen), Monica Parker (Ladonna), Michael Puttonen (Motel Manager), Gabrielle Rose (Anita Budahas)

Mulder is contacted by the mysterious Deep Throat, a government source who is willing to provide tidbits of information to help the agent in his quest to discover the truth about UFOs and a far-reaching government conspiracy. As a result, Mulder and Scully travel to

36

Idaho to investigate the disappearance of a pilot from Ellis Air Force Base. What they (Mulder in particular) discover is that the military is performing mind experiments on pilots who have been flying new vehicles apparently created from alien technology.

❊ ❊ ❊

"The character of Deep Throat of course came from the infamous Watergate figure, who may or may not have existed," offers Chris Carter, who also cites Donald Sutherland's portrayal of "Mr. X" in Oliver Stone's *JFK* as inspiration. "I felt that we needed a connection: somebody who would come from this mysterious, shadowy government; somebody who works in some level of government that we have no idea exists, and he comes to Mulder and Scully and leads them carefully, selectively, without giving them too much and making them work for the answers, but helping them when they reach a dead end or helping them when they make a wrong turn."

Also pleasing to Carter was the fact that Daniel Sackheim returned to direct the episode. "It was a natural and worked well," Carter enthuses. "We were of one mind as to what the show is about, so I wrote this episode that he thought was great and he did a wonderful job directing it. The episode also further served to establish the landscape we were going to be working in with *The X-Files*: the introduction of Deep Throat, and the idea

that the government knows even more than we established in the pilot and that they will go to any length to protect that information."

While the notion of the government utilizing alien technology to improve its own aircraft seems highly original, Carter demurs. "Believe me," he says with a laugh, "when you start reading the material that's out there, anything you can imagine has either been imagined or experienced by some folks."

Howard Gordon views "Deep Throat" as part two of the pilot, with Carter attempting to reestablish the themes of a government UFO conspiracy. "The Army using alien technology is what made it most interesting," he opines. "The whole Roswell thing and Ellis Air Force Base are the pillars of UFO mythology, so it was an appropriate and smart first choice for Chris. And then the idea of the government doing mind control . . . People really responded to Mulder's putting his neck on the line, seeking the truth and then getting taken himself and having his brain subjected to the same thing these pilots were subjected to."

Co–executive producer Robert Goodwin, who supervises physical production of the series, found "Deep Throat" to be a particularly challenging episode.

"We had to put together a new crew, and

"We wanted to get right out of the box after 'Deep Throat' and do something that *wasn't* an alien story."

'Deep Throat' was a break-in period where everybody came to learn the kinds of demands of quality that we were making," he explains. "They'd worked on several shows prior to ours that hadn't been as challenging or demanding. There was a certain level of quality that they had to step up to, and in all honesty, virtually all of the departments did that. But it was a learning experience.

"My most vivid memory of the episode was a sequence in which Mulder is out on the tarmac at this Air Force base where this UFO hovers over him," Goodwin continues. "We had that, plus about three shots where this UFO hovers over him, and then a few more scenes where these two teenage kids show Mulder where the base is. We started shoot-

ing ten o'clock Friday morning and we finished shooting eight o'clock Saturday morning. It was amazingly difficult. We had one scene where these two kids lead Mulder to the edge of the base. Originally it was written that they would lead Mulder up to a certain point and say, 'We'll leave you here; we're not going any farther. Go through that part of the fence when it gets dark.' And we were supposed to dissolve to night. Well, as we were progressing we realized we weren't going to get it shot that afternoon and we had to turn it into a night scene. Then we had to turn it back into a day scene because we couldn't get it shot before the sun came out."

Rating/Audience Share: 7.3/14

Episode 1.3
"Squeeze"
Original airdate: September 24, 1993
Written by Glen Morgan and James Wong
Directed by Harry Longstreet
Guest starring: Henry Beckman (Det. Frank Briggs), James Bell (Johnson), Gary Hetherington (Kennedy), Doug Hutchison (Eugene Victor Tooms), Paul Joyce (Mr. Werner), Terence Kelly (George Usher), Donal Logue (Tom Colton), Kevin McNulty (Fuller), Rob Morton (Kramer), Colleen Winton (Lie Detector Technician)

Mulder and Scully travel to Maryland, where they go up against Eugene Tooms, a mutant who can squeeze his body through any space and who comes out of hibernation every thirty years to devour the livers of five victims. Tooms must be stopped before he vanishes again for another three decades.

❀ ❀ ❀

"Squeeze" was significant in the development of *The X-Files* in that it informed the audience that the show wasn't just going to be a UFO series. As Glen Morgan explains it, "I remember I read an article about Richard Ramirez, the Night Stalker of LA, in the middle eighties, and the rumors were that he was climbing in those little windows everyone has in their bathroom above their shower. Supposedly he would climb in through those windows and the dust and soap grime on the sill was undisturbed. He was a pretty big guy. I think we took it from there. That was when it was Jim and Chris and I sitting around saying, 'How about this, how about that?' Some things we thought would be too far out there."

"An okay episode," adds Jim Wong, "but I was very disappointed by its production. There were a lot of things that didn't work for us and we had to go back and reshoot. The production of it left such a nasty taste in my mouth that I've never really thought it was

that good, but we've gotten a lot of [positive] reaction to it. It *was* creepy, though, and in that way it worked really well. All I can see is what it should have been. It should have been more than it was, though it did do its job."

Morgan notes that the episode was truly saved in postproduction, and that editing made the show. "I think it's been so long since television has done horror, and it's been an area for low-budget features for so long, that people have forgotten how to do it well. We

> **"We found this Canadian contortionist named Pepper. We said, 'Here's the little opening, see what you can do.' All we added were some sound effects of bones snapping and cracking."**

wanted certain things which weren't agreed with, and when we watched the episode it wasn't scary. It was a show that taught us all a lot."

The casting of Doug Hutchison as Tooms stands out in Morgan's mind. "When the actor came in to read," he recalls, "we said, 'No, no, he looks like he's twelve years old.' Then I said, 'Come to think of it, he looks forty.' Then the director said, 'Can I see you go from a neutral position to one of attacking me?' Doug just sat there and said, 'A neutral position?' a couple of times. And the director said, 'And then you're going to attack me.' 'I'm going to attack you?' Doug responded. All of us react-

ed, 'Oh, brother, here's a nut.' Then he was immediately into it and he really scared the shit out of us. He just started off as if he didn't understand what we were talking about. What he was really doing was showing us how he was building up to being a maniac. Naturally we said, 'He's the guy.'"

Chris Carter recalls that when the series was okayed by Fox, he had been on vacation with his wife in France and had to head back to California a week earlier than expected. "Which didn't go over well with my wife." He smiles. "So she stayed and traveled around the country while I came back and started to work with Glen and Jim. We wanted to get right out of the box after 'Deep Throat' and do something that *wasn't* an alien story. It was a story that expanded the realm of what an X-File could be. As far as the germ of the idea, I had eaten some foie gras in France and I thought, 'Wouldn't it be intriguing if some human was interested in eating the livers of other humans?' That was the kernel of the idea, and they turned it into a terrific, dramatic, and very scary episode."

From Robert Goodwin's point of view, the chief challenge of "Squeeze" was designing the scene in which Tooms climbs up onto the roof of a house, squeezes into a very small opening in the chimney (dislocating most of the bones his body), enters the house, and chows down on his victim's liver.

"Somehow," Goodwin says, "we found this contortionist named Pepper. So we brought Pepper to the set, thinking we could get at least part of the scene with him as a photo double. We said, 'Here's the little opening — see what you can do.' Well, Pepper squeezed right down inside the damn thing, right in front of us. He got his whole body inside of there. That's what you see. All we added were some sound effects of bones snapping and cracking. We didn't do any visual effects at all. It was amazing."

Despite the incredibly flexible Pepper, effects supervisor Mat Beck and his team did get some work. "Mat Beck did this wonderfully subtle computer effect of Tooms's fingers stretching as he climbs up the house," says co-producer Paul Rabwin, who supervises post-production. "The viewer actually had to wonder if those fingers really were stretching. I think that's a real key to our show. As opposed to saying with red lights and sirens that the fingers are stretching, you make the audience ask, 'Is that happening? Am I seeing that?' It's a very effective way of doing visual effects."

Referring to a later shot in which Tooms fluidly erupts from a heating vent, Beck explains that the show is careful not to take any effects shots over the top. "Hutchison came rocketing out of the vent we built six different ways from Sunday. It was pretty intense, even unstretched. We then shot a clean background plate of the apartment, added a bunch of blue-screen material around the grate, and shot him again coming out of the grate against the blue so we could stretch him [on the computer]. We squeezed him a bit when we put him back in the scene, but not a lot, because Chris Carter insists that less is more: just a hint of the unnatural is all that is required."

A hint was all that *was* needed, as most viewers felt that combination of terror and fascination Carter is always aiming for. Tooms became the show's most identifiable demonic figure — no small feat in a series devoted to such characters. Even the normally stoic Gillian Anderson was a bit unnerved. "It was just incredibly creepy to me." She laughs. "I think it was one of the first scripts I read where I was nervous afterward."

Rating/Audience Share: 7.2/13

Episode 1.4
"Conduit"
Original airdate: October 1, 1993
Written by Alex Gansa and Howard Gordon
Directed by Daniel Sackheim
Guest starring: Michael Cavanaugh (Sheriff), Charles Cioffi (Section Chief Scott Blevins), Taunya Dee (Ruby Morris), Don Gibb (Kip), Anthony Harrison (Fourth Man), Mauricio Mercado (Coroner), Akiko Morison (Leza Atsumi), Shelley Owens (Tessa), Joel Palmer (Kevin Morris), Glen Roald (M.E. Worker), Carrie Snodgress (Darlene Morris), Don Thompson (Holtzman)

In Sioux City, Iowa, Mulder's feelings for his abducted sister are reawakened when he learns of a teenage girl who has apparently been abducted as well. He and Scully check

out the story of the girl's mother, Darlene Morris, who was an abductee herself but is reluctant to talk about it. At episode's end, Scully does her best to account for everything scientifically, but she is confronted with information that has no rational explanation.

❋ ❋ ❋

"Alex [Gansa] and I made an effort to play to our own strength, which is character," says Howard Gordon. "We thought this was an interesting place to reiterate Mulder's quest for his sister. We set out to tell a simple abduction story, which was played out behind the shadows. We wanted to create an air of tension. With everything that happened, we wanted to explain what it could be. At every point, everything can be explained. Was she taken or killed by her boyfriend, who she was seeing against her mother's wishes? Is it *Twin Peaks* or an alien abduction? That was the theme of the show.

"We also used UFO lore," he continues, "like the idea of repeat abductions and mother–daughter abductions. Apparently you're taken and sometimes several members of the family are taken as well. I think we're most proud of the ending: Mulder's quest is reestablished (and Daniel Sackheim directed it beautifully) with Mulder sitting alone in a church with only his faith. The story, again, was fueled by Mulder's belief and emotional connection with this case. Another girl taken from her family. And, in a way, the little boy

who is the conduit, who is also perhaps touched by the aliens, is essentially Mulder. Those little touches the fans seem to respond to. It was difficult for us, but in the end satisfying. It came out of frustration on our parts, and creative uncertainty."

Most significant about "Conduit" for Glen Morgan was the fact that it drove home the notion of strength in diversity in terms of the writing staff.

"Alex and Howard worked on *Beauty and the Beast* and *Sisters,* and they have a better character-dramatic sense," he muses, "and I think 'Conduit' really helped define Mulder. Those guys are Princeton-educated, Ivy League, with a literature background. Jim and

43

I are more blue collar, from San Diego. I grew up on Hammer horror films and things like that. Everybody on staff was kind of teaching everybody else."

For Carter, one of the episode's highlights was its conclusion and "the realization by Scully that Mulder may not be a crackpot. The science that she so depends on points to an abduction. The girl's physiology and body chemistry at the end of the show says that she may have been in a state of weightlessness. It really helped to define something that was very important to the show, which was its point of view. It was, I think, a very defining episode in terms of how to tell these stories using these characters we had put in motion."

Rating/Audience Share: 6.3/11

Episode 1.5
"The Jersey Devil"
Original airdate: October 8, 1993
Written by Chris Carter
Directed by Joe Napolitano
Guest starring: Andrew Airlie (Rob), Bill Dow (Dad), Tamsin Kelsey (Ellen), Jayme Knox (Mom), Michael MacRae (Ranger Peter Boulle), Hrothgar Mathews (Jack), Gregory Sierra (Dr. Diamond), Claire Stansfield (Jersey Devil), Jill Teed (Glenna), Wayne Tippit (Det. Thompson)

A murder similar to one in 1947 leads Mulder and Scully to New Jersey, where Mulder wants to investigate the legend of the "Jersey Devil," a supposed beast who has been stalking human prey for some time. They learn that the subject of their search is actually a primitive woman, a genetic mutation or throwback to humanity in its previous incarnation.

❄ ❄ ❄

"I had read an essay by this guy E. O. Wilson, who writes about bugs — particularly ants — and he had written a story that posed the question of whether or not man is hellbent on his own extinction," Chris Carter recalls. "There's this idea that we, being carnivores, start to eat our own tails because we're so gluttonous. I mean that not in the eating sense but what we do to the land. I thought of the curious idea, 'What if evolution had provided us with an evolutionary mutation which is almost a throwback to the Neanderthal?' The idea that there's a de-evolutionary bent in nature that, in order to survive, we would actually go

One of the episode's highlights was its conclusion and "the realization by Scully that Mulder may not be a crackpot."

backwards. So I had the idea that we could do a sort of caveman in the woods of New Jersey. The little twist, of course, is that it's not a man, it's a woman. I think the episode was very well directed, and I think it was a little different approach for us. It was a little more poetic and didn't have the 'boo,' which is the big effect or the big scare.

"I also think it further established the relationship between Mulder and Scully," Carter continues, "and expanded the idea of what an X-File is and where it can take place."

James Wong didn't share Carter's enthusiasm for the episode. "Beautifully shot," he says, "it started off great, but I felt the story ran out of steam in the middle. It didn't go anywhere; there weren't enough complications to it."

"That was a difficult show because it was the death of a thousand cuts," Robert Goodwin recalls with a laugh. "To make that work, it required so much shooting, so much film at different angles. I do, however, remember a personal experience making that episode. We needed more footage of this wild woman stalking Mulder as he's walking through the forest at one particular point. I was sent off into the woods with a second unit and a six-foot-tall naked woman to do this filming. However, it was at this forest up here called the Greater Vancouver Regional District. It's not open to the public because it's a preserve. So I get to the gate and my two sons, who are at that time twelve and eight, are with me that day. I said, 'Come on, guys, we're going to shoot some film of the big, tall naked lady.' We get to the gate and the guard won't let the kids in because they're not covered for liability insurance. He said the kids were going to have to wait in the parking lot several miles from where we were shooting, and then he said, 'You don't want them in there, anyway, because we've had several mountain lion attacks over the last week and it was just spotted a half a mile down the road.' I said, 'You want me to leave my two kids standing in a parking lot, telling me that there are mountain lions half a mile down the road?' They wouldn't let them go, so I'm up there, and I should have been having the time of my life with this naked lady, and all I can think about is how my two little boys are stuck at the gate, about to be mauled by a mountain lion."

Adds Glen Morgan with a smile, "They had a naked woman running around the set, so people were pretty thrilled."

Rating/Audience Share: 6.6/12

Episode 1.6

"Shadows"

Original airdate: October 22, 1993
Written by Glen Morgan and James Wong
Directed by Michael Katleman
Guest starring: Anna Ferguson (Ms. Winn), Kelli Fox (Pathologist), Lorena Gale (Ellen Bledsoe), Deryl Hayes (Webster), Tom Heaton (Groundskeeper), Nora McLellan (Jane Morris), Tom Pickett (Cop), Barry Primus (Robert Dorland), Veena Sood (Ms. Saunders), Lisa Waltz (Lauren Kyte), Janie Woods-Morris (Ms. Lange)

A young woman named Lauren Kyte seems to be under the protection of a ghostly force. Mulder and Scully investigate and learn that Lauren's employer, Howard Graves, who was like a father to her, supposedly committed sui- *cide. In actuality, the man was murdered by his business partner and is reaching out from the beyond to make sure that justice is done.*

❊ ❊ ❊

"It wasn't a great script," a candid James Wong admits, "although I thought the director did a good job with it. It was entertaining, but not my favorite episode. The network wanted a lot more relatable things. Originally we made this girl a lot more interesting, but because they wanted relatable things, we made her a secretary, and it wasn't really involving. An average episode."

Glen Morgan notes that a big influence on the episode was *The Entity*, though on the surface of things it looked like their take on *Carrie*. "That's what Chris wants, the idea: 'Can it be this thing and then become that?' I never realized that's what experts think poltergeists are. Usually poltergeists are around younger kids. They have a telekinetic ability

"A big influence on the episode was *The Entity,* though on the surface of things it looked like their take on *Carrie.*"

and don't know how to control it or don't realize it. That's another criterion in writing a script for this show: try and have a way for Scully to explain it. As a writer you're saying, 'If we go in this direction, it allows Scully to say this. If we go in that direction, it allows her to say that.'"

"A very popular show," says Carter. "Very well done, really great effects, and more of a meat-and-potatoes kind of story. An FBI sting and a good mystery that Mulder and Scully investigate. Overall, a really solid episode."

Michael Katleman, who went on to co-create the short-lived Fox series *VR.5,* directed the episode. "As a director," he explains, "you go into some things in episodic television where it's laid out very clearly. The great thing about *The X-Files* is that it *wasn't* laid out. There were a lot of ways to go from a directorial standpoint. You could shoot things in a lot of different ways because you were going into the psyche. You had a lot more freedom to

explore certain areas that haven't been explored yet. For instance, 'Shadows' was about a woman being haunted by her ex-boss. In the beginning it appears she's being haunted by him, but he's really protecting her. When you look at that situation, how do you show that? Which way do you show that someone is possessing someone or protecting them? It's really wide open as to the ways you can explore this psychological dilemma. In that sequence where the attackers come into her house, how do you tell that story? It's done from a psychological perspective, so there are many different ways to do it."

Rating/Audience Share: 5.9/11

Episode 1.7
"Ghost in the Machine"
Original airdate: October 29, 1993
Written by Alex Gansa and Howard Gordon
Directed by Jerrold Freedman
Guest starring: Gillian Barber (Nancy Spiller), Marc Baur (Man in Suit), Wayne Duvall (Jerry Lamana), Bill Finck (Sandwich Man), Jerry Hardin (Deep Throat), Rob Labelle (Brad Wilczek), Blu Mankuma (Claude Peterson), Theodore Thomas (Clyde)

Deep Throat informs Mulder that the Defense Department is extremely interested in computer genius Brad Wilczek, who has mastered computer intelligence. Proof of this comes in the form of the high-tech Eurisko building, whose Wilczek-developed computer command system has taken control of the building and is killing anyone who attempts to tamper with its programming.

❉ ❉ ❉

"My least favorite episode," offers Howard Gordon, who co-wrote the script with Alex Gansa. "I think Chris Carter and I argued what the worst episode of the first season was. Alex and I contend that it was 'Ghost in the Machine,' and Chris insists it was 'Space.' This is easily and clearly our worst. It's basically uninteresting. Some of the concepts may have been interesting, maybe the idea of artificial intelligence. But it's an old idea. There may have been a more interesting way of doing it."

Glen Morgan agrees. "I think parts of the episode worked. What maybe fell a little flat is that we were a little too afraid of doing HAL [from *2001*] and, in a sense, I think that's what the building needed: to have a scary personality. I think we could have given the building a little bit more of a mean-spirited personality to get it away from HAL. HAL, even when he was being dismantled, was very soft-spoken and was never angry.

There's a line between something being an influence and just taking an idea. I don't think we've taken. At least I hope we haven't."

"It had some neat stuff at the end," James

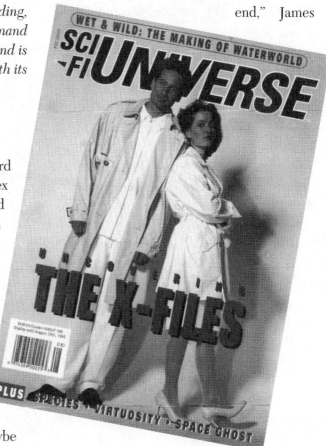

Wong adds, "although I think the ending was a little unsatisfying to me visually, as well as in terms of how Mulder comes to dismember the machine. It was either a little too easy or maybe we could have thought of something more fun to do with the machine. Actually the script was a lot more fun, but it ran into production problems in terms of the budget and we had to devise something that was a little more straightforward. They reprised some of the elevator stuff and it was just a lot more complicated. Overall a fun episode."

One major supporter of "Ghost in the Machine" is Chris Carter, who thought the script effectively addressed the question of just what made up an X-File. "It doesn't have to be paranormal," he notes. "In this case it's technology run amok. X-Files involve lots of different scientific and technological and natural anomalies, and this is just another case of that. I think the action scenes and the abduction of Scully were great. A very successful episode on many levels. Some people didn't think so, but I did. There are some computer buffs who question a few things we had done. Maybe they have some valid arguments, but I think as a dramatic piece it was strong and good."

One difficult aspect of the episode, according to Robert Goodwin, is the fact that the story is told primarily from the point of view of the computer that has taken over the building.

"It's almost like we were shooting two different shows," Goodwin says, "because in any given scene you're showing two or three monitors which show something different happening. So you're spending forever prefilming a scene, transferring it over to video, and playing it back over the monitor. It was a very complex show. Jerry Freedman directed that. If you didn't have a good strong director with

a lot of years of technique behind him, that could have easily been brought to its knees."

Rating/Audience Share: 5.9/11

Episode 1.8

"Ice"

Original airdate: November 5, 1993
Written by Glen Morgan and James Wong
Directed by David Nutter
Guest starring: Xander Berkeley (Dr. Hodge), Felicity Huffman (Dr. Da Silva), Steve Hytner (Dr. Denny Murphy), Ken Kirzinger (Richter), Jeff Kober (Bear), Sonny Surowiec (Campbell)

When communication is cut off with a research facility in Alaska — and the last words of anyone stationed there are, "We are not who we are" — Mulder and Scully, accompanied by a team of physicians and scientists, proceed to Alaska, where they discover a parasitic wormlike creature that takes control of the human mind and intensifies feelings of fear and paranoia, with deadly results.

❊ ❊ ❊

An early high-water mark for the team of Morgan and Wong, "Ice" inspires Carter to enthuse, "They took to the show like crazy, and they're one of the reasons we've done so well and are being so well received. They just outdid themselves on this show, as did director David Nutter, who really works so hard for us. They had worked with David before, and it was a nice partnership that came to *The X-Files*. I think they wrote a great script and he did a great job directing it, and we had a great supporting cast. I think that the cast, directing, and writing came together. 'Ice' was inspired by *The Thing*, as anyone who knows the genre will tell you, but I think it was even better as an X-File. It pitted the characters of Mulder and Scully against each other in a way that was very interesting and a new look at their characters early on in the series. It's the stuff of great drama."

"To me," says Nutter, "the real great thing about 'Ice' is that we were able to convey a strong sense of paranoia. It was also a great ensemble piece. We're dealing with the most basic emotions of each character, ranging from their anger to their ignorance and fear. The episode also showed a real trust between Mulder and Scully. It established the emotional ties these two characters have with each other, which is very important. Scaring the hell out of the audience was definitely the key to the episode. The main thing is that it really had to scare the hell out of the actors on the show. Their fear

had to relate with [the audience's], and I think it did that."

Gillian Anderson can concur with that. "It was very intense. There was a lot of fear and paranoia going on. We had some great actors to work with, and the way the set was built was like a bunker almost. We felt like we were really in that place, as opposed to many of the sets, which are three-quarters walls. This was the Antarctic — for all we knew, that's where we were shooting. And it was cold. That particular studio was the old Spelling studio, and it doesn't have heat."

The script for "Ice" was inspired by an article in *Science News* about a group of scientists

"'Ice' was inspired by an article in *Science News* about a group of scientists in Greenland [who] found these worms frozen that later came back to life."

in Greenland drilling into 250,000-year-old ice. "The Greenland Ice Project was taking core samples from deep within the ice to study," James Wong says. "We started with that. The amazing thing is that they apparently found these frozen worms that later came back to life. It was *after* we wrote the episode that we found it out, which was a little scary."

The entire Arctic complex was created by production designer Graeme Murray, who had worked on John Carpenter's remake of *The Thing*. "That kind of a one-set show works quite well for the series," Murray opines. "You

put a bunch of people into a claustrophobic space and set something loose in there. There's nowhere to go. They can't run. They have to stay and confront it, and that makes for a very tense and exciting episode."

Interestingly, "Ice" was originally conceived as a so-called bottle show, one that would take place in a single location, because it would be cheaper to produce.

"There was a budgetary concern at that point," Wong agrees. "Our shows were going over budget and we needed to do a show that was more contained. We were going to do this one later in the season, when there was the possibility of snow in Vancouver, so we could have some exteriors with snow. As it turned out, we were over budget and we liked this idea, so we had to do it all inside."

But did it save money? "It really didn't," Carter recalls with a chuckle. "We got such production value, and production value costs money. There's no tricks involved. Every dollar we spend shows up on the screen. That's why the show looks so good. We are actually a pretty low budget show, but we've brought a lot of folks together who have given us the most for our money."

Upon receiving the script, Robert Goodwin was immediately struck by its power and the question of how they were going to bring it to life.

"You've got these worms which are living inside of bodies and you can see one wriggling under the skin of a dog and then under a couple of people," he says with a sigh of mock exhaustion. "There's a scene where they pull one of the worms out of the guy's neck. It was a combination of rubber worms and, in some shots, those completely generated by computer. [Makeup artist] Toby Lindala really saved us. For the scene where you see the worms in the back of the neck, one process you can do is build an entire body from a mold made of the actor, so what you're shooting is a very detailed mannequin that looks very realistic. But Toby came in and said, 'Let me try something,' and he actually created a process in which he created false skin that went over the real neck of the person and he built a channel with this worm in it. Actually right there on the actor's neck you could see the worm. It was disgusting, but it was cool. It was one of those things where going in to it you didn't know how you were going to do it. What I was deathly afraid of was that we would do something that looked so cheesy that it would just take away from the story. But everyone delivered, and it's a classic episode."

Rating/Audience Share: 6.6/11

Episode 1.9

"Space"

Original airdate: November 12, 1993
Written by Chris Carter
Directed by William Graham
Guest starring: David Cameron (Young Scientist), Paul DesRoches (Paramedic), Alf Humphreys (Second Controller), Ed Lauter (Lt. Col. Marcus Aurelius Belt), Tyronne L'Hirondelle (Databank Scientist), Tom McBeath (Scientist), Terry David Mulligan (Mission Controller), Susanna Thompson (Michelle Generoo), French Tickner (Preacher), Norma Wick (Reporter)

When Mulder and Scully are secretly informed that a deliberate string of sabotage attempts on America's space shuttle program seems to be taking place, they come into contact with former astronaut and current head of the shuttle program Lieutenant Colonel Marcus Belt. This former hero, it turns out, may be possessed by an extraterrestrial spirit that does not want anyone to join it in outer space.

❈ ❈ ❈

"The conceit was taking a space shuttle up into space and saying that it was essentially hijacked by an alien," Chris Carter says. "It took a lot of research on my part, and I was under a tremendous amount of pressure to get that script done and do a lot of things that an executive producer has to do as well. I didn't know if it was going to work, and I'm still not very happy with some of the special effects in it. We were under a tremendous time crunch in postproduction. I was working until four in the morning two or three nights to make the effects right. I should mention that I was working with the guy who really means a lot to the show and added a lot to it in terms of special effects, Mat Beck, the special effects producer. He was responsible in the pilot for the wonderful vortex in the forest, which took more coordination than the invasion of Normandy. He has just continued to come through with great special effects. But we were both under time pressure here that didn't allow us to do what either of us would have liked to.

"The show comes down to scripts. They have to be really tight and well conceived in order to tell a good story so that you don't have to rely on the special effects. I think we've done that. 'Space' was the first time that I thought the effects didn't live up to my

Noting that Carter likes to take his ideas from the newspaper, Glen Morgan points to the disappearance of the Mars Observer around the same time "Space" was being written.

"Chris wanted to use that as well as the other elements that maybe we're all familiar with, such as the face on Mars," Morgan says. "Even if you're not familiar with it, you kind of learn about it from the show. I thought it was a really great idea, that there must be a saboteur in NASA, because people must have wondered what the hell was going on. I think we maybe could have done a better job of conveying that the aliens were controlling this guy. Ed Lauter did a good job, though."

Referring to the lackluster special effects job on the episode, Morgan notes that in recent years Fox has produced straight series like *L.A. Law* and *Picket Fences*. "Suddenly they're doing an effects show and everyone thinks that you can have a regular postproduction schedule," he muses. "I think that was a nutty episode, with like four days for the effects. A lot of times you've got the show cut and you still don't know what the effects are — they run higher than you anticipated; sometimes they turn out crummy. In that case, we ran out of time and money and were stuck with some effects that didn't work. Hopefully we learned from that. I think

expectations, but I think the rest of the episode was very strong."

James Wong opines, "It was a great script and a pretty good episode. The problem came from the fact that some of the special effects were farmed out and they just didn't turn out well, so they looked cheesy and made the show less effective. I thought it was really neat the way they incorporated all the NASA footage in that episode. When I look at it, though, all I see are the problems."

on a show like this, when you really take chances, sometimes you're going to embarrass yourself and other times you hit a home run. You knew every week what *The Commish* was going to be, and it just wasn't as much fun."

For Robert Goodwin, the biggest challenge of the episode was re-creating NASA Mission Control in Houston, which involved video playback and machines with techno graphics. "Because everyone has seen so much of it on TV, you had to do something worthwhile or it would become a joke. In that show, I think the art department really came through. They vacuum-formed all these computers, stations, and everything else. I thought it was all very effective. A real tour de force for the art department."

About the set that became Mission Control, Graeme Murray explains: "It was an empty room in a public building here that is used, I believe, for theater presentations, that we converted. We got what photographs [of Mission Control] we could, and there's actually a fair amount of them. It's reasonably easy to re-create, like the Oval Office seems pretty easy to re-create. It was an interesting show, but a little confusing, because at the end you kind of say, 'Now what the hell was that about?'"

Rating/Audience Share: 6.5/11

**Episode 1.10
"Fallen Angel"**
Original airdate: November 19, 1993
Written by Alex Gansa and Howard Gordon
Directed by Larry Shaw
Guest starring: Marshall Bell (Commander Henderson), Scott Bellis (Max Fenig), Frederick Coffin (Chief Joseph McGrath), Jerry Hardin (Deep Throat), Jane MacDougall (Laura Dalton), William McDonald (Dr. Oppenheim), Tony Pantages (Lt. Fraser), Sheila Paterson (Gina Watkins), Freda Perry (Mrs. Wright), Michael Rogers (Lt. Griffin), Alvin Sanders (Deputy Wright), Bret Stait (Corp. Taylor), Kimberly Unger (Karen Koretz)

Mulder has twenty-four hours to prove that a spaceship has crashed — this despite a large military presence that is evacuating a small Wisconsin town, claiming that a toxic spill endangers the population. Things intensify when Mulder learns that Commander Henderson and his soldiers are in pursuit of the powerful alien pilot. Amid all of this, Mulder and Scully encounter Max Fenig, a man who claims that he has been abducted by aliens and that this situation mirrors that of Roswell, New Mexico, in 1947.

❋ ❋ ❋

"Right away we established that there was a cover story, that this town was being evacuated based on a supposed toxic spill," Howard Gordon explains. "This, of course, played right into the paranoid aspect of the show. And it was a pretty straight-ahead story, with Mulder operating covertly in a quarantine zone. It's an episode we're proud of. Alex and I like to dig our teeth into a character that interests us, where there's some emotional resonance. Scott Bellis was one of those discoveries we get sometimes in casting."

Notes Chris Carter with a wry smile, "Everyone keeps saying, 'This is my favorite episode.' Leaping forward, each one becomes people's favorite episode. I think we were helped by the great direction of Larry Shaw. And actor Marshall Bell, who played Henderson, was also great. I think it was very suspenseful right out of the box. You were headlong into the story and it never let up

> **"Something invisible is much more interesting. Certainly more than something that is very real and has a fur coat or a wagging tail."**

until the end. We also got to expand Deep Throat's involvement, raising the question that he may not be what he appears to be. I think it really played into an expansion of his character — who he is and why he's doing

this, all of which was explored later. I think the episode had great effects, and it enlarged our alien repertoire."

Of Deep Throat, Gordon adds: "We took the character and pushed him forward a step. Is he ally or foe? We weren't sure at that point ourselves what he was, and we thought we'd couch it in the demise of the X-Files. So we had a frame within a frame that we worked in."

Robert Goodwin remembers writing a memo on the episode about the several sequences where the alien is on the loose and is invisible.

"You really can't see it," Goodwin says, "and then he goes through a laser beam that's up as protection around this Army base. As he goes through, the base buzzes and he becomes visible. Mat Beck, who does our visual effects, needed to create this thing as something actually there which he could take with his visual effects afterwards and completely change its appearance. But at least it gives him something to start with. Here's a memo I wrote on the show: 'Page 15. Shape that distinguishes itself. The effect we are after here is that as the alien moves towards the laser beams, we see its hazy aura approaching. As it crosses through the laser beams we'll see its central anthropological shape. It's a dinosaur-like shape with a large head, a humped back, wing-like webbed limbs as opposed to arms, and long skinny legs. It moves like a dinosaur. To

achieve this effect, Mat Beck needs an image of this creature on film that he can morph and distort in postproduction. He says the best color would be orange, so we need to hire a woman who can move well (probably a dancer) and create an orange-colored, hump-backed, big-headed, webbed-armed, pointy-butted outfit for her. And that's exactly what we did. If you could see the dailies of this woman in this orange outfit with a bicycle hat, her arms pinned back, humped over and stuffed full of pillows, you would be hysterical. It was the craziest thing you've ever seen. But the final effect was very good."

According to Carter, the invisibility of the extraterrestrial was quite deliberate. "I always think what you don't see is scarier than what you do see," he explains. "You need a good otherworldly effect; otherwise it's going to look like a monster of the week. As soon as you create a monster and give it shape, you can know it or you can catch it. Something invisible is much more interesting. Certainly more than something that is very real and has a fur coat or a wagging tail."

From a design standpoint, Graeme Murray recalls: "We did what was supposed to be a mountaintop surveillance center in Colorado that was seen in the opening of the show. It was a wall set with no walls to it that was really just kind of plunked into the middle of a black stage and we put up pieces of glass and made reflections of computer monitors and dials and gauges and that kind of thing and tried to build a set that didn't have any boundaries to it. In kind of the flipside to 'Ice,' which was one set, this was a whole bunch of different, interesting things. It's the only time we've done a UFO crash, although you weren't really sure if it was a UFO or an airplane crash."

Rating/Audience Share: 5.4/9

Episode 1.11

"Eve"

Original airdate: December 10, 1993
Written by Kenneth Biller and Chris Brancato
Directed by Fred Gerber
Guest starring: Garry Davey (Hunter), Tina Gilbertson (Donna Watkins), Jerry Hardin (Deep Throat), Harriet Harris (Dr. Sally Kendrick), Maria Herrera (Guard #2), Janet Hodgkinson (Waitress), David Kirby (Ted Watkins), Erika Krievins (Cindy Reardon), Sabrina Krievins (Teena Simmons), Robert Lewis (Officer), Joe Maffei (Guard #1), Tasha Simms (Ellen Reardon), Gordon Tipple (Detective), George Touliatos (Dr. Katz), Christine Upright-Letain (Ms. Wells)

A pair of men are murdered by their eight-year-old daughters in, respectively, Connecticut and California. What draws Mulder and Scully to the case is the fact that the two little girls are exact twins. Upon further investigation, they discover that both of their families had been involved in a 1950s genetic experiment known as the Litchfield Project, which resulted in the creation of boys and girls referred to as Adams and Eves, who have heightened strength and intelligence, and who are psychopathic in nature and look exactly alike.

❊ ❊ ❊

"A freelance episode, and Jim [Wong] and Glen [Morgan] came in at some point on and did an interesting rewrite on it," Chris Carter recalls. "We also had a first-time director in Fred Gerber, who brought some interesting stuff to it. I liked the episode, the casting in particular, with the twin girls. We had to cast in Vancouver and so you're limited in the twins you find up there, because the labor laws are different. It's just difficult to shoot with kids in any case. Also Harriet Harris was excellent."

Robert Goodwin agrees that the biggest challenge of the episode was the casting. "It's hard enough to find one good kid actor, but to find twins who can act is really tough," he says. "At one point I thought we should cast one actor and then do a photo double and split screen, but there was so much with the two of them together that it was impossible. It also would have been very expensive. We just got very lucky that we found these little girls who were terrific. 'Eve,' like most of the scripts, was so goddamned good that our job was not to screw it up. If we can do it without screwing it up and deliver what's on the page, we're going to have a good show. 'Eve' in particular was a very good show."

"I loved the teaser," Carter recalls with a smile, "where the little girl is hugging her teddy bear out in the street and two joggers come by and find that her daddy is sitting, slumped, in the swing set. It's kind of a horrific image and not something you see on your regular network TV show."

Rating/Audience Share: 6.8/12

Episode 1.12

"Fire"

Original airdate: December 17, 1993
Written by Chris Carter
Directed by Larry Shaw
Guest starring: Lynda Boyd (Bar Patron), Duncan Fraser (Beatty), Christopher Gray (Jimmie), Phil Hayes (Driver #1), Dan Lett (Sir Malcolm Marsden), Keegan Macintosh (Michael), Laurie Paton (Lady Marsden), Amanda Pays (Phoebe Green), Alan Robertson (Gray-Haired Man), Mark Sheppard (Cecil L'ively/Bob)

Mulder is visited by an old girlfriend, Phoebe Green, who is trying to protect a British lord after several members of Parliament have been burned to death. When Scully joins the investigation, they learn that the suspect is Cecil L'ively, the caretaker of the lord's Cape Cod retreat, who apparently has the ability to create flames from his mind.

✿ ✿ ✿

"This is an episode that people were mad at me from the beginning for because I wanted to do something with fire and it's very hard to work with," says Chris Carter with a laugh. "Fire is much hotter than you think it's going to be. Actually, it's amazingly frightening when you're around it and it's burning things down in your studio. Until you're actually confronted with those balls of flame, you can't imagine it. So that was an interesting thing. It's a very popular episode, and I'm just somewhat happy with the way it turned out. Having written it and imagined it in certain ways, I think it could have been a lot better. Although I thought it was generally well directed, the show felt very 'wide' to me — very loose and lacking some things."

"Boy," Robert Goodwin moans in mock weariness, "that was a hard one. Any kind of a fire stunt is a major undertaking, because it involves so many overlapping things. First of all, it is a stunt, so you have to have a stuntman who can work fire. A lot of them can't. We had two full body burns in that show and those were people inside those flames. If it's inside, which many of the film sequences were, because of natural concerns for safety and all the legal concerns by the fire department, you have to carefully design and build the sets in such a manner that they're fireproof and the fire can be controlled. It was a major feat, a real logistical and creative feat, because you wanted it to look good. Mark Sheppard is at the far end of the hall and Mulder is in the foreground. He waves with his arms and these flames come racing down the hallway and along the ceiling. It's just a spectacular moment, but it got to be so hot that the actor could not stand it any longer and had to duck

out of the show. I remember that there was a whole lot of trickery we had to pull off because he was supposed to be standing there when he wasn't. Director Larry Shaw, with very short time to prepare, was able to pull it off."

One aspect of the show that Carter did enjoy was the attempt to explore a little more of Mulder's background and personality. "I thought it was interesting to show a little bit of Mulder's history by bringing an old girlfriend back," he notes. "I've always wanted to do a Scotland Yard detective who was a woman. I also thought it was an interesting chance to use Amanda Pays and to make a villainess of her."

James Wong doesn't feel that the relationship was conveyed effectively. "I thought there was so much more in the script in terms of emotions that Mulder and Amanda Pays's character were supposed to have. There's a lot more to their relationship in the script than there was on the screen. It didn't play at all, and that should have been the subtext of the whole show. We ended up cutting a lot of stuff that just didn't work."

"The weird thing about that script," adds Glen Morgan, "is that Chris had that concept and started writing it, and then LA started burning. I think that fueled him a bit. And I think Chris would acknowledge that Jim Wong is a very good editor. At one point the story was muddled and Jim, in editing, put things in a different way and it came out good. That was a situation where you didn't have the time to do an insert and fix it. People have written that they like it. I like that bit with the cigarette in the beginning where it lights itself. Little things like that are effective."

Rating/Audience Share: 6.8/12

Episode 1.13
"Beyond the Sea"

Original airdate: January 7, 1994
Written by Glen Morgan and James Wong
Directed by David Nutter
Guest starring: Katherynn Chisholm (Nurse), Don Davis (Capt. William Scully), Brad Dourif (Luther Lee Boggs), Fred Henderson (Agent Thomas), Lawrence King (Lucas Jackson Henry), Sheila Larken (Margaret Scully), Randy Lee (Paramedic), Don MacKay (Warden Joseph Cash), Len Rose (Emergency Room Doctor), Lisa Vultaggio (Liz Hawley), Chad Willett (Jim Summers)

Mulder and Scully, who is coping with the death of her father, take on a kidnapping case that leads them to a prisoner on death row named Luther Lee Boggs. Claiming to be psychic, Boggs tells the duo he'll help solve the case if they can get his sentence changed. In the midst of the investigation, Scully — the skeptic — sees visions of her dead father and, despite Mulder's claims she's being manipulated, she turns to Boggs as a possible channel to her father's spirit.

❀ ❀ ❀

"I'm uncomfortable talking about my own work, but I am proud of this episode," Glen Morgan admits. "Jim and I have written maybe thirty hours of television, and before working on this series there were maybe three *21 Jump Streets* which I can say I'm proud of. 'Beyond the Sea' is another show I'm proud of. We fought pretty hard for Brad Dourif, and Chris came through for us. [*One Flew Over the*] *Cuckoo's Nest* is a movie that means a lot, and to have Brad Dourif [a star of that movie] saying our lines just meant the world to me. If you had someone crummy in there, that's where the show would have fallen apart. The story provided us with a chance to deal with Scully and expand her role a bit and change the rules around. If people say it's derivative of *Silence of the Lambs*, that's just a brilliant idea Thomas Harris came up with. I hope it's not seen that way, and it's something I tried to avoid as much as possible. I just thought that Brad Dourif and Gillian's performances were great, and David Nutter did a great job directing."

For his part, Nutter is justifiably proud of the show. "To me," he says, "I think it's the most accomplished piece of directing of actors I have been able to do. I thought Brad Dourif was brilliant, and I thought I helped bring him to where he should have been, and we were able to capture what he could really do onscreen. I very much enjoyed working with Gillian on the show. I think she's a young actress with a lot of talent but not a lot of experience prior to this show. I think this episode really made a difference in how the audience looks at Scully. I think it brought a lot of dimension to her character, and for her as a person it definitely had a lot of impact. It also allowed us to explore the emotional side of things, which we don't talk that much about. To me it's right up there with 'Ice.' Certainly one of the most enjoyable shows I did."

Robert Goodwin recalls, "The whole thing was spellbinding. One of those episodes where a guy in my position just has to get the sets built, stick the actors in, let the director do his job and let the actors do theirs."

"My favorite episode of the first year," Chris Carter enthuses, "and one of my favorites overall, flipping the Mulder and Scully points of view. Actually, the network did not want to do that episode. They had turned it down because they thought it was too much like *Silence of the Lambs*. I was so sure this was a great episode that I remember running up to the executive building — literally running — into Dan McDermott's office and saying, 'These guys believe in this episode, I believe in this episode, we've got to do this episode.' They finally let us do it, although there was a question of whether or not we'd have Brad Dourif. I remember calling Peter Roth, the president of Twentieth Century Fox, at home on Thanksgiving and saying, 'This is the guy we need for this episode.' There was a money issue. He was the person who signed off on that. I pulled him away from the Thanksgiving table and he said, 'Just cast him,' and that was it. The tim-

ing to call him was perfect, though it was inadvertent."

Rating/Audience Share: 6.6/11

Episode 1.14
"Genderbender"
Original airdate: January 21, 1994
Written by Larry Barber and Paul Barber
Directed by Rob Bowman
Guest starring: Doug Abrahams (Agent #2), Paul Batten (Brother Wilton), Grai Carrington (Tall Man), Lesley Ewen (Agent #1), Michele Goodger (Sister Abigail), Brent Hinkley (Brother Andrew), Mitchell Kosterman (Det. Horton), Nicholas Lea (Michael), Aundrea MacDonald (Pretty Woman), Tony Morelli (Cop), Peter Stebbings (Male Marty), John R. Taylor (Husband), David Thomson (Brother Oakley), Kate Twa (Female Marty)

When five people die during sex — and there is evidence of an impossible amount of pheromones — Mulder and Scully proceed to a Massachusetts religious sect known as the Kindred. There, Scully nearly falls victim to one of the sect, but is rescued by Mulder. What they discover is that members of the Kindred have the ability to switch genders at will, with the implication at episode's end being that they are actually an alien race.

✼ ✼ ✼

"We had brought in a couple of writing producers, Paul and Larry Barber, who came up with the idea of gender-shifting characters in a sort of Amish setting," Chris Carter recalls. "I think the idea is pretty good, and there are some interesting visual moments. Rob Bowman really rose to the occasion and showed us what he is capable of, which is why he's on the show as a producer now. A terrific episode given real style and passion by Rob."

One bit of criticism Carter has received about the episode is its conclusion, with circular burn marks in a field that indicate a UFO may have been involved in the scenario. "I like that ending, though a lot of people complained," he says. "I think it's vague: Is it or isn't it? That ambiguity is a hallmark of some of our best episodes."

James Wong doesn't agree. "There were problems with the ending of the show," he says, "in that we pretty much wrapped it up relatively quickly and just threw in something [the burn marks]. Those things always seem like a little trick. It's like we tried to play a trick on the audience to make them say, 'Ooh, what the heck was that?' But when it's not integral to the story, it lessens the impact. You don't get a sense of a cathartic moment, because we kind of blew it."

"Initially," Glen Morgan adds, "we said we wanted an episode with more of a sexy edge, but it was difficult to find a story that shows sex as scary. As a result, it kind of veered off to, What if there are people like the Amish who are from another planet? I think people have said that we overstepped the bounds on that one. Maybe we went too far. At what point do we become unbelievable?"

Rob Bowman was the best of the early directors of *Star Trek: The Next Generation*, helming episodes in that show's first two seasons that were visually unlike those of anyone else working on the series. Feeling stifled, he left in the middle of year two and was creatively reborn when he joined *The X-Files*.

"At the time of 'Genderbender,' *The X-*

"We wanted an episode with more of a sexy edge, but it was difficult to find a show that shows sex as scary."

Files was a series that hadn't fully defined itself," Bowman explains. "The script I received was from outside writers who, in Chris's mind, hadn't fulfilled his wishes, whatever they were. The concept of the show was a low-tech episode where they didn't want to have any high-tech anything. They wanted

mostly lantern light, and the only tech you would have would be the contrast between the city life and this very primitive farm life. There was a deliberate attempt to come up with swirling lights, multicolored things, people wearing shining clothes, lots of steel and shine and some Gigerisms with very sexual connotations, and you slam that against people carrying lanterns around in these monk-like outfits.

"It was a very bizarre story," Bowman elaborates, "especially for me, because it was my first episode. The story challenges were to examine the influence of a superficial society,

with its vanity and sex and what's trendy. That's what the Amish people found in the magazine the one guy is enticed by. Reproduction was a very significant part of their culture, as indicated by the cave and the very phallic, lubricated cave walls that were found. I suppose the trick that I had to pull off was to draw the greatest contrasts between the two worlds.

"The difficulties of shooting it were just that the cave was so small that we had guys crawling around there and there was no light. Lantern light is not enough to light up a face for film. Production-wise, it was very difficult to get enough light in the cave. I had to go back an extra day and fill out quite a bit of the stuff with Mulder and the cave because it took too long to get the stuff I needed. I'd say that seventy-five percent of the stuff with Mulder down in the caves was shot another day with a smaller unit."

For Robert Goodwin, "Genderbender" was an artistic triumph, primarily in terms of art direction. He also cites the female-to-male switch as being a technical challenge.

"One of these guys has gone haywire because he's tasted sex and he's off and his pheromones are so strong that they can kill anyone he has sex with. He/She doesn't care because they're overpowered by lust. To really pay off the business about this person being able to change gender, we decided we'd have one shot where we would actually morph the female into the male. We wanted to be as believable as possible. We'd already cast the female, who had a very distinct look, and we searched around and found this wonderful young actor who looked very much like the girl. There was a very strong resemblance. In the scene, Mulder has trapped this person and she morphs into the male and comes out, knocks him down, and takes off. When we shot the two parts of the morph and put it together, the two actors really looked so much alike that it didn't look like a morph. It looked like this girl was just standing up. We were *too* good at casting, I think, and it zapped the energy out of the moment."

Graeme Murray notes that the design of this particular episode was a true hybrid. "We were working with an Amish kind of look, also a sleazy downtown look, and a kind of alien center where they brought people to be revived," he says. "It has a nice feel to it. That kind of Amish culture is sort of alien anyway, and combining real alien on top of that was interesting."

Rating/Audience Share: 7.2/12

Episode 1.15
"Lazarus"

Original airdate: February 4, 1994
Written by Alex Gansa and Howard Gordon
Directed by David Nutter
Guest starring: Christopher Allport (Agent Jack Willis), Alexander Boynton (Clean-Cut Man), Jay Brazeau (Professor Varnes), Lisa Bunting (Doctor #1), Brenda Crichlow (Reporter), Jackson Davies (Agent Bruskin), Russell Hamilton (Officer Daniels), Peter Kelamis (O'Dell), Callum Keith Rennie (Tommy), Mark Saunders (Doctor #2), Jason Schombing (Warren James Dupre), Cec Verrell (Lula Philips)

In a Maryland bank, Scully and FBI agent Jack Willis are drawn into a shoot-out with a robber named Warren Dupre. Both Willis and Dupre are wounded and brought to the emergency room. Willis dies, but suddenly "comes back" after Dupre jumps up and dies himself. Shortly thereafter, Willis begins acting differently, with Mulder concluding that Dupre's spirit has somehow taken over the agent's body.

✵ ✵ ✵

Chris Carter enthuses, "A very good and well-acted episode. I like it because it actually seemed so real to me. It played less as a paranormal science fiction show than as whether or not something could really happen. The entire cast was wonderful. Overall that was a terrific episode."

According to Howard Gordon, the story initially had Mulder possessed by the person he was hunting. Fox didn't really like the notion of their hero experiencing, firsthand, such a supernatural occurrence. "I think that was a wise decision," Gordon admits, "though at the time we were angry and up in arms."

Director David Nutter notes, "Pacing was the key for that show. It was the opposite of 'Beyond the Sea.' I thought a lot of movement had to happen. The camera was moving, the actors were moving, all of which was designed to move the script along. It wasn't one of the more involved scripts. Just a pretty basic, straightforward story."

Rating/Audience Share: 7.6/12

Episode 1.16
"Young at Heart"
Original airdate: February 11, 1994
Written by Scott Kaufer and Chris Carter
Directed by Michael Lange
Guest starring: Courtney Arciaga (Progeria Victim), Alan Boyce (Young John Barnett), William B. Davis (Cigarette-Smoking Man), Robin Douglas (Computer Specialist), Christine Estabrook (Agent Henderson), Merrilyn Gann (Prosecutor), Jerry Hardin (Deep Throat), Graham Jarvis (Dr. Austin, NIH), Robin Mossley (Dr. Joe Ridley), David Petersen (Old John Barnett), Gordon Tipple (Joe Crandall), Dick Anthony Williams (Reggie Purdue)

Mulder finds himself going up against a killer from his past, John Barnett, whom he had put behind bars several years earlier, prior to taking on the X-Files. Barnett supposedly died in prison, but all clues are indicating that he is back, stalking Mulder and his friends, primarily Scully. They ultimately discover that Barnett has actually been a participant in a genetic experiment that is reversing the aging process, supplying him with the perfect means of disguise.

❂ ❂ ❂

"I liked the script very much," recalls director Michael Lange, "and I think I stayed fairly close to the original draft. I liked it because it had a lot of good spookiness to it. To me, the intriguing part was the doctor's research into being able to reverse the aging process, which I wish we could have explored more.

"In my first meeting with Chris Carter on the tone of the show," he adds, "Chris said, 'Remember one thing: On *The X-Files,* the Devil is in the details.' I write it big on my script whenever I do the show, because it's the details that make it work, as opposed to broad strokes. As a director, you really have to pay attention to all those details, or else no one is happy."

One problem, according to Glen Morgan, was the fact that the episode aired right after "Lazarus," and there were certain similarities between the shows. "When I looked at my bulletin board at the time," he reflects, "I saw that there was a pattern of 'Shadows' through 'Space' where we were trying to scare people. Then starting with 'Beyond the Sea' I think we were trying to do more intellectual stories. Then we tried to go back to a little more visceral storytelling. I think we may have been a little off course on some of them. Chris had said, 'Where's the big boo? Where's the real scare scene?' And I don't know if they had those."

For Robert Goodwin, "Young at Heart" is one of the most emotional episodes of the first season. "When Mulder and Scully are finding out about this doctor, they're running this old scratchy black and white footage of him in the institute he ran back in the fifties and sixties, in which he was working with children who had progeria, the disease that aged them, so that by the time they're ten they're like seventy-year-olds. We needed that footage to run, and Paul Rabwin contacted the Progeria Society and we actually brought a darling little girl up from San Diego who had the disease. We shot this footage with her. Michael Lange directed. He has two little girls and I have a couple of kids, and it was a very, very touching moment for all of us. We felt it was good

> **"Chris said, 'Remember one thing: on *The X-Files,* the Devil is in the details.'"**

because it made the disease visible, so it helped create more public awareness of it. On an individual basis, when we contacted the parents we found out they were big fans of the show, as was the little girl. It was almost like a 'Make a Wish' kind of thing; it was wonderful."

Rating/Audience Share: 7.2/11

Episode 1.17

"E.B.E."

Original airdate: February 18, 1994
Written by Glen Morgan and James Wong
Directed by William Graham
Guest starring: Tom Braidwood (Frohike),
Dean Haglund (Langly), Jerry Hardin (Deep
Throat), Bruce Harwood (Byers), Peter
LaCroix (Ranheim/Druse), Allan Lysell (Chief
Rivers)

Claiming it's a means of protecting Mulder, Deep Throat sends Mulder and Scully on a wild UFO chase, diverting them from a military operation to contain an extraterrestrial retrieved from a UFO crash over Iraq. By the time Mulder figures out the truth, the E.B.E. (extraterrestrial biological entity) has been exterminated. Deep Throat reveals that he is one of three people who has participated in the extermination of extraterrestrials in the past, and his helping Mulder is an attempt to make amends for what he has done.

Note: This episode introduced the Lone Gunman, a conspiracy-obsessed organization that is well aware of Mulder's efforts.

✿ ✿ ✿

"When we tested 'Squeeze' with an audience," Glen Morgan recalls, "they said, 'Well, it was okay. I don't know if a person could stretch like that. But I like the UFO and conspiracy stuff,' so Jim and I had a chance to do one, and 'E.B.E.' was the result. A lot of that was from fan mail, what people wanted us to deal with. I think 'E.B.E.' was written for people who we felt were hardcore *X-Files* fans: people into UFOs and every conspiracy imaginable. The thing is, they screened 'E.B.E' and people were saying, 'I like the UFO episodes, but there was one where this guy kind of stretched . . .' C'mon, make up your mind. Anyway, the movie I kind of really looked at in order to catch the tone for 'E.B.E.' was *All the President's Men*, dealing with dark parking lots and that kind of paranoia."

James Wong isn't as pleased with the final product. "I really felt we didn't do a great job on the script," he says. "We wanted to do a show that's all about paranoia and a conspiracy theory, but at the end I felt like we didn't really gain a lot of new ground or learn a lot of new things. I think we played a lot of texture instead of substance."

"Another of our most popular first-season episodes," says Chris Carter. "Jim and Glen wanted to do an alien episode, and this is what they came up with. I thought it was well directed by Bill Graham. I thought there were some really memorable scenes in it, particularly Deep Throat and the shark tank, also the teaser with the Iraqi pilot. Some really wacky stuff: the UFO party, and the introduction of the Lone Gunman, and they've served us well since then. Glen and Jim had both gone incognito to things like UFO conventions and saw folks setting up their booths, selling rather paranoid literature. These guys represented a certain type that we had run across."

Says Graeme Murray, "A lot of the episode took place in a facility in Vancouver where they do high-voltage electrical research, which is where we created the containment facility where they hold the alien. That was a fascinating kind of place, where they create lightning and high-voltage electrical effects. A wonderful location for us. Then we built a couple of things. There was a forty-foot truck that transported the alien, and we built an interesting room in there, although you didn't see much of it actually in the show. It was like a traveling life support room for an alien."

Rating/Audience Share: 6.2/9

Episode 1.18
"Miracle Man"

Original airdate: March 18, 1994
Written by Howard Gordon and Chris Carter
Directed by Michael Lange
Guest starring: Scott Bairstow (Samuel), Lisa Ann Beley (Beatrice Salinger), Iris Quinn Bernard (Lillian Daniels), R. D. Call (Sheriff Daniels), Chilton Crane (Margaret Hohman), Alex Doduk (Young Samuel), George Gerdes (The Rev. Cal Hartley), Roger Haskett (Deputy Tyson), Campbell Lane (Margaret's Father), Dennis Lipscomb (Leonard Vance), Walter Marsh (Judge), Howard Storey (Fire Chief)

A faith healer named Samuel who, in 1983, brought a man back to life by praying over him, finds himself the subject of a Mulder and Scully investigation after he attempts to heal a woman who dies instead. Seeming miracles turn out to be quite man-made, and there is much skepticism over Samuel's "powers," even as he cryptically mentions Mulder's sister and the fact that she was taken away by strangers within bright lights. In the end, though, his true spiritual abilities are revealed.

✵ ✵ ✵

"Miracle Man" marked the first collaboration between Howard Gordon and Chris Carter, following Alex Gansa's departure from the series.

"Howard came to my house," Carter says, "and said, 'Help me out,' so we went to my living room and put up this bulletin board and in a matter of hours we came up with this story. Then Howard and I split up the scenes. It was a blast, because Howard and I had never written together before. We had a great time. And I think it set the tone and laid a foundation for what our relationship is. Besides that, we wanted to do something with the bright side of the paranormal, and of course we had to contrast it against the dark side, with this kid who had been able to heal people with his hands and believed he had lost his gift. It was really a story about human nature, jealousy, and the tragedy of this kid's death set against the idea of Mulder and Scully's faith and the appearance of Mulder's sister."

Of the scenario itself, Gordon adds: "We said, 'This is a show about belief, about possibilities.' We're all believers at some level. There's healing beyond what you get at your local MD. Given that, I think there's a power of faith, and so we set out right away to not do the obvious, which would be to make these people into buffoons. In a way, it was a kind of Jesus story. You don't have to look too hard to see the parallels. Samuel was a kid who was given a gift. Our premise was, What if a prophet or someone with special powers was set down on Earth? What would happen to him?"

"On an intellectual level," says director Michael Lange, "it really dealt with the subject of God — the power of God — and the power of man in kind of a neat way. There were a lot of things to think about, working on it as a director, and also for the viewer. If you want to go along with it, it can really take you to some neat places. I was trying to kind of create the image of the son of Jesus, basically. Some of the things I put in were actually pulled back by the network when they saw it. Networks, and I think human beings in general, always have a problem with compositing violence with religion. There was one scene where Samuel was beaten up by the guys in the jail cell and was killed, as we find out in the next scene. I had this one image that I shot, which was the silhouette of him against the wall with the bars, and he actually had

taken a crucifix pose, and that of course went bye-bye. Even the bold Fox network couldn't handle that one.

"All of the tent stuff with the faith healing was done in one day," he continues. "We had three hundred extras and managed to get it done in one day. I, myself, have a kind of skepticism about all these faith healers, but by the end of that day I could see how people would be drawn into it, because it's very compelling. There were some very inspirational things in there, and everyone became so infused with this fervor that you really could understand how it could all happen. It doesn't happen often on TV that you can explore an area of the human experience and feel it that much."

Glen Morgan is a little more critical of the episode. "I think it's kind of easy to pick on religion," he says, "especially one of the fundamentalist backgrounds. It's easy to portray them as Bible thumpers. To tell you the truth, there are a lot of people for whom it's their faith, and I would like to have had a little more respect towards that. Overall, my personal belief is that some of the phoniness needs to be exposed; however, it's just kind of easy to say this is all that it is. I think there is more to it. There are good people who have Christian faith in their background. They're not just on bad cable. It's a tough challenge because, really, on network TV they don't want you to deal with religion."

Robert Goodwin's difficulties with the episode were of quite a different nature. "The problem with 'Miracle Man' is always a problem when you shoot a show that's set in the South anywhere but in the South," he explains. "It's really easy to do a bad Southern accent. That, for me, was one of the bigger challenges, because a lot of the supporting actors come from Vancouver, but there are also people up here who come from the South. I hired a dialect coach to help even it all out so it didn't sound like they were coming from fifteen different parts of the South."

"Setting up the tent and getting that Southern atmosphere in Vancouver was kind of interesting," says Graeme Murray. "That episode was kind of difficult to put together logistically. There were a lot of different little places, and trying to get that Southern atmosphere was a little tough. It was a real location show. A lot of time in the shows like that is spent trying to put together a day of shooting where you have what are supposed to be four or five different locations and we don't really have the time to move during a day. You pretty much have to shoot a day in the location, so everything has to be found within walking distance of the major set of that day. 'Miracle Man' was particularly like that, and putting it all together was very tricky."

Rating/Audience Share: 7.5/13

Episode 1.19
"Shapes"

Original airdate: April 1, 1994
Written by Marilyn Osborn
Directed by David Nutter
Guest starring: Jimmy Herman (Ish), Michael Horse (Charley Tskany), Dwight McFee (David Gates), Paul McLean (Dr. Josephs), Ty Miller (Lyle Parker), Renae Morriseau (Gwen Goodensnake), Donnelly Rhodes (Jim Parker)

Reports of a strange beast that has attacked a man reach the desks of Mulder and Scully, who proceed to the Two Medicine Ranch in Browning, Montana. There they learn that rancher Jim Parker shot the beast that attacked his son, Lyle, and the creature turned out to be an Indian named Joseph Goodensnake. Eventually, Lyle — the victim of the beast's bite — finds himself transforming into an Indian manitou.

❊   ❊   ❊

"People would say to me, 'When are you going to do the vampire and werewolf thing?'" Glen Morgan recalls. "Well, here it is. Like a good rock band should be able to play standards by Chuck Berry, I feel we should be able to do the basics. I think there's room for the straight-out, scare-the-hell-out-of-people type of show."

"The network wanted a monster show,"

notes David Nutter, "and that's what they got. The main crux for me on that show was to create an atmosphere that would make it as different as possible from other episodes. Also, the manitou wasn't too much in your face. You only saw a little bit of the monster here and a little bit of it there, and it was all very well handled."

"The manitou is a combination of eleven or twelve different sounds of varying degrees, varying pitches, and varying speeds."

The visual execution of the manitou especially pleased Robert Goodwin. "That monster was put together in a combination of traditional and computer ways," he says. "We had a man in a suit with an articulated mask. Then we had a dog's-head mask that was also articulated for the teeth and the fangs, and those elements were brought together."

The final ingredient needed to bring the manitou to life came in postproduction, where Paul Rabwin supervised the sound effects. "We needed a combination of sounds in order to make it frightening," he recounts. "A sound that was part animal and part human. We had several groans and screams from different animals, ranging from a hawk's screech to a lion's roar. Then I had an actor who specializes in voices do a number of different screams and sounds. In the end, the manitou is a combination of eleven or twelve different sounds of varying degrees, varying pitches, and varying speeds. The sound was familiar in that we heard elements of the Wolf Man, but different in that it was definitely *The X-Files*."

"I thought Jim and Glen, in rewriting Marilyn Osborn's script, did a terrific job of giving us a good sort of meat-and-potatoes werewolf story by calling it a manitou, which was our *X-Files* twist on it," says

Chris Carter. "I thought it was very well directed by David Nutter. Glen's right in his feeling that this show should be able to deal with more traditional monsters. I defend that.

When you do twenty-five episodes a year, you are going to get some that are a little more down the pipe, and I think this one is an example of that."

Graeme Murray explains, "We were trying to re-create this big-sky Montana ranch country in Vancouver. We shot in a town that was created for a show called *Bordertown*. It was one of those shows where you just try and get it done on schedule and on budget."

Rating/Audience Share: 7.6/14

Episode 1.20
"Darkness Falls"
Original airdate: April 15, 1994
Written by Chris Carter
Directed by Joe Napolitano
Guest starring: Jason Beghe (Larry Moore), Barry Greene (Perkins), David Hay (Clean-Suited Man), Tom O'Rourke (Steve Humphreys), Ken Tremblett (Dyer), Titus Welliver (Doug Spinney)

Mulder and Scully are drawn to the Olympic National Forest in northwest Washington State, following up a report that loggers have been attacked and killed by a mysterious entity. Once there, they find themselves essentially trapped with several other people, the victims of phosphorous insects that have seemingly been unleashed from a recently felled tree, and that feast on human flesh.

✿ ✿ ✿

Chris Carter reflects, "This came right from my college biology class, where we studied the reading of tree rings. I thought, 'Let's go to the woods and cut open one of these big trees, which are really historical time capsules of everything that has gone on in the past couple of thousand years. What if there are these bugs that escape and hold everyone hostage?' It was supposed to be a bottle show, but in fact it turned out to be one of our hardest shows. The first day of that episode, I woke up and looked out the window and there was a blizzard and I thought they were never going to make it; that nothing would match from that day on. You see some scenes where the actors are just miserably soaked. *We* didn't make that rain."

Indeed, "Darkness Falls" is probably most noteworthy for the physical hardships it imposed on the cast and crew.

"It was the dead of winter," Robert Goodwin moans. "Out of eight days of shooting, six of them were in the forest. There were terrible rainstorms and mud, and it became a logistical nightmare. On a television series you don't usually tackle that kind of thing. That's usually reserved for big-budget features. In any case, at one point I just sent the company home because it was raining so hard. It was like trying to see through a waterfall. But it all came out in the end, and the episode was pretty scary."

"It was very tough on the crew," seconds

Glen Morgan. "No one wanted to go through that again. The next episode was 'Tooms,' and Bob Goodwin called me up and said, 'You know those keys on your typewriter that spell

"Rabwin cast 10,000 mites, which were very temperamental."

EXT for exterior? They're now broken.' So 'Tooms' had a lot of interiors."

Perhaps the producer with the most legitimate reason for complaining about the episode is Paul Rabwin, who had to cast 10,000 extras for the episode — without getting an increased budget. "I spent a lot of time trying to find the right stock footage of the thousands of insects we needed for the show," he says. "Ninety-five percent of the insects you see are computer generated, particularly the descending swarm and the specks in the corner of the room. But there were a couple of shots where we wanted to see thousands of bugs up close, and we couldn't find any stock footage that had the feel we were looking for."

Rabwin ultimately hooked up with a cameraman who specializes in microscopic photography, which in turn led to his "casting" 10,000 mites, which were extremely temperamental.

"They tend to shy away from the light," he points out. "And photographing them was dif-

ficult — they were so small you couldn't corral them. We finally figured out that they're slowed down by the cold, so we took this nitrogen solution and placed it on the bottom of the slide, and all these little buggers congregated around the nitrogen. Then we removed the nitrogen and quickly put it on the microscope, and we had about a thirty-second window of opportunity to photograph them before they started to disperse. It was an effects-heavy show, and there were a number of scenes that these insects were in, so it had to be staged properly."

Rating/Audience Share: 8.0/14

Episode 1.21
"Tooms"
Original airdate: April 22, 1994
Written by Glen Morgan and James Wong
Directed by David Nutter
Guest starring: Steve Adams (Myers), Henry Beckman (Det. Frank Briggs), Pat Bermel (Frank Ranford), Gillian Carfra (Christine Ranford), Andre Daniels (Arlan Green), Jan D'Arcy (Judge Kann), Glynis Davis (Nelson), William B. Davis (Cigarette-Smoking Man), Mikal Dughi (Dr. Karetzky), Doug Hutchison (Eugene Victor Tooms), Catherine Lough (Dr. Richmond), Mitch Pileggi (Assistant Director Walter S. Skinner), Frank C. Turner (Dr. Collins), Paul Ben Victor (Dr. Aaron Monte), Jerry Wasserman (Dr. Plith), Timothy Webber (Det. Talbot)

Eugene Tooms, who was arrested and placed in a sanitarium at the conclusion of "Squeeze," is released for good behavior, and attempts to go back to his old ways, doing his best to get Mulder out of the picture by making it seem that the FBI agent has been stalking and threatening him, resulting in the desired effect. However, when Tooms kills his doctor, chows down on the man's liver, and goes back into hibernation, Mulder and Scully discover his nest in an area beneath a building, where they have a final confrontation.

✻ ✻ ✻

"Here's the weird thing," muses Glen Morgan, "and I can't explain it. When we were finishing 'Shapes,' I said, 'This is really good; I like it.' When I saw it aired, I said, 'Kind of a letdown. I don't know why.' When we were doing 'Tooms,' I was disappointed, and then we were mixing in the sound and I thought, 'Man, I love this.' Doug Hutchison really stole the show. He had the character down.

"Jim and I had never done a follow-up to a show we had written. You have the challenge that you just assume that a lot of people hadn't seen the first one, so you have to quickly recap what this guy is about and that's why act one is at Tooms's trial. You could recap what the rules were with this monster. With this character, it's kind of like, 'What would you like to see him do?'

"The other thing was that the first show ['Squeeze'] had a director who was a problem, so this was a real chance to correct that part of it and do some of those things that were cut out of the first episode. I cannot tell you how unwatchable the first cut of 'Squeeze' was. When I watch it, I can't even follow the story. I just see where we solved problems, or hope that we solved problems."

Robert Goodwin says, laughing, "Nothing brilliant to say about the episode. We brought back Pepper, our contortionist from Seattle. My kids and their friends kept showing up at the set, because Tooms is their hero."

Chris Carter admits, "This was sort of the command performance of Tooms. We had had such a difficult time with 'Squeeze' — it took so much care in postproduction to make it what it was — that this was an opportunity to take the character and do a sequel using David Nutter, who that season was definitely our best director. To have him come in and give it his take. In a way, it was almost a vindication episode. I think it turned out very well, and Tooms remains a very popular character."

"The main thing for me on that show," says David Nutter, "was knowing how popular this character was, I felt it was important to give him his just deserts on the second show. The producers weren't so happy with how the first show turned out. The character caught on; they had worked very hard to make it work to the point they wanted. But for the second show, they really wanted to make it good. I'm lucky I was available to do that one. I think it's a real classic horror story; I think Tooms is a real classic character in the horror genre, and

I wanted to punch that up as much as possible. I think I'm really happy with the finale of that show."

Rating/Audience Share: 8.6/15

Episode 1.22
"Born Again"
Original airdate: April 29, 1994
Written by Alex Gansa and Howard Gordon
Directed by Jerrold Freedman
Guest starring: Leslie Carlson (Dr. Spitz), P. Lynn Johnson (Dr. Sheila Braun), Dwight Koss (Det. Barbala), Peter Lapres (Harry Linhart), Andre Libman (Michelle Bishop), Mimi Lieber (Anita Fiore), Brian Markinson (Tony Fiore), Richard Sali (Felder), Maggie Wheeler (Det. Sharon Lazard), Dey Young (Judy Bishop)

An eight-year-old girl with a penchant for disfiguring dolls is linked to a series of deaths, all of which are reminiscent of the work of a serial killer who is now dead. An investigation by Mulder and Scully seems to indicate that the serial killer has been reincarnated in the body of the little girl.

❊ ❊ ❊

Says Howard Gordon, "The idea of reincarnation hadn't been done yet, and there were parts of it that I think were interesting, but I don't think it was very well executed on any front. It was a pretty classic back-from-the-dead revenge tale, and not done particularly interestingly. And it had elements that were repetitive to one of my previous [*X-Files* episodes], 'Shadows.'"

"One of our least successful episodes," Chris Carter admits. "I thought the direction was a little sloppy, but it's one of those episodes that plays a little closer to reality and I like that about it. There's a nice twist in it about a man marrying the wife of another man he had killed. There were actually some nice effects. Just not one of my favorites."

Robert Goodwin's strongest memory of the episode was its teaser, in which a police officer went through a window. "We were shooting the exterior portion of the body exploding out this window. There were actually a pair of windows in this room. We took out the glass from one of them and put in what we call candy glass. And we used this cannon that blasted the debris out the candy-glass window. We had three or four cameras shooting the thing. They call 'Action,' the window blows out, and we realize that the force of the concussion from this cannon has also knocked a hole about three feet across and a foot high in the real window next to our phony window. Al Campbell, our key grip, sort of a Will Rogers kind of guy, says, 'I have a perfect solution for this. When the woman goes to the window, and looks down to see the dead guy, just pan over and next to him will be his dead dog.'"

Rating/Audience Share: 8.2/14

Episode 1.23
"Roland"
Original airdate: May 6, 1994
Written by Chris Ruppenthal
Directed by David Nutter
Guest starring: Garry Davey (Dr. Keats), Dave Hurtubise (Dr. Lawrence Barrington), Zeljko Ivanek (Roland Fuller), Sue Mathew (Lisa Dole), Micole Mercurio (Mrs. Stodie), Kerry Sandomirksy (Tracy), James Sloyan (Dr. Nollette), Matthew Walker (Dr. Surnow)

At a propulsion laboratory, a scientist is trapped in a wind tunnel and is killed through the actions of a severely handicapped janitor named Roland. Upon checking out the situation, Mulder and Scully learn that Roland's brother, Dr. Arthur Grable, recently died in an apparent accident and that the man's head is being kept in a jar of liquid nitrogen. When they learn that Grable's research is being pilfered by his fellow scientists, Mulder concludes that somehow Grable's brain is reaching from beyond the grave (or perhaps the liquid nitrogen) to control Roland's actions.

❖ ❖ ❖

"Probably the weakest script from start to finish that I got," David Nutter admits. "I was really fortunate to get a really fine actor named Zeljko Ivanek, who was wonderful. I thought he was just great. Basically when I knew I had him, I thought it was important to push that as much as possible, to help outweigh the frailties in the script. I felt like it was a real strong character piece. Some of the shows are going to be like that. You're not always going to get the best scripts in the world, but if you get a good actor involved with it and really push that aspect of it, it will definitely help to make it better."

Chris Carter concurs. "Just an amazing performance. This guy, Zeljko, should have won an award for this. I thought he was just fantastic. He was actually the first person to come in and read for this part, and then we had about ten people come in after him, but they just didn't get it. We cast this guy and he turned in a terrific performance which, for me, made the episode. Hats off to David Nutter and to the writing staff for falling in and making the episode really work."

Glen Morgan offers, "Overall, ultimately it probably wasn't completely effective, but I think the show should do some softer, so to speak, episodes; episodes that demonstrate the paranormal isn't always horrifying. It can offer different notions of hope, a life afterwards, consciousness, and things like that."

"You may not notice it in the episode, but there were a lot of scientific rooms and a wind tunnel to be created," says Graeme Murray.

"It was all kind of fun. It was interesting for us just learning some of these things; we spent a lot of time in some of the scientific research places around Vancouver and in the universities."

Rating/Audience Share: 7.9/14

Episode 1.24
"The Erlenmeyer Flask"
Original airdate: May 13, 1994
Written by Chris Carter
Directed by Robert Goodwin
Guest starring: William B. Davis (Cigarette-Smoking Man), Anne DeSalvo (Dr. Carpenter), Lindsey Ginter (Crew-Cut Man), Jaylene Hamilton (Reporter), Jerry Hardin (Deep Throat), Ken Kramer (Dr. Bérubé), Jim Leard (Capt. Lacerio), Phillip MacKenzie (Medic), Mike Mitchell (Cop), John Payne (Guard), Simon Webb (Dr. Secare)

Mulder and Scully investigate a government scientist, Dr. Bérubé, who has cloned extraterrestrial DNA recovered from an alien embryo and is injecting it into terminally ill humans. Those subjects return to complete health, but are stronger than they originally were. And the government's reasons for the alien DNA experiments go beyond the goal of advancing medical science. Guided by Deep Throat, both Mulder and Scully (seemingly no longer the skeptic she once was) are determined to reveal the truth before it's completely and ruthlessly covered up. Shockingly, the episode ends with Deep Throat's death, the disposal of the alien embryo, and the closing of the X-Files, with Mulder and Scully being reassigned.

❊ ❊ ❊

Says Chris Carter, "'Erlenmeyer Flask' brings back nothing but good memories. It just has terrific images in it; it really brought the series in its first year full circle. It was successful in doing what we wanted to do, which was to close down the X-Files. It shocked a lot of people. Glen told me he got a message on his machine when the show ended, a woman with a shaky voice saying, 'What have you done?' They couldn't believe we had killed off a very popular character and closed the X-Files. I think it led us into the second season in a very interesting way."

"That was another case where we had to fight the network," Glen Morgan notes. "They said, 'Closing the X-Files is completely unacceptable. We will not air it because people will believe the show's been canceled.' My response was, 'It's your job to let them know it hasn't, and this is the best way to end the season.'"

"That was a big show for us," says Graeme Murray, "creating all the tanks that the bodies were floating in. We tried to make this kind of life support facility that looked real but also had an eerie aspect to it as well. That was a big set show and pretty interesting; a show where the script really inspired everybody to do the best job they could do."

For Robert Goodwin, who directed this season finale, the episode held special meaning. "In terms of a challenge, and coming at the end of the season — after a real long, tough time — this was a very difficult show, demanding physically, mentally, and every other way. It's the hardest series I've ever worked on. At the end of a very long year, the cast and crew were so tired, yet they all took a deep breath and just said, 'Here we go, guys,' and they gave the finale a two-hundred-percent effort. There's not one department that fell down. Everything about that episode is absolutely first class. The acting, the art direction, the camera work. There's nothing in it that isn't the best you can get, and that's really a credit to a lot of very talented people."

A highlight of the production for Goodwin was a sequence in which Scully is sitting on a bridge, waiting for Deep Throat to show up. His car finally arrives and she crosses the bridge to reach him.

"She's now got the alien fetus she's taken from a top-secret facility," Goodwin explains, "and he says, 'Okay, give it to me, I'm going to make the exchange [for Mulder].' She says, 'No, I'm going to do it.' Scully's very distrustful of him. Mulder's disappeared, she's

"'The Erlenmeyer Flask' shocked a lot of people. Glen told me he got a message on his machine when the show ended, saying, 'What have you done?'"

stressed out. What happened was, the night we shot that scene, we had a little scene to shoot somewhere else and we had to move over to this bridge. The plan was to get there an hour before it got dark so we could block the scene, and I had one shot I wanted to do, which was way up high on this crane elevator. We got to the location to block the scene. One end of the bridge was handled by the Vancouver police, and they didn't show up. By the time they got there, I had lost an hour. My plan had originally been to shoot this high scene, get down on the bridge and shoot this dialogue scene, the little piece with the two of them at the car where she's not going to give him the embryo. Then we go and do all the physical stuff that was needed for the whole sequence.

"Because of the hour lost," Goodwin continues, "I realized that the one part of it I could shoot on a stage was the dialogue: essentially two close-ups of them talking. So I didn't do the dialogue. I did everything else first. What happened was, I finally got to the dialogue and it was five in the morning. All night long, all these actors have been running back and forth and getting shot and dropping dead and doing all the things they had to do. And Gillian was very tired. Now I wake her up — she's been sleeping in the back of the car — and I say, 'Okay, let's do the dialogue.' And she got angry, rightfully so. Actually, not really angry. She was tired. I said, 'Listen, we're about to lose the darkness. The sun is going to come up in about twenty minutes. Let's just shoot it. If it's no good, I promise you we won't use it.' She said okay. The same thing with Jerry. We shot the scene and the both of them were so tired and stressed that it came out so strongly on film and was great. It taught me a lesson. If I'm in a similar situation, I'm going to do the same exact thing. If you look at her performance, she's just wonderful. We never had to reshoot it."

CHAPTER FIVE
Year Two: The Cult
Goes Mainstream

"During our first year," says co-producer Paul Rabwin, "the industry said *The X-Files* was a cross between *The Twilight Zone* and *The Night Stalker*. By our second season, *TV Guide* said that a new show, *The Kindred*, was 'a feeble attempt to imitate *The X-Files*.' Now the industry is saying the other networks are trying to launch shows that will take the eighteen-to-forty-nine audience away from *us*. We were even spoofed in *Mad* magazine. I guess we've made it!"

Even the FBI opened its door, inviting Carter in from the cold.

They certainly have. But with all due respect to Alfred E. Neuman, *The X-Files'* arrival in the big time of network television probably had more to do with winning the 1994 Golden Globe award for best drama than it did with a *Mad* magazine parody. It marks one of the few instances where critical attention significantly altered public awareness.

Many television viewers who had only vaguely heard of the Fox network show decided that if it could win a prestigious industry award against such highly acclaimed competition as *Chicago Hope* and *NYPD Blue*, there must be something to it. "The Golden Globe made a lot of people take notice," explains Rabwin, who supervises postproduction of each episode of *The X-Files*. "When we won, you could hear a pin drop. It was like the longest shot in the world coming in, and everyone was dumbfounded. It's given us wonderful credibility."

The momentum quickly transformed the creepy cult show into a ratings juggernaut. Soon after the Golden Globe victory, Viewers for Quality Television nominated the series for best drama and David Duchovny and Gillian Anderson as best actor and actress. Public approval followed critical acclaim, and the series went up 42 percent in the ratings during its second season, the highest gain of any show. "We became contenders." Rabwin smiles. "Suddenly, we were in a very different position than we were during the first year."

Even the FBI, which had refused to help Chris Carter when he was researching the show for its launch, opened its door, inviting the *X-Files* inner circle in from the cold.

"It was funny," Carter says of his tour of FBI headquarters in Washington, D.C., shortly after the second season began, "because when I was first preparing the show, they were very reluctant to give me any information. They didn't know who I was or what I wanted or what I was doing, and they really wouldn't

Co-Executive Producer Robert Goodwin

"Essentially, I'm the commander of the invasion of Normandy, and at the same time I'm worrying about the forces in Italy."

Although this sounds like a bit of self-importance from an ego in overdrive, everything is put in perspective when one realizes that the speaker is Robert Goodwin, co–executive producer of *The X-Files*.

Goodwin, a veteran of such quality television fare as *Hooperman; Mancuso, FBI; Eddie Dodd;* and *Life Goes On*, is the guy who supervises all aspects of physical production of the Fox sensation, taking the various scripts and somehow seeing that they are brought to life on film.

"On a show like *Life Goes On*, the biggest problem we had was whether we were shooting the kitchen or the living room," says Goodwin. "We had two stages at Warner Brothers, the house on the back lot, and that's it. It was essentially the same cast every week. All of which means it was much easier to produce, as opposed to *The X-Files*, which is murderous. We have eight days of shooting, so we potentially have eight days to prepare each episode. I have casting to do, the locations, various and sundry meetings regarding special effects or stunts, then we use the last day to have a production meeting and go over the script page by page with all the heads of production to make sure everyone is prepared for what they have to do. Then we have a 'tone' meeting, which usually involves the writer, the director, myself, and Chris Carter. What we do in the tone meeting is go through the script and make sure that the director and writer are on the same page. Sometimes it's not completely clear what the writer had in mind, so this is an opportunity to take care of that. We discuss characterization, what the actors require, what we hope to get out of it. Then we have our final 'show and tells' with prop support and special effects, and then they're off shooting."

Part of the challenge for Goodwin is that there are two units usually shooting simultaneously, which means he is responsible for getting sets, wardrobe, props, actors, and directors to two different locations at the same time. "It's like doing the *New York Times* crossword puzzle every day," he says with a laugh. "For instance, on a day like today, [producer–director] Rob Bowman is finishing up an episode he's just done that involves a mysterious discovery at the bottom of the ocean, so we have a lot of underwater photography. We finished the principal photography last Wednesday; yesterday he was out on a boat in Vancouver harbor. Meanwhile, [producer–director] Kim Manners started principal photography on his episode yesterday, and he'll shoot for eight days. Then we have a bunch of other second-unit sequences being prepared for next week, all of which [producer] J. P. Finn has to keep in his head at once. And I have to oversee all of this to make sure that when the crew gets there, they have something to shoot."

Back in the 1970s, Goodwin was under contract at Paramount Pictures, where he supervised the production of a variety of television movies. Each movie, naturally, was an entirely different experience, which he credits for preparing him for the daily challenges of *The X-Files*.

"It's not difficult keeping the show new, because it always is new," he notes. "There are different genres of *X-Files* stories. There are funny ones, mythology stories, the monster/scary stories, and that sort of thing. The only thing repetitive about the show is some of its thematic material. But each week, you're always being faced with something new and different to work out. What makes it a little harder is that the natural tendency is that when you've done one thing, you want to try and top yourself. Because of that, the shows have gotten bigger. If you look at some of the first-year shows compared to what we're doing now, there's a *huge* difference in terms of the amount of work that has to be done. But I think we've got a lot more self-confidence than we used to have. Before, it seemed we were always teetering on the edge of a precipice and now, having done so many of them, the stress factor — for me, personally — is a lot less. For the most part, we handle whatever they give us.

"I've been fortunate to have a very long career, I think, because I know how to select material and I have always associated myself with shows that have tried harder," he adds. "Shows that have wanted to be more than just standard television."

One quality production Goodwin will probably *not* be involved with is the proposed *X-Files* feature film. The reason is simple: The film would have to be shot during the show's hiatus (likely between the fourth and fifth seasons), which means preproduction would have to begin during the television season, and there simply wouldn't be time for anyone involved in the show's production to work on the film.

"To be honest with you," Goodwin observes, "I find the pace of life on a feature film — prepping, production, and postproduction — a little too lethargic. I wouldn't have that much interest in it. Besides, on a very pragmatic level, this show takes almost eleven months a year to shoot. When I get those five or six weeks off, all I want to do is go lie down somewhere. The movie Fox just did based on *Power Rangers* didn't do very well, and that may support the line of thinking that if you can watch it on TV every week, why would you want to pay to see it at the movies? Of course, *The X-Files* does have a huge following and there would be tremendous interest.

"Whatever happens," he says with a grin, "I'll certainly go see it. Hey, I'm a big fan."

cooperate with me at all. So beyond a little protocol or procedure that they described to me, I didn't know this institution. I was sort of writing about it blindly, having only what I had read and the little they had told me. A year goes by, and all of a sudden the phone calls start coming from FBI agents who are secret fans, and we developed a few relationships with these people. Finally, at the end of the year, a couple of them became such big fans that they were able to coordinate an *X-Files* tour of the FBI for Gillian Anderson, David Duchovny, and me, and *TV Guide* was allowed to come in and document the whole thing.

"I made some notes," he adds, "but mostly it was just a chance to see up close what I had been writing about. I have developed contacts since then, so if I need to know something about ballistics or DNA testing or fingerprinting, I've been able to call and get good expert advice or information from these people. Still, officially they can't say they endorse the show or that they are in any way connected to the show."

Producer J. P. Finn, who works in collaboration with Robert Goodwin on the physical production of the series, acknowledges the critical kudos as a key to the show's becoming a mainstream hit, but he also says there was more to the ratings explosion than simply recognition of good work. "I think the success of the show has a lot to do with the quality, because we do great work. But I also think our timing was great. We arrived at the same time

Howard Gordon.

the Internet took off. We were probably the first show to be adopted by the Internet, and that drove the underground word of mouth. Those good vibes permeated through the audience we first attracted, and Fox paid attention to it. It kept us going when the ratings weren't so great, and so we survived, and in the second year the general public became more aware of us."

Producer–director Rob Bowman observes

that prime-time episodic television is dominated by statistical concerns: age and wealth demographics and so forth. "That eliminates anything that's really a fringe or risky kind of idea," he says. "Being that *The X-Files* opened on Fox, which already likes to try different things, we were never intended to be anything except something dark, mysterious, intelligent, and fun. I don't think we ever expected to be as popular as *Melrose Place* or any of the shows like that. If that was the original goal, we wouldn't have the show we have."

Howard Gordon, who was promoted from supervising producer to co–executive producer in the third season, agrees with Bowman. "It's a fairly intelligent show," he observes. "People know they're going to be turned on to part of our world that they don't normally see. Whether it's government conspiracy or ghosts, they're going to see something that will take them to a place they don't usually see. There are so many shows on television, and so little that distinguishes one from the other. This is one of those shows that's different, and as long as you deliver on the product, people will come."

"A lot of it has to do with the stories we tell and how we tell them," Carter opines. "I think the writers on the show have hooked in to what really scares people. We try to stay away from horror conventions, and I think we've been very successful at that; I think we've been very successful at finding the universal, real scariness out there and plugging in to it."

Despite ubiquitous press (*Entertainment Weekly* and *TV Guide* featured cover stories the same week *People* profiled Anderson on its cover) in the aftermath of the Golden Globe breakthrough, the show's creators didn't allow success to pull them away from the game plan.

"We don't listen to our own press," Carter proclaims. "We're still the same people, and we don't sit on our laurels. I think all of us realize we did real good shows as well as shows that could have been better. None of us likes to feel we've done anything less than our best, and there's a nice little competitive thing going on. We all want to one-up the other guy, in the most constructive way imaginable. We push each other, so all this attention doesn't necessarily bring any additional pressure. I pressure myself more than anyone or anything. I want to make sure we're happy with what we do. I just do what I feel is right and hopefully people will like it. You can't succumb to the pressure."

Co–executive producer Goodwin actually found himself more confident as the second season dawned, in spite of the sudden attention of the press and the public. Staying within the budget, he says, had never been a problem — the show's makers had proved themselves capable of consistently producing quality work for about $1 million per episode.

"I became immune to the pressure of accomplishing the impossible." Goodwin laughs. "After getting twenty-three impossible-to-produce scripts that first year, by the second year it didn't matter what they sent. So the stress level has changed. Second year we were so much more confident, because we had pulled so many amazing things off. Some

"*The X-Files* could be like an Ed Wood movie if you're not careful."

of the guest directors who come in start hyperventilating. They say, 'Oh my God, have you read this script?' and I would respond, 'Yes, you've got an easy one.'

"[The second-season episode] 'The Host' is a perfect example," he continues. "The script required a large humanoid flukeworm that's going to be moving through all these sewers and Russian freighters and so on. Sure, it was hard, but in the end we did it. There was none of the panic or disbelief that was there the first year. Now I say, 'Okay, if that's what you want, that's what we'll do.' But that doesn't mean we became complacent. If you don't do it right, it becomes laughable. It could be like an Ed Wood movie if you're not careful."

Hoping to avoid making *Plan 9 from Prime Time,* Carter instituted an unusual policy at the beginning of the second season, giving directors the additional authority and responsibility of producing. For half the season,

David Nutter was employed this way until he moved over to *Space: Above and Beyond*. He was followed by Rob Bowman and Kim Manners, both of whom have remained under contract with *The X-Files*.

"I think Chris Carter is starting a real smart trend here," says Manners. "I believe he feels that directors make good producers in a creative sense, which is really not normal network thinking. The truth is that a director has so much more knowledge of what it takes to bring it all together on a set, and he also has much more knowledge in the cutting room. Let's face it, from the time that script is written until the public sees it on the air, it's either been filmed on the set or redirected in the editing room."

Bowman notes that the difference between being a producer-director on a show as opposed to being a freelance director on assignment is a distinct and powerful one, both psychologically and practically. First of all, a producer–director has "made the roster" and is no longer a free agent, he says, thus removing the pressure of needing to sell his services to different series during the course of a season.

"As a result," Bowman says, "the only thing I've got to think about is *The X-Files*. My allegiance changed; this was now my show, and I was fully committed to it. So now I'm trying to keep my ears open for Chris Carter, Howard Gordon, and the other writers. How do we tell the stories better? Who are the directors I need to look at to hire on to the show? Who are the best storytellers? There are a lot of guys who can shoot nice film, but there aren't very many who can tell a story. I think the trick is to find directors who can think like writers. I need to talk to the newcomers, even though they may be twenty-five-year vets, and say, 'This is how we like to have it done on our show.' It's a highly creative show, and I don't want to stifle anybody's creativity, as long as they're paddling in the same direction we are, because we know how to get there."

"Gillian came back ten days after giving birth."

And if Robert Goodwin's stress level has dropped since the first season, it may be because he's spreading it around to more people. For the second season, the average episode of the series was still scheduled for just eight days of production, which Kim Manners terms "a joke," but by this time, cast and crew had figured out how to stretch production as much as possible. Second-unit photography, for example, typically has a separate deadline, which usually brings production up to about ten days. "Sure, it's second unit," Manners says of the crew that shoots backgrounds and various periphery scenes that usually don't include the principal actors, "but they've still got their own crew, and they're shooting with cast and sound." This core work

Designing The X-Files

Creating the impossible is the everyday objective of the cast and crew of *The X-Files*, which strives for, and often achieves, a feature-film-quality look with each new episode. While no single person is more important than another in bringing the show to life, one can't help looking to the series's production designer as playing an integral role in its success.

"I kind of ended up here semi-accidentally," says production designer Graeme Murray with a shrug. "I just feel like we're a bunch of little kids making forts in the woods. You get to build some weird stuff and you have the budget to kind of build the fort you want — plus, you're old enough to have girls in, too."

Upon graduating from art school, Murray, a Vancouver native, began his professional career as an illustrator with a serious interest in printing. "I enjoy fine typography and old-style engraving," he says. "I honestly thought I was going to do book illustrations and make my own books, but you start off one way and if the road goes a different way, you follow it."

The road first led him to a local television station in the days before computer graphics, when illustrators would create station slugs and promotional images. This ultimately led to his becoming art director of the Canadian series *Beachcombers*. From there he took on two projects he considers the most prestigious of his pre–*X-Files* career, the feature film *Never Cry Wolf* and the CBS crime series *Wiseguy*, starring Ken Wahl. Shot in Vancouver, *Wiseguy* brought Murray a tremendous amount of recognition that piqued the interest of other production companies shooting in Canada, and that eventually brought him to the attention of Chris Carter and co–executive producer Robert Goodwin.

"The art director they had for the first five or six

shows wasn't getting along with Bob Goodwin," says Murray. "Once you don't get along with Bob, it's not Bob who's going to go. I met with him, and here we are."

But the road from "there" to "here" has been a challenging one as his imagination has been unleashed on a weekly basis. "Chris Carter's ambition has always been that these are little features," Murray says, "and we all try to approach it that way. For instance, I like layering things. I like to see things through glass or through doorways, and place other elements behind, so the set has a bit of depth and it's not just flat walls or anything real straight. As much as possible, we try to make it feel like there's a world beyond the little room you're actually in. The set also has to feel right for the story. We try to give each episode an individual look, so we use different colors or different moods to make each one stand by itself, which is unusual for most episodic stuff. I think that fits in with Chris's thinking. He's always felt that if he could get that kind of feature quality and as long as the show's popular, he can push. That's what he's been doing.

"But I'm not complaining," Murray concludes. "There's nothing else you can liken this show to, where you're in a completely different arena every time. It is never the same, and you get the opportunity to do things you've never had a chance to do before. Most series work, for example, kind of takes place in and around a police station where everything is street-related or police-related. This show just goes everywhere. It's the variety that keeps it interesting. I think there are a lot of shows you do so that you can pay the rent or buy groceries, but *The X-Files* is much more than that. It's a series you're proud to be a part of."

Chris Carter.

shows are a huge undertaking. They are not episodic television shows in the traditional sense. These are small features or movies of the week that we're trying to turn out. That's the challenge we face."

It all works, says Manners, who began directing television almost two decades ago, because of the guidance and encouragement that come from the top. "Not only is it a vision that Chris shares, but also the opportunity to actually be a filmmaker. He encourages everybody — not just the directors — who works with him. 'Hey, you're a filmmaker, you have good ideas,' he tells us. 'Do your best work. Make this your best effort.' He inspires that from us."

Such testimonials would sound a tad disingenuous coming from an underling trying to snare a promotion, but that's pretty clearly not the origins of such kudos for Carter. From the top to the bottom of the creative ladder, the commitment to Carter and to *The X-Files* is complete.

"It's a seven-days-a-week job," says Rob Bowman. "I've totally sacrificed my personal life for the show. I was dating somebody for five years who had incredible patience, but still we couldn't hold on. You may ask if that kind of commitment is worth it. Well, to me, it is. It's an expensive personal contract, but I can't imagine anything else I'd rather be doing."

is mirrored by a separate shot-insert unit that can shoot up to five days a week. "The shows have just gotten enormous," Manners says. "When we had our second-season wrap party, Chris Carter commented, 'Man, there's a lot of people that work for me that I don't even know.' He thought he knew everybody, but there's the construction crew, the special-effects crew, the makeup crew. Frankly, these

✿ ✿ ✿

All that dedication was to be tested in the second season, which saw the core premise of the series turned on its head by the events of the first season's finale as well as Gillian Anderson's real-life pregnancy. In "The Erlenmeyer Flask," the X-Files was closed down by the FBI bosses, and Mulder and Scully were separately reassigned, allowing Carter to write Anderson out of the show (via an apparent alien abduction in "Duane Barry" and "Ascension") during the latter stages of her pregnancy.

"In the beginning of the season," says Carter, "we did what producers are supposed to do, which is turn problems into assets. I thought it was really a testament to both David and Gillian's dedication to us. First of all, David had to carry a tremendous amount of work because Gillian's availability was limited. But Gillian was such a trouper in that she wanted more work and worked right up until she just couldn't anymore. Then she came back ten days after giving birth."

For Howard Gordon, Anderson's pregnancy brought back memories of his tenure on *Beauty and the Beast,* where star Linda Hamilton's similar announcement essentially sounded the death knell for that show.

"Obviously, there was an immediate feeling of déjà vu," Gordon says with a laugh.

"The difference — and it was a significant one — was that Gillian wanted to be on the show. We were clearly working with someone who would be game for doing whatever she could. We were able to block out not only the episodes that would have to exclude her, but

Scully's limited involvement [resulted in] increased exposure for some of the ancillary characters, which gave substance and depth to the *X-Files* universe.

ultimately it sort of was a blessing in disguise because it forced us to contrive something that has been grist for the mill and will continue to be, in terms of her abduction or disappearance. As it turned out, her pregnancy not only gave birth to [Anderson's daughter] Piper, but to a whole new avenue of possibilities on the show. I really love most of the first seven or eight episodes of the season, because they dealt so profoundly with the main characters: her disappearance, Mulder working with [Agent] Krycek, who was a Judas among them . . . it was all very exciting stuff."

Former co–executive producer Glen Morgan, who left *The X-Files* midseason with partner James Wong to create the Fox series *Space: Above and Beyond,* admits he was

Paul Rabwin.

crossed our fingers. We were just hoping that people would hang in there until she got back."

What Anderson's departure did allow for was a renewed enthusiasm for one of the show's staples: government conspiracies.

"What those episodes, and the show in general, made me realize was that *The X-Files* almost seems like the kind of show that would have gone over during the Reagan years," says Morgan. "Films like *JFK* and *Silence of the Lambs* — Scully, especially in the beginning, was very much like the Jodie Foster character — and older films like *Parallax View, The Conversation, Three Days of the Condor,* and *Klute* are all conspiracy-oriented, weird, paranoid movies that I think Chris tapped in to."

An additional result of Scully's limited involvement was the increased exposure offered to some of the ancillary characters, which gave substance and depth to the *X-Files* universe. Among the peripheral characters who stepped up in the second year were rogue agent Krycek (Nicholas Lea); his mysterious, enigmatic boss, the Cigarette-Smoking Man (William B. Davis); Mulder's superior, Assistant Director Walter S. Skinner (Mitch Pileggi); and Mr. X (Steven Williams), who replaced Deep Throat as Mulder's chief inside informant.

Strangely, the conspiracy arc that Carter so carefully charted during Anderson's pregnancy was shelved when she returned midseason. When Mulder and Scully were finally reunit-

quite concerned about the temporary loss of Anderson.

"No matter how good David is, *The X-Files* is a two-person show; that's what makes it work," he says. "And suddenly we're turning it into a one-person show. We were really messing with the concept. The whole business of splitting them up is the kind of thing you would do at the beginning of year three. So we

ed in "Firewalker," the two agents largely left government intrigue behind and headed out into the hinterlands to pursue a wide variety of paranormal phenomena in a series of stand-alone episodes. Besides confronting Flukeman ("The Host"), they had close encounters with Vietnam veterans who hadn't slept in twenty-four years; sexy vampires; reincarnated serial killers; a boy-next-door necrophiliac; Satan worshipers who doubled as members of the PTA; deadly viruses and parasites; and a scientist whose experiment caused his shadow to suck unsuspecting passersby into a black hole.

But while the change of emphasis was jarring to many viewers, the show didn't completely abandon Mulder's search for the truth about UFOs and the government's efforts to suppress that information. The two-part "Colony" and "End Game" was probably as ambitious as *The X-Files* can get, with Mulder seemingly reunited with his long-missing sister, only to be forced to give her up to an alien bounty hunter. Samantha, he finally becomes convinced, isn't really his sister, but an alien clone. The season finale, "Anasazi," brought Mulder to a buried boxcar containing what appear to be alien corpses. Investigating further, he learns that they might be human beings who had been subjected to government experiments involving alien DNA.

Before he can uncover the truth, he is either killed in the boxcar or abducted by aliens, in either case paving the way for the third season and the frustrating problem of maintaining Scully's skepticism in the face of all she's encountered.

Once again citing his concern that success can breed complacency, Carter took a fairly unorthodox approach to forming the writing staff for the third year. Contributing writer Frank Spotnitz became story editor, and Carter added writers such as Darin Morgan (who brought a quirky sense of humor to the show with episodes like "Humbug"), *Northern Exposure*'s Jeff Vlaming, *Chicago Hope*'s Kim Newton, and John Shiban to the full-time staff. There was not one genre writer among them.

"I chose to go with unknown quantities," Carter says. "This isn't a sci-fi genre show, as far as I see it. It's a cross-genre show. It's some kind of a suspense thriller–espionage crossbreed. If I get [an established] science fiction writer, that could work to the show's disadvantage, because you can't approach *The X-Files* as straight science fiction.

"Ultimately," he concludes, "my goal then was the same that it's always been: to create twenty-two to twenty-four really scary shows. I just want to scare the hell out of the audience. That's all."

The X-Files

Episode 2.1 (#25)

"Little Green Men"

Original airdate: September 16, 1994
Written by Glen Morgan and James Wong
Directed by David Nutter
Guest starring: Raymond J. Barry (Sen.
Richard Matheson), William B. Davis
(Cigarette-Smoking Man), Mike Gomez (Jorge
Concepcion), Vanessa Morley (Samantha, age
8), Mitch Pileggi (Assistant Director Walter S.
Skinner)

*The X-Files remain closed, with Mulder and
Scully given other assignments. At the same
time, Mulder begins to lose faith in his own
beliefs — that, essentially, the truth is out
there — until he is contacted by Senator
Richard Matheson and finds himself heading
out to a supposedly abandoned SETI program
site in Puerto Rico where a message has been
received from the Voyager spacecraft. Scully
arrives to help him, and together they must
flee government agents who are out to capture
them.*

❊   ❊   ❊

"I thought it was a great first episode, coming
off of 'The Erlenmeyer Flask,'" says Chris
Carter, "and it established what was going to
be the Scully–Mulder relationship for at least
the first eight episodes. I thought the script by
Glen and Jim and the direction of David
Nutter were terrific, and that David and
Gillian's performances were excellent. I'm
very proud of that show as a season opener."

Glen Morgan explains that "Little Green
Men" began life as a feature he and Jim Wong
were attempting to write. "But we liked the
idea so much," he explains, "that we decided
to do it for Mulder. The other thing is that I
was irked that the government had shut down
the SETI project and I wanted to address that.
Most important, I was on the set first season
once when Duchovny was talking about the
episode 'Beyond the Sea' [which focused on
the Scully character] and he said, 'That was a
pretty good episode. When are you going to
write one like that for me?' Well, I liked him,
he deserved it, and I thought that's what
'Little Green Men' was trying to be."

One interesting aspect of the show is that
Mulder has waited years for contact, but when
it's about to happen he freaks out.

"Although I don't think it came across as
well as we wanted it to," Morgan says, "we
were trying to work up the notion, 'Was that
even there? Is this real?' At some point in
editing I realized that it didn't play that way.
Earlier in the show Mulder has said to Scully,
'I'm starting to doubt that my sister was
abducted.' So you're trying to say, 'Is this in

his head? Do we create these kinds of fear ourselves?'"

Director David Nutter admits that he had become a bit nervous tackling the show because it had grown so popular between seasons. "I wanted to avoid the pitfalls of these shows that become phenomenons — really hot — and then fade away really quickly. I, like everybody else, wanted this to be a long-running program. By the end of the first season, it was like a ship pulling away from port: 'There it goes!'

"I thought 'Little Green Men' was a tough show to do. I thought the introduction of the show was wonderful, and I loved the paranoia we were able to generate in that episode,

"I was irked that the government had shut down the SETI project and I wanted to address that."

especially during the first meeting between Mulder and Scully. I thought Mulder was very good in the scene with Senator Matheson.

There was also a lot of action, what with the car chase and all. I also very much liked the bookending of the show, opening with Mulder on a mundane surveillance assignment and closing the same way."

For producer J. P. Finn, perhaps the most difficult aspect of the episode was trying to achieve Puerto Rico in Vancouver. "Which I guess we pulled off, though if you look closely you'll see pine trees in the back." He laughs. "Anyway, a great little show to get going with. A typical *X-Files* show, where more is suggested than you actually see."

Interestingly, actor Darren McGavin (forever known as Carl Kolchak) was approached to play Senator Richard Matheson (whose namesake adapted Jeff Rice's *Night Stalker* novel for TV).

"We tried very hard to get him," says James Wong. "I'm not sure what happened. Our casting director called before we started second season and spoke to McGavin's agent and said, 'We want him for the first show; lock him up, and we're willing to pay the price.' By the time it came down to getting him, suddenly the agent said, 'He doesn't know about the show' or 'He's not available.' It became some kind of weird thing and it just didn't happen."

Rating/Audience Share: 10.3/19

> **Episode 2.2 (#26)**
> **"The Host"**
> Original airdate: September 23, 1994
> Written by Chris Carter
> Directed by Daniel Sackheim
> Guest starring: Freddy Andreiuci (Det. Norman), Marc Bauer (Agent Brisentine), Darin Morgan (Flukeman), Mitch Pileggi (Assistant Director Walter S. Skinner), Gabrielle Rose (Dr. Jo Zenzola)

When the decomposed body of a man is found in the sewers of Newark, Mulder is given what seems to be a routine murder case to investigate — punishment, he believes, for his work on the X-Files — but it turns out that the perpetrator is actually a flukeworm mutated into humanoid form by radioactive material being transported on a cargo vessel from Chernobyl.

❋ ❋ ❋

Chris Carter notes, "'The Host' has become a real popular episode. That's one of our traditional monster shows — although we don't do *traditional* monsters, obviously. I was in a

funk when I wrote that episode, actually. We were coming back from hiatus and I was trying to find something more interesting than just the Flukeman. I was irritated at the time, and I brought my irritation to Mulder's attitude. Basically he had become fed up with the FBI. They had given him what he felt was a low assignment, which was sending him into the city after a dead body. But lo and behold, he finds that this is a case that for all intents and purposes is an X-File. It's been given to him by a man he's never looked at as an ally, Skinner. So it's an interesting establishing of the relationship between them."

"A Carter script, but a bit of a departure for a Carter script," says J. P. Finn. "Chris's scripts tend to deal with alien subject matter. Although we had done some creature parts the first year, this time we got to see more of the creatures than we had before. That was a departure. Graeme Murray did a great job building those sewers. It was very cleverly designed. On one of our stages we have a pit, which is about ten feet deep, sixteen by sixteen wide. He basically built two sewers, with one main sewer that he renovated to a central area. At one point, we actually went into a real sewage plant for those exterior shots. That was the real McCoy. It was also a hot summer day — about ninety degrees — and it was a pretty difficult and smelly day for the cast and crew."

Emmy-winning director Daniel Sackheim enjoyed the episode as much as anyone. "It's classic Chris Carter," he says. "I remember when I read the script I said, 'You've got to be kidding me.' It has elements of *Creature from the Black Lagoon*. It's what makes the show the show. Nobody else would attempt to do something like that. It has to be done with a fine touch so that you wouldn't be laughed off of the screen. The concept is fairly preposterous, and the subject matter is a little stomach-churning. I think he wrote a terrific script, and I would like to think it was handled adeptly.

"You know, there was one thing that was a great thing Chris taught me, and I think it is the signature of the show. I don't know what he would call it, but I call it event writing. What I mean by that is two or three times during the course of an act, he would have an event transpire that would always get the audience's attention. A lot of the show is expository, with Mulder talking about how this project happened, and Scully responding. In 'The Host,' the event is when the guy is brushing his teeth and he starts to choke. Blood starts to

"I remember when I read the script I said, 'You've got to be kidding me.' It has elements from *Creature from the Black Lagoon*."

come out of his mouth, he goes into the shower, and this fluke comes out of his mouth. It's

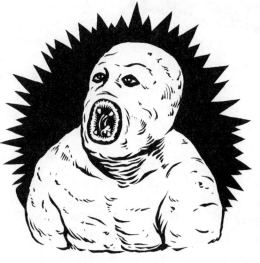

such a testament to what is great about the writing of the show: these events that don't require any dialogue."

"I will *never* forget that toothpaste scene," adds James Wong. "I thought that was the grossest piece of television ever put on the air, so that was cool."

Glen Morgan proclaims, "My brother the Flukeman! My brother Darin wore the costume of Flukie. At one point, I saw Darin getting made up at five o'clock in the afternoon. After dinner and a few drinks, I went back to Darin's trailer at like one in the morning, and there's this thing in a rubber suit with my brother's voice. I said, 'I really can't deal with this; I've got to go.'"

During the shooting of "The Host," David

said, 'I'm Flukeman!' Duchovny was quite impressed that Darin was willing to wait a half hour into the flight before he pulled the joke."

For his part, Darin Morgan doesn't remember his actual work as Flukeman with such levity. "It was hell! The suit required a very long makeup job. It was very uncomfortable, I couldn't breathe, and it smelled bad. I couldn't urinate or anything else. It was just sort of generally unpleasant being in that suit. I started suffering from sensory deprivation, where I couldn't really feel anything. It was a very bizarre experience which I hope never to repeat."

But, it's pointed out, Chris Carter has said that they might bring back Flukie. "If they do, it won't be me," Morgan says matter-of-factly.

Rating/Audience Share: 9.8/17

Duchovny never saw Darin Morgan outside of his Flukeman suit. They spoke and got along — in fact, Darin was asked to join the writing staff. When Darin was flying to Vancouver to prep "Humbug," by coincidence he sat next to Duchovny, who didn't know who he was. About a half hour into the flight, Darin leaned over to Duchovny and said, "Could you sign an autograph?"

"David made the best of the situation and said, 'What do you want me to write?'" Glen Morgan recounts. "Darin said, 'I want you to write, "To my nemesis — Fox Mulder."' Duchovny is like, 'What nut am I next to?' and he said, 'Why am I your nemesis?' And Darin

94

Episode 2.3 (#27)
"Blood"

Original airdate: September 30, 1994
Story by Darin Morgan
Teleplay by Glen Morgan and James Wong
Directed by David Nutter
Guest starring: Tom Braidwood (Frohike), John Cygan (Sheriff Spencer), Andre Daniels (Harry McNally), Kimberly Ashlyn Gere (Bonnie McRoberts), Dean Haglund (Langly), Bruce Harwood (Byers), John Harris (Gary Taber), William Sanderson (Ed Funsch), Diana Stevan (Mrs. Adams), George Touliatos (County Supervisor Larry Winter)

A string of seemingly random killings occur in a small Pennsylvania town, which brings Mulder in to profile the murderers. He discovers that not one of them had a history of violence, and all died at the end of their sprees. The only clues available are destroyed electronic devices — whose LCDs triggered the murders — and an unknown organic substance.

❋ ❋ ❋

"Darin was supposed to write that one," Glen Morgan recalls, "but scheduling wouldn't allow it. We wanted to do something about postal workers and paranoia about pesticides and decided to merge the two ideas. We worked with Darin on the story, but we needed a script really fast, so Jim and I did it. We took some heat for the ending when William Sanderson climbs a tower and starts shooting people. On the Internet people would say, 'Couldn't they come up with something more original?' But that was the point. It's almost like the joke that people at work who are stressed say: 'I'm going to go up in a tower with a gun.' That's what everyone points to when they're going to flip out. We really lucked out getting William Sanderson."

According to Glen Morgan, director David Nutter and Sanderson were working so well together that Nutter was seemingly reaching out to him personally for the ending sequences in the tower. "Almost all of that stuff that's in the end was pre-slate; it wasn't in the take. Jim and I had read a lot about the beginning of *Apocalypse Now* when Martin Sheen puts his hand through the mirror. He had cut himself in reality and the camera operator stopped. [Director Francis Ford] Coppola said, 'No, no, keep going.' Which is why they put jump cuts in that scene, because they had a moment where the camera stopped. So Nutter said, 'Why don't we cut the best psychotic moments that this actor is

Playing the Flukeman, Darin Morgan said, "I was suffering from sensory deprivation, where I couldn't really feel anything."

feeling and we'll put them all together like that?' That's why this act is cut like that. We spent a lot of time on it, and that's something I was very happy with. None of that stuff is between 'Action' and 'Cut.'"

Nutter explains, "I always love to get a hold of an actor like William Sanderson. At the ending, what I tried to do was allow him to get into it and let the camera roll while he did so.

Different actors you treat in different ways. He was the kind of actor that wanted to, emotionally, get into it. I let him get pumped up

for it, and filmed what he was doing. Most of the stuff you see in the episode came during the prep."

Chris Carter offers that the genesis of the story came "from films Darin Morgan had seen of pesticides being sprayed on unknowing populations by a government who said this was good for you, and what the effect of our government spraying may be now on some level. I think it works because it feels like it can happen in your own backyard." David Nutter notes, "Glen, Jim, and I had talked about doing shows that were very different from each other. I thought 'Blood' was a real throwback to *The Twilight Zone*. It was a show shot in a standard way, where a lot of editing was involved."

"When we did that show, we were of the opinion that it should feel different in style than the other episodes," says James Wong. "We wanted a more sterile, static kind of feel to it. I'm not sure if we were able to get that with the direction. We missed communication with David in terms of what we felt it should look like. I liked the idea of the show, and I really liked William Sanderson. I don't think it was the most successful, but it wasn't the worst."

Controversy arose when Morgan and Wong cast former porn star Kimberly Ashlyn Gere as a suburban housewife.

"She was trying to go legitimate, and we were trying to be punks and ruffle feathers," recalls Glen Morgan, who later cast her in several episodes of his series *Space: Above and Beyond*. "She said, 'What's the sex thing I have to do in it?' and I said, 'We wouldn't be that obvious. You play a housewife.' I was very proud of her and scared to death, because Bob Goodwin said, 'Why are we casting this girl?' I think people suspected monkey business, but I said, 'We're casting her for the same reason *Miami Vice* cast Gordon Liddy — it's a weird, cool thing to do, and she's a better actress than Gordon was.'"

Rating/Audience Share: 9.1/16

Episode 2.4 (#28)
"Sleepless"

Original airdate: October 7, 1994
Written by Howard Gordon
Directed by Rob Bowman
Guest starring: William B. Davis (Cigarette-Smoking Man), Jonathan Gries (Salvatore Matola), Nicholas Lea (Agent Alex Krycek), Mitch Pileggi (Assistant Director Walter S. Skinner), Don Thompson (Henry Willig), Tony Todd (Augustus Cole), Steven Williams (Mr. X)

Mulder and Agent Krycek, the new partner who has been foisted on him, investigate a series of bizarre deaths that don't make sense: for instance, a scientist whose demise is consistent with burning, although there is no evidence of fire or burns. Ultimately, it is discovered that a series of Army experiments to create a better soldier during the Vietnam War induced permanent insomnia in some soldiers. None of them have slept in twenty-four years, and one of them, Augustus Cole, has moved to a higher plane, where he can make dream and reality one. His goal is to bring salvation — through some fairly violent means — to his comrades.

❉ ❉ ❉

For supervising producer Howard Gordon, "Sleepless" was significant in that it represent-ed the first time in nine years he was writing without a partner.

"I had some insecurity in the beginning," he admits. "I was now on my own and had to investigate all new processes. I did a story on agricultural engineering. It was a good idea, but a very oblique script. I did the outline with Chris, but as I wrote the story I knew something was wrong. I spent an undue amount of time on it, really stressed out over it, and gave it to Jim Wong to read and said, 'This isn't very good, is it?' He read it and said, 'No, it's not.' Meanwhile, I was two weeks away from prepping on my first episode as a solo person, and I had a script that sucked. I basically couldn't fall asleep for two nights straight, I was so anxious. I figured that my career was over, I figured I was done, I had no talent, and I was history. Not being able to sleep for two nights, I began to think, 'Gee, what if somebody couldn't ever sleep?' So I went to Chris and said, 'I'm putting a pin on that other script and I'm writing this story.' Chris could have thought, 'Oh man, we're dead.' Not only was I insecure about my solo act, but Chris might have been as well. But he had this really great confidence in me and said, 'Whatever you want, just do it. I trust you're going to do it.' It's that kind of trust that just gave me the confidence to do it. I beat out the whole story in twenty-four hours and it came out well."

"I really love that show," Christ Carter enthuses. "It's a great idea, well executed. I guess the hardest part was that it required a lot of night shooting, and of course we were shooting in the middle of the summer in Vancouver, where it's the land of the midnight sun. That was a challenge for the cast and crew. We had a good cast; Tony Todd was wonderful. Production-wise, I think there's a lot of suggestion of violence there rather than what you see. You're shown what's going to happen, but you don't actually see it."

they know they're going to be killed, there should be a moment of release there. I found that very interesting, and it made the audience think for a second as to who was right and who was wrong."

In one particularly memorable scene, a soldier is greeted by armed Vietnamese men, women, and children who seem ready to exact revenge.

"He's out killing people, but the reason he's killing people is well supported. His victims *want* to die."

"None of the people could speak English," Bowman recalls. "I think it was the first time any of them had been on a set, so they were looking at the camera, the people, and the hardware. I had to reshoot it another day, and it was an exercise in blank expressions and nonresponsive looks from all of them. But the little boy right in the foreground of the shot seemed to understand through an interpreter what the scene was about. The direction was along the lines of, 'This man has hurt your family and you've come to make him pay his debt.' This boy gave one of these steely-eyed, dagger-filled stares. He did it every time. I remember saying to all of them, 'Hold court with your eyes, by looking very final in your conclusion that he has to pay his debt.' A little smoke, a little crosslight, a little blood and some prosthetics, and you have it. The other thing is to put so many people in the room that they could only have

For director Rob Bowman, an enjoyable aspect of "Sleepless" was the ambiguity of the drama. "You couldn't tell who the good guy was and who the bad guy was. The apparent antagonist, played by Tony Todd, was on a mercy mission. You could absolutely endorse this guy's point of view. He's out killing people, but the reason he's killing people is well supported. His victims *want* to die. We even added something to the first killing, the soldier in the apartment. Just at the moment he realizes he's going to be killed, he closes his eyes, rolls his head back, and thinks to himself, 'It's over. Finally, relief. I can sleep.' That was something I put in there because Howard Gordon had talked a lot about how these guys have been suffering for twenty-four years. If

appeared magically. I think originally there were like three people on the set and it looked like they could have walked in there. We put nine people in there, literally in the blink of an eye, and there's no way they just walked in."

James Wong says, "Stylistically, it had some very strong shots. We also introduced Mr. X in that episode. Mr. X, originally, was a woman. But when we watched the dailies, we realized that it wasn't going to work."

Glen Morgan adds, "Chris didn't like her, and I said, 'How about Steve Williams? He's a great guy and an intense actor.' As a result, X's scene with Mulder was actually David playing against an actress, but then we went back, shot Steven Williams, and inserted the footage."

Rating/Audience Share: 8.6/15

Episode 2.5 (#29)
"Duane Barry"

Original airdate: October 14, 1994
Written and directed by Chris Carter
Guest starring: William B. Davis (Cigarette-Smoking Man), Nicholas Lea (Agent Alex Krycek), CCH Pounder (Agent Lucy Kazdin), Steve Railsback (Duane Barry), Frank C. Turner (Dr. Del Hakkie)

Episode 2.6 (#30)
"Ascension"

Original airdate: October 21, 1994
Written by Paul Brown
Directed by Michael Lange
Guest starring: William B. Davis (Cigarette-Smoking Man), Sheila Larken (Margaret Scully), Nicholas Lea (Agent Alex Krycek), Mitch Pileggi (Assistant Director Walter S. Skinner), Steve Railsback (Duane Barry), Steven Williams (Mr. X)

In part one, Former FBI agent Duane Barry escapes from the mental hospital where he's being held, and takes several people hostage. Blaming his erratic behavior on the fact that he was abducted by aliens, Barry is convinced he must find someone else to sacrifice to the aliens to save himself, and he finds that some-one in Dana Scully.

In the second part, Mulder pursues Duane Barry and the captured Scully, a chase that leads him to the mountains and near-death on a tram car. It is revealed that Agent Krycek is

actually working for the Cigarette-Smoking Man, who seems to be pulling everybody's strings. At episode's end, Scully is gone, Barry claims she's been taken by a UFO, and Skinner reopens the X-Files.

❋ ❋ ❋

Chris Carter, who directed "Duane Barry" as well as wrote it, says he's very proud of the episode. "It was a chance for me to show people what I thought the show could be and should be, and I think I was very successful. I had a lot of help from a very dedicated crew and really nice technical help from David

Nutter as far as the economy of direction and where to put cameras at certain times. Ultimately, though, it was me on the set directing. No one can do it for you. I was very pleased that when I first said 'Action,' no one laughed. From that point on, I knew I was going to be okay."

"Directing for the first time is a nightmare for anyone," says Robert Goodwin. "So to make your first time an episode of *The X-Files* is crazy. We have sent so many directors home in body bags, but Chris came in and did a very good job."

Carter did find some significant differences between just writing and both writing and directing a show. "There are so many different problems to solve," he notes matter-of-factly. "As a director, you have to solve them practically. As a writer, you have to solve them creatively. When you're a writer, you put everything on the page and hope that everybody does exactly what you've asked them to do. But when you're a director, you take it to the set and discover that some things written on the page just won't work and you have to be able to rework them."

J. P. Finn admits, "We were all pretty nervous doing that one, because Chris Carter was a new director and not so much because he's the boss. It turned out that he directed very well. In fact, that's the episode that won the Golden Globe. It was a great script, a great cast, and he ended up directing a home run. One of the charming things about it was the end, where we had these alien heads placed on young children. It was so endearing to see them on the set between takes, playing with Chris and everyone. They were more like lep-

rechauns than aliens; they were the most charming aliens you've ever met, because they were just a great bunch of kids that we adopted for three or four days of the show. A big highlight of the year."

"The difficult part of the episode ['Ascension']," reflects J. P. Finn, "was to get the stunt gag on the cable car. At first we had written the scene for night, which would have been impossible, given our schedule. So we went for a transition period over late afternoon to twilight. Production-wise, given that we couldn't light a whole mountaintop and shoot the cable car at night — besides, you wouldn't be able to see the mountain at night anyway — there wouldn't be any sense of jeopardy. The production point of view was timing it all out so that you were right on the money as far as finishing

each segment by the beginning of twilight. There was a bit of a stopwatch there. A pretty good two-parter, though the first part might have been a little better than the second."

"I think Duchovny is a very brave and dedicated actor to hang off of that tram car," muses Glen Morgan. "Jim Wong made that scene work because he's a really good editor. It was missing a lot of stuff. If you go back, you see all kinds of little insert things. Jim said, 'You've got to show the dial, you've got to see the other car' — that kind of thing. And that ending is the kind of thing I wish I had done. A guy just standing at a point where he

"Duchovny is a very brave and dedicated actor to hang off that tram car."

feels he's completely lost. Let's face it, Mulder loves Scully. It's the same thing he felt for his sister, and now he's just looking into the abyss. I thought that was wonderful."

Says Wong, "I thought 'Duane Barry' and 'Ascension' worked together relatively well. 'Ascension' was kind of an ambitious show to do. We had sky-tram stuff, and that made it difficult. But Steve Railsback was really good. It was interesting, because that was one of the few times that we really see aliens, so we didn't know whether or not it was going to work. Ultimately I think it's okay, because you don't know whether it's reality or not. What I really remember is the nightmare of post[production]. We were doing the sound dub on 'Ascension' and running late and the guy from Twentieth kept saying, 'I'm going to shut you down at twelve! You better be done!' It's that kind of stuff I remember more than anything."

Rating/Audience Share ("Duane Barry"): 8.9/16
Rating/Audience Share ("Ascension"): 9.6/16

Episode 2.7 (#31)
"3"
Original airdate: November 4, 1994
Story by Chris Ruppenthal
Teleplay by Glen Morgan and James Wong
Directed by David Nutter
Guest starring: Frank Ferrucci (Det. Nettles), Tom McBeath (Det. Munson), Frank Military (The Son/John), Gustavo Moreno (The Father), Perrey Reeves (Kristen Kilar), Justina Vail (The Unholy Spirit)

To keep his sanity after Scully's disappearance, Mulder continues his work on the X-Files. He recognizes that a series of murders follow the patterns of the Trinity Murderers, a trio of killers with a fetish for drinking blood. While investigating, he finds himself drawn into their circle by the mysterious Kristen Kilar.

❄ ❄ ❄

"Several mistakes took place," says Glen Morgan. "Howard Gordon was supposed to do episode seven, but it wasn't going to happen. There was a script by Chris Ruppenthal that was sitting around, and we said, 'Look, we'll do number seven and eight back to back.' Howard agreed, and then I read the script and said, 'Oh my God!' It was a lot of work to do. That was mistake number one. I think mistake number two was to just do a vampire show, which to me shouldn't be a mistake. If there's one thing that's kind of a letdown about the *X-Files* audience, it's that even though it's a show that should be able to do anything, the Internet and feedback tells me, 'You just shouldn't do vampires.' My feeling is, Why not? We did the manitou last year, which was essentially a werewolf, and they hated that too.

"My feeling," he elaborates, "is that it's a legend that's been around since the eleventh century. In starting to do research, I began to find out about these people who felt it was a sexual fetish to ingest blood. Obviously the [Broadcast] Standards people say, 'Huh? What the . . .' I think we caved in on too many points to the Standards people. In the first draft it was a really kinky, erotic episode. It lost that because we didn't battle hard enough with the Standards people. Then we took heat for Mulder falling for this woman. People said, 'How could he sexually accept someone so soon after he lost Scully?' but to me that would be the perfect time. Another problem is that Perrey Reeves is David's real-life girlfriend. I think because the two of them have a sexual relationship offscreen, there's a tension that's missing that you'd have with two people who *haven't* messed around. The whole thing is that she should have been so alluring and there would be a chemistry between them, and there wasn't at all. That's why I think it wasn't successful."

James Wong admits that the episode was disappointing in the sense that "the script was much better than the show. The problem is twofold. Broadcast Standards really had lots of problems with that show. We had the blood fetish stuff going on. When you took away all that stuff, it really didn't make any sense anymore. Also, the blood kinkiness really helped the vampire aspect of it work as well as made the show a lot more interesting, because it's not something you normally see. We had to take that away and by doing that, it really lessened any impact that might have been there."

Notes David Nutter, "A very different show, because it's the first one without Scully. She's been away for quite some time. It's a situation where Mulder is in a dark place, doesn't know which way to turn, and is really very much on his own. The whole vampire thing happened because he went to a dark place that he normally wouldn't have gone to. For some people it worked, for a lot of people it didn't. I thought it worked pretty well."

Rating/Audience Share: 9.4/16

Episode 2.8 (#32)
"One Breath"

Original airdate: November 11, 1994
Written by Glen Morgan and James Wong
Directed by Robert Goodwin
Guest starring: Tom Braidwood (Frohike), Jay Brazeau (Dr. Daly), Nicola Cavendish (Nurse G. Owens), Don Davis (Capt. William Scully), William B. Davis (Cigarette-Smoking Man), Dean Haglund (Langly), Bruce Harwood (Byers), Sheila Larken (Margaret Scully), Melinda McGraw (Melissa Scully), Mitch Pileggi (Assistant Director Walter S. Skinner), Steven Williams (Mr. X)

Scully mysteriously appears in a Washington, D.C., hospital, where she is being kept alive by life support devices. Relieved that she's back but frustrated that he doesn't know what happened to her, Mulder begins trying to uncover the truth, leading him to a confrontation with the Cigarette-Smoking Man that could take Mulder down the path of darkness and make him resemble those he despises. In the end,

Scully's spirit is visited by her late father, who nudges her back to the world of the living.

✿　✿　✿

"One of our most popular episodes," says Chris Carter. "I guess that's really the third episode of the 'Duane Barry'–'Ascension' trilogy. It's the return of Gillian, and it has very little paranormal stuff in it. I think there were some people at Fox who didn't like it for that reason, but on the Internet it was received as one of our best."

Glen Morgan explains, "Duchovny challenged us to do a 'Beyond the Sea' for him. The show had been so dark and bleak, and Jim [Wong] and I feel that there is a side to the paranormal that's very hopeful — the phenomena of angels and hope and peace. We wanted to do that side of it. I had read a book called *Raising the Dead,* about a guy who was a surgeon and a writer. He was in his study and the next thing he knows, he's lying on the floor, there's a paramedic over him, and his wife is freaking out. What happened is that it was Legionnaire's disease. He had gone into a coma. The guy wrote a diary of his time in that state of consciousness, which is fascinating. The original intent was that was what the whole episode was going to be. I had wanted to do this from the beginning of the year. I thought it would

be a great opportunity for Duchovny, but then the situation came up with Gillian's pregnancy. We needed to get her off her feet anyway. There's a line in there where Scully's sister says, 'Just because the belief is positive and good doesn't make it silly or trite.' It was the whole theme of the show."

"I really love that show," says James Wong. "I thought David did a wonderful acting job. The biggest problem we had was in postproduction when we saw Gillian just lying on the table. I want to put this tactfully, but she had just had a baby and her breasts were enormous, and she was wearing a tight hospital gown. There was nothing we could do about it, but it was *very* noticeable."

"Bill Davis was hired to smoke a cigarette. That's what his job was."

"One Breath" also marked a significant development of the Mr. X character, as he executes — in front of Mulder — two men who have seen him.

Morgan explains, "At first, Steve [Williams] wasn't going over too well, and they were unhappy with him. I said, 'Jerry Hardin brought so much to Deep Throat, and we're kind of giving Mr. X Jerry's lines.' That's why they didn't use X for a while. But Steve is a good actor, which is why we could do the scene in this episode where he performs an execution. Deep Throat was a guy willing to lose his life for letting out the secret, whereas X is a guy who's still scared. He's somewhere between Mulder and Deep Throat."

"What's so unusual about 'One Breath' is that it had very little to do with our usual X-File stuff," says Robert Goodwin, who directed the episode. "It was more about human emotions, drama, relationships."

A real highlight of the episode is when Mulder confronts the Cigarette-Smoking Man. Ironically, for quite some time Glen Morgan and James Wong were told not to give the actor, Bill Davis, much to do. "They thought he might not be a good actor," says Morgan. "I said, 'He's great. He's an acting teacher,' but that's how they felt. When it came time to do 'One Breath,' Bob Goodwin said, 'Cut down his scene,' and I said, 'No, he can pull it off,' and he did."

Goodwin explains, "Bill Davis was hired to smoke a cigarette. That's what his job was. He was hired for the pilot and told to stand there and smoke a cigarette. He didn't even say a word. Gradually, over the course of the show, we gave him a scene here or there, but he was never expected to do very much. Frequently when you hire an actor for a part where he has to smoke a cigarette, you find out that that's basically all he can do. We had no idea if this guy was going to be able to come up to the plate and handle this kind of stuff. But he's just fabulous. He evolved over the course of

the series as this sort of Nazi figure.

The easy thing to do in that kind of role is twist your mustache, arch your eyebrows, and overplay it. He and I talked about it, we talked about the kind of power this guy has, and he just gave us an incredible performance in 'One Breath.' And he continues to do it."

Rating/Audience Share: 9.5/16

Episode 2.9 (#33)

"Firewalker"

Original airdate: November 18, 1994
Written by Howard Gordon
Directed by David Nutter
Guest starring: Hiro Kanagawa (Peter Tanaka),
David Kaye (Eric Parker), David Lewis
(Vosberg), Tuck Milligan (Dr. Adam Pierce),
Leland Orser (Jason Ludwig), Torben Rolfsen
(Technician), Shawnee Smith (Jesse O'Neil),
Bradley Whitford (Dr. Daniel Trepkos)

When a robot designed for volcanic explo-
ration yields evidence of a life-form living
within the caves of a volcano, Mulder and
Scully — reunited at last — begin an investi-
gation to see whether they can discover the
identity of this life-form. Once there, they
begin working with the remnants of the
research team, who all seem delusional.

❉   ❉   ❉

"A very successful episode," notes Chris
Carter. "David Nutter added a nice directorial touch; the guest performances were very
good. We had a cool interior of a volcano set.
When I walked on that set, I had no idea how
the hell they were going to shoot it, but they
utilized a special crane to do it. I think that's
the first time in our second season that we
were telling what's one of our serial stories
rather than our mythological stories. In other

words, it was an X-File rather than one of the
cosmology shows that explore the characters."

"It was a tough shoot at the beginning,"
says David Nutter, "because it was a situation
where they were trying to redo 'Ice.' What
happened, though, is we got a terrific group of
actors who pulled it out for us, and I thought
the volcano stuff was real interesting and different. I think it all worked out pretty well. It
was not a painfully bad show, but if there had
not been an 'Ice,' it would have been wonderful."

Says J. P. Finn, "That was a big production
number. We built the volcano, and there was
another great job of makeup done. The cave
was the biggest part of the job. Whenever you
do any special effects or visual effects, it takes
more time. So from a production point of
view, it's not easy to pull off the building of a
cave that size on a TV schedule."

While "irked" at the similarities to "Ice,"
Glen Morgan nonetheless enjoyed the parasitic creature the episode presented. "A nearby museum said there is an ant in Africa that
once it ingests this virus, it climbs up to a tree,
hangs from it, and this spike juts out of its
head. Howard and I talked about that, and he
put it out through the neck, which is gorier."

About the similarities to "Ice," James
Wong says the primary problem is "if the show
starts to cannibalize itself, there's going to be
trouble."

"I know there are some similarities to
'Ice,'" says Howard Gordon, "but I think once
you get beyond the similarities of a group of

people in a confined space going up against a creature, there are enough differences to separate the two."

Rating/Audience Share: 9.0/16

Episode 2.10 (#34)
"Red Museum"
Original airdate: December 9, 1994
Written by Chris Carter
Directed by Win Phelps
Guest starring: Gillian Barber (Beth Kane), Steve Eastin (Sheriff Mazeroski), Lindsey Ginter (Crew-Cut Man), Mark Rolston (Richard Odin), Paul Sand (Gerd Thomas)

Reports of cows being injected with alien DNA lead Mulder and Scully to a Wisconsin town, where several teens are found wandering outside in their underwear, with the words "HE IS ONE" or "SHE IS ONE" scrawled on their backs. What the duo encounter is a strange vegetarian cult in a meat-producing township.

✧ ✧ ✧

"Red Museum" brings back the Crew-Cut Man, the guy with the gun who blew away Deep Throat at the end of season one. According to Glen Morgan, however, this wasn't exploited as effectively as it could have been.

"My feeling, and Chris knows this, is that to bring this guy back, his presence should have been better developed," Morgan says, "and he's shot offscreen. I thought, 'Geez, this is the guy who killed Deep Throat, who the audience loved, and it's kind of tossed away.' The episode just seems like half of one thing for a while, then half of something else. I think that was a curious choice for Chris. He wanted to take a real left turn, but I'd rather have seen a whole episode about that guy showing up and Mulder getting back at him."

"A pretty straightforward show," says J. P. Finn. "I think the meat plant was the hardest part for the cast and crew. We went to a real meat plant to shoot that, and it was tough for David and Gillian. We learned our lesson: when we did 'Our Town' later in the season and needed a poultry factory, we created our own."

Adds James Wong, "I think that was one of the most confusing episodes I've ever seen. It had some really neat ideas in it, but I don't think it pulled together finally."

This episode was at least partially designed to serve as a crossover with David Kelley's CBS series *Picket Fences*. The episode for that show, "Away in the Manger," had cows giving birth to human children — which is actually par for the course for life in Rome, Wisconsin. Kelley's concept was for Mulder to come to Rome to investigate the situation, believing it would provide information on the "Red Museum" case. The search is fruitless, however, when the cow phenomenon turns out to be human embryos placed in the cows' wombs by a wannabe-mother. Both episodes were ultimately produced, but without Mulder on the CBS show.

"I spent days on the phone with a producer of *Picket Fences*," says Robert Goodwin. "We spent days organizing our schedules. Then at the very last minute, of course, we found out that no one had told CBS, and they said, 'Forget it. We're having enough trouble on Friday nights without publicizing *The X-Files*.' It's too bad."

Chris Carter was disappointed as well. "I'm sorry it didn't happen," he says. "But I still like to think the crossover happened. We just didn't see Mulder in Rome, Wisconsin."

Rating/Audience Share: 10.4/18

Episode 2.11 (#35)
"Excelsis Dei"
Original airdate: December 16, 1994
Written by Paul Brown
Directed by Stephen Surjik
Guest starring: Frances Bay (Dorothy), Eric Christmas (Stan Phillips), David Fresco (Hal Arden), Teryl Rothery (Nurse Michelle Charters), Sab Shimono (Gung Bituen)

Mulder and Scully proceed to a Massachusetts convalescent home, where a nurse claims she *was raped and beaten by an invisible force. They learn that a mystical drug is allowing one of the residents to unleash his psychic desires as well as the spirits of former residents.*

❊ ❊ ❊

"Kind of a troublesome episode," says Chris Carter. "The original script came in and I didn't like it. It was completely unproducable. It was just too big and all over the map. During the week of prep there were changes made in the script, and I actually think that, in the end, it turned out to be an interesting and touching episode that had some pretty good effects in it. The story also had a nice resonance to it."

James Wong offers, "It was one of the hardest shows we've put on, because the script came in in really bad shape and Chris was rewriting it until the last minute, even while we were shooting it. Again, I think that show had some neat stuff in it, but I don't think it came together at the end either."

One feature of the episode that J. P. Finn points out is that most of the guest actors were more "senior than I think the audience is used to. I don't think they're used to seeing older people act. Everything was different and odd.

"I guess the hardest part of the production was when David was in a room that was flooded with water. On location we had a tank dressed as the room, which we lowered into a pit of water to give the impression of flooding.

108

When the door is opened and the water comes flooding into the hallway, that was shot on location. The overall image worked really well."

Rating/Audience Share: 8.9/15

Episode 2.12 (#36)

"Aubrey"

Original airdate: January 6, 1995
Written by Sara B. Charno
Directed by Rob Bowman
Guest starring: Joy Coghill (Ruby Thibodeaux), Terry O'Quinn (Lt. Brian Tillman), Deborah Strang (Det. B. J. Morrow), Morgan Woodward (Old Harry Cokely)

While dreaming, a policewoman experiences the memory of a serial killing and discovers the body of an FBI agent who was assigned to investigate it nearly fifty years earlier. Then the serial killer strikes again, drawing Mulder and Scully into the investigation and raising the issue of a killer's genes being handed down to his descendant.

✵ ✵ ✵

"Sara Charno's first effort, something she had been working on for several months," Chris Carter recalls. "By the time we got to produce it, it was a finely honed script. There was a lot of help given to Sara by Glen Morgan and James Wong, who helped shepherd that script along. I think it came out great, and the casting was terrific. Deborah Strang, who played B. J., was top-notch, and we put her in for an Emmy nomination. Morgan Woodward was excellent as well. Rob Bowman came through for us and gave us an excellent job, following on 'Sleepless,' which was wonderful as well."

Says Bowman, "'Aubrey' was set in the Midwest. My father's family is all in Kansas, so I knew the look this episode had to have. I knew what these people needed to be like, these smalltown people. I also thought that it was the most horrorlike

episode I had done. I thought, 'Okay, let's make a good slasher episode.'

"With that episode," he continues, "I felt more confident and freer to experiment. Some of that experimentation I blew, and I managed to learn a lot from that episode about what Chris Carter wants, how his taste had evolved, how to do a slasher episode that was truly scary. I'm proud of the sequence that begins when B. J. is in her bedroom and she wakes up, there's blood on her chest, she goes to the bathroom and sees that she's slashed herself. She comes out, closes the door, and there's Harry Cokely. The script girl couldn't watch us shoot the scene because it was too scary."

Bowman has high praise for guest star Deborah Strang, who he feels tracked herself

through a very complex storyline that originally was *too* complicated for a one-hour TV show.

"We had to simplify it just a little," says Bowman. "She was always very careful about making sure one scene went into another logically. I remember the character was always in some kind of state, so at some point in the script I felt she had to be a totally ordinary person. So when she's in the hospital after finding a dead body, I wanted the scene to be totally normal, absolutely believable, no great storytelling techniques. There was a lot of nice shading of her character and peeling away of different sides of her. I just thought she did a great job of coloring the character and making her believable."

Rating/Audience Share: 10.2/16

**Episode 2.13 (#37)
"Irresistible"**

Original airdate: January 13, 1995
Written by Chris Carter
Directed by David Nutter
Guest starring: Nick Chinlund (Donald Eddie Pfaster), Robert Thurston (Jackson Toews), Bruce Weitz (Agent Moe Bocks), Christine Willes (Agent Karen E. Kosseff), Denalda Williams (Marilyn)

Mulder and Scully are called to Minnesota by an agent who believes that a mutilated body might have been ravaged by a paranormal phenomenon. What they find instead is that they're up against a necrophiliac — Donald Pfaster — who has begun a killing spree, with a captured Scully one of his intended victims. The only paranormal aspect of the story is that Pfaster sometimes appears as a demonlike creature for an instant, which could be Scully's subconscious mind dealing with her supposed abduction by aliens.

✿ ✿ ✿

"My first chance to work with David Nutter in a long time, and I wanted to give him something he could sink his teeth into," Chris Carter recalls. "It's a little bit different for us. It doesn't really have a paranormal aspect, except for Scully's perceptions of her deepest fears. I felt that I had to figure out what she is most afraid of, and she is most afraid of those things that most of us are afraid of. The idea of dying at the hands of someone — creature or not — and she is helpless to do anything about it. I thought it was a very good way to explore Scully's character. I thought it was a wonderfully creepy villain, played by Nick Chinlund. The casting of that show was very difficult. We saw many actors, but there was a quality I was looking for and I couldn't put a name on that quality. I finally figured out what it was when Nick came in and he had a kind of androgynous quality that worked. I thought he looked like Joe College, but he could scare the hell out of you."

Glen Morgan enthuses, "I think that's David Nutter's best episode in that when you read the script you said, 'Yeah, that's okay,' but he just gave it the whole atmosphere it needed. And the actor — Nick Chinlund — was outstanding. They just made it work."

"I was leaving the show," says Nutter, who departed to direct the pilot of Space: Above and Beyond, "and I didn't know if I would ever be coming back. I was hoping that it was a good script, because I wanted to go out with, as they say, a bang. The script was very good, but a lot of it depended on the actor. Chris was adamant about getting the right guy for the role. Well, Nick Chinlund was wonderful to work with; the guy was like putty in my hands. He was great. If you're looking for someone to underline the weirdness and strangeness of the character, he did that.

"I really worked hard to make a special show, because I thought it *was* special. It was Gillian's post-traumatic-stress episode, because she had not really had the opportunity to vent her feelings about the whole Duane Barry situation. This was an opportunity to sit back and let all that happen."

Some criticism was leveled against the show in terms of Pfaster appearing as a demon to someone besides Scully, thus negating the possibility of its being a purely psychological reaction on her part.

"In many ways," says Nutter, "Chris wanted to sell the idea that, as established in Mulder's closing dialogue in the show, not all terror comes from the paranormal. It could

"The idea [behind 'Irresistible'] is that sometimes our deepest fears are collective fears."

come from the person next door. The other part of that is, obviously, the pressure to show something different and paranormalish about

the demon. I thought it was really a matter of perspective."

Carter supports the aired version, stating, "The idea is that sometimes our deepest fears are collective fears."

Rating/Audience Share: 9.2/15

Episode 2.14 (#38)
"Die Hand Die Verletzt" (The Hand That Wounds)
Original airdate: January 27, 1995
Written by Glen Morgan and James Wong
Directed by Kim Manners
Guest starring: Susan Blommaert (Phyllis H. Paddock), Dan Butler (Jim Ausbury), Shawn Johnston (Pete Calcagni), Heather McComb (Shannon Ausbury)

Some teenagers pretend to perform an occult ritual in an effort to impress some of their classmates, when they inadvertently cause the death of one of the group. Mulder and Scully discover that members of the PTA are actually practicing Satan worship.

✿ ✿ ✿

"We were leaving the show," says Glen Morgan of his and James Wong's departure, "and ever since *21 Jump Street* we had wanted to do a script about Satanic cults kidnapping people and burying them. I wanted that to be the hoax episode — that Mulder was so sure it was going to be something and it became something else. Jim and I felt the things people liked out of the two of us were the Tooms episodes ['Squeeze' and 'Tooms']. It just seemed like the time for a scary episode. I don't know if it was the mood we were in, but except for the situation with the girl who confesses how she was molested, it was almost a comedy. A comedic premise that PTA members are Satan worshipers. I like that. Of course we had fights with Standards on that as well.

"We had to let the leader get away at the end," he continues. "How are you going to catch the Devil? The self-indulgent part of the episode comes from the fact that we love the crew and the show so much, we wanted a message, so at the end when Mulder reads the note Blommaert's left on the blackboard that says, 'It's been nice working with you, see you soon,' that's really from Jim and me to the crew. I remember there was one take where David and Gillian come up to the blackboard, they're looking at it, and David says, 'Goodbye, it's been nice working with you. Thanks for using us to get our own show.' Gillian says, 'Fuck off — the Wongs.' Then David says, 'I'm going to miss those guys,' and she says, 'Me too,' and they both start laughing."

Says Chris Carter, "It was a fun script that turned this big corner when the girl had the emotional breakdown. It suddenly became a very creepy, dark, disturbing episode. It was vintage Glen and Jim, and we had a great, great performance by the guest stars. A really good, solid episode that actually veered a little more toward the horror genre. But it worked because of Mulder and Scully."

For J. P. Finn, a couple of snakes used in the episode stick out in his mind more than anything. "John Bartley, our wonderful director of photography, was shooting at really low light levels," says Finn. "We had this twenty-foot, two-hundred-fifty-pound snake coming down the stairs. We had two cameras on it. The dolly grip, who was underneath the stairs, said, 'Can't see it, can't see it.' He turned around and the snake was about six inches from his face. The crew just cleared out of there."

Rating/Audience Share: 10.7/18

Episode 2.15 (#39)
"Fresh Bones"

Original airdate: February 3, 1995
Written by Howard Gordon
Directed by Rob Bowman
Guest starring: Roger Cross (Pvt. Kittel), Katya Gardner (Robin McAlpin), Matt Hill (Pvt. Harry Dunham), Peter Kelamis (Lt. Foyle), Adrian Malebranche (Skinny Man), Callum Keith Rennie (Groundskeeper), Jamil Walker Smith (Chester Bonaparte), Steven Williams (Mr. X), Bruce Young (Pierre Bauvais)

After a soldier stationed at a North Carolina resettlement camp for Haitians drives himself into a tree, Mulder and Scully are called in when the man's widow contacts the agency. The duo investigate and find themselves immersed in the world of voodoo, practiced by local residents and the colonel commanding the refugee area.

❄ ❄ ❄

Chris Carter says, "I would say that ranks as one of the best of our series episodes — not the mythology episodes. They're stand-alone episodes that don't push forward the mythology of the Mulder–Scully search for the truth against the wishes of those who don't want them to know it. 'Fresh Bones' is one of the episodes I'm most proud of this season. I thought Howard did a good job with the script and Rob did a great job with the directing. I just love the darkness of the episode."

"The story came very much out of the newspaper," Howard Gordon explains. "During the invasion of Haiti, several servicemen died at their own hands in a very short period of time. It was a tragic event, but also an interesting speculation: Could there have been something unsavory, more centered on a cultural phenomenon, at work here too? Since we couldn't shoot it in Haiti, we thought about the refugee situation with the Cubans and Haitians. These were all real stories happening on the front pages, and we approached it from a voodoo angle, because voodoo is an

obvious area for an X-File. The trick was to do it with some kind of fidelity."

"Agony," moans Rob Bowman, "because it was such an enormous episode. There were lots of extras, and it was difficult to shoot. First of all, find two hundred black people in Vancouver. We did it, but it felt like an impossibility. Make an internment camp in Vancouver that looks anything like Virginia or the Carolinas.

"The goal was to create believability in this voodoo storyline and not to make it silly, filled with bloody chickens and all of the things we've seen before. We wanted to create a very believable scenario."

One of the most frightening sequences in the episode is when Scully suffers a vision in which she's looking at her hand and another hand bursts through the skin and begins choking her, with blood pouring out of her mouth.

"Our editors are wonderful cutting things together," comments makeup maestro Toby Lindala. "We had a mechanical hand and had a guy doubling the actor's hand stuff his fingers up through it. There was gelatin skin on the hands, which I thought played very well and was believable and fleshy. The hand double had tubes attached to his fingers, so as he pushed up it tore it open a little bit and you see the plasma and the skin rips. They played that so well in the final cut."

Robert Goodwin says, laughing, "Gillian loves doing those scenes. We've got her in the car at one in the morning, it's sixteen degrees, and she has to have blood gushing out her mouth over and over again. She just thought that was great."

Rating/Audience Share: 11.3/19

Episode 2.16 (#40)
"Colony"
Original airdate: February 10, 1995
Teleplay by Chris Carter
Story by Chris Carter and David Duchovny
Directed by Nick Marck
Guest starring: Tom Butler (CIA Agent Ambrose Chapel), Peter Donat (Mulder's Father), Dana Gladstone (Dr. Landon Prince/Gregor), David L. Gordon (FBI Agent), Bonnie Hay (Field Doctor), Tim Henry (Federal Marshal), Andrew Johnston (Agent Barrett Weiss), Megan Leitch (Samantha Mulder), Michael McDonald (Military Policeman), Capper McIntyre (First Jailer), Mitch Pileggi (Assistant Director Walter S. Skinner), Rebecca Toolan (Mulder's Mother), Brian Thompson (Pilot)

Episode 2.17 (#41)
"End Game"
Original airdate: February 17, 1995
Written by Frank Spotnitz
Directed by Rob Bowman
Guest starring: Colin Cunningham (Lt. Terry Wilmer), Peter Donat (Mulder's Father), Tim Henry (Federal Marshal), Megan Leitch (Samantha Mulder), Mitch Pileggi (Assistant Director Walter S. Skinner), Brian Thompson (Pilot), Steven Williams (Mr. X)

In part one, a series of murders occur after an ad is placed in a newspaper seeking out a particular doctor. Especially unusual about the deaths is that all of the victims have the same face! Mulder and Scully start looking for yet another clone in order to get some answers, when Mulder is contacted by his father and told that his sister, Samantha, has come home.

Part two has an alien bounty hunter determined to get Samantha Mulder — a clone — back. To gain the upper hand with Mulder, he abducts Scully and will return her only in exchange for Samantha. When Mulder learns that the hunter knows where the real Samantha is, he travels to the North Pole for a final battle with this extraterrestrial.

✺ ✺ ✺

"I think the two-parter of 'Colony' and 'End Game' was extremely ambitious," says Chris Carter. "It encompassed a couple of desires from the first year which I couldn't fulfill. In 'Ice' I wanted to be in the North Pole, which is something we couldn't do. Nick Marck did the first episode, which had some cool effects.

"I also thought it was an interesting exploration of Scully and Mulder's different perspectives as well. I wanted to reestablish what their points of view were; to reaffirm her belief in science and his belief in the paranormal.

"It was a different way to tell a story. I've always wanted to tell a story backwards like that, an inspiration I took from the original *Frankenstein,* which is told the same way."

Producer–director Rob Bowman notes, "It was around this time that *The X-Files* finally exploded into bigger than life. These were the sweeps episodes, and the scripts became enormous, requiring several units to shoot them."

For most of the staff, "End Game" was the ultimate *X-Files* episode because of its incredible production values.

"We rented a submarine that was being decommissioned from the Canadian Navy," says J. P. Finn. "We used it on three different episodes: as an icebreaker in 'Colony,' the submarine in 'End Game,' and as a ship in 'Dod Kalm.' It was just an incredible set piece that we were able to use."

Robert Goodwin points out that in many cases — particularly in this two-parter — there is no need for special effects on the show because the crew physi-

"*The X-Files* finally exploded into bigger than life. These were the sweeps episodes, and the scripts became enormous, requiring several units to shoot them."

cally does what is seen on film. "In 'End Game,' there was a nuclear submarine coming up through the polar ice cap. In the last act, Mulder and this alien hit man are having a vicious fight and Mulder is dangling off the top of this conning tower when the thing starts to submerge. He drops to the ice and is nearly crushed to death. I swear to God, it was like something out of *Die Hard,* and we did it on a stage."

Adds Bowman, "'End Game' really is an example of what *The X-Files* can do best, because it was a huge, huge production. We had a hundred and fifty tons of snow shipped in to us down to a stage that was refrigerated. We had built a full-scale mock-up of a conning tower with articulated wings!"

Writer Frank Spotnitz explains that shortly after he was hired, he went to Chris Carter and said, "'It's been so many years since Mulder has seen his sister — what if someone shows up and says she's his sister? What would he make of this?' Chris saw how that could immediately fit in to what he and David had already been talking about for the two-parter — the bounty hunter and the alien clones — and I was brought on to do the second part.

"As big as the episode was," Spotnitz adds, "my initial draft was even bigger. There were two scenes that I had to cut out because there wasn't time to shoot them. One was going to take place very early in the story, after Mulder bursts into the motel room and Scully has already been taken. He walks out into the breezeway and he sees the federal marshal we had seen at the end of 'Colony,' and he's very paranoid that this could be the bounty

> **"'It's been so many years since Mulder has seen his sister — what if someone shows up and says that she's his sister?'"**

hunter, because he could be anyone. So there's this big thing where he draws his gun on a federal marshal and there's a showdown between the two of them. Ultimately it turns out to be the marshal and not the bounty hunter. The other sequence that was going to be really big is at the top of act two. It's the morning after the hostage trade (when Mulder has traded his sister for Scully). I was going to have him meet his father at the bridge and as he's driving he sees his sister, wet and cold on the side of the road. He pulls over, she gets in, and he's driving, when he suddenly realizes it's *not* her, it's the bounty hunter. She morphs into the bounty hunter right before his eyes, they struggle for the wheel of the car, they end up jumping out of the car, the car crashes, and then he rushes to the abortion clinic where the other clones are, and the bounty hunter is right after him. We ended up cutting all of that. Great stuff, but the story really didn't *need* either of those scenes. I didn't realize it when I was writing that you *can't* do a show of that size in eight days."

Rating/Audience Share ("Colony"): 10.3/17
Rating/Audience Share ("End Game"): 11.2/19

Episode 2.18 (#42)
"Fearful Symmetry"
Original airdate: February 24, 1995
Written by Steve DeJarnatt
Directed by James Whitmore, Jr.
Guest starring: Charles Andre (Ray Floyd), Jayne Atkinson (Willa Ambrose), Tom Braidwood (Frohike), Lance Guest (Kyle Lang), Bruce Harwood (Byers), Jack Rader (Ed Meecham)

A series of animals, ranging from elephants to tigers to gorillas, are blamed for a string of murders, though witnesses claim not to have seen any animals. Investigations seem to indicate that aliens are involved, abducting animals to perhaps create their own version of Noah's ark.

❄ ❄ ❄

"A quirky little episode for us," Chris Carter recalls with a smile. "It had kind of a cool teaser, which featured an elephant running down the highway. I thought it was a touching episode and a very original idea. Right now I'm reading this book about the paranormal, and there's this idea that aliens are working like Noah with his ark to collect us. I thought it was, by and large, a successful episode, and a little bit of a diversion for us after coming off of 'Colony' and 'End Game.' A lot of people really responded to it."

Says J. P. Finn, "A tough show schedulewise. We had to shoot everything second unit because of the animals. The hardest part was getting the elephant here. I started working on getting a permit for the elephant to come across the border to Vancouver way back at the first of December. Right up until the day it had to leave Los Angeles to be here, we finally got the permits from the proper government agencies. Once she got here — her name was Bubbles — she was fantastic to work with."

Rating/Audience Share: 10.1/17

Episode 2.19 (#43)

"Dod Kalm" (Dead Calm)

Original airdate: March 10, 1995
Teleplay by Howard Gordon and Alex Gansa
Story by Howard Gordon
Directed by Rob Bowman
Guest starring: Mar Anderson (Halverson),
Dmitry Chepovetsky (Lt. Richard Harper),
David Cubitt (Capt. Barclay), Stephen
Dimopoulos (Ionesco), Vladimir Kulich
(Olafsson), John McConnach (Sailor), Bob
Metcalfe (Nurse), Claire Riley (Dr. Laskos),
John Savage (Henry Trondheim)

The U.S.S. Argent's last position was in the Norwegian Sea, and a boatload of survivors are discovered — all of them apparently having aged decades in only a few days. Mulder and Scully board the vessel and suffer the same fate, desperately searching for a cure before they die.

❈ ❈ ❈

"Back on the ship again," says Rob Bowman. "The episode from hell, because it was seven or eight days straight on that battleship. On 'End Game' the ship had been white, the color the ship actually is. For 'Dod Kalm' we painted it rust brown. It was dark and depressing every day. The work was very slow in coming because David and Gillian both had hours of makeup every day. They're tired by this time of the season anyway, but to put a pound

of makeup on their face and then act had to be too much. I was pretty tired too, because the prep of 'Dod Kalm' was completely filled with shooting second unit for 'Fearful Symmetry.'

"Ultimately it ended up being one of my favorite episodes, filled with atmosphere. John Savage proved to be a very interesting man to work with. He is very intelligent, but he's used to a feature schedule. I've had that before, when people who aren't used to a TV schedule are forced to learn so much dialogue for a single day. But I think he did the show proud. His being slightly uncomfortable helped in the playing of the character."

Of the makeup task, Toby Lindala explains: "There's kind of a standard when you're aging someone, but this was a little different. It was supposed to be caused by dehydration rather than actual aging, so you don't have the effect of the hair graying. You don't have a lot of form change, so we tried to focus more on texture. We didn't want a cheesy aging effect, although we still tried to cheat a little bit while keeping it stylized where we didn't age their noses. Both David and Gillian have quite distinctive noses, so their characters are identifiable through that, and then we stylized it, and we didn't age their ears either. Just to keep the idea of the textural age rather than the form age. You're not getting that big wattle under the neck, but rather more a wrinkling of the skin."

Says Chris Carter, "Although we had used that ship for 'Colony' and 'End Game,' what I had planned to use it for all along was an episode like 'Dod Kalm.' I didn't want to do a Bermuda Triangle episode per se, because I thought that was an obvious way to go with it. So what looks like a Bermuda Triangle story turns out to be something else. I thought it would be a great money saver, and production value would be built in, but it ended up being very expensive, very costly time-wise. For one thing, the makeup for David and Gillian took a long time to put on, and they were miserable. The boat was cold inside; it was cramped, tight quarters. It's one of those situations where you think you're brilliant, but things don't go exactly like you planned."

Rating/Audience Share: 10.7/18

Episode 2.20 (#44)

"Humbug"

Original airdate: March 31, 1995
Written by Darin Morgan
Directed by Kim Manners
Guest starring: Michael Anderson (Mr. Nutt),
Alex Diakun (Curator), The Enigma (The
Conundrum), Wayne Grace (Sheriff
Hamilton), John Payne (Jerald Glazebrook),
Jim Rose (Dr. Blockhead, a.k.a. Jeffrey
Swaim), Vincent Schiavelli (Lanny), Debis
Simpson (Walter), Blair Slater (Glazebrook,
older), Gordon Tipple (Hepcat Helm), Devin
Walker (Glazebrook, younger)

Investigating a long series of ritualistic killings that follow no particular pattern, Mulder and

Scully proceed to Gibsonton, Florida, a town built around a carnival and its sideshow acts. Mulder suspects the paranormal — particularly when he watches the bizarre Crocodile Man — but he is completely off base this time.

❁ ❁ ❁

"Darin Morgan writes with a very comedic voice," Chris Carter explains. "When he handed me this script, he didn't know how I was going to respond to it, because it is so whacked. But I read it and I laughed out loud. I thought it was wonderful, but I thought to try and do it any time sooner would have been too big a risk, because its tone was so different from what has become a traditional *X-Files* script. But I figured that by the forty-fourth episode, we had earned that right, so I stood behind it, despite head-scratching and resistance from the studio. What you get from Darin's scripts are pretty offbeat shows. I think it's a nice ingredient to add to the show."

Darin Morgan explains, "One of the reasons I was uncomfortable joining the staff is that I'm a comedy writer and this *isn't* a comedy show, so I was trying more or less to have an episode with a little bit of humor, without telling anybody what I was doing. They asked me to do something about freaks and gave me a tape of one of Jim Rose's stage performances. I watched the tape and started doing research on sideshows, and that's where the script developed."

"I love 'Humbug,'" says Robert Goodwin.

"Talk about offbeat. It's very theatrical and grandiose. The trick was being careful that it

> **"The trick [with 'Humbug'] was being careful that it didn't become like a bad Vincent Price movie, but it really worked."**

didn't become like a bad Vincent Price movie, but it really worked out well."

Producer–director Kim Manners thought "Humbug," as the first *X-Files* that was a comedy, was particularly challenging. "A bizarre show," he recalls with a laugh. "Chris said he was throwing the audience a curveball. Well, he threw a whole lot more than a curveball. There I am, I'm a new producer and I'm directing my second episode, and it's a comedy. I'm working with Jim Rose, who's an entertainer, not an actor, and he's got five pages of dialogue, exterior, days. He's outside in just a pair of pants, hanging upside down over a boiling cauldron, and it was like fifty degrees out. At night, the Enigma, who plays the Conundrum, is running around literally in a loincloth and it's thirty-three degrees. These

were the challenges of 'Humbug,' and I've got to tell you, I was scared to death. The sun was going down and Jim Rose couldn't remember his dialogue and I had to give him a hug and say, 'It's okay,' and literally give him off-camera line readings in order to get the show done. We got it done and Jim Rose came off terrific. Everyone was great."

Rating/Audience Share: 10.3/18

Episode 2.21 (#45)
"The Calusari"
Original airdate: April 14, 1995
Written by Sara B. Charno
Directed by Michael Vejar
Guest starring: Lilyan Chauvin (Golda), Helene Clarkson (Maggie Holvey), Jacqueline Dandenau (Nurse Castor), Bill Dow (Dr. Charles Burk), Kay E. Kuter (Head Calusari), Joel Palmer (Charlie/Michael Holvey), Ric Reid (Steve Holvey), Oliver and Jeremy Isaac Wildsmith (Teddy Holvey), Christine Willes (Agent Karen E. Kosseff)

When a child is killed under mysterious circumstances, Mulder and Scully discover that the boy's older brother is possessed by an evil spirit. The parents contact a group of Romanian ritualists to perform an exorcism, in which Mulder participates.

❈ ❈ ❈

"Accomplishing this episode was really arduous," says Robert Goodwin. "There were *so* many special effects to be coordinated, and we had a teaser involving a toddler wandering onto a railroad track in an amusement park. In making that a believable sequence, you have to work from the framework that kids are restricted by child-labor laws in terms of how much time they can work. A good episode, but a tough one to make happen."

Adds Chris Carter, "Sara Charno and I had gone to lunch and she hit on the evil-twin idea and how best to approach that. We worked on that idea, she wrote the story and came back, and I felt that it wasn't quite scary enough. I wanted her to add the Calusari, and their addition really upped the stakes. I think the episode came out to be one of the best of the season. It's funny sometimes how some of the most difficult episodes turn out to be some of the best. It felt like it should have been a very contained episode, but it didn't work out that way. During the exorcism — if you want to call it that — there were so many elements to it. It's a show that never let up."

Rating/Audience Share: 8.3/16

Episode 2.22 (#46)

"F. Emasculata"

Original airdate: April 28, 1995
Written by Chris Carter and Howard Gordon
Directed by Rob Bowman
Guest starring: William B. Davis (Cigarette-Smoking Man), Kim Kondrashoff (Bobby Torrence), Dean Norris (U.S. Marshal Tapia), Morris Paynch (Dr. Simon Auerbach), Mitch Pileggi (Assistant Director Walter S. Skinner), John Pyper-Ferguson (Paul), Bill Rowat (Dr. Robert Torrence), Charles Martin Smith (Dr. Osborne), John Tench (Steve), Angelo Vacco (Angelo Garza)

Mulder and Scully are sent into a prison from which two prisoners have escaped. At first they're completely confused as to why they're involved in this situation, until it's revealed that a highly contagious and deadly disease has infected many of the inmates and, quite possibly, the escapees as well.

❋ ❋ ❋

"Howard Gordon and I teamed up again after having not teamed up for a while," says Chris Carter. "I think we work well together, and having Rob Bowman as director made it delightful. Rob loved directing it, saying that it came to him easily. He and Kim Manners are producer–directors on the show and both are top-notch and they'll give you everything they've got. Anyway, I think it was a very successful show, very creepy. One thing I'm astounded at is what we pull off in an hour of television. The look of that episode was wonderful."

Rob Bowman notes, "I had begun to change my diet and working out, because after 'Dod Kalm' I was in such bad shape that I

"I knew I was working on *The X-Files* when I heard myself say, 'I need the pus to go from left to right.'"

needed to do *something*. I kind of got my legs beneath me again when it came time to do this episode. Not a particularly emotional show, but it's a great X-File because there are some things in it that are just about as disgusting as anything you could imagine. It's about cover-ups, viruses; it's a chase. Basically it was a cops-and-robbers show with an *X-Files* twist. It was one of those episodes that seemed to go easy for Chris when he wrote it, it was easy for me to shoot, and Chris and I were absolutely in sync. I think we needed an episode at that time that didn't kill everybody in production or editing. It just came together and was a gift for everyone."

For Toby Lindala, "F. Emasculata" was a "fun" episode. "Bladder effects had become a standard for us." He smiles. "But the idea of actually using a bladder and a virus as a weapon while holding a hostage is wonderful.

We had actors rigged with bladder boil pieces on their faces, going through up to three different phases each. The boils just keep getting larger until they blow pus. We rigged each of the pieces with two different tubes so that they could spew different distances."

Speaking of pus, Robert Goodwin has one particular memory of the making of this episode. "Rob Bowman was doing shots of the boils exploding on one of the dead victims. He said, 'I knew I was working on *The X-Files* when I heard myself say, "I need the pus to go from left to right."' I love that show. It was disgusting, but so well done. Toby really outdid himself. He loves to do things that seem like they're impossible, especially impossible given the time frame. These guys who work on films have months to set themselves up. We usually have a week or two at the most. The thing with Toby is sometimes he really grosses me out and I tell him so, and his response is, 'Thank you.'"

Rating/Audience Share: 8.9/16

Episode 2.23 (#47)
"Soft Light"

Original airdate: May 5, 1995
Written by Vince Gilligan
Directed by James Contner
Guest starring: Forbes Angus (Government Scientist), Steve Bacic (Second Officer), Nathaniel Deveaux (Det. Bradley Baron), Guyle Frazier (Barney), Kevin McNulty (Dr. Christopher Davey), Robert Rozen (Doctor), Tony Shalhoub (Dr. Chester Ray Banton), Kate Twa (Det. Kelly Ryan), Steven Williams (Mr. X), Donna Yamamoto (Night Nurse)

Scully is asked by a former student to investigate a series of mysterious disappearances in which the only thing that remains from each victim is a black spot on the ground. Mulder suspects spontaneous human combustion, but the truth is that a scientist finds himself trapped in his own experiment, resulting in his shadow drawing in anything that gets in its way — essentially a mini–black hole.

❋ ❋ ❋

"A tough show from the point of view of visual effects," says J. P. Finn. "That was the technical challenge there. It's very tough to light a show in an interesting way, while not having the actor cast a shadow."

Explains Graeme Murray, "A fair amount of work for us on that one. We did some work on a nuclear research facility, a particle accelerator, and the necessary computers. It was a good high-tech set, and as contrast we had to build a hospital and government facility where the investigations took place. A good show for us in terms of contrast."

"This show was written by a writer whose work I admired before I even began working on *The X-Files,*" says Chris Carter. "I think 'Soft Light' is a real popular episode. Maybe a little more science fiction than our other episodes, but I think there's some really good scientific principles involved that helped to make it believable. The lighting problems were difficult to work out, but luckily the director we had was a former DP [director of photography], so he could solve them."

Rating/Audience Share: 8.5/15

Episode 2.24 (#48)
"Our Town"

Original airdate: May 12, 1995
Written by Frank Spotnitz
Directed by Rob Bowman
Guest starring: Gary Grubbs (Sheriff Tom Arens), Caroline Kava (Doris Kearns), John MacLaren (George Kearns), Hrothgar Mathews (Creighton Jones), John Milford (Walter "Chic" Chaco), Gabrielle Miller (Paula Gray), Robin Mossley (Dr. Vance Randolph), Timothy Webber (Jess Harold)

When they are informed of a missing poultry inspector, Mulder and Scully come to Dudley, Arkansas, where — they eventually learn — cannibalism is a way of life.

❈ ❈ ❈

"Frank Spotnitz wanted to do a cannibalism episode, and I guess this is it." Chris Carter laughs. "He had done some research on chicken processing plants and discovered that they were perhaps the most despicable and vile things you could imagine — therefore perfect *X-Files* material. This idea of a town protecting its deepest, darkest secret and Mulder and Scully getting involved while we were making our move toward the season finale was wonderful. Standards was a little concerned, but I think our handling of cannibalism was tastefully done."

Spotnitz explains, "I knew I wanted to do something about cannibalism, because it was something we hadn't done and I think it's one of those things people are naturally morbidly fascinated by. I was reading articles trying to think of a way into this story, when I came across something about salamanders eating other salamanders. There are very few cannibals in nature, but there sometimes are, and they get sick when they consume sick members of their species. That was it for me. What if you're a cannibal and you get food poisoning? That was my way into the story, and the rest was figuring out how cannibalism got to the United States and who would be an interesting person to give them food poisoning. The story sprang from there. The only supernatural aspect to the story was the idea that if you ate other people and performed this magic ritual, it would prolong your life, which is sort of stretching real beliefs from cannibal tribes.

"I was very pleased with the way it was executed, and I think it was a good mystery," he adds. "Some people have complained about seeing Scully in jeopardy again, and I've got to say that they have a good point. After having seen her abducted twice, beaten up, and all the things she had been through, I could understand why some fans didn't want to see that again. If I had that to think over, I'd probably come up with another way to get out of that story."

Rob Bowman terms "Our Town" "a sick little episode. I have to classify this as a classic X-File where Mulder and Scully are handed a case and they search out the creepy aspect of whatever the situation is and solve the crime. I must admit to being very tired and not very inspired. I felt my job on this one was to do the best I could with a tired crew. We didn't want to create too many waves; we just wanted to get it done. It ended up taking a lot of extra time to finish because we were all so brain-dead. And it took us a while to figure out how to make it end. A fastball-down-the-middle kind of X-Files; no skew to it."

Rating/Audience Share: 9.4/17

Episode 2.25 (#49)
"Anasazi"

Original airdate: May 19, 1995
Teleplay by Chris Carter
Story by David Duchovny and Chris Carter
Directed by Robert Goodwin
Guest starring: Tom Braidwood (Frohike), Bernie Coulson (The Thinker, a.k.a. Kenneth Soona), William B. Davis (Cigarette-Smoking Man), Aurelio Dinunzio (Antonio), Peter Donat (Mulder's Father), Dean Haglund (Langly), Bruce Harwood (Byers), Nicholas Lea (Agent Alex Krycek), Paul McLean (Agent Kautz), Byron Chief Moon (Father), Renae Morriseau (Josephine Doane), Mitch Pileggi (Assistant Director Walter S. Skinner), Michael David Simms (Senior Agent), Floyd "Red Crow" Westerman (Albert Hosteen)

At first Mulder is overjoyed when he is given a computer disk that supposedly contains classified government information on UFOs, but the fact that it's encrypted begins a downward spiral for him: he starts behaving erratically, culminating in his punching out Skinner. Scully eventually learns that Mulder has been drugged. Upon recovering from its effects, he proceeds to the Nevada desert, where he finds a buried boxcar that seemingly contains the bodies of numerous extraterrestrials — although further examination indicates that they could conceivably be humans who had undergone government experimentation. The Cigarette-Smoking Man shows up and orches-

trates what could be Mulder's death in the boxcar.

❀ ❀ ❀

Robert Goodwin, who directed this season's finale and the first year's, finds that whereas season one's "Erlenmeyer Flask" was a locomotive that couldn't be stopped in terms of its pacing and the physical action it presented, "Anasazi" was more dramatic, focusing intensely on the characters. "From the moment you see Mulder, you get the feeling that something is wrong," he says. "When he hits Skinner, it's a genuine shock for the audience. I thought David and Gillian were both great. While Mulder is going through what he's going through, Scully is really caught between a rock and a hard place. She's trying to protect him, but at the same time she knows there's something wrong with this guy and she's got to figure out what it is, or she's going to go down with him. I just thought there were a lot of personal things happening for both of them."

In reflecting on this episode, Glen Morgan brings up the interesting notion that, after all she's seen and been through, Scully could — if Mulder were actually dead — step into his shoes. "It's almost as though she's in the position where she would have that cynicism, that

darkness, yet she would now have the hopeful, believing edge," he muses. "To me, Scully's in a position to become Mulder. I just don't believe she's a skeptic anymore. I thought there was a possibility after 'One Breath' for her to be thrown back to her skeptical state, her really hardcore position, because she was in such denial over what had happened to her. But it didn't come out that way."

But Chris Carter, holding fast to the believer-versus-skeptic relationship that underpins the show, doesn't agree with Morgan. "My feeling is that she acknowledges there is definitely someone trying to keep certain things from us," he says. "But her bias is a scientific one. She admits there is a conspira-

> **"'Anasazi' was the culmination of a lot of ideas. Darin Morgan called this the kitchen sink episode."**

cy afoot, but is she able to take Mulder's place? I would say no. She's not willing to take his place as a believer. She's still a skeptic."

Of "Anasazi" itself, Carter observes: "This episode was the culmination of a lot of ideas. Generally, when we pitch stories to the staff everyone comments on them, and Darin Morgan called this the kitchen sink episode, because it had so much in it, he didn't know how we would pull it off. But I'm very proud of the script. David Duchovny and I worked quite closely on the story and he had a lot of input, and then I sat down and wrote the script, which is always tough. You write the words 'fade in' and realize that you have *not* asked yourself so many questions. But I'm proud of the way it came together, what it did for the series, and the overwhelmingly positive response it has gotten. I'm very pleased beginning season three with where this episode put us — which is that it posed more questions than it answered."

Rating/Audience Share: 10.1/18

the X-Files

CHAPTER SIX
Year Three: The Mythology

Now that *The X-Files* has established a secure foothold for Fox on Friday nights — a prime-time slot when audiences have historically been difficult to pin down — the young network is looking for its big show to do some more heavy lifting in the 1996–97 season. With NBC's *Mad About You,* CBS's *60 Minutes,* ABC's *Lois & Clark: The New Adventures of Superman,* and a regular lineup of high-profile movies and miniseries, the Big Three networks

haven't allowed Fox to lure a regular viewership on Sundays. So Fox is throwing its best at the competition — a risky move that surprised many industry watchers, including Chris Carter.

"I had heard rumors about the move [before it happened]," says Carter. "Fox had mentioned it to me and I was not pleased with the suggestion. Now that it's happened, of course, I've got to live with it. But it's not something that I had anticipated or welcomed. I just love that Friday-night slot for *The X-Files.* Once a show proves that it works somewhere, I'm loath to [move it around]. Maybe it's a part of me that's resistant to change, but I just hate to see *X-Files* leave its Friday slot."

Lessening the sense of dislocation for Carter, the network has put his new show, *Millennium,* in *The X-Files'* Friday slot. "*Millennium* is a scary show too," he says, "so I believe it will work there."

What Fox execs are banking on is their belief that *The X-Files* will work anywhere. After all, it has worked not only on Friday nights, but in retail shops, bookstores, and Blockbuster Video. The comic book series that's based on the show more or less saved the hemorrhaging Topps comic line, HarperCollins has scored big with hardcover *X-Files* novels, videocassettes of the series's early episodes are also hot sellers (even more so overseas), and merchandise inspired by the show has become ubiquitous. "I'm always nervous about merchandising the show," Carter says. "I don't want the show to be perceived as shameless commerce, but there's a demand for mer-

Millennium

Chris Carter is attempting to capture lightning in a bottle a second time with the creation of a new Fox series, *Millennium*, which will be assuming *The X-Files'* Friday-night time slot as that show shifts to Sunday.

"It's about a former FBI agent who is working with a kind of mysterious group of men," Carter says. "He is using his expertise, which he gained in the FBI and which has actually evolved into a kind of intuition where he can get into a criminal's head, to solve cases."

As Fox's official press release notes, many prophecies have predicted that the approach of the millennium will coincide with the demise of humanity, a fact apparent each night on the evening news. In *Millennium*, a force is at work to reverse the seemingly inevitable. Lance Henriksen (*Near Dark; Aliens; The Terminator*) stars as Frank Black, whose uncanny ability to enter the minds of criminals and capture them has led him to leave the FBI out of fear that something could happen to his wife or daughter. As a result, he leads an enigmatic — and secret — task force to strike back at those who would prey on society's fears. At the same time, the series will contrast its darkness with Black's suburban Seattle home life, and look at the relationship between him and his wife, Catherine (Megan Gallagher), and daughter, Jordan (Brittany Tiplady). Catherine is a social psychologist who has to help Black in his struggle to retain his humanity by overcoming his inner demons.

David Nutter, who directed the pilot episode of the series, believes *Millennium* owes a tip of its hat to such features as *Manhunter* and *Silence of the Lambs*, as well as the *X-Files* episode "Grotesque."

"We have gone for a compelling reality in the creation of this show," Nutter explains. "The characters are people who have seen things; people who have lived a life and have so much to offer from their experience. Lance is an actor with caliber and strength who could really portray a character burdened by his experience in many ways, but who can offer us hope and is fighting for right. We needed someone who would be able to go in and out of characters and make them believable. You can trace the idea to the notion 'When you want to study Picasso, study his paintings.' To study serial killers, you need to study victims. So basically, what happens is that Frank Black is the kind of character who looks into the grotesque — the things you and I would turn away from — in order to find an MO, find that signature, find that *something* you can track the serial killer down with. He basically gets into their head by being able to retrace their steps, put on their shoes, and live in their environment. These killers don't see the world as we do. They don't hear the world as we do. It's a situation where he really immerses himself until he finds them."

"I've just always been a fan of his work," adds Carter of Henriksen, who seems like an odd choice for the lead of a prime-time series, given his offbeat, eclectic film roles. "He brings to the role, for me, a clarity, maturity, and a centered quality I was looking for. A very reserved and masculine heroic quality that I felt was really the character I wanted to create."

Both Carter and Nutter agreed that *Millennium* needed to have its own signature, much as *The X-Files* did when it began. To this end, they spent a great deal of time putting together a production crew and creating a look the show could call its own.

"My attitude is that whenever you turn on *The X-Files*, you know what you're watching before you see a title or before you see a main character," says Nutter. "This show has to have the same attitude, and I'm really happy that it does. People are very, very excited by the look and the style of it."

Carter notes that there is, nonetheless, a certain sense of kinship between the two series. "It's going to be scary," he says matter-of-factly. "It's going to deal with some elements of psychological terror that *The X-Files* sometimes delves into. I think the associations will be made, but the differences are greater than the similarities."

chandise based on the show. I guess we're just satisfying that demand."

"What's amazing to me," offers co-producer Paul Rabwin, "is that in its third year *The X-Files* clearly became a part of the cultural lexicon. You cannot get an issue of *TV Guide* or *Entertainment Weekly* or *People* without someone referring to the show. There have been political cartoons, references in the funnies, and newspaper headlines. It's no longer something that needs explanation."

Story editor Frank Spotnitz muses that the enormous popularity of the show is, in some ways, a little bit painful for longtime fans. "I think there's a nostalgia for the first season, when *The X-Files* was their own little discovery and there was a very small but intensely loyal audience for the show. Now I think a lot of people feel it's not just their private 'find' anymore. They are sharing it with a mass audience and seeing it on magazine covers everywhere."

To Carter, all this attention isn't simply momentum, but a reward for discipline. "I think it's all because we are still doing what we set out to do, which is to tell very good stories. I think that's what

"What's amazing is that in its third year *The X-Files* clearly became a part of the cultural lexicon. It's no longer something that needs explanation."

series's moral compass. And yet, paradoxically, it is the remarkable popularity of these conspiracy-themed episodes — what Carter calls *The X-Files*' mythology — that threatens to undermine the show's original premise: the believer, Mulder, and the skeptic, Scully, investigating individual cases of the paranormal each week from their very different vantage points.

The mythology episodes, which feature the enigmatic Cigarette-Smoking Man, were originally designed to be just one of many thematic arcs in the series. But by the latter part of the second season, it was clear that the mythology had become the show's guiding force, leading some of the *X-Files* writers to puzzle over how to handle it. With all that Scully has seen and experienced (see "Duane Barry," "Colony," "End Game," and "Paper Clip"), how does she remain a skeptic? And how do the duo return to individual cases after some of their astonishing discoveries in pursuit of the conspiracy? The official line out of the *X-Files* office rejects such concerns. "If you look at the series in a linear fashion, I agree that it's a problem," producer–director Rob Bowman says. "But God only knows when these things occur in terms of chronology; who knows in what order of the fictional lives of Mulder and Scully these events take place? If you look at this in terms of a person's life, in the end it doesn't make sense. You go from Scully seeing aliens in the tunnel in 'Paper Clip' to rock-

we're doing, and now a lot of talented people have come to work on the show and the cumulative power of that talent has made the show better and better. All that I do, to be honest, is try and make this TV show as good as it can possibly be. All of these other things that have come from it are the rather improbable offspring of a good idea well realized."

In the third season, Carter continued to embroider on his good idea, ratcheting up the pressure on Mulder and Scully to face down the government conspiracy that serves as the

and-roll boy in 'D.P.O.' How come there is no carryover? Well, because we never said that that was week two and this is week three in their lives. We are just saying that that was episode two and this is episode three and it happened *whenever*."

Carter, meanwhile, points to the tidy voiceover at the close of "End Game" as a defining moment, where he "reaffirms [Scully's] belief in science and [Mulder's] belief in the paranormal."

Not everyone on the creative staff, however, can dismiss the contradiction so easily. Says co–executive producer Howard Gordon, who wrote "D.P.O.," the first stand-alone episode of the season, "The third year really gave rise to the mythology episodes in a more concerted fashion. I think we started building a much more sustained narrative, a kind of ladder that Chris describes as the scaffolding from which the rest of the series is hung. We don't have the isolated abduction stories anymore. In fact, I think that's why [the stand-alone episodes sometimes can be] disappointing, because the mythology episodes are not only dealing with the broad conspiracies, they are also the stories in which we weave in the main characters' families. The mythology shows have an emotional power

Miran Kim, illustrator for Topps' *X-Files* comic books series.

that the stand-alones simply cannot have. I think some of the stand-alone episodes that are the best are the ones that involve one of the characters in a very deep way, where you find an 'in' that can exploit some emotional adrenaline for our main players. But it is definitely difficult to compete with those [mythology] episodes, there's no doubt about it.

"That being said," he adds, "in some ways I think the stand-alones are going to be the ones that survive in syndication. Ultimately, when people rediscover the show in syndication, a lot of the mythology episodes will be a prob-

The Triumph of Evil

"The world isn't safe at all," Chris Carter says. "Good doesn't necessarily win. In fact, it wins a surprisingly paltry amount of the time — and we often live in denial of that."

Not anymore. If you watch television, the presence of evil is undeniable. Just as Carter found seeds of inspiration in such '60s and '70s scare fare as *The Invaders* and *The Night Stalker*, his colleagues are now trying to imitate the dark cynicism of *The X-Files* with their own sinister offerings in prime time. Among the recent launches — some of them limited to a single season — designed to provoke paranoia and fear are *American Gothic*; *Nowhere Man*; *Poltergeist: The Legacy*; *Strange Luck*; and *Dark Skies*. All were born from the success of *The X-Files* and viciously play upon our feelings of helplessness against a power structure that is increasingly faceless, remote, and unaccountable.

"We never say that evil is more interesting than good," Carter asserts. "We don't try to make a statement about evil and good per se; we just try to do scary stories each week." And Carter understands that the best way to scare people is to hit them where it already hurts: the very real fears — about crime, money, technology, officialdom — that keep them up at night.

And thanks to Carter and his admirers in the television industry, this many Americans haven't been wide awake at night since Johnny Carson was in his prime.

Karl Schaefer, creator of the Fox series *Strange Luck*, calls Carter's legacy the "new noir," which he says is driven by "the ambiguity of our times. There are no clear-cut bad guys any-more. The Soviet Union is gone, and it's a big mess. Things used to be pretty simple, and now it's a little bit like when the original noir came along at the end of World War Two. Women were in the workplace, we were rebuilding Germany and Japan, and nobody knew exactly what shape the world was going to take. Even though it was ostensibly a happy, peaceful time, there was this undercurrent of darkness and fear beneath that. I think that's similar to the times we live in now. There's not one big enemy to focus our energies on, so we're turning on each other."

The original film noir was indeed a by-product of the Second World War and the birth of the nuclear age. The movement was tethered to the notion of a civilization in decline and gave rise to the antihero. In the 1960s, TV shows like *The Invaders* and *The Prisoner* could connect with viewers as Cold War or even apocalyptic metaphors. But now, in the wake of Watergate, Iran-Contra, Whitewater, even Ruby Ridge (to name just a few prominent examples), Americans fear that the threat to their security doesn't come only from outside the country, it also comes from within their own government. The government, many people believe, is no longer just unresponsive, it is playing an active part in the subversion of our values and way of life.

"The government is really hurting in terms of public relations," says Stuart Fischoff, professor of media psychology at California State University, Los Angeles. "It's come to the point where if you make the argument that the government is behind a conspiracy or is covering up something, people are immediately ready to believe you. Government conspiracies seem much more likely today — at least that's what people believe. When you had Patrick McGoohan and

The Prisoner, you didn't have the pervasiveness of electronic surveillance capability. Today the big thing is that government, corporations, computer hackers, and everybody else can get access to your private life. Their reach is far more pervasive now than it was back in the sixties and seventies when people who were good didn't really have to worry. Today it doesn't matter if you're good or not. People want a big uncle to look out for them, but they feel that all they're getting is Big Brother."

Leo Braudy, professor of English at the University of Southern California and the author of *The World in a Frame: What We See in Films*, concurs, adding that the idea of Big Brother has taken on dimensions above and beyond government and technology. "People are more apt to believe in conspiracies now because of the information superhighway," he says, "because the technology seems so powerful and there are so many organizations out there that seem to be coercive and repressive." But the true source of this fear is not the government, he adds. "It's the all-powerful eye of God — but it's some malevolent God who not only has his eye on the sparrow but wants to squash the sparrow."

The show's ongoing thematic arc — or mythology, as Carter refers to it — has revealed a government conspiracy involving alien corpses recovered by the U.S. military from Roswell, New Mexico, the location of an alleged UFO crash in 1947. Mulder's personal crusade to obtain proof of both the crash and government experiments involving human and alien DNA gives the show its driving force.

"Mulder represents the current seeker of the American dream," says *X-Files* producer–director Rob Bowman. "And he can only achieve it by finding the truth. There's something very classic and American about Mulder. If you strip away the obsession with the paranormal, he's a very ordinary person who is kicked about by a big, dark overseer that doesn't necessarily have the best interests of the people in mind. It's hard for him to handle. 'I thought you were supposed to represent the people,' he says to them. 'Why do I find constant cover-up? I'm really confused by this.' I identify with him completely, and I think the audience does as well."

Professor Braudy suggests that Mulder's appeal comes from his willingness to battle insurmountable opposition, his willingness to continue to fight evil even though he knows he cannot obliterate it. "The genie is going to get out of the bottle again," Braudy says. "The whole approach [of the show] is to stanch the flow but not stop the seepage. *The X-Files*, in that regard, is the most realistic show on the air right now, because it understands that evil is a multiheaded hydra. If you chop off one head, another one is going to appear somewhere else."

And so Mulder's battle continues.

the simple reason that they've begun to figure out how the series operates. At the beginning of the first season, he says, viewers thought of *The X-Files* solely as a UFO series. "Then we got 'Squeeze,' which made it a monster show," he says with a laugh. "Then we got 'Ice,' which is really a suspense thriller; and 'Erlenmeyer Flask,' which was a government paranoia show. Then Darin Morgan came along and suddenly we have humorous, ironic episodes, and so it has really gotten so that you turn on the show and it could be one of five different genres. People don't know what to expect, so the mythology episodes are the core [of the series] that people have been able to pin down."

Former story editor Jeff Vlaming adds, "Next year will be a tough nut to crack, because it's getting to the point where you almost can't believe that Mulder is doing anything but pursuing these monumental discoveries he is making in search of the conspiracy. Why is he worrying about fat-sucking vampires when he knows that his father was involved in his sister's disappearance?"

Kevin Anderson, author of a number of *Star Wars* and *X-Files* books.

lem, because they rely too much on what came before. For die-hard fans it's great, but, ultimately, when people watch these shows chopped up, I think the stand-alones are the ones that are going to have a longer shelf life."

Spotnitz believes that the tension between the two types of episodes has become more noticeable to viewers in the third season for

And yet Carter is determined to prevent *The X-Files* from becoming *The Conspiracy Show*. It's the thematic and narrative variety of the series, he believes, that keeps it creatively fresh.

"The truth is, you can't have Mulder and Scully pursuing the conspiracy forever. Those episodes, even though they're very popular, have to come along only occasionally in order to give the show its breadth, its life, and its longevity. From the beginning, the search for

Carter is determined to prevent *The X-Files* from becoming *The Conspiracy Show*. It's the thematic and narrative variety of the series that keeps it creatively fresh.

the truth about what the government may or may not know about the existence of extraterrestrials has been the backbone of the series. The stand-alone episodes have become the all-important search for other truths that may in fact impact on those larger truths. I think the audience has to be forgiving and is — wonderfully so — because if we just made this a mythology show, it wouldn't be as good a show as it is."

None of which means he doesn't like the twists and turns of the mythology any less than the next guy. "I think from the beginning to the end [of the third season], we brought things to an interesting point," Carter says. "We learned more about the Cigarette-Smoking Man, what Mulder's past is — his personal history is now seemingly quite intertwined with some early government stuff. We know now that Mulder's father had connections to these men. We know there's an international cabal of sorts, a syndicate, that has spread the conspiracy beyond the borders of the U.S., and I think we see that there are improbable alliances between people in the scientific community who in fact may be conducting a much larger conspiracy than what was once imagined."

And such labyrinthine intrigues, of course, go to the heart of what *The X-Files* is all about. "As we know," Carter says with a smile, "the truth is very difficult to arrive at. In fact, there are *many* truths. I think that what we're playing with here is the complexity of what the truth is."

SEASON THREE
Episode Guide

Episode 3.1 (#50)
"The Blessing Way"

Original airdate: September 22, 1995
Written by Chris Carter
Directed by R. W. Goodwin
Guest starring: Forbes Angus (MD), Tom Braidwood (Frohike), Lenno Britos (Luis Cardinal), Mitch Davies (Camouflage Man), William B. Davis (Cigarette-Smoking Man), Peter Donat (William Mulder), Ernie Foort (Security Guard), Benita Ha (Tour Guide), Jerry Hardin (Deep Throat), Dakota House (Eric Hosteen), Alf Humphreys (Dr. Mark Pomerantz), Sheila Larken (Margaret Scully), Nicholas Lea (Agent Alex Krycek), Melinda McGraw (Melissa Scully), Tim Michael (Albert's Son), John Moore (3rd Elder), John Neville (Well-Manicured Man), Mitch Pileggi (Assistant Director Walter S. Skinner), Michael David Simms (Senior Agent), Rebecca Toolan (Mrs. Mulder), Ian Victor (Minister), Stanley Walsh (2nd Elder), Floyd "Red Crow" Westerman (Albert Hosteen), Don Williams (1st Elder)

While Mulder lies somewhere between life and death as his spirit undergoes a Navajo healing ceremony conducted by Albert Hosteen (during which Mulder is visited by the spirits of his father and Deep Throat), Scully finds herself pitted against her superiors as the search for the MJ documents DAT intensifies. Later, she is warned by the Well-Manicured Man, part of an international group of conspirators, that her life is in danger. Indeed, Agent Krycek assassinates her sister, Melissa, by mistake when he breaks into Scully's apartment. At the same time, Skinner has obtained the DAT and comes to Scully with it, but she believes he's attempting to kill her, and it ends in a standoff with the two of them aiming guns at each other's head.

❋ ❋ ❋

According to story editor Frank Spotnitz, "The Blessing Way" represented a difficult challenge due to the fact that it was the middle chapter in a trilogy of episodes.

"The expectations were very high coming after a summer's worth of anticipation to see how Mulder got out of the boxcar," he says. "We knew that we had to answer that question and still leave an intriguing enough dilemma at the end of the show to bring viewers back for the third and final part. I also thought it was a big gamble to do all of that Indian mysticism stuff. It was very spiritual, which is not something the show is usually about. I thought a lot of people would not necessarily respond to that. There is nothing cynical about spiritualism. There is nothing dark about it. It appeals to a different part of our nature. So I was nervous about that, but very excited about the Scully storyline and the way all of that played out with Mulder and Skinner."

Co-producer Paul Rabwin notes that for the Blessing Way ceremony, a sand painter was brought on location and spent a full day creating two paintings. "One of them was preserved so that it wouldn't move, and then he had to create another one that could be wiped out at the end. But there were two intricately designed sand paintings utilized."

For co–executive producer Robert Goodwin, who also directed the episode, a disappointing aspect of production was the sequence in which Mulder is floating in a netherworld and encouraged in his search for the truth by his late father and Deep Throat.

"On a technical level," he explains, "it is the kind of thing that is basically a monologue. To make it interesting, I wanted to keep the camera moving. I wanted to be circling around and floating and all of that, but because of the technical difficulties they had with the special effects, I was forced to make it much more static than I wanted. That's just a minor thing, though. That is a case where a technical aspect overrides the creative aspect. Nobody's fault; that's just life. Frankly, I thought the third part of the story, 'Paper Clip,' was just sensational. Rob Bowman did a great job with that."

Rating/Audience Share: 12.3/22

Episode 3.2 (#51)
"Paper Clip"

Original airdate: September 29, 1995
Written by Chris Carter
Directed by Rob Bowman
Guest starring: Tom Braidwood (Frohike), Lenno Britos (Luis Cardinal), Peta Brookstone (ICU Nurse), William B. Davis (Cigarette-Smoking Man), Martin Evans (SM), Walter Gotell (Victor Klemper), Dean Haglund (Langly), Bruce Harwood (Byers), Sheila Larken (Margaret Scully), Nicholas Lea (Agent Alex Krycek), Robert Lewis (ER Doctor), Melinda McGraw (Melissa Scully), John Moore (3rd Elder), John Neville (Well-Manicured Man), Mitch Pileggi (Assistant Director Walter S. Skinner), Rebecca Toolan (Mrs. Mulder), Stanley Walsh (2nd Elder), Floyd "Red Crow" Westerman (Albert Hosteen), Don Williams (1st Elder)

The standoff between Scully and Skinner comes to an end when Mulder enters the scene, returned to health by the Navajo. As Skinner attempts to negotiate the DAT for Mulder and Scully's reinstatement with the Cigarette-Smoking Man, the duo make their way to a mine in West Virginia, where they make a number of incredible discoveries. First off, Mulder sees what can only be described as a UFO taking off, Scully catches sight of what appears to be a group of aliens running by her, and the two of them find a series of filing cabinets. Within the innumerable cabinets are folders containing medical information, including DNA samples. Among the files are ones for Scully (dating back to her abduction by Duane Barry in season two) and Samantha Mulder, though Fox's name was on the folder first. Later, Mulder confronts his mother and learns that his father had been a part of the government conspiracy and had been forced to give up one of his children to ensure his silence about "the project" known as Operation Paper Clip, inviting scientists from Nazi Germany and Japan.

Meanwhile, agent Alex Krycek manages to beat the hell out of Skinner and obtains the DAT, and Krycek in turn barely avoids being killed by agents of the Cigarette-Smoking Man. Then, when Skinner tries to make his deal with the CSM, his bluff is called — until Skinner informs him that Albert Hosteen has decoded the tapes and, "in the oral tradition of his people," has shared its con-tents with many other Navajo. Should any-thing happen to him, Mulder, or Scully, all of that information will be available with a sim-ple phone call.

❋ ❋ ❋

Frank Spotnitz enthuses, "I love 'Paper Clip.' I was thrilled with the plot. I know it moved very fast for some people, but I actually think that for some of these shows you don't need to understand everything. I think it is more excit-ing to go at rocket speed. Everybody was on the mark in that one: David and Gillian's per-formances, Rob Bowman's direction, Chris Carter's writing — everything was just terrific in that show."

Says Bowman, "I was disappointed that my

"We have done several aliens in the past, where we used a bunch of little girls, like nine or ten years old. Because we had so much fighting and struggling in the mine scene, we used boys."

first episode of the season wasn't going to be a mythology episode, then Chris Carter writes 'Paper Clip.'" He laughs. "There were ele-ments of that show that really stretched the boundaries of the series, what with the space-ship, the shooting we did in the mine, and so on. First of all, I think the episode gave the audience something they have waited for, which is 'Let's watch Mulder have a protract-ed encounter.' Several of the other episodes have had brief, fleeting glances and it's over.

140

Let's get a long, drawn-out orgasm and we'll make it glorious, but we will do it in the style that we usually do it. We will tease the hell out of the audience. There is proof. It is theory no more. It is not hypothesis. There is the ship. Mulder runs upstairs and he comes outside and our challenge was showing the ship without actually showing the ship.

"Then there's Scully's little encounter. How does she react to this? It was up to me to provide these different points of view. The aliens are whipping around and we just see body parts and pieces. It sure looks like something there, but it's kind of like a deer in a headlight because they are just charging. I think that opened the season with something very cinematic. When I finished 'Paper Clip,' I thought, 'I don't know what else I am going to do this year to top this.'"

Another highlight for Bowman was a sequence in a small diner where Skinner is meeting with Mulder and Scully to discuss the deal he will try to arrange with the Cigarette-Smoking Man.

"I just think Mulder is a very calm person in there," he explains, "not screaming and yelling. There is this quality in the scene. People are expressing their heartfelt emotions. Scully is saying she thinks they should take the deal because, damn it, she wants to see her sister. Well, what human being in that situation wouldn't say the same thing? There was a certain rhythm to that scene that was not rushed or skipped through that I liked, and David had a lot to do with that.

"'Paper Clip' had all the big characters in it," Bowman continues, almost giddily. "And the storyline was almost *Godfather*-like, with Krycek and Skinner, Skinner getting beaten up, and then the attempt made on Krycek in his car. It was a big, sweeping show with many locations, interesting people, and full of great drama. There were a lot of beautiful things in the episode too. Even the scene with Scully in the hospital. I have to tell you, I hate hospital scenes. Every time I see one I just cry, because they're so dull; somebody is going to one day tally up how many times Mulder and Scully did a hospital scene. So every time I see one I say, 'Do we have to do this in a hospital room?' And they'll say yes or no, and then I'll take it from there. But I feel the hospital scenes in 'Paper Clip' are probably the only hospital scenes I have directed in this whole series that I liked just because of the emotion of the scene."

"One other thing that comes to mind about that episode," Robert Goodwin adds, "is the little aliens in the mine. We have done several aliens in the past; the first group we did was in 'Duane Barry,' where we used a bunch of little girls, like nine or ten years old. Because we had so much fighting and struggling in the mine scene, we used boys. I'll tell you something, and I hate to say it, but girls are a hell of a lot smarter than boys. They were born smarter and they always stay smarter. Girls are just a lot easier to direct, especially the younger ones. We just kept shooting and shooting and shooting. Next time we need a

bunch of aliens, you can count on them being played by girls."

Of the mine itself, production designer Graeme Murray says it was actually an old mine in Vancouver that has become a museum. "We got into some of the old tunnels and built all of those filing cabinets and the doors that led into it. When we started in there, we were actually going to bring in real filing cabinets and line them up against the wall there. On the survey day, Chris looked at it and thought, 'It would be way better if they were built into the mine itself.' They were kind of false fronts for the whole thing built into the rock, and I thought it looked pretty interesting.

"We also put together a spaceship — really just a framework with a bazillion lights on it. Those were quite huge kinds of effects — or rather, on other shows they would be huge, but on this show they seem to have become pretty standard."

Rating/Audience Share: 11.1/20

Episode 3.3 (#52)
"D.P.O."

Original airdate: October 6, 1995
Written by Howard Gordon
Directed by Kim Manners
Guest starring: Peter Anderson (Stan Buxton),
Mar Andersons (Jack Hammond), Jack Black
(Bart "Zero" Liquori), Brent Chapman (Traffic
Cop), Cavan Cunningham (2nd Paramedic),
Jason Anthony Griffith (1st Paramedic),
Bonnie Hay (Night Nurse), Ernie Lively
(Sheriff John Teller), Steve Makaj (Frank
Kiveat), Giovanni Ribisi (Darin Peter Oswald),
Kate Robbins (Darin's Mom), Karen Witter
(Sharon Kiveat)

Mulder and Scully investigate a series of deaths by lightning, and are led to Connerville, Oklahoma, where a teenager, Darin Peter Oswald (hence the title "D.P.O."), seems to have acquired the ability to control lightning and is using it to seek retribution against anyone who crosses him.

❈   ❈   ❈

"This was an idea floating around the office for some time," Howard Gordon explains. "There was literally an index card that said 'Lightning Boy,' but no one had come up with a way to crack the story. I wanted to use the idea of lightning as a metaphor for the collision of boredom and hormonal anxiety. That's what it felt like, and lightning seemed like the perfect analog for that kind of thing. The idea was Beavis and Butt-head electrified. That was really the germ of the idea. It was a way to investigate with a tragic and comic lens what it's like to be numb from television and video games, and it dealt with illiteracy and single parenthood and everything else."

Story editor Frank Spotnitz admits there was some discussion among the staff as to how "D.P.O." could possibly follow the trilogy of mythology episodes in which so much had happened to Mulder and Scully. "Originally," he explains, "we said we should try to incorporate those events into the story of 'D.P.O.,' but then we decided it didn't make sense for a variety of reasons, because, ultimately, each episode has its own integrity and has to stand alone.

"I also thought it was a risky show for us to do, which is something I feel whenever we go to a high school setting. This is an adult show, and you need to find a way to make it interesting to adults. The storyline was really about adolescence and the violent impulses you have when you're a kid. But if you take it a step further and imagine yourself having the powers this kid did, it suddenly becomes an X-File. I thought the actor, Giovanni Ribisi, was really, really good. We also used the music differently in that show than we ever had before."

Director Kim Manners notes that the episode was an incredibly emotional experience for him because on the third day of shooting, his best friend and that man's son were killed in a drowning accident.

"He was my best friend for thirty-one years and he died and I was stuck in Vancouver," he says. "I couldn't leave the show, though I did leave it in the sense that my body was there while my mind was elsewhere. I hardly remember the shoot, but the show worked, miraculously. My wife came up and kind of babysat me so that I could get through it, and I learned a great lesson in life. I should have left the show and let somebody else take over and dealt with my emotions. I guess that's the 'show-must-go-on' attitude. I think 'D.P.O.' could have been much better than it was, though the fans liked it."

Co–executive producer Robert Goodwin opines, "An interesting show, though a little difficult to do all of the effects work that was required. They were done through physical effects of sparks and explosions and stuff that we shot right on film with the actors, combined with individual lightning effects that were put in after the fact. It was a real coordination between the two departments. One without the other would be nothing. I think the best thing about it was the lead and his sidekick, both of whom were great. One interesting thing is that it took us forever, but we finally got permission to use a real dead cow for a scene where a cow had been struck by lightning. All these animal rights people are very, very watchful. We had a phony cow originally, but it *really* looked phony, so we got permission from a slaughterhouse to use a real cow."

Graeme Murray offers, "It was a 'small-town America' type of show. Probably the biggest construction event for us was the crossroads where the traffic lights were. The kids are sitting there and triggering the lights to cause accidents. That was a big setup for us. We had to plant telephone poles and build this billboard. The road was there; it had been married people's quarters during the war, but all the houses had been torn down. We've used it for a couple of shows. It was just an overgrown vacant lot, basically, with three or four roads crisscrossing through it. We also used it in 'Apocrypha' for the exteriors of the missile silo."

Rating/Audience Share: 10.9/20

Episode 3.4 (#53)
"Clyde Bruckman's Final Repose"
Original airdate: October 13, 1995
Written by Darin Morgan
Directed by David Nutter
Guest starring: Greg Anderson (Photographer), Peter Boyle (Clyde Bruckman), Jaap Broeker (Yappi), Frank Casini (Det. Cline), Stu Charno (The Puppet), Alex Diakun (Tarot Dealer), Karin Konoval (Madame Zelma), Dwight McFee (Det. Havez), David Mackay (Mr. Gordon [Young Husband]), Doris Rands (Mrs. Lowe), Ken Roberts (Clerk)

A serial killer is stalking fortune tellers in Minneapolis. When an insurance salesman named Clyde Bruckman comes across one of the bodies, he gets in touch with Mulder and Scully and ultimately reveals that he himself has the ability to foresee how people will die. When Bruckman leads them to two additional bodies, Scully becomes convinced that he just might be the man they're seeking, but Mulder doesn't accept that theory, believing instead that Bruckman can lead them to the real killer.

❈　❈　❈

"A show that worked on every level," says story editor Frank Spotnitz. "Actually, that's my favorite of Darin Morgan's shows, because there are so many levels to it. He is really literate in the way he constructs things, and it also just has so much heart. Peter Boyle was a great success, particularly after we agonized over who we should cast in that role. Darin had originally written the part with Bob Newhart in mind, which probably would have been great, but we ended up going with Peter Boyle. In the end, everybody thought that show was just thrilling.

"One thing about Darin," he continues, "especially since 'Clyde Bruckman,' is that he's always tried to do something the show would never think of doing and he's pulled it off. I think he really helped people see that this show was even more versatile than they imagined it could be."

Amazingly, the person most disappointed with the episode is Morgan himself. "I wanted to do an episode that was more serious and more depressing and more along the lines of [season one's] 'Beyond the Sea,'" he explains. "My original idea was to do one without any jokes. I was just so depressed over the whole writing of the script. It was so painful I didn't even bother to watch it when it first aired. Some of the script really works, but I just felt it didn't come out as good as it should have.

"I just wanted it to be the most depressing thing ever. I guess part of it comes from the fact that when I was writing [season two's] 'Humbug,' the feeling was that it was going to be funny and a lot of the fans would have a problem with the comedy — which they did. They were worried it was going to ruin the show and I felt, after it was done, that maybe they were right. So after it aired, I went back and watched 'Beyond the Sea' and said this is *really* what the show should be like. So I wanted to do something that was much more serious. Of course I ended up putting jokes in it anyway. The thing is, I got away with it on this one because the story was much more similar to a standard X-File, so people didn't have any problems with it. The difference between the two seasons I've been involved with the show is that when I turned in 'Humbug,' everyone said, 'This is funny; we can't do this.' When I turned in 'Clyde Bruckman,' everyone said, 'I love this. This is so funny.' It was the difference between before and after.

"The other main gist of 'Clyde Bruckman' was the research," he continues. "We have these books on homicide investigations and they have these crime scene photos of dead bodies and how you are supposed to conduct an investigation. The book is so disturbing that when people look through it they say, 'Oh, that doesn't bother me,' then they come back a day or two later and say, 'You know, there is a picture in that book that I just can't get out of my head.' I really can't describe how disturbing some of these photos are. So I was just thinking about psychics, people claiming to see other people's future. If they really could, they should be able to see a person's ultimate future, which is their death. If they could see exactly how people will die, just like these crime photos, they would just go insane. They would be depressed to the point of suicide. So that was really what that whole show was about."

The finished product, however, once he finally did see it, is something he's proud of. "That was totally my favorite episode that I wrote, and Peter Boyle was great. I guess another reason for writing it was we had been going over budget and I wanted to see if I could write something that could be done very, very simply. So a lot of the scenes take place in Bruckman's apartment or a hotel room. It came in under budget and on schedule. It was just a very easy show to do."

For director David Nutter, the script was definitely the thing. "The writing was so tight and so crisp and so fresh that I think, as a director, the only thing you have to do is create the atmosphere, set up the characters, set up the shots, and you are basically invisible," he says. "Then you step back and just let it happen. Find the moment, know how you are going to cut it; know how you are going to outline the sequences, and so forth. Know all that before you do it, of course, but when you do it, let it happen and use a very free hand on it, because it is a situation where some of it is really created on the set with respect to the attitude and the characters."

"Clyde Bruckman" was fairly character-intensive, which Nutter feels provided him the opportunity to take a slightly different directorial approach. "A lot of time people in Hollywood classify you and categorize you. He does drama. He does horror. She does comedy. Whatever. With this show, you definitely get to see that I can handle all aspects. I'm very, very proud of it."

In designing Clyde Bruckman's apartment, Graeme Murray notes, the idea was to "keep things as bland as possible. He's kind of hiding in this little bland place, whereas everything else around him is strange and brightly colored, with odd stuff going on. One of the more meaningful shows for me; it had some real depth to it."

For Robert Goodwin, the most interesting aspect of the episode was Peter Boyle, particularly given the fact that Boyle didn't really want to do the show.

"Peter is not interested in episodic television," he explains. "He is more interested in theater and features, but somehow he did it. I don't know whether it was a combination of coercion and bribery or what, but when he first arrived, you could tell that he didn't want to be there. But he melted and thawed out very quickly, and by the end of the show he was very exuberantly thanking me for the wonderful experience and asking for T-shirts. Peter's been telling people that he's gotten more response from that show than anything he had done in his entire career."

Rating/Audience Share: 10.2/18

Episode 3.5 (#54)
"The List"
Original airdate: October 20, 1995
Written and directed by Chris Carter
Guest starring: Michael Andaluz (Tattooed Prisoner), Denny Arnold (Key Guard), Craig Brunanski (Guard), Badja Djola ("Neech" Manley), Ken Foree (Parmelly), April Grace (Danielle Manley), Mitch Kosterman (Fornier), Don Mackay (Oates), Bruce Pinard (Executioner), Paul Raskin (Dr. Jim Ullrich), Greg Rogers (Daniel Charez), J. T. Walsh (Warden Leo Brodeur)

Immediately before his execution, prisoner Napoleon "Neech" Manley swears he will seek vengeance beyond the grave against his enemies — a very personal hit list of those who he feels have wronged him. Naturally the warden and everyone else dismiss this, but then guards begin dying under mysterious circumstances. Mulder and Scully are called in to investigate before the so-called list expands.

❊ ❊ ❊

Story editor Frank Spotnitz opines, "I think this is a vastly underrated episode. I also think it was a very brave and different show to do and that it will weather the test of time very well. I think it was brave because there is not a single likable character — nobody you can root for. Mulder and Scully do not solve the case, and that is something I had been interested in doing for some time. I originally wanted [season two's] 'Our Town' to end with them not solving the case, but we changed that at the last minute.

"'The List' is not scary in a big flashy way. It is more sneaky and ominous. It also had a look to it that was unlike any other show we had done, using greens — which is a very hard color to work with, especially in television. On the level of performance, writing, the way it was shot and directed, I think it was a standout episode. I was initially surprised that more people didn't just flock to it because of all the qualities, but I think because Mulder and Scully didn't solve the case and because there was nobody to root for, it made it harder for some fans to jump up and down about it."

"The hardest part about 'The List,'" says co–executive producer Robert Goodwin, "was the set design, because we built this big, expensive two-story prison, and it was a major undertaking. And once it was built, it was very tough to work in, because you've got to deal with these tiny cells. Physically, it was a nightmare, and extremely difficult to work in. I

"How do you make a prison sound unlike a typical prison?"

sympathize with Chris. But I thought there was a great performance from J. T. Walsh as the warden."

The episode marked Chris Carter's second writing-directing effort, following season two's "Duane Barry."

"I wanted to give it a look like no other X-File," Carter says. "First of all, the color palette is green. John Bartley and I lit it with pink light, and then in the postproduction process that pink was taken out, which saturated the green, giving it a submarine quality. In the sound of the show, too, I added a submarine quality. I wanted it to feel like you were compressed at the bottom of the sea. There were just things I wanted to do that were different from other episodes we'd done. I feel very proud of the results. I felt more assured as a director this time, but it's extremely hard and demanding physically."

According to co-producer Paul Rabwin, particular attention was paid to sounds in this prison. "There were tons of levels of sounds," he says. "How do you make a prison sound unlike a typical prison? We wanted to get lit-

tle subtle sounds from these prisoners, but we didn't want it to sound like a James Cagney picture. Throughout the prison there was a deep, dark, rumbly kind of an effect that we put in. You could never really put your finger on it, but there was something uneasy and cavernous about the sound on that show. If you listen to it very carefully, you would notice that if you turned the bass up a little bit it was almost like the inside of a submarine. We just permeated the whole soundtrack with that, and that was kind of interesting."

Rating/Audience Share: 10.8/19

Episode 3.6 (#55)
"2Shy"
Original airdate: November 3, 1995
Written by Jeffrey Vlaming
Directed by David Nutter
Guest starring: Lindsay Bourne (Hooker's John), Timothy Carhart (Virgil Incanto), Glynis Davies (Monica Landis), Beverly Elliot (Raven), James Hardy (Det. Alan Cross), Suzy Joachim (Jennifer Workman), Randi Lynne (Lauren Mackalvey), William MacDonald (Agent Dan Kazanjian), Dean McKensie (Lt. Blaine), Aloka McLean (Jesse Landis), Jans Baily Mattia (Hooker), Catherine Paolone (Ellen Kaminski), P. J. Prinsloo (Tagger), Kerry Sandomirsky (Joanne Steffen), Brad Wattum (Patrolman)

Mulder makes the connection between the disappearance of a lonely, overweight woman and that of several women before her, who all had made contact with someone over the Internet. The investigation leads Mulder and Scully to a killer who has the unimaginable ability to suck the fat out of his victims' bodies.

❀ ❀ ❀

Of the episode's genesis, Jeff Vlaming explains that he had been working at Universal on *Weird Science,* when he got the opportunity to pitch to Chris Carter.

"Originally," he explains, "the guy wasn't sucking fat out of his victims as much as he was sucking the oil from them. Everybody has body oil, and he would suck that. He preferred women, but he wasn't doing fat women. Just who this guy was went through some changes as well. At first he was creepy-looking, wearing a turtleneck up to his chin, sunglasses, and a hat — very much like the Phantom of the Opera — and then we changed him to a good-looking guy who stays behind his computer and only meets these women after he's charmed them with his words and his voice. Finally, we went with a fairly normal-looking guy. Originally he was a butcher, literally working in a butcher shop, so he knew how to get fat out. It went through a number of permutations and just got better and better."

One of the grossest *X-Files* moments occurs in this episode, when Scully opens a morgue drawer and finds that the woman's body that had been there has dissolved to a puddle of muck.

"People like that disgusting stuff," says David Nutter. "They liked Flukeman [in season two's 'The Host']. They are into this stuff, so I definitely wanted to give the audience what they wanted with this episode. I also really love the teasers of the show. When I read the script and it was so soft and wonderful and warm at the outset, I knew I just wanted-ed to really hit the audience with *something* by the time the teaser ended."

Story editor Frank Spotnitz reflects,

"When Jeff Vlaming initially came up with the idea of a fat-sucking vampire, I had my reservations, because the idea of somebody preying on fat women can be very offensive. But one thing I've got to say for Chris is that he never

"One thing I've got to say for Chris is that he never worries about whether something is going to be politically correct."

worries about whether something is going to be politically correct. He just trusts in his ability to tell a good story and, the truth is, if you tell a good story, you don't need to worry about [being offensive] because the story has its own integrity. In the end, I thought that was a fun, old-fashioned sort of X-File."

The notion of the killer getting his victims from the Internet was an inventive one. "Chris's approach to the show is to base everything in reality," says Spotnitz, "and it just seemed so believable that somebody would pick victims that way. It was also topical."

"I think the idea of using the Internet was Chris's," adds Vlaming. "He liked the vulnerability of it. Anybody could be on the other end of the computer, which really freaked out a lot of people who were on-line."

Co–executive producer Robert Goodwin

remembers the woman the vampire is kissing in the teaser pulls back in horror and there is slime covering her mouth. "That poor girl," he says. "She almost lost it. All of that slime was Jell-O, but it was disgusting, and she had to do this thing where she could barely breathe and see the slime coming in and out. We felt bad for her, and even sent her flowers. I thought the guy who played the lead, Timothy Carhart, was terrific. A very nice guy, extremely gentle. Every time I saw him I said, 'You are the most disgusting human being I have ever seen.' 'Well, thank you. Thank you.'"

"That was an episode," says co-producer Paul Rabwin, "where you had to ask, 'What is the sound of sucking fat and wrapping people up in mucous membrane?' How stretchy do you want to make it? It was a fun sound show for us."

He also notes that this episode, which on a surface level reminded many people of season two's "Irresistible," actually had more than a few things in common with that episode. "Besides being directed by David Nutter again, there were two blatant 'Irresistible' moments. One was the hooker scene, where this guy is trying to pick up a hooker and your reaction is, 'My God, it's the same scene that was in "Irresistible."' Number two is that the woman who is the landlady in this episode was the same actress who made the cookies and invited Donnie in in 'Irresistible.' The truth is, when you have the limited talent pool of actors in Vancouver, you tend to use the same ones periodically. On very small parts we have used an actor more than once in a season. But in the end, '2Shy' was quite different."

Rating/Audience Share: 10.1/17

Episode 3.7 (#56)
"The Walk"

Original airdate: November 10, 1995
Written by John Shiban
Directed by Rob Bowman
Guest starring: Andrea Barclay (Frances Callahan), Pat Bermel (Therapist), D. Harlan Cutshall (Guard), Paul Dickson (Uniformed Guard), William Garson (Quinton "Roach" Freely), Deryl Hayes (Army Doctor), Thomas Kopache (Gen. Thomas Callahan), Brennan Kotowich (Trevor Callahan), Rob Lew (Amputee), Paula Shaw (Ward Nurse), Nancy Sorel (Capt. Janet Draper), Don Thompson (Lt. Col. Victor Stans), Ian Tracey (Sgt. Leonard "Rappo" Trimble), Beatrice Zeilinger (Burly Nurse)

Mulder and Scully are drawn into the investigation of a number of Gulf War veterans who have tried to commit suicide but have, strangely, been unable to do so because of an invisible presence. They are inescapably drawn to a quadruple amputee, whose physical limitations seem only to have enhanced his psychic powers of astral projection.

❊ ❊ ❊

This episode was somewhat rushed due to the fact that "731" was originally scheduled for this production slot but was pushed off when the producers decided to turn it into a two-part episode.

"The last thing to happen is the director gets to sit down and figure out a scene," Rob Bowman reflects. "He is so busy putting out fires for the various departments before he can sit down and say, 'Okay, go shoot it.' Now that I have everybody else taken care of, what about me? How about the tone of the take? We kind of rushed into this episode, but I felt that we made the most of it and got some very good performances.

"Graeme Murray really performed way above the call of duty. We were ripping ceilings out of hospitals to get more pipes, and painting walls metal gray, coming up with scenes of reflection. Every time you turned around there was a mirror, so Graeme suggested that we paint everything high gloss and play lots of reflections. I thought about it and then I put it in every shot that I could. I just kept putting in reflections. If you watch that episode, and if you look for reflections, you will see they are in windows, they are here and there, and it's done to keep the audience wondering when this guy is going to show up."

Graeme Murray elaborates, "We wanted to

make everything shiny and see if we could get odd reflections everywhere to give off the idea of ghostly reflections all around these guys who had ghost pains and the one guy who was able to astral project. The result, hopefully, is that you weren't quite sure what was real and what wasn't, who was real and who was a reflection."

"There was only one element of that episode that I didn't agree with," says Bowman. "A friend of mine lost his son in a beach accident where the boy was accidentally buried in the sand — he dug a hole and it caved in. There was a scene in the script that was very similar. I called the writers and said, 'Hey, listen, I can't shoot this scene.' 'Why?' I told the story and said I didn't want my friend to think I was using that tragedy for creative material. I was very averse to doing it and asked, 'Why do we have to kill kids anyway? Can't we think of a story that doesn't involve killing a kid?' I was opposed to it but had to shoot the scene, so I tried to be as oblique about it as I could."

Conversely, Bowman is pleased with a sequence in which a woman is swimming in a pool when the spirit attacks her. It's a moment that suggests the opening scene of Steven Spielberg's *Jaws.*

"It was a challenge to create tension with somebody swimming around in a pool," he admits. "That script needed help visually, because it is all interior, and when you get interior you get claustrophobic. So I just felt that it was my job to breathe life into it visually, create a show that would be uncomfortable

"I had trouble watching the dailies of that episode because the armless and legless guy was so realistic, it was very upsetting."

for people to watch. In the end, I was very proud of the episode."

Co–executive producer Robert Goodwin admits, "I had trouble watching the dailies of that episode because the armless and legless guy was so realistic, it was very upsetting. That was really an incredible piece of work by Toby Lindala. You make the beds so that the arms and legs go through holes and are hidden underneath, but, man, was it realistic. The guy who played him, Ian Tracey, is someone we've been trying to cast for three years. He's a local guy out of Canada who could probably be the star of a series or something, but he refuses to move to Los Angeles. The episode was also a tricky combination of physical and visual effects, but Rob Bowman really pulled it off."

Rating/Audience Share: 10.4/18

Episode 3.8 (#57)
"Oubliette"

Original airdate: November 17, 1995
Written by Charles Grant Craig
Directed by Kim Manners
Guest starring: Sidonie Boll (Daphne Jacobs),
Michael Chieffo (John Wade), Tracey Ellis
(Lucy Householder), David Fredericks
(Photographer), Jaques LaLonde (Henry),
Alexa Mardon (Sadie Jacobs), Ken Ryan
(Banks), Dollie Scarr (Supervisor), Jewel Staite
(Amy Jacobs), Dean Wray (Tow-Truck Driver)

Scully believes Mulder is allowing his obsession with his sister's abduction to cloud his thinking, but he is convinced there is a psychic connection between a woman named Lucy Householder, who had been kidnapped and held prisoner by a madman for five years as a child, and a little girl who was recently abducted. Lucy seems to be feeling the girl's pain and bleeding her blood. Given that situation, she is their only hope of locating the kidnapper and his victim.

❊ ❊ ❊

By the time "Oubliette" came along, Kim Manners had had the opportunity to deal with his emotions following the death of his best friend (see "D.P.O.").

"I was very much in touch with my emotions, very sensitive," he says,

"and here we have a story about a woman who gives her life so that another young girl might live. The actress, Tracey Ellis, was phenomenal. She was very fragile, very sensitive, and really got into the role. David responded beautifully to her acting, and in the scenes they did together, he got down as an actor. Just a fabulous experience. It was the first *X-Files* in a long while that was based strictly on an emotional level, and it worked like gangbusters.

"With the mythology shows," he

adds, "when Mulder's father was killed, he broke down; the scenes where he dealt with his sister being kidnapped, he broke down. Here he breaks down over a complete stranger; a girl who is basically a drug addict and whore, but he is so touched by her giving her life for this little girl, and he played such a big part in her decision to do so. I thought that was a special moment for *The X-Files,* and David just did a great job. But he's always wonderful when he's not doing one of those — as I call them — Joe Friday scripts, 'Just the facts, ma'am.' And David makes no bones about it, either. We did an episode [later in season three] called 'Quagmire' and in the entire third act it's just David and Gillian stranded on a rock together and they have a conversation for about nine and a half pages. After we shot it I told him that he and Gillian had kicked the shit out of that scene. David looked at me and said, 'Well, Mulder finally had a conversation.'"

Says Robert Goodwin, "'Oubliette' was terrifying because it was a little more reality-based than most of our shows. The abduction of a young girl and holding her hostage in the basement and all of that stuff just touched on reality. A terrible thing had happened two weeks earlier up in Vancouver to a little girl who was a friend of our construction coordinator's daughter: She was abducted and killed, so it hit very close to home. I remember that being a somber experience.

"The biggest problem, physically, with that episode is in the last act where they find the kidnapper in the river, drowning her, and they come on, shoot him, and she comes back to life. I think we shot that in October. The rivers up in Vancouver are glacially fed, so they are all very, very cold. As a consequence, it is difficult for actors to work in them for any length of time, but this particular spot was a shallow part of the river, about eighteen inches deep. In sunlight it would warm up a bit. Anyway, the bottom line is that it started raining like hell. We got up there on the day they were supposed to shoot and it was suddenly like the Colorado River. It was completely impossible to put anybody in that water. It went on for weeks — we kept trying to find a time when the water would drop so we could shoot it. We barely got the damn thing done before we went on the air. We were shooting that river sequence up to the very last minute. In the end, though, I think it looks great."

Rating/Audience Share: 10.2/17

Episode 3.9 (#58)
"Nisei"

Original airdate: November 24, 1995
Written by Chris Carter, Howard Gordon, and
Frank Spotnitz
Directed by David Nutter
Guest starring: Roger Allford (Harbormaster),
Gillian Barber (Penny Northern), Raymond J.
Barry (Sen. Richard Matheson), Brendan
Beiser (Agent Comox), Tom Braidwood
(Frohike), Dean Haglund (Langly), Bruce
Harwood (Byers), Robert Ito (Dr. Ishimaru),
Corrine Koslo (Lottie Holloway), Paul McLean
(Coast Guard Officer), Yasuo Sakurai (Kazuo
Takeo), Carrie Cain Sparks (Train Station
Clerk), Warren Takeuchi (Japanese Escort),
Lori Triolo (Diane), Bob Wilde (Limo Driver),
Steven Williams (Mr. X)

A mail-order alien autopsy tape leads Mulder and Scully to investigate a salvage ship that may have raised an alien ship from the ocean floor. Separating as a means of furthering their investigation, Scully checks out a woman involved with the salvage company but, instead, finds a group of women who claim to know her, who have all had computer chips implanted in their necks, and who have been abducted on numerous occasions. Mulder, meanwhile, finds himself on a train that may very well be carrying a living alien.

❋ ❋ ❋

As Frank Spotnitz explains it, the "Nisei" follow-up, "731," was originally intended to be a one-part episode.

"The script was written that way," he says, "and we discovered that it was just impossible to do all the stuff we wanted to do with the train, in terms of both logistics and expenses, as a one-part show. Chris made the decision to expand it to a two-parter and push it back until we had time to prepare. So we ended up working backwards, taking elements from that single-episode script and spreading them out over two parts, then adding new elements. The idea of the alien autopsy video came in late, as well as adding these other women who have had the same experience Scully had. These were things we did to expand the story, and so we ended up writing episode nine very quickly; it became a group effort for me, Chris, and Howard."

Howard Gordon became involved with the writing of this episode when he complained a bit to Chris Carter that he wanted to participate in the mythology episodes. Carter's response was for Gordon to simply join in on this script. "I think 'Nisei' and '731' knocked the audience off balance," Gordon says. "It allowed us to retrench and ultimately answer questions from Scully's point of view. She had it her way, basically, proving that the aliens are not coming down and that they are genetic experiments. That science is responsible."

David Nutter admits, "This was the first of the mythology shows that I directed, and I was nervous about it, believe it or not.

Fortunately, it turned out very well, I thought. I just wanted to do the best job I could, because of the mythology episodes directed by people like Rob Bowman, Kim Manners, and Bob Goodwin, which I think really brought scope to these shows and made them, in a sense, mini-features."

For Robert Goodwin, the guy supervising physical production of the series, the real challenge of "Nisei" was the fact that the episode involved a train, and a climactic moment when Mulder has to leap on top of it.

"We had to use three different train cars," he recounts. "We had a freight car, a car that had the laboratory in it, and a sleeper car. They had to be built on great big inflated inner tubes so that we could rock it. You have to rock it to feel like it was really moving. So we shot a portion of it, including the portion in the passenger car, on a real train. The real train is a nightmare because it is a train. You do take one and the train comes around the bend and [a stuntman] jumps on top of it and it's 'Okay. Cut. Let's go to take two.' Well, that means you have to stop the train, roll it two miles or however far it is to get it back around the bend, and start it up again. In between takes it could be an hour and a half, and we have to shoot thirty takes a day to get the show done. That was difficult, plus I was very nervous about the stunt with Mulder jumping on the train. David, if you would let him, would do everything himself. So it was a combination of safety and visual effectiveness. I insisted on a number of tests, and I'm glad I did, because

we found out that the manner in which we were going to shoot this, which was basically have the camera mounted on top of the train shooting straight back, was very ineffective. Even a train going sixty miles an hour, if you are shooting straight back it doesn't appear to be going that fast. In reality, you can't get it going much more than twenty to twenty-five miles an hour in order to do the stunt. It would almost look like he was standing still, whereas if you come around on a side angle, say somebody standing on top of the train and you shoot him from the side, you are seeing the trees and houses and everything on the side whisk past. They sort of blur and you could be going fifteen miles an hour, but it looks as though you are going much faster.

"The one place where it worked," Goodwin elaborates, "was just after Mulder does his jump and he sees the overhead footbridge go by and disappear behind him. At that moment, looking straight back, you have a sense of speed, because you have that bridge just suddenly going backward, but as soon as it was gone it became nothing. So I designed a shot where we had a crane mounted on top of the train, we were shooting back initially, and as soon as Mulder landed at the end of the shot (David actually was standing and just dropped to the top of the train, because we did the stuntman part of the jump prior to that), the crane swung out around the side of the train so you were shooting over to the side of it. If you look at it again, it's a very effective shot. Timing-wise it was perfect. He lands, you see the bridge go by, and then you swing around to the side. In the end, it worked out great."

Rating/Audience Share: 9.8/17

Episode 3.10 (#59)
"731"

Original airdate: December 1, 1995
Written by Frank Spotnitz
Directed by Rob Bowman
Guest starring: Brendan Beiser (Agent Pendrell), Sean Campbell (Soldier), Colin Cunningham (Escalante), Robert Ito (Dr. Shiro Zama), Stephen McHattie (Red-Haired Man), Victoria Maxwell (Mother), Mike Puttonen (Conductor), Don S. Williams (Elder), Steven Williams (Mr. X)

Mulder finds himself trapped in a bomb-rigged train car with an apparent assassin who, he assumes, has been sent to kill an apparent alien locked in a compartment of the area they're in. Scully calls Mulder on her cell phone and provides him with what she feels is convincing proof that alien beings do not exist; that the government has been performing genetic experiments with human beings and has used the notion of aliens as a smokescreen. Trying to piece it all together in his mind, Mulder suggests to the assassin — though he is never told for sure — that the creature locked in the compartment was created to be a test subject that would survive the fallout of any weapon known to man. Nothing is ever proved, however, when X arrives, kills the assassin, and removes Mulder from the train just before it explodes.

❊   ❊   ❊

In reflecting on his inspiration for the episode, Frank Spotnitz notes: "I read an article in the *New York Times* a year earlier about these Chinese war crimes that I had never even heard of before. I was just shocked, first of all, that I had never heard of them, and then by the details. Prisoners of war were exposed to bacterial agents; experiments were done on children. Just unbelievably cruel and horrible experiments. So there was something new there to be dealt with. I ended up reading books on it, and part of the aftermath was that our government basically pardoned these people in exchange for their science. One of the leaders of this unit — called 731 — that conducted this experiment was spotted in the United States at an Army base in the 1950s, presumably to share this information with our military. Anyway, I thought there was something in there, and that is where the character in 'Nisei' came from. Also, I love train movies, particularly *North by Northwest* and *The Train*, an old John Frankenheimer film. So I just loved the idea of Mulder on a train.

"What ended up particularly interesting about the episode," he continues, "is that it really gave us a chance to set the counter back.

"I read an article in the *New York Times* a year earlier about these Chinese war crimes that I had never heard of before . . . so there was something new there to be dealt with."

I think after 'Paper Clip' people thought, 'That's it. Scully saw aliens and both of them are going to be believers now,' and this gave us a chance to say, 'Wait a minute. You can't be sure of that. What did she, in fact, see? Were they aliens, or were they people who were disfigured, subjects in an experiment?' I think we concluded the two-parter with Scully believing that alien abduction is all a hoax, a sham, a cover-up for government experiments which our government has actually admitted to, as Scully referred to when she was talking about the president admitting that we were doing experiments on innocent civilians. That was in the news a few months prior to that. So it is a credible alternative theory for Scully to have and an opportunity to say, No, she has not been corrupted into being a believer like Mulder. She has a very compelling real-world alternative explanation for what she has seen."

When shooting the episode, Rob Bowman took two different approaches to a significant scene, when Mulder is on the train and Scully is telling him over the cell phone that there are no aliens, just a government conspiracy.

"I shot Mulder with a Steadicam, which is a kind of handheld camera but it floats a bit," says Bowman. "And I shot him off center. He is kind of paranoid because the assassin may come in the room and jump him. I wanted a completely different feeling with Scully. I wanted Scully to feel like the Rock of Gibraltar. I wanted her to feel symmetrical, balanced, confident, strong — how do I do that? Well, all of her shots are on the dolly and are very graphically balanced."

Rating/Audience Share: 11.9/20

Episode 3.11 (#60)
"Revelations"

Original airdate: December 15, 1995
Written by Kim Newton
Directed by David Nutter
Guest starring: R. Lee Ermey (Rev. Patrick Finley), Nicole Roberts (Mrs. Tynes), Hayley Tyson (Susan Kryder), Kenneth Welsh (Millennium Man/Simon Gates), Selina Williams (School Nurse), Kevin Zegers (Kevin Kryder)

A *bit of role swapping for Mulder and Scully, with Scully believing that their current case involves religious phenomena, while Mulder thinks there is a more earthly explanation. Eleven reported stigmatics are stalked and killed by a religious zealot, and the FBI duo find themselves protecting a twelfth, a young boy who just may be the real thing, exhibiting blood from the same kinds of wounds that were inflicted upon Jesus Christ when he was crucified.*

✧ ✧ ✧

Official alien wear.

"'Revelations' was tough at first because it was kind of a softer show, and you have to be really careful with the softer shows so that they don't lose the overall *X-Files* edge," says David Nutter. "There always has to be a taste of horror in there somewhere.

"The relationship between the boy and Gillian was very strong, with much of it not actually being stated. There was just a connection between them. I also love the performance of R. Lee Ermey, who was the drill sergeant in *Full Metal Jacket.* He was also in the pilot of *Space: Above and Beyond,* and he

has always wanted to do an *X-Files,* so it was wonderful to get him."

Offers co-producer Paul Rabwin, "A show with script problems. It's difficult to sell the concept of religious magic and people appearing in two places at one time. It was a very emotional show, because it got into an important area of Scully's background, but trying to pull off the mystical parts was problematic. The script went through several rewrites and was still being worked on until the time of production. We figured, 'Nutter is a strong guy; he'll bring that in okay.' It did come off

"Some of us thought ['Revelations'] was DOA. We were on the operating table with that show and had it on life support."

very well, but there were some inconsistencies and pieces in it that just didn't seem to make sense to me. We went into a very detailed editing marathon, and we ended up with a show that just didn't work on a number of different levels. At one point, we couldn't sell the idea of this kid being in two places at the same time. There were some things missing that really tied together the kid and Owen, who's this mystical bald-headed character — just a number of things that weren't satisfactory about it. Some of us thought that show was DOA. We were on the operating table with that show and had it on life support.

"But I think it's one of the better examples of what happens when all of the creative forces come together. The kid had already gone home to Toronto. We flew him back to Vancouver, wrote some detailed lines for the Millennium Man. We had people writing new sequences; our second-unit crew was set up to shoot some stuff. We went back in and recut and restructured and the show started to make sense. By the time that show came out,

we were in awe because it played well. It amazed us. The response on-line was, 'Great show,' 'Meaningful show,' and people just loved it. We thought it was going to be one of the dogs of the season, and it turned out to be a very popular episode."

Rating/Audience Share: 10.1/17

Episode 3.12 (#61)
"War of the Coprophages"
Original airdate: January 5, 1996
Written by Darin Morgan
Directed by Kim Manners
Guest starring: Dion Anderson (Sheriff Frass), Raye Birk (Dr. Jeff Eckerle), Alex Bruhanski (Dr. Bugger), Alan Buckley (Dude), Bill Dow (Dr. Rick Newton), Tom Heaton (Resident #1), Ken Kramer (Dr. Alexander Ivanov), Tyler Labine (Stoner), Tony Marr (Motel Manager), Nicole Parker (Chick), Bobbie Phillips (Dr. Bambi Berendaum), Wren Robertz (Orderly), Bobby Stewart (Resident #2), Norma Wick (Reporter)

Mulder and Scully are drawn to Miller's Grove, Massachusetts, responding to reports of a town being overrun by cockroaches. Upon further investigation the question arises: Are these insects man-made robotic creatures, or alien probes sent to Earth as a means of terrifying us?

❋ ❋ ❋

"I came across a picture on the cover of an old magazine of a robotist named Rodney Brooks who was creating these robots that looked like insects, and he was giving them artificial intelligence that tried to duplicate the way the brain works," says Darin Morgan. "He decided to give the machine the most simple of programs, almost buglike, and these creatures actually appeared to be thinking. They appeared to be living, because they were reacting to things in the environment, which gave them a sort of lifelike quality. So you look at that and you say, 'There's a story in there somewhere.' An interesting science that somehow got crossed with cockroaches only because the place I was living in for a while had cockroaches.

"Even though I do funny shows, there always has to be a certain scare element," he adds. "The cockroaches are the built-in scare factor. So there was that, and I also wanted to do something like *War of the Worlds*, in a sense. Not a hoax, but people having mass hysteria. I don't know how I made the connection, but humans often think they have a highly developed brain and always think things out clearly and rationally. Yet in the case of mass hysteria, they really react like insects, swarming around. Somehow I made the connection between that and this artificial intelligence research. Robots and thought patterns — somehow that all came together to make the episode what it was."

Kim Manners deems this episode incredible due to the luck they had with the required cockroaches.

"You can't imagine how lucky we were. Debbie Cove, who is our animal trainer, has got around four hundred cockroaches. Two hundred from one school and two hundred from another, and we can never intermingle them. We also have to be careful not to hurt them. There were some shots where I wanted to tie cockroaches into the scene with actors, and every time we set up to do what I wanted to do, we were unsuccessful.

"There is one story I have to share because it's a classic," Manners continues. "We did a shot where I had Bill Dow, a local Vancouver actor, sitting on a toilet and the camera was outside the stall doors. We dollied into his face and he is sitting there reading a magazine. We went up and over his head and tilted the camera down to the back of the toilet tank. At that point on cue I needed about a half dozen cockroaches scurrying up on top of the tank. The minute I cleared Bill's head, they had to be there. Well, we were releasing them through a hole in the back of the set and so they had about a one-inch gap between the set and the toilet. Anyway, we did the shot four or five times and the trainers were releasing the cockroaches when I called 'Action,' but they weren't there. So, after five takes, we gathered them all back up and put them in a plastic bucket. Debbie Cove walked out of the set to go behind the wall. I said, 'Just come here a minute.' I stuck my head in the bucket and said, 'Listen, you sons of bitches. There are two cues. The first one is for camera. The second one is for you. When I say "Action," you guys run your asses to the top of the toilet

"The sounds of cockroaches were also great fun. Since these were alien mechanical cockroaches, we ended up taking a combination of something organic and something metallic."

tank. Do you hear me?' Now, the crew got a big kick out of that. Well, the next take, I said, 'Camera action' and 'Action,' and the little bastards did exactly what I told them to do."

Co-producer Paul Rabwin recalls with a laugh, "A Darin Morgan show — what can I say? It had at the same time among the funniest material in *The X-Files* as well as the most horrific sequences ever. I think the scene in which the cockroach crawls *into* someone's arm affected more adult professional people I work with than any other sequence we've ever done. When we see things happen to other people, usually we don't relate them to something that could happen to us. One of the things *The X-Files* tries to do is get into every-

body's psyche. Well, everyone has bug nightmares. Spielberg knew this when he did *Raiders of the Lost Ark*. So cockroaches are something near and dear to everyone's heart, and we all get freaked out by them. To relate to one crawling up our arm — and then into the arm — is unbelievable, and people went nuts. It was well done.

"The sounds of cockroaches were also great fun," he continues. "Since these were alien mechanical cockroaches, we ended up taking a combination of something organic and something metallic. We took a cicada sound and then we took some metallic scrape sounds and combined them and played them up about three octaves and got a little echo to it. We did about five or six different versions of this combination of organic and metallic sounds. We tried different pitches and speeds and came up with one we thought was really cool. That became the signature. Then we had to run it through the multiplier and create thirty or forty different sounds working simultaneously. It worked well and had a nice feel to it. And then we wanted to make sure it had a sound that was reminiscent of a cell phone, because of the big joke at the end where Mulder's cell phone goes off and the doctor thinks he's a cockroach. So we used an element of the cell phone blended in with the cockroach chirp."

Rating/Audience Share: 10.1/16

Episode 3.13 (#62)
"Syzygy"

Original airdate: January 26, 1996
Written by Chris Carter
Directed by Rob Bowman
Guest starring: Wendy Benson (Margi Kleinjan), Richard Brown (Minister), Garry Davey (Bob Spitz), Tim Dixon (Dr. Richard Godfrey), Lisa Robin Kelly (Terri Roberts), Gabrielle Miller (Brenda J. Summerfield), Russell Porter (Scott Simmons), Ryan Reynolds (Jay "Boom" DeBoom), Dana Wheeler-Nicholson (Det. Angela White), Denalda Williams (Zirinka)

Fears arise in a small town that a Satanic cult has taken root in the local high school, particularly in a pair of teenage girls. Mulder and Scully become convinced of this as well, although a local astronomer seems to answer some questions by explaining that once every eighty-four years a planetary alignment — a syzygy — occurs and that this town's location makes it a "cosmic G-spot" for the repercussions.

✹ ✹ ✹

Rob Bowman is not a fan of this particular episode. "The show proved to be much more difficult than I anticipated, and there wasn't enough time to shoot the show properly, because we were so close to the Christmas break. I felt extremely pressured and frustrated, although there are things in it I love, particularly the banter between Mulder and Scully. But overall, I thought the show was very oblique. I don't feel that the characters ever knew what was going on, and I don't think it is all that cool that kids are murdering people. I didn't feel like I was shooting an episode of *The X-Files,* and I think I let Chris down a little bit. Truth is, I don't like doing episodes I don't want to watch. I don't like doing episodes I don't feel like I can do a great job on, and I didn't do a great job on it. I don't think it is representative of me or the show.

"When you go too fast, you make mistakes," he continues. "Like in movies, you do half a page a day and you do it right. Here is a storyline where at one point the girls split off and at the same pace of shooting — one page of shooting is credited as one page of production time. Well, unfortunately, we had parallel action. I had to shoot two scenes in two separate locations. I had to go out in the countryside and shoot the people on the road, and that is counted as one page. Unfortunately, I also had to go back to the garage for Mulder and the other girl telling the other side of the story. So instead of shooting one scene and completing that page, I wound up shooting many pages twice. The result is that what appears to be a fifty-page script is actually closer to seventy-five or eighty pages. Well, I'm sorry, we can't shoot eighty pages. I am responsible for my own goofs on that episode, and I just couldn't enjoy it."

Co–executive producer Robert Goodwin reflects, "The hardest part of the show was the whole sequence at the police station where the girls go against each other psychically and all of the guns are going off. It was just a combination of physical effects and special effects, and it all worked really well."

Rating/Audience Share: 10.8/17

Episode 3.14 (#63)

"Grotesque"

Original airdate: February 2, 1996
Written by Howard Gordon
Directed by Kim Manners
Guest starring: Paul J. Anderson (Paramedic), Susan Bain (Agent Sarah Sheherlie), John Milton Brandon (Rudy Aguirre), James McDonnell (Glass Blower), Kasper Michaels (Young Agent), Amanda O'Leary (Doctor), Levani Outchaneichvili (John Mostow), Mitch Pileggi (Assistant Director Walter S. Skinner), Kurtwood Smith (Agent Bill Patterson), Greg Thirloway (Agent Greg Nemhauser), Zoran Vukelic (Peter [Artists' Model])

Mulder and Scully find themselves working with Mulder's former mentor, agent Bill Patterson of the behavioral sciences unit, when Patterson arrests a serial killer obsessed with gargoyles. But the killings nonetheless continue. What they need to know is whether the confessed killer, John Mostow, had an accomplice or has inspired someone to pick up where he left off. Using an expertise not often demonstrated in the series, Mulder essentially allows himself to get into the killer's mind, thinking as he would think and beginning to act in a peculiar manner. The descent into madness gives hints of possible demonic possession.

✲ ✲ ✲

For Howard Gordon, "Grotesque" was a personal crowning achievement of the season. "I had spent the better part of a month writing a story that really involved a possession, about the spirit of one particular gargoyle. I wrote a whole draft and literally three days before prep I said to Chris, 'This episode just is not working.' He sat with me on a Saturday, and we retrenched. It occurred to me on that morning and at the eleventh hour that this was not a story about an actual demon, but the demon of one man's mind. It was roughly the same structure I had done before, but with a completely different and much more internal and psychological story. On *The X-Files* we have often decided that the psychological is less interesting than the paranormal or external phenomena, but in this case the internal was really the way the story needed to be told, about the duality of people. It's a story that's been done before, but I think we added a really unique twist to it.

"This being *The X-Files*," Gordon continues, "I was looking for something visual, something that would ground you in the episode. I was walking the streets of New York and was looking up, noticing these gargoyles at every corner staring down at me. I was just fascinated by that. That's really where the episode was born. I also thought that in many ways, getting into the mind of a criminal is a kind of sculpture, so the idea of a sculptor came to me. I also thought people really enjoyed the fact that the episode told something about Mulder before Scully, which is always interesting. We also saw some of what made Mulder the man we know."

"David Duchovny drove himself, and he was brilliant in that show," adds Kim Manners. "I also think 'Grotesque' may have been the template for Chris Carter's new show, *Millennium,* because it is quite the same storyline, with someone becoming the person he's hunting; driving himself into the darkest, deepest corner of his mind. Asking the question, What is evil? And then experiencing evil so that he can recognize it and therefore capture it. I think 'Grotesque' is a frightening show. I think it is a disturbing show, and I think that's why — for me — it's such a good show. We pulled off making the viewer feel uneasy. *I* even found it a difficult show to watch. Yeah, it was a pretty dark hour

of television, and I would like to do more of those."

Co-producer Paul Rabwin recalls, "In one of the last scenes, when we pan up to see a gargoyle on top of a building, it happened to be shot on a particularly windy evening in Vancouver. The gargoyle was flopping around in the wind because there was no way to secure it. So optically we had to basically freeze the gargoyle itself and keep it in the shot because the camera was moving. It's supposed to be a big stone gargoyle attached to the building, and it was moving around like the papier-maché that it was."

Rating/Audience Share: 11.6/18

Episode 3.15 (#64)

"Piper Maru"

Original airdate: February 9, 1996
Written by Chris Carter and Frank Spotnitz
Directed by Rob Bowman
Guest starring: Jo Bates (Jeraldine Kallenchuk), Paul Batten (Joan Gauthier), Lenno Britos (Luis Cardinal), Robert Clothier (Commander Chris Johansen), Russell Ferrier (Medic), Rochelle Greenwood (Waitress), Richard Hersley (Capt. Kyle Sanford), Darcy Laurie (2nd Engineer), Nicholas Lea (Agent Alex Krycek), Robbie Maieri (World War II Pilot), Tegan Moss (Young Dana), David Neale (Guard), Morris Paynch (Gray-Haired Man), Mitch Pileggi (Assistant Director Walter S. Skinner), Tom Scholte (Young Johansen), Peter Scoular (Sick Crewman), Joel Silverstone (1st Engineer), Ari Solomon (Gauthier), Christine Viner (Young Melissa)

A French salvage ship discovers a World War II plane at the bottom of the ocean, its pilot somehow still alive. However, a transfer takes place, with an alien force going from the pilot to the diver, eventually to the diver's wife, and then to agent Alex Krycek, who is in Hong Kong. That is where Mulder finds Krycek and

brings him back to the United States to turn over the DAT. Unbeknownst to Mulder, however, the alien has taken possession of Krycek's body.

❋ ❋ ❋

"'Piper Maru' began with two things that Chris had known for a while he wanted to do," says Frank Spotnitz. "One, he knew he wanted a diver to go down in one of these deep-diving suits and find a World War II plane with the pilot alive in the cockpit. He hadn't thought about how that would work, like what the explanation was, whether this was a real thing the diver was seeing or an illusion. He just knew he wanted that image. Two, he wanted to have a flashback in black and white aboard a submarine.

"That was it. That was my assignment, and I had a number of false starts. I started working on it immediately after we finished '731,' and, finally, flying back from a convention in Minneapolis, I realized I didn't have any paper with me. I just had a pen and a magazine that was on the plane. During the flight it occurred to me that Scully's sister had been dead for many months and we hadn't dealt with it. Death — that was what the show should be about. Death and dealing with the dead. So I started thinking about Mulder and Scully, and then Krycek came to mind, and very quickly I started writing all over the white spaces in the magazine. 'Piper Maru' came together very quickly, as dealing with the dead behind you seemed to tie in nicely with the idea of this buried secret at the bottom of the ocean. Something terrible had happened there and the people who knew about it had to live with it the rest of their lives. That became a theme through both episodes ['Piper Maru' and 'Apocrypha']. Krycek in the missile silo, still alive, at the end of 'Apocrypha' was a nice period on that thought.

"Rob Bowman directed the first part, and it was a big, big deal shooting underwater," Spotnitz continues. "It was a very complicated sequence — actually having a tank, a P-51 the art director had designed, and having a diver go down there. We shot water and smoke and used every trick in the book, which was great. What's amazing to me is that we write these things in Los Angeles and then we go to Vancouver and in a matter of eight days — eight working days — the crew has turned the scripts into the episodes you see. It never ceases to amaze me. It is this huge operation; they build these sets and find these props and locations. They not only do good work, but they do it week in and week out and in such a short time period."

Rob Bowman enthuses, "'Piper Maru' was sent from heaven. Part of the story was based on my very first night scuba dive. Everything

was pitch black except for the little glow lights on the tanks and the bright flashlights used to light the water. I thought it was cool, and that we should do an episode where they go down into the ocean and discover something creepy. I mentioned that to Chris. He took it and said, 'Let's put a P-51 Mustang in there with a guy in the cockpit.' That is basically 'Piper Maru.' The rest of the script was generated from that. Here is a show where we got great mythological scenes with Mulder, and then a wonderful

"What's amazing to me is that we write these things in Los Angeles and then we go to Vancouver and in a matter of eight days — eight working days — the crew has turned the scripts into the episodes you see."

balance of the emotional storyline for Scully. And, again, great performances by all."

An interesting moment for Bowman was a Scully flashback when she's visiting the place where she grew up, and remembers playing with her late sister.

"These little girls playing were not there that day. We're driving up the street; the sun is gone. We're waiting for our light to get this shot. I'm in the back seat of the car, operating the camera that shoots over her shoulders, and I'm directing Gillian while we're driving, and I say, 'Okay, here we go. Here come the kids. Up there on your right is a tree — make that tree you and your sister.' The idea was that the close-up of Gillian would be reflective and loving toward her sister — and she was acting to a tree! I saw the dailies of that and called her up and said, 'You are my hero. No one will ever know what you did, and I'm going to tell everybody I can that you just did that great reaction to a tree.' Two weeks later, our second unit went out and shot the girls and then put it together and you say, 'Oh, my God.'

"In terms of the mythology," says Bowman, "once again we're going forward and it feels natural. At the end of '731' you're confused because of everything Scully has told Mulder, but with 'Piper Maru' you feel that it's the truth; that there are aliens. I also love the end of it with Krycek coming out of the bathroom and he and Mulder are walking along. You always have to be ready to fix something that's not right. They are walking along and David says, 'You feel better?' Nick [Lea] says, 'Like a new man,' they walk past the camera, and that's the end of the episode. *I don't think so.* What am I going to do? I jump on the camera and, of course, we're behind schedule and everybody is looking at me like, 'Rob, we don't have time for you to fix this.' But we did it again, and I remembered a moment in a film

I had seen that was the same kind of long walking shot and I thought, Well, this is really going on too long. There has to be something going on here. I told Nick to plant his face right in the camera. Nick will jump in front of a truck if he thinks it will make a scene better. So he walked right up to the camera; he shot his head forward into the camera and I came off the camera after rehearsal and said, 'Now we have an ending,' and then it was a matter of asking Mat Beck if we could make his eyes go with the moving camera, filled with that black oil stuff that represented the alien presence. All of a sudden we went from, 'Oh shit, we can't end the episode this way,' to one of my favorite endings ever."

Rating/Audience Share: 10.6/18

Episode 3.16 (#65)
"Apocrypha"

Original airdate: February 16, 1996
Written by Frank Spotnitz and Chris Carter
Directed by Kim Manners
Guest starring: Brendan Beiser (Agent
Pendrell), Tom Braidwood (Frohike), Eric
Breker (Ambulance Driver), Lenno Britos
(Luis Cardinal), Jeff Chivers (Armed Man #1),
Harrison R. Coe (3rd Government Man),
William B. Davis (Cigarette-Smoking Man),
Martin Evans (Major Domo), Francis
Flanagan (Nurse), Dean Haglund (Langly),
Bruce Harwood (Byers), Richard Hersley
(Capt. Kyle Sanford), David Kaye (Doctor),
Nicholas Lea (Agent Alex Krycek), Brian Levy
(Navy Doctor), Kevin McNulty (Agent Brian
Fuller), Sue Mathew (Agent Linda Caleca),
John Neville (Well-Manicured Man), Mitch
Pileggi (Assistant Director Walter S. Skinner),
Peter Scoular (Sick Crewman), Stanley Walsh
(2nd Elder), Craig Warkenten (Young
Cigarette-Smoking Man), Don Williams (1st
Elder)

Skinner is wounded in what appears to be a random shooting, but as Scully investigates, she learns that the shooter, Luis Cardinal, is the same man who was working with Krycek and who pulled the trigger on her sister, Melissa. Meanwhile, Mulder and the alien-possessed Krycek return to America from Hong Kong to retrieve the DAT, but their car is run off the road by agents of the Cigarette-Smoking Man. While Mulder is unconscious,
Krycek irradiates the agents, retrieves the tape on his own, and strikes a deal with CSM: The alien will be told where its spacecraft is in return for the tape. Eventually, Mulder and Scully proceed to a missile silo in North Dakota in pursuit of Krycek, but they are restrained by CSM's men and taken away. Unbeknownst to them (though Mulder suspects it), the silo actually contains an alien spacecraft and now the completely mortal Krycek, who will apparently be trapped for the rest of his life.

✿ ✿ ✿

"I actually think you didn't learn a lot more about the conspiracy in these two episodes ['Piper Maru' and 'Apocrypha']," says Frank Spotnitz, "but, emotionally, I think they were really good episodes. 'Nisei' and '731' were good for advancing Mulder and Scully's attitude toward what is really going on, but these shows were much more emotional, focusing on the consequences of the quest they are on. It is really easy to go through a lot of these action things with people dying and never addressing them. So I thought it was very interesting to do so."

Kim Manners was intrigued by the episode because it was his first mythology. "Rob Bowman had done 'Piper Maru.' I read the script, and I said, 'Well, Robbie's got this bitchin' underwater sequence where they find the monster and we see the monster transfer from body to body.' Then I got Krycek, and now I had to put the whole thing to rest. That was a show I really directed from instinct alone."

He notes that he approaches the mythology shows differently from the stand-alones. "Each stand-alone has to have, for me, a different means of presenting the story to the audience. With the mythology shows, you don't have to find an approach. What you need to do as a director is to be sure that the performances are there and the camera is working well and that the yarn is presented in its cleanest and most interesting fashion. It is not as creative a thing for us, but we've got to make sure that it is a damn good quality hour of television, whereas with the monsters of the week there is some individual creative contribution from the directors. The mythology shows are spooky or disturbing or interesting on their own. They really are, I think, easier to direct, and there is something about them that's of a better quality."

Rating/Audience Share: 10.7/18

Episode 3.17 (#66)
"Pusher"

Written by Vince Gilligan
Directed by Rob Bowman
Guest starring: Julia Arkos (Holly), Steve Bacic (Agent Collins), Meredith Bain-Woodward (Defense Attorney Brent), Roger R. Cross (SWAT Lieutenant), Ernie Foot (Lobby Guard), Janyse Jaud (Nurse), Darren Lucas (Lead SWAT Cop), Don Mackay (Judge), D. Neil Mark (Deputy Scott Kerber), Mitch Pileggi (Assistant Director Walter S. Skinner), Vic Polizos (Agent Frank Burst), J. D. Sheppard (Prosecutor), Henry Watson (Bailiff), Robert Wisden (Pusher/Robert Modell)

Mulder and Scully go up against a man named Robert Modell, who refers to himself as "Pusher" and has the ability to control people's minds with the sound of his voice (for example, inducing a police officer to drive his squad car into the path of a truck; giving an FBI agent a heart attack over the phone simply by describing arteries shutting down and his heartbeat slowing). The stakes become personal when Pusher uses his power to turn Mulder and Scully against each other.

✿ ✿ ✿

"This was, I believe, a pure *X-Files* script," says Rob Bowman. "What if we don't have a train? What if we don't throw all the money in Fort Knox into an episode? How well can we do it? So Vince Gilligan sat down and arced out an episode about this character. Directorially, this was a time for me to step out of the way. It's the opposite of many other shows, where it is about embellishment. This was one where I just had to make sure that the performances were well timed. Also, I was just so tired. 'Piper Maru' was a killer, just brutal, and thank God 'Pusher' came along, because I had just enough energy to walk up and talk to the actors but not enough energy to create a visual palette of colors and light and everything else. I was really challenged by the idea of fulfilling the expectations for an *X-Files* episode but without any hardware — no aliens, no spaceships. I also thought Robert Wisden was great as Pusher. He is a very energized kind of confident actor with lots of ideas of his own. It took me about a day and a half to get him into it, and then I never had to speak to him again, because he had that look in his eyes. I would walk up to talk to him about the scene and I could see that he was already there."

Rating/Audience Share: 10.8/18

Episode 3.18 (#67)
"Teso dos Bichos"
Original airdate: March 8, 1996
Written by John Shiban
Directed by Kim Manners
Guest starring: Garrison Chrisjohn (Dr. Winters), Tom McBeath (Dr. Jerrold Lewton), Janne Morth (Mona Wustner), Alan Robertson (Dr. Carl Roosevelt), Ron Sauve (Mr. Decker), Gordon Tootoosis (Shaman), Vic Trevino (Dr. Alonso Bilac)

When ancient archaeological items are removed from a sacred burial ground in Teso dos Bichos, Ecuador, those involved in the expedition begin to disappear, leaving a trail of blood. Mulder and Scully are sent in to investigate, and find themselves up against spirits, rats, and multitudes of savage cats.

❊ ❊ ❊

An episode, according to Kim Manners, marred by one distinct problem: cats. Although the ending sequence involving hundreds of them seems quite effective, he suggests that viewers turn off the sound to see how tame it really is.

"Do you know what's scary about that scene?" he asks rhetorically. "One full day on the dubbing stage mixing act four. What is scary, what is frightening, is the sound you hear, not at all what you see. It's ridiculous. I thought the first three acts were terrific, though. I pulled out all the horror stops and I thought it worked rather well until the fourth act."

Co–executive producer Robert Goodwin concurs, noting that it is extremely difficult to make domestic cats look dangerous.

"If you thought cockroaches were tough to shoot, cats are forty times harder," he says. "First of all, they don't look that scary. They look like cats, and you can never get all of those cats to do the same thing at once. I mean, if you have eighteen cats in a scene, it would take you half a day just to get them all in one place and roll the camera. You get ready to go, and three of them disappear on you. One of the things that was pointed out to me is that they all looked fluffy and clean. I wanted to go back and reshoot the cats, but I wanted them greased down and dirty. No more white cats, only gray cats and black cats and brown cats. I wanted them really scruffy and greasy. So we've got twelve cats in a scene, all greasy and scruffy but, like I said, it takes forever to get them all in place so that we can shoot. While we're taking forever to get them in place, what do cats do? They clean themselves. So we have these scruffy, dirty cats, but by the time we get to shoot, they've

"If you thought cockroaches were tough to shoot, cats are forty times harder."

cleaned themselves up and look absolutely beautiful. We had to build a little cat puppet that I thought was marginal, but it actually did work. But it was something I thought we would never be able to pull off."

Co-producer Paul Rabwin elaborates, "We probably spent twenty hours just filming cats, trying to get them to react and behave a certain way. Trying to get cats milling around, looking evil, which is difficult, because cats are basically domesticated. We ended up having Mat Beck take a certain group of cats that were holding still and multiply them optically. So one of the cat shots we saw looking down through a grate was something Mat had to create."

Rating/Audience Share: 10.7/18

Episode 3.19 (#68)
"Hell Money"
Original airdate: March 29, 1996
Written by Jeffrey Vlaming
Directed by Tucker Gates
Guest starring: Doug Abrahams (Lt. Neary), Stephen Chang (Large Man), Donald Fong (Vase Man), Dina Ha (Dr. Wu), James Hong (Hard-Faced Man), Ed Hong-Louie (Money Man), Lucy Liu (Kim Hsin), Graham Shiels (Night Watchman), B. D. Wong (Det. Glen Chao), Paul Wong (Wiry Man), Michael Yama (Shuyang Hsin)

Mulder and Scully are called in to a situation where a Chinese immigrant has been burned alive in a crematorium and another dead man has a living frog inside his body. What seems to be a Chinese spirit at work turns out to be an ancient secret cult that holds a lottery in which participants wager parts of their body against the financial jackpot.

✲ ✲ ✲

"I had two different ideas," says writer Jeff Vlaming. "One dealt with a lottery in a small town — you know, Nowhere, USA — and the other was about the goings-on in Chinatown where a corporate being assembles the destitute. It was all very mystical, and Chris just combined the two ideas, turning it into a lottery story involving organs. I thought this would be the episode the audience has been waiting for, where Scully is right. But in the end, Mulder came out to be the guy who put it all together."

At the end of this episode one is left wondering just what the hell that show was about.

Co-producer Paul Rabwin admits to not being a fan of this episode, primarily because he feels it was never really an X-File. "If you can take Mulder and Scully out of the show and it doesn't change anything, it's not an X-File. They weren't affected personally, and the other characters weren't affected by them. That's what makes the series unique: it's got great interaction."

Like season two's "Irresistible" and "Grotesque" earlier in season three, "Hell

Money" represented a show that suggests the paranormal without completely filling that bill.

"I think the paranormal is a great big all-encompassing label," offers Chris Carter. "I still feel that 'Grotesque' and 'Hell Money' in fact were paranormal. Though they may not have been directly or high conceptually paranormal, they both have elements of the paranormal. I like those episodes very much, much like I'm very fond of 'Irresistible,' which other people have cited as a non-paranormal X-File. But I still think those are, for me, certainly another way to look at the show, just as Darin Morgan has found a unique way of looking at the show."

Rating/Audience Share: 9.8/17

Episode 3.20 (#69)
"Jose Chung's *From Outer Space*"
Original airdate: April 12, 1996
Written by Darin Morgan
Directed by Rob Bowman
Guest starring: Terry Arrowsmith (Air Force Man), Jaap Broekar (Yappi), Alex Diakun (Dr. Fingers), Michael Dobson (Lt. Jack Sheaffer), Jason Gaffney (Harold Lamb), William Lucking (Roky Crikenson), Mina Mina (Dr. Hand), Larry Musser (Det. Manners), Charles Nelson Reilly (Jose Chung), Sarah Sawatsky (Chrissy Giorgio), Andrew Turner (CIA Man), Jesse Venture (Man in Black #1), Allan Zynyk (Blaine Faulkner)

174

Alien abductions or a government campaign of disinformation? That is the question addressed in what is undoubtedly the most bizarre and surreal episode of The X-Files *ever produced. Scully is interviewed by famed author Jose Chung, who is trying to expose the truth about alien abductions. A variety of conflicting stories unfold and grow more strange as they go on, leaving the viewer with just one question when the episode concludes: What the hell was that show about?*

❀ ❀ ❀

"I had the pieces for that script for a really long time," says Darin Morgan. "Where Gillian's abductors get abducted — I really thought that was neat. I had done research on hypnosis, and I'd read a book about government cover-ups of UFOs. The author believes UFOs exist, but doesn't think there are alien craft or beings from some other planet. He believes it's a phenomenon that somehow manipulates time and space. His point is that our government doesn't know what to believe or what to do about it, so they try to use it for their own purposes. Talking about whether or not it is true is something I found interesting.

"Some people like the show, some people hate it. I really like the show. For whatever reason, this one required me to watch it. I had to watch it so many times before it was finished that I got sick of it, but I think it turned out good. It was jam-packed with stuff. You usually don't see that on an hour television show. I actually learned a great deal about production, which you can't really learn as a writer until you do it. Writing is one thing and production is another. Overall, I learned that some of my stuff will work. When you are writing scripts you have no idea whether or not it is going to work or whether people will understand it. So this show provided me with a chance to see that people will understand my stuff."

One person who barely "understood his stuff" was director Rob Bowman. "A difficult show," he says, "because I had to speak to the writer and say, 'What was your intention here?' I can honestly tell you that there was probably not one person in Vancouver and probably one or two in Los Angeles who knew what the hell was up with that script. Darin Morgan has his own voice, and maybe his scripts are not quintessential X-Files, but they are certainly entertaining. After reading the script fifteen times, and then having about an eight-hour session with Darin in my hotel room, I was into this script deep. I did a great deal of storyboarding and whatnot, because this was a puzzle. This was an episode that was not 'follow-the-bouncing-ball.' We were going to present different pictures to you. It would be up to you to line them up. So it is my job to make sure each one of those pictures is perfect and that the transition from scene to scene propels you

forward or backward clearly, and to get the tone of every actor and every line perfectly, because it affects the overall concept. So it was a mind-blowing episode. It was a ball-buster, but that is not to say this script is a better or worse script than 'Pusher.' It's a

different script. This is more of a mosaic, and it is so thick and complicated that it is up to me, the storyteller, to be as simple and direct as I can. A very difficult show to do, but a very satisfying one as well.

"As wacky as the episode was," Bowman continues, "it still had the X-Files creepiness and truthfulness to it, and I think it could have easily been screwed up and become a comedy. I was hellbent on making sure that Mulder and Scully were true to themselves. They were not going to be funny, they were going to be real. They were on a case. Mulder and Scully had to drive us to this thing, so they had to be themselves so we could trust them. Then

ducer says sheepishly. "Even Darin Morgan, who wrote it, didn't understand it. In reality, it is one of those shows you have to see to get. You can't get it by reading it. It is extremely confusing, because so much of it is flashbacks told from one character's point of view or another character's point of view. Until you put it all together and can visually follow what is happening, it doesn't make any sense. So the biggest problem we had was understanding what the hell they were talking about. What was going on, who was doing what to who, is this scene real or someone's point of view? It became a true challenge, I think, directorially more than anything else, because the director had to keep all these lines going as to which was the flashback and which was real.

"The most fun on that episode," Goodwin adds, "was the casting of Charles Nelson Reilly. I couldn't wait to watch dailies, because he is hysterical when he is doing the dialogue, but even funnier when he goes off it. He forgets his lines. If you saw the dailies, you would die. I don't know how Gillian could continue to act because it was so funny. As opposed to Peter Boyle, who arrived not wanting to do the show, Charles definitely wanted to do it, was thrilled doing it, and could not thank me enough."

Of Darin Morgan's overall contribution to the series, Chris Carter notes, "It's been a wonderful coincidence of timing, talent, and the success of the show, allowing it to stretch in a direction it would never have been able to

I had to see how I could color it. It was just a fun bit of orchestration, and it was very expensive. But it is an episode that really puts a spin on the expectations of an *X-Files* viewer. They turn on the show on Friday night and they see that episode and think, 'Boy, you can never predict what you are going to get on this show.'"

Another member of the totally confused "Jose Chung" fan club is Robert Goodwin. "I must have read that script a dozen times and never understood it," the co–executive pro-

if it had been less successful or if it had been a younger show. Darin is a truly original comic mind. I don't know anybody in the world working in film, and that's what we work in here even though it appears on television, who has the voice Darin has. He is one in many million."

Co-producer Paul Rabwin proclaims, "An instant classic. One of those seminal episodes. You know, when people talk about *The Twilight Zone*, they say 'Remember "Eye of the Beholder"?' Or 'Trouble With Tribbles' on the original *Star Trek*. 'Jose Chung' is going to be one of those episodes that is immediately revered."

Rabwin also remembers a particular post-production challenge of the episode. "There's a sequence where this guy is found wandering naked on the streets. Mulder passes by him. We had this very long shot of this naked man coming out of the bushes. In fact, he was really in a body suit, so it didn't show anything anyone might care about, but he appeared to be without clothes. Standards and Practices came down and scrutinized it. We couldn't see anything, but as far as they were concerned it was the *impression* of a naked person, and they didn't want to show that. So we had Mat Beck, our visual effects producer, take the headlight beam from Mulder's car from the distance and put one of these big left-to-right horizontal beams that totally wiped out the whole center of the screen. So we had this headlight beam covering the man's body between his belly button and his knees. It looks okay, but that's about as big a stretch that they've had us go."

Rating/Audience Share: 10.5/19

Episode 3.21 (#70)
"Avatar"

Original airdate: April 26, 1996
Teleplay by Howard Gordon
Story by David Duchovny and Howard Gordon
Directed by James Charleston
Guest starring: Brendan Beiser (Dr. Rick Newton), William B. Davis (Cigarette-Smoking Man), Stacy Grant (Judy Fairly), Jennifer Hetrick (Sharon Skinner), Tom Mason (Det. Waltos), Morris Paynch (Gray-Haired Man), Mitch Pileggi (Assistant Director Walter S. Skinner), Bethoe Shirkoff (Old Woman), Michael David Simms (Senior Agent), Tasha Simms (Jay Cassal), Malcolm Stewart (Special Agent Bonnecaze), Amanda Tapping (Carina Sayles), Cal Traversy (Young Detective), Janie Woods-Morris (Lorraine Kelleher)

Walter Skinner is accused of murder when he awakens in a hotel room next to the corpse of a slain prostitute. Suspicion of him mounts when it's revealed that he doesn't remember what happened to the woman, his marriage is about to end in divorce, and he is seeing a psychiatrist for a severe sleep disorder. Mulder and Scully try their best to clear him of these charges, but things don't look good. Skinner's salvation lies in the apparition of an elderly woman who continues to materialize before him.

❈ ❈ ❈

"This began as a germ of an idea that David Duchovny came up with," says Howard Gordon. "It came from David saying, 'Mitch [Pileggi] is a great guy and Skinner is a great character; we don't use him enough.' He and I had been talking about doing another episode entirely, but we felt it was a good time in the season to deal a little more with Skinner rather than his just being a curmudgeonly foil for them.

"The story evolved and, again, I think it became more psychological than supernatural. I think in the best *X-Files* fashion it left to the imagination whether these apparitions Skinner was seeing were for real or not. What's interesting is that it examined this character in some depth. We saw what work meant to him and how this closed-off part of him had forced his marriage to end, even though this apparition came to him begging him to open himself up to the possibility of love, basically. In a very broadstroke way it attached the idea of a conspiracy to him. It then of course touched on Skinner's function in the *X-Files*. He served as Mulder and Scully's patron, sort of, and knocking him out was one way to weaken the power of Mulder and Scully."

Robert Goodwin notes that the episode introduced a new director to the series, James Charleston. "He came in and worked very hard during prep and he had great ideas," says Goodwin. "He shot it very visually and right on schedule. The funny part about that show is that the whole episode was written for rain. It was about how the constant rain was driving people to madness and depression. Every day we shot, it was bright and sunny and we had to keep making our own rain — in Vancouver! People always talk about how the rain always helps with the mood of the show. It is true, but we're fighting sunlight just as often as we fight the rain."

Rating/Audience Share: 9.3/16

Episode 3.22 (#71)
"Quagmire"
Original airdate: May 3, 1996
Written by Kim Newton
Directed by Kim Manners
Guest starring: Mark Acheson (Ted Bertram), R. Nelson Brown (Ansel Bray), Chris Ellis (Sheriff Lance Hindt), Peter Hanlon (Dr. William Bailey), Terrance Leigh (Snorkel Dude), Murray Lowry (Fisherman), Nicole Parker (Chick), Timothy Webber (Dr. Paul Farraday)

A "frog holocaust" in Georgia draws Mulder and Scully in, particularly after reports of a

Loch Ness Monster type of creature in the waters. Scully is more skeptical than ever, though that skepticism is put to the test when body parts start appearing, and she and Mulder witness actual attacks.

✵ ✵ ✵

"Not a great show, but a good one," opines Kim Manners. "It's a lighter show. There is a lot of humor in it, but I think it's a hit with fans because there is some wonderful Mulder and Scully relationship stuff. The entire third act is just the two of them talking, which is actually kind of interesting.

"The episode was a challenge to me because it is what I call a 'blue sky' show. There are very few interiors. It is all outside on a lake, and that is tough. One of the reasons *The X-Files* works is that it's dark and we're in tight, cramped, scary places. Now suddenly you are under a canopy — how do you make that scary? I just had to do my best to make the attack scenes scary with this secret monster. It actually does chew up quite a few people, so that part of it worked nicely. Overall, though, it is not the way I would have chosen to go out of the season. I would have liked to have another 'Grotesque.'"

Notes Robert Goodwin, "It's always difficult working with water, on water, around water — anything to do with water, especially up here because, as I've said, everything is glacially fed so it's freezing cold. Everyone has to have wetsuits, and you can only be in the water for a certain amount of time. So that was the big challenge. I also happen to like the very last shot of the show: Mulder kills this creature that has been killing off these people and it's a huge fourteen-foot alligator, and the last shot as he walks by, you hold on the water and see this sea monster go by."

Rating/Audience Share: 10.2/18

Episode 3.23 (#72)
"Wetwired"

Original airdate: May 10, 1996
Written by Mat Beck
Directed by Rob Bowman
Guest starring: Linden Banks (Joseph Patnik), Tom Braidwood (Frohike), Colin Cunningham (Dr. Henry Stroman), William B. Davis (Cigarette-Smoking Man), Dean Haglund (Langly), Bruce Harwood (Byers), Sheila Larken (Margaret Scully), Zinaid Memisevic (Lladoslav Miriskovic), Mitch Pileggi (Assistant Director Walter S. Skinner), Sandy Tucker (Helene Riddock), Steven Williams (Mr. X)

A wide variety of sudden homicides in Maryland attracts the attention of Mulder and Scully. They learn that everyone involved watched an awful lot of televison. When Scully begins acting erratically and, eventually, psychotically, Mulder comes to the conclusion that somehow the populace is being manipulated by their television signals.

❖ ❖ ❖

"I dug the script," says Rob Bowman. "I felt it was a good old-fashioned show, and people who didn't like 'Jose Chung' would like 'Wetwired' because all the bad boys are back. Again, the objective was to guide the performances so that Scully proceeds into her state of paranoid delusion naturally. A good clean steak-and-potatoes type of episode."

Interestingly, the episode ends with X getting into a car with the Cigarette-Smoking Man, adding further layers to this enigmatic character.

"Wetwired" was written by special-effects producer Mat Beck, whose imagination was obviously piqued from working on the series.

Rating/Audience Share: 9.7/17

Episode 3.24 (#73)
"Talitha Cumi"
Original airdate: May 17, 1996
Teleplay by Chris Carter
Story by David Duchovny and Chris Carter
Directed by R. W. Goodwin
Guest starring: Brian Barry (Last Man), Ross Clarke (Pleasant Man), William B. Davis (Cigarette-Smoking Man), Stephen Dimopoulos (Detective), Bonnie Hay (Night Nurse), Hrothgar Mathews (Galen Muntz), Mitch Pileggi (Assistant Director Walter S. Skinner), Roy Thinnes (Jeremiah Smith), Angelo Vacco (Doorman), Steven Williams (Mr. X)

The notion of aliens among us intensifies when Jeremiah Smith heals the wounds of several shooting victims with the palms of his hands. Later, we learn that he is well known to the Cigarette-Smoking Man, and the implication is that CSM is working closely with the aliens in preparation for the day of colonization. Meanwhile, Mulder's mother is hospitalized with a stroke shortly after meeting with CSM (where it's revealed that they knew each other far better than anyone previously suspected), and Mulder sees the healing powers of Smith as her only hope. He never finds out, however, because he and Scully discover themselves about to engage in a deadly tug of war with the Pilot, the alien bounty hunter (from season two's "Colony" and "End Game"), whose mission is to kill Smith.

❀ ❀ ❀

For Robert Goodwin, who directed the episode, the toughest part was the opening sequence in the fast-food restaurant where several people are shot and Jeremiah Smith heals them.

"If you watch it closely," he explains, "you see that the scene is made up of a trillion tiny pieces of film, and in order to get a trillion tiny pieces of film, you have to shoot them all. That's the way I thought it should be shot to be most effective. It's all handheld. I used two cameras. If you look at it, you'll see all these little cuts where it actually jumps and cuts from one position to another. That makes it more scary. The Jeremiah Smith character, who's supposed to be Godlike, was always on Steadicam. Everybody else was jumping, moving, fast, panning, jump to that, and he was always rock steady. In his first appearance I overcranked, which means he was actually in slow motion. The music helped that too. It is very quick and something that is only subliminal, but I think it has a psychological impact on the audience. It makes the Roy Thinnes character something other than real."

Another highlight for Goodwin was a scene between the Cigarette-Smoking Man and Jeremiah Smith, in which the latter morphs into the image of Deep Throat.

"It was hard to do only because when you do those things, you have to use a video splitter and basically do the first half of the morph," he explains. "So you film the first half of the scene with Roy Thinnes. He lowers his head into position, and then you cut. Then you put Jerry Hardin [Deep Throat] in, and you get him into the chair and everything else ready to go. You run a videotape of what you shot with Thinnes, freeze that moment at the end where he has his head down, and then you can have Jerry on a separate scene just to

the right of that, getting into position. They are also about to superimpose one over the other on the video, so you are lining them up almost perfectly. The problem was that Jerry had a movie he had to do when we were shooting. We shot all that stuff in the prison on the last day and Jerry couldn't work that day. So Chris had to direct Jerry's part in the scene three days earlier. He videotaped that and I had to do the morph backwards: I had to match Roy to Jerry instead. That was actually quite difficult to match up. I got Jerry on tape and froze him in position. Of course, it's not just a question of position, but you have to have the same lens size, the camera position has to be the same, everything has to line up where it will work seamlessly. So that was difficult.

"The other morph, where Smith changes into Mulder's father and then back again was easier," he adds. "He looks down and he then looks back up and he's the father. That was easy because I had both of them there. In that case you set up the camera, stop, cut, put in the actor, and do it again. The camera is already in the correct position."

There are moments in "Talitha Cumi" that indicate alien colonization is a process that may be starting shortly. Indeed, it's an accusation Mulder actually makes in the episode. Chris Carter, however, just smiles when it's brought to his attention.

"If you go back and look at that episode very carefully, you'll see there were things posited but nothing ever addressed," he says. "I would suggest that anyone who feels they are now zeroing in on what we are doing, make sure they stay tuned for the opener of season four."

Rating/Audience Share: 11.2/21

The X-Phile Encyclopedia
SEASONS ONE–THREE

All entries are based on the original shooting teleplays.

001013: FBI Special Agent Dana Scully's e-mail account number. ["End Game"]

000517: FBI Special Agent Fox Mulder's e-mail account number. ["End Game"]

Note: The pilot episode (episode #1 in the series) is the only one that has no story title.

[A]

ABRAMOWITZ PLUMBING: The name on the side of a panel truck that is actually being used as cover by government agents. ["The Erlenmeyer Flask"]

ADAMS, MRS.: She is working at the blood drive table at a department store in Franklin, Pennsylvania. ["Blood"]

ADULT VIDEO NEWS: The trade magazine of the adult movie industry. Scully catches Mulder reading a copy. ["Beyond the Sea"]

ADVANCED RESEARCH PROJECT AGENCY: The government agency behind the **Arctic Ice Core Project.** ["Ice"]

AHAB: Scully's pet name for her father, taken from the main character of Herman Melville's novel *Moby Dick.* ["Beyond the Sea"]

AIKLEN, STAFF SGT. KEVIN: A soldier whose case is oddly similar to that of **Lt. Col. Victor Stans.** His family died in a fire, and Aiklen tried to commit suicide by throwing himself into a wood chipper. Like Stans, Aiklen claims that someone would not let him die. ["The Walk"]

AIR FORCE: One of the people who interrogates **Chrissy Giorgio.** At first she remembers him as looking like a Gray Alien. ["Jose Chung's *From Outer Space*"]

AGUIRRE, RUDY: The instructor of the art class at **George Washington University.** ["Grotesque"]

AL-HADITHI, MOHAMMED: An Iraqi military officer who sees UFOs on radar which apparently attack a jet. ["E.B.E."]

ALLEGIANCE, USS: The U.S. Navy nuclear submarine on a cartography mission that encounters the **Pilot**'s submerged spacecraft and is disabled by it when the sub tries to follow orders and destroy the UFO. When Mulder reaches the submarine stranded in the ice, he finds all its crew members dead, apparently done in by the Pilot, an alien assassin. The sole survivor, Lt. **Terry Wilmer,** is actually the Pilot, who uses the vessel to get back to his own ship. ["End Game"]

ALIEN AUTOPSY: Captured on videotape, it was conducted inside a train car on a siding in Knoxville, Tennessee. Soldiers dressed in black burst into the train car in the middle of the autopsy, shot the four Japanese doctors, and took the Gray Alien corpse away in a body bag. A satellite dish on the top of the train car had been broadcasting the autopsy at the time of the hit on the doctors, and this broadcast was intercepted by someone in **Allentown, Pennsylvania.** ["Nisei"]

ALIEN BOUNTY HUNTER: An alien who hunts down and kills alien clones. ["Talitha Cumi," "Colony," and "End Game"] He reappears in "Talitha Cumi" and is clearly bent on assassinating the gentle alien clone, **Jeremiah Smith.**

ALLENTOWN POLICE SUB-STATION: Where Mulder and Scully take the Japanese man they catch at the scene of a murder. Not only does the man turn out to supposedly be a diplomat, but Assistant Director **Walter S. Skinner** comes to Allentown himself to secure the man's release (see also **Rat Tail Productions** and **Kazuo Takeo**). ["Nisei"]

ALLENTOWN, PENNSYLVANIA: Where a man intercepted the satellite transmission of an alien autopsy. He sells copies of it on videotape for $29.95 plus shipping. ["Nisei"]

ALTA: A Navy icecutter that observed a UFO going down in the Beaufort Sea, north of the Arctic Circle; the crew of the *Alta* rescued the alien **Pilot,** who led them to believe he was the survivor of a Russian plane crash. ["Colony"]

ALT.-FUELS INC.: Runs a **methane research facility.** Their motto is "Waste is a terrible thing to waste." ["War of the Coprophages"]

AMARU: A powerful female shaman, whose remains are discovered in their sacred burial urn in Ecuador by **Dr. Alonso Bilac** and **Dr. Carl Roosevelt.** Roosevelt is killed under mysterious circumstances at the dig where the Amaru Urn was discovered; it is brought to the Boston Museum of Natural History in

accordance with his final wishes. His body was never recovered. ["Teso dos Bichos"]

AMBASSADOR HOTEL: Where Walter Skinner picks up a woman, takes her to his room, and wakes up the next morning to find her lying dead next to him. ["Avatar"]

AMBROSE, WILLA: A naturalist brought in by the Board of Supervisors to oversee activities at the **Fairfield Zoo** in Idaho. She's questioned about how **Ganesha,** an elephant, somehow escaped from her locked cage. When Ambrose began working for the zoo, one of the first things she did was to prohibit the use of chains holding elephants in place. ["Fearful Symmetry"]

AMERICAN RONIN: A guns-and-mercenaries magazine Robert Modell used to advertise his talents as a killer. The ads lead Mulder and Scully to a pay phone in Virginia, where Modell calls to taunt them and leave a clue. ["Pusher"]

AMRITH: A viscous, honeylike substance sometimes produced during magical rituals. Amrith oozes from the walls of **Charlie Holvey**'s hospital room when the **Calusari** perform the Ritual of Separation. ["The Calusari"]

AMROLLI, MOHAMMED: A terrorist linked with the radical

Iranian group known as Isfahan. He and an accomplice attempted to kill **Lauren Kyte,** only to be killed by the ghost of **Howard Graves.** Mulder identifies the body by covertly getting a fingerprint on his glasses. ["Shadows"]

ANAPHYLACTIC SHOCK: Fatal reaction to an insect bite. ["War of the Coprophages"]

ANASAZI: A Native American tribe that vanished from the New Mexico area some six hundred years ago. Anthropologists have determined that the Anasazi practiced cannibalism. ["Our Town"] According to **Albert Hosteen,** their name means "ancient aliens." Hosteen claims the Anasazi were carried away by aliens. ["Anasazi"]

ANKUSES: Poles used by animal trainers to control elephants. ["Fearful Symmetry"]

ANNAPOLIS SAVINGS AND LOAN: The first bank robbed by **Warren James Dupre** and **Lula Philips,** on May 9, 1993. ["Lazarus"]

ANTHROPOMANCY: The ancient art of predicting the future by studying the entrails of a disemboweled human being. Mulder refers to this practice at the scene of the **Doll Collector**'s murder. The killer (see **Puppet**) has left part of his victim's intestines sitting on a table next to her eyes. ["Clyde Bruckman's Final Repose"]

ANTONIO: A subordinate of a high-ranking Italian diplomat in the United Nations, Antonio informs his superior that the **MJ documents** have been stolen. ["Anasazi"]

ARCTIC ICE CORE PROJECT: A scientific expedition to study the Earth's past climate by drilling for samples of very deep Arctic ice. After several months, the project team, headed by **John Richter,** draws samples from depths of nearly two miles. This unusual depth is due to a meteor strike eons earlier; the samples contain an ancient alien microorganism that infects the team members with a parasite that encourages violent behavior, resulting in their deaths. Two more victims succumb to the virus in the course of the X-Files investigation: **Bear,** a pilot, dies, while **Dr. Nancy Da Silva** is cured. The site is destroyed by the government after the survivors are airlifted out. ["Ice"]

ARDEN, HAL: A seventy-four-year-old Alzheimer's patient at the Excelsis Dei Convalescent Home for eight years. Nurse **Michelle Charters** claims he raped her, only he was invisible at the time of the attack

. . . or so she says. Shortly thereafter, Arden is killed by an unseen force after he threatens to reveal a secret about the capsules of drugs **Gung Bituen** has been giving them. Traces of ibotenic acid, a powerful hallucinogen, are found in his body. ["Excelsis Dei"]

ARGENT, USS: A destroyer escort, commissioned in 1991 by the U.S. Navy and commanded by **Capt. Phillip Barclay,** the *Argent* was reported lost in the North Atlantic. By the time Mulder and Scully reach it, it looks as if it had been there for thirty years. Advanced corrosion has caused the ship to "bleed" rust. Mulder and Scully are rescued by Navy SEALs and taken to Bethesda, where Scully's detailed notes on their experience help save their lives. The ship sinks after its inner hull corrodes away. ["Dod Kalm"]

ARECIBO IONOSPHERIC OBSERVATORY: Site of a radio telescope in Arecibo, Puerto Rico, which is shut down after the project designed to scan the sky for radio transmissions of an intelligent extraterrestrial origin is terminated by **Sen. Richard Bryon.** This dormant station becomes mysteriously reactivated when it receives a trans-

mission recorded from the Voyager spacecraft years after the Voyager left our solar system. ["Little Green Men"]

ARENS, SHERIFF TOM: The seemingly friendly sheriff of **Dudley, Arkansas,** who explains away the scorch marks in a nearby field as illegal trash burning. As the masked executioner in the cannibalistic rituals performed in Dudley, Arens is on the verge of decapitating Scully when he is shot dead by Mulder. ["Our Town"]

ARGOTYPOLINE: A highly flammable rocket fuel that **Cecil L'ively** [a.k.a **Bob**] mixes with paint in order to accelerate fires started with his pyrokinetic powers. ["Fire"]

ARLINGTON, VIRGINIA: The Washington suburb where the **Holvey** family lives at the time of the deaths of Teddy, Steve, and Golda. Scully encounters the malevolent ghost of Michael Holvey in the Holvey house. ["The Calusari"] Also the location of a fast-food restaurant where a robbery and shootings take place. But the victims do not die because **Jeremiah Smith** is there and he heals all the injured. ["Talitha Cumi"]

ARMY: One of the people who interrogates **Chrissy Giorgio.** At first she remembers him as looking like a Gray Alien.

["Jose Chung's *From Outer Space*"]

ASTADOURIAN LIGHTNING OBSERVATORY: A scientific facility located near **Connerville, Oklahoma,** where scientists study lightning, and produce it with hundreds of ionized rods pointed at the sky. ["D.P.O."]

ASTRAL PROJECTION: The psychic ability to leave one's physical body. **Sgt. "Rappo" Trimble** has this power, which he uses to murder the families of his enemies. Mulder carries dental x-ray film to various murder scenes in order to detect radiation traces associated with this phenomenon. ["The Walk"]

ATKINSON, MIKE: Employee of the Mutual UFO Network (MUFON). ["Irresistible"]

ATLANTIC CITY, NEW JERSEY: The police here covered up a series of brutal murders involving the homeless. ["The Jersey Devil"] Bank robbers **Warren James Dupre** and **Lula Philips** were married here in May 1993. ["Lazarus"]

ATSUMI, LEZA: The special agent who explains, with considerable skepticism, that all of the binary figures written down by **Kevin Morris** can be deciphered, including fragments of Shakespeare's sonnets, the Koran, and Bach's

Brandenburg Concertos. ["Conduit"]

AUERBACH, DR. SIMON: One of the doctors involved in **Pinck Pharmaceuticals'** unethical test of a newly discovered disease at the **Cumberland State Correctional Facility,** and the ensuing cover-up. ["F. Emasculata"]

925 AUGUST STREET: The address in Dinwiddie County, Virginia, of **Elizabeth,** the girlfriend of the escaped convict **Paul.** Mulder and U.S. marshals arrest her here, and find another escapee dead of *F. Emasculata.* ["F. Emasculata"]

AUSBURY, JIM: A member of a coven in Milford Haven, New Hampshire. His sixteen-year-old stepdaughter, Shannon, accuses him of having abused her when she was a small child. He is eaten by a python and reduced to bones. ["Die Hand Die Verletzt"]

AUSBURY, BARBARA: Jim's wife. She doesn't believe the accusations against him. ["Die Hand Die Verletzt"]

AUSBURY, SHANNON: She complains of witnessing occult rites as a child and claims she had three babies who were killed by the coven, and that her sister was murdered when she was eight. Shannon is later

killed by the black magic of the demon in the form of **Phyllis Paddock.** ["Die Hand Die Verletzt"]

AUSTIN, DR.: A physician at the National Institutes of Health who provides Mulder and Scully with information about **Dr. Joe Ridley**'s progeria studies and the unethical activities that led to his dismissal. ["Young at Heart"]

AVALON FOUNDATION: A cryogenics facility where the head of **Dr. Arthur Grable** is preserved in liquid nitrogen. Grable died in a car accident and his body was too badly damaged to be frozen as well. ["Roland"]

[B]

BAILEY, DR. WILLIAM: Member of the U.S. Forestry Service. He rejects **Dr. Paul Farraday**'s request to place the frog known as the *Rana Sphenocephala* on the endangered species list, deeming Farraday's results inconclusive. Moments later, something comes out of the lake and drags him into the water to his doom. ["Quagmire"]

BAKER, DR. AARON: One of the **Gregor** clones, killed by the **Pilot** in his home in Syracuse, New York. ["Colony"]

BALBOA NAVAL HOSPITAL: Military hospital in San Diego where the crewmen of the *Piper Maru* are treated for radiation burns. [*"Piper Maru"*]

BANANA CREAM PIE: The dessert Mulder steps in shortly before being attacked by the **Puppet** in a hotel kitchen, as predicted by **Clyde Bruckman.** ["Clyde Bruckman's Final Repose"]

BANTON, DR. CHESTER RAY: A brilliant scientist who built an incredibly compact particle accelerator for use in his studies of subatomic particles, particularly dark matter, at Polarity Magnetics. While bombarding an alpha target with beta particles, Banton got in the way and received a massive dose of particles, which burned his shadow onto the wall but miraculously did not kill him. Instead, his shadow somehow became a separate entity of dark matter, which can kill people by completely absorbing their mass and energy. Banton suspects that the shadow might be able to survive without him. Abducted by **X,** he is now undergoing top-secret government testing at an undisclosed location. ["Soft Light"]

BARBALA, RUDY: Detective at Buffalo's 14th Precinct. He is killed by the psychic powers of eight-year-old **Michelle Bishop.** We later learn that he was responsible for the murder of a police officer nine years before. ["Born Again"]

BARCLAY, CAPT. PHILLIP: Commander of the *USS Argent.* His alcoholism actually prolongs his life when his ship's crew experiences accelerated aging due to **free radicals** in their drinking water, but it does not keep eighteen crew members from abandoning ship. Found on his ship by Mulder and Scully, he tells them the ship has begun to bleed. Barclay is the last of his crew to die. ["Dod Kalm"]

BARNETT, JOHN EARVIN: A dangerous criminal from New Hampshire whose extremely violent armed robberies have taken the lives of seven people. Barnett, Mulder's first assignment out of the FBI academy in 1989, killed his hostage and FBI agent **Steve Wallenberg** before being apprehended, convicted, and sentenced to 340 years in the Tashmoo Federal Correctional Facility, where he is experimented on by prison doctor **Joe Ridley,** who reverses his aging process and amputates his right arm, replacing it with one grown from salamander cells. Reported dead of cardiac fail-ure on September 16, 1989, and supposedly cremated and scattered along the Delaware River, Barnett is actually alive — and younger than ever. Several years later he returns to get revenge on Mulder, killing a jewelry store clerk and FBI agent **Reggie Purdue** and shooting Scully before his death. Scully is saved by her bulletproof vest. ["Young at Heart"]

BARNEY: A purple TV dinosaur popular with children, but eight-year-old **Cindy Reardon** prefers to watch congressional investigations on television. ["Eve"] Also the name of one of the Richmond, Virginia, policemen killed by **Chester Ray Banton**'s shadow. ["Soft Light"]

BARON, DET. BRADLEY: A senior detective on the Richmond, Virginia, police force who supervises **Kelly Ryan**'s first (and last) case. He is perplexed to learn of Mulder and Scully's involvement when he comes to arrange **Chester Ray Banton**'s transfer from the Yaloff Psychiatric Hospital to the city jail. ["Soft Light"]

BARRINGTON, DR. LAWRENCE: A doctor at the Avalon Foundation, a cryogenics institute. ["Roland"]

BARRY, DUANE: A former FBI agent with an impeccable

record who left the Bureau in 1982. The official story is that he was shot in the brain with his own weapon while on a drug stakeout in the woods, rendering him a dangerous psychotic with severe delusions. Barry believes himself to have been abducted by aliens on numerous occasions and implanted with various devices. He escapes from the Davis Correctional Treatment Center on August 7, 1994, with his psychiatrist as hostage and holes up in a travel agency, taking other hostages; Mulder negotiates with him until a marksman shoots Barry in the chest. Medical examinations reveal mysterious pieces of metal in his gums, sinuses, and abdomen. The wounded Barry escapes from Jefferson Memorial Hospital in Richmond, Virginia, and kidnaps Scully from her home. ["Duane Barry"] Mulder later finds Barry on top of Skyland Mountain in Virginia, site of his first abduction by aliens; seemingly freed from his mental problems, Barry claims that aliens have taken Scully away in his place. Barry dies shortly afterward, possibly poisoned by **Alex Krycek.** ["Ascension"] Barry's name appears in the most recent entries of the encoded **MJ documents**

passed on to Mulder by the **Thinker,** alongside Scully's name ["Anasazi"]

BAUER, ERIC: A basketball player at Grover Cleveland Alexander High School in Comity. During a practice game he crashes into a table on the sidelines, spilling lemonade all over **Terri Roberts** and **Margi Kleinjan.** When he later goes to retrieve a basketball under the bleachers, the bleachers close on him, crushing him to death. ["Syzygy"]

BAUVAIS, PIERRE: A Haitian witch doctor and voodoo high priest. He's kept imprisoned by **Col. Jacob Wharton,** who is also secretly into voodoo. ["Fresh Bones"]

BAYSIDE FUNERAL HOME: San Francisco mortuary where a Chinese man is murdered in the crematorium. ["Hell Money"]

BEAR: The civilian pilot who flies Mulder, Scully, and their team from **Jimmy Doolittle Airfield** in Nome, Alaska, to Icy Cape. When an infected dog attacks him, Bear becomes infected by the ice worm microorganism, but covers up his symptoms. While he does not harm anyone as a result of his infection, he dies when the ice worm is removed from his

neck, making him its sixth victim. ["Ice"]

BEAR CREEK STATE PARK: Two escaped convicts from the **Cumberland State Correctional Facility** kill a father of two in the men's room at this Virginia park and steal his family's motor home, leaving the widow and orphans stranded. ["F. Emasculata"]

BEATTY, MELVIN: The FBI's arson specialist at the Washington office, he does not believe in spontaneous human combustion and postulates the use of an accelerant, such as argotypoline or other rocket fuel, in a series of arsons and murders later linked with the pyrokinetic **Cecil L'ively.** Beatty helps Scully devise a character profile of the arsonist. ["Fire"]

BEHEMOTH: A.k.a. Lord **Kinbote;** a.k.a. the Behemoth from the Planet Harryhausen. A real alien who kidnaps **Harold Lamb** and **Chrissy Giorgio,** along with two military men disguised as aliens (**Lt. Jack Sheaffer** and **Col. Robert Vallee**). ["Jose Chung's *From Outer Space*"]

BELIEVER: The name of one of the phony Gray Aliens who interrogate people they abduct. ["Jose Chung's *From Outer Space*"]

BELLEFLEUR, OREGON: The site of five mysterious deaths, where Scully and Mulder have their first mission together. [Pilot]

BELT, LT. COL. MARCUS AURELIUS: A former astronaut who went on to become head of the Viking Orbiter project, and eventually headed the space shuttle program. As head of the Viking program, Belt denied that the giant sculpted face reported on Mars was anything more than an optical illusion created by erosion. However, he knows this is not true: while spacewalking as an astronaut, he was possessed by a mysterious space entity, somehow related to the face, that has controlled him ever since. This almost leads him to sabotage a shuttle mission in the 1990s, but he unconsciously alerts communications commander **Michelle Generoo,** who in turn alerts the FBI. Realizing almost too late what he has done, he provides the information needed to save the shuttle flight, then jumps out a thirtieth-floor window in Houston. ["Space"]

BENNETT, DR. M.: Director of the **Luther Stapes Center for Reproductive Medicine.** Explains in vitro fertilization, or egg implantation, to Mulder and Scully and reveals that the

Simmons family used the same procedure. Also reveals the reasons for **Dr. Sally Kendrick**'s dismissal from the Center. ["Eve"]

BERENDAUM, DR. BAMBI: A beautiful entomologist from the USDA Agricultural Research Service, she is studying what cockroaches respond to in order to better determine how to eliminate them. ["War of the Coprophages"]

BERNSTEIN, DANIEL: A cryptologist at FBI headquarters in Washington. He agrees to examine **Kevin Morris**'s handwriting in exchange for Mulder's tickets to a Redskins–Giants game. ["Conduit"]

BERTRAM, TED: The owner of Ted's Bait & Tackle on Heuvelmans Lake in Georgia. He's a huge **Big Blue** fan, although he's never actually seen it. He sells Big Blue souvenirs in his store and makes fake Big Blue footprints around the lake to maintain interest and lure tourists. One night while he's making the tracks, something snatches him and pulls him into the lake. Was he eaten by his hobby? ["Quagmire"]

BERUBE, DR. TERRENCE ALLEN: Graduated Harvard Med in 1974. Works on the **Human Genome Project** in

the Molecular Research Lab at the EmGen Corporation in Gaithersburg, Maryland. He conducts experiments on human beings by injecting them with extraterrestrial DNA. ["The Erlenmeyer Flask"]

BETA TEAM: A military unit involved in **Operation Falcon,** headed by a **Lt. Fraser.** This unit corners the alien pilot, only to be blasted by an intense white light. Team members closest to the blast are obliterated; Fraser and Jackson suffer severe burns. Four members of Beta Team survive and are sent to the Johns Hopkins Burn Unit; they have not been identified. ["Fallen Angel"]

BETHANY MEDICAL CENTER: In Aubrey, Missouri. Where **Det B. J. Morrow** is taken after she claims she was attacked by **Harry Cokely.** ["Aubrey"]

BETHESDA NAVAL HOSPITAL: A renowned hospital in Bethesda, Maryland, where U.S. presidents are often treated. Mulder and Scully are called there to take a look at two corpses whose throats seem to have been crushed from the inside. ["Shadows"] FBI agent **Jack Willis** is revived here after being shot by **Warren James Dupre** in a bank shootout. ["Lazarus"] **Lt. Richard Harper** dies here, apparently of accelerated aging; Scully and Mulder are treated here for the same affliction, but survive, thanks to Scully's field notes and **Dr. Laskos.** ["Dod Kalm"]

BETHESDA SLEEP DISORDER CENTER: Where **Walter Skinner** had been receiving treatment for three months prior to the mysterious murder of **Carina Sayles.** Skinner had been experiencing a recurring dream in which he's confronted by an old woman. ["Avatar"]

"BEYOND THE SEA": A song recorded by Bobby Darin. It was playing on the radio when **William Scully** proposed to his wife in the late 1950s, and was played at his funeral service as well. **Luther Lee Boggs** sings it when he first meets Dana Scully. ["Beyond the Sea"]

BIG BLUE: The name given by locals to a mysterious serpent that lives in **Heuvelmans Lake** in Georgia. Mulder thinks Big Blue might just be a serpent serial killer, after people start vanishing at the lake and some turn up dead. Mulder thinks it might be a prehistoric plesiosaur. The killer in the lake turns out to be an alligator, and Mulder

just misses catching a glimpse of Big Blue when he turns away moments before it appears on the surface of the lake under a full moon. ["Quagmire"]

THE BIG BOPPER: Stage name of J. P. Richardson, best known for his 1950s hit "Chantilly Lace." The Bopper was a passenger on the doomed airplane flight that also claimed the life of Buddy Holly. The young **Clyde Bruckman** was a big fan of the Bopper. Believing that the Bopper was on that airplane thanks to a fateful coin toss, he tells Mulder that his obsession with the chance nature of the Bopper's death eventually triggered his own psychic ability to foresee people's deaths. (In reality, it was Ritchie Valens who won his seat through the flip of a coin. The lucky person who lost the coin toss was Waylon Jennings.) ["Clyde Bruckman's Final Repose"]

BIG CITY HOSPITAL: In Providence, Rhode Island, where Mrs. Mulder is taken after she has a stroke. ["Talitha Cumi"]

BILAC, DR. ALONSO: A brilliant and impetuous archaeologist born in Brazil. He opposes **Dr. Carl Roosevelt**'s plans to take sacred Secona artifacts from Ecuador to the United

States. He may have killed several people, including Roosevelt, because of his beliefs in this matter . . . or he may have been possessed by an ancient jaguar spirit. His mutilated body is found in the sewers beneath the Boston Museum of Natural History. ["Teso dos Bichos"]

BINGHAMPTON GLOBE & MAIL: A local newspaper in Binghampton, Pennsylvania, upstate from Scranton. It runs an ad featuring the face of the three identical doctors murdered by the **Pilot;** the ad leads Mulder to **Dr. Aaron Baker** in Syracuse, New York, but he arrives too late. The ad may have been placed by the Pilot, masquerading as CIA agent **Ambrose Chapel.** ["Colony"]

BIODIVERSITY PROJECT: The research project that brings **Dr. Robert Torrence** to Costa Rica in search of new biological samples. Presumed to have been sponsored by **Pinck Pharmaceuticals.** ["F. Emasculata"]

BISHOP, JUDY: The mother of **Michelle Bishop.** ["Born Again"]

BISHOP, JIM: Father of Michelle, who is now divorced from Judy. ["Born Again"]

BISHOP, MICHELLE: An eight-year-old girl in whom the

psychic spirit of a murdered policeman has emerged. She lives at 121 Shady Lane, Orchard Park, New York. When she is found alone near the 14th Precinct station in Buffalo, New York, and is taken into the station, she is interviewed by **Rudy Barbala,** whom she kills by using psychic powers to hurl him through a window to the street below. She is terrified of water and refuses to go swimming. ["Born Again"]

BITUEN, GUNG: An Asian orderly at the **Excelsis Dei Convalescent Home.** He's helping the old men who live there by giving them a special drug he extracts from mushrooms in the basement. The drug contains ibotenic acid, a powerful hallucinogen. ["Excelsis Dei"]

BLACK CROW MISSILE COMPLEX: Allegedly abandoned military site in North Dakota where a recovered alien craft is stored. Also the last resting place of **Alex Krycek.** ["Apocrypha"]

BLAINE, LT.: A Cleveland policeman who informs Mulder and Scully of the 911 call that leads to **Virgil Incanto.** ["2Shy"]

BLEDSOE, DR. ELLEN: The Philadelphia county medical examiner, who confirms that

Howard Graves is dead and provides the autopsy report to prove it. ["Shadows"]

THE BLESSING WAY: A Navajo Indian healing ceremony for those who are near death. It is used to save Mulder's life and give him insight into his mission. ["The Blessing Way"]

BLEVINS, SCOTT (SPECIAL AGENT IN CHARGE): Advises Scully that Mulder should not investigate events at **Ellens Air Force Base** in Idaho, as the case has been reclassified as a strictly military affair, but does not interfere, hoping the case will discredit Mulder. ["Deep Throat"] Intends to deny Mulder permission to pursue the disappearance of **Ruby Morris,** but is convinced otherwise by Scully. ["Conduit"] Arranges for Mulder and Scully to assist CIA agents Webster and Saunders. ["Shadows"] Blevins works in the violent-crime division of the FBI training facility at Quantico, Virginia, and assigns Scully to work with Mulder on the X-Files. [Pilot]

BLOCKHEAD, DR.: An escape artist who emerges from the ground beneath **Jerald Glazebrook**'s coffin at his funeral and proceeds to pound a spike into his own chest. **Sheriff Hamilton** is not amused. Dr. Blockhead claims to be from Yemen. His real name is Jeffrey Swaim and he's from Milwaukee. ["Humbug"]

BLUE BERET UFO RETRIEVAL TEAM: A secret government force dispatched to the site of any detected contact with extraterrestrials where evidence might be found. This team has the authority to kill any unauthorized personnel discovered at the site of a genuine UFO crash. ["Little Green Men"]

BLUE DEVIL BREWERY: In Morrisville, Virginia. **Lucas Jackson Henry** dies there while fleeing the law. As predicted by **Luther Lee Boggs,** he dies under the sign of the devil: the brewery's logo. ["Beyond the Sea"]

BLUE EARTH, IOWA: After Mulder is rescued from the **Quarantine Car** by **X,** an anonymous 911 call is placed from Blue Earth, Iowa, to come and pick up the injured FBI agent. ["731"]

BLUE RIDGE MOUNTAINS: The location of Heuvelmans Lake. ["Quagmire"]

BLUE "SAMANTHA": An alien clone in blue surgical garb whom Mulder meets at the **Women's Health Services Center** in Rockville, Maryland. She, along with the rest of the "Samantha" clones, is killed by the **Pilot.** ["End Game"]

BOAR'S HEAD: A tavern in Sioux City, Iowa, where Mulder goes to look for **Ruby Morris**'s alleged boyfriend, **Greg Randall.** Instead he meets a biker named **Kip,** who has a UFO tattoo. ["Conduit"]

BOB: The name used by **Cecil L'ively** during his activities in the United States. This is probably the name of the caretaker he killed and replaced at Lord and Lady **Marsden**'s Cape Cod retreat. ["Fire"]

BOCKS, MOE: A special agent for the FBI who calls on Mulder and Scully after he finds a grave desecrated in Minneapolis. ["Irresistible"]

BOGGS, LUTHER LEE: A multiple murderer who killed all the animals in his housing complex when he was a child of six; strangled five relatives at a Thanksgiving dinner when he was thirty; and embarked on a serial-killing spree, committing many more murders before being apprehended in 1985. Boggs was about to be executed in 1992 but the execution was stayed; he claims this near-death experience provided him with psychic channeling abilities. Boggs leads lawmen to the fugitive **Lucas Jackson Henry,** but whether this was due to psychic knowledge or to communication with Henry is uncertain. Boggs's second trip to the North Carolina gas chamber, in 1993, is not interrupted. ["Beyond the Sea"]

BOISE STREET: The escaped tiger from the **Fairfield Zoo** turns up near a fast-food restaurant here. **Ed Meecham** is forced to shoot and kill the tiger when the big cat moves to attack **Willa Ambrose.** ["Fearful Symmetry"]

BONAPARTE, CHESTER: A ten-year-old boy who greets Mulder and Scully at the Folkstone Processing Center. He sells Mulder a magic charm of protection. Chester later turns out to be a ghost. ["Fresh Bones"]

BONNECAZE, SPECIAL AGENT: He is going through the material in **Walter Skinner**'s office after the Assistant Director becomes the suspect in a murder. He tells Mulder that Skinner is also being investigated by the FBI in this matter. ["Avatar"]

BOSHAM, ENGLAND: A town seventy miles southwest of London, where **Cecil L'ively** was employed as a gardener on the estate of an aristocrat, whose death by fire he caused. ["Fire"]

BOULLE, PETER: A park ranger who found the body that attracted Mulder to the Atlantic City murders. At first he is tight-lipped, but later admits that he's seen the Devil and his traces. Close to retirement, he doesn't want to jeopardize his retirement benefits, but later goes out on a limb for Mulder and Scully. ["The Jersey Devil"]

BOZOFF, AGENT: Relieves Mulder of his boring surveillance duty so that he can go on his new assignment. ["The Host"]

BRADDOCK HEIGHTS, MARYLAND: A small town where some TV sets have been wired to receive a special signal that drives viewers to kill. ["Wetwired"]

BRAIDWOOD: One of the phony names used by Mulder and Scully to get inside a complex where an E.B.E. (extraterrestrial biological entity) is apparently being held. Braidwood is the name of the actor who played Frohike. ["E.B.E."]

BRAUN, DR. SHEILA: Developmental psychologist at Brylin Psychiatric Hospital who sees **Michelle Bishop** twice a week. ["Born Again"]

BRAY, ANSEL: A photographer who is an expert on **Big Blue,** the mysterious serpent that lives in **Heuvelmans Lake.** He's determined to get a photo of Big Blue that will leave him set for life, but gets swallowed by his ambition. ["Quagmire"]

BREM: FBI agent in charge of the tactical (SWAT) operations aspect of the **Duane Barry** hostage situation. ["Duane Barry"]

BRENMAN: A graduate student whom Scully interviews as a possible suspect in the fat-sucking-vampire murders. The real perpetrator is **Virgil Incanto.** ["2Shy"]

BREWER, WESLEY: A trucker barreling down Route 7 near Fairfield, Idaho, who suddenly sees a ten-foot-tall elephant in the road in front of him. He's barely able to stop in time, whereupon the elephant turns and runs past the truck. ["Fearful Symmetry"]

BRIGGS, FRANK: A police detective who once hunted **Eugene Tooms,** he now lives at the dilapidated Lynn Acres Retirement Home, where Scully goes to see him to obtain information on one of the earlier crimes committed by Tooms years before. When Briggs was a sheriff investigating the Powhattan Mill murders in 1933, he suspected Tooms but could not indict him; he has collected evidence over the years, however, including photos of Tooms at the time of his 1963 murders. ["Squeeze" and "Tooms"]

BRIGHT WHITE PLACE: Where abductees claim they have been taken, but were they taken there by humans or by aliens? ["Nisei"]

BRISENTINE, AGENT: Tells Mulder that his new assignment is a murder in Newark, New Jersey, and that the reassignment request was made by Assistant Director **Walter Skinner** himself. ["The Host"]

BRODEUR, LEO: The warden of **Eastpoint State Penitentiary,** who oversees the execution of **"Neech" Manley.** He believes the murders committed after Manley's death are the work of an accomplice, not of a reincarnated spirit. He beats the prisoner **Sammon Roque** in an attempt to find out who's on Manley's revenge list. Brodeur is number five on Manley's list, and dies in a car wreck with Manley's fingers around his throat. ["The List"]

BROTHER AARON: The member of the **Kindred** who collapses during Mulder and Scully's dinner with the religious group. His body is subjected to a strange ritual and placed in a hivelike crypt, where it undergoes an apparent gender transformation and is revived. ["Genderbender"]

BROTHER ANDREW: The member of the **Kindred** who offers to help Scully and Mulder, but then tries to seduce Scully with his pheromonic powers—possibly an attempt to kill her. He was the closest friend of the runaway Kindred named **Marty.** ["Genderbender"]

BROTHER OAKLEY: The member of the **Kindred** who

insists that Mulder and Scully give up their guns. ["Genderbender"]

BROTHER WILTON: The member of the **Kindred** who becomes angry at Mulder's questions but is censured by **Sister Abby** for expressing rage. Mulder suspects that the outbreak was an act intended to put an end to his questions. ["Genderbender"]

BROWN, DEBORAH: Member of a witches' coven. **Calcagni** kills her while he is under the domination of the demon. ["Die Hand Die Verletzt"]

BROWNING: The police pathologist who examines the burned and blackened body of the Son. ["3"]

BRUCKMAN, CLYDE: The first genuine psychic encountered by Mulder, Bruckman is an aging insurance salesman who possesses one paranormal ability: he can see the way people are destined to die. His greatest regret is his inability to guess the winning Lotto numbers. Scully mistakes Bruckman's prediction of his own final moments as a pass at her. After helping Mulder and Scully capture the serial killer known as the **Puppet,** Bruckman commits suicide with sleeping pills and a plastic bag. When Scully discovers his body, she is next to him, fulfill-

ing his prediction that they would wind up in bed together. ["Clyde Bruckman's Final Repose"]

BRUMFIELD, ELLEN: A customer on **Donnie Pfaster**'s frozen food delivery route. He steals some discarded hair from her bathroom wastebasket. ["Irresistible"]

BRUMFIELD, LISA: The sixteen-year-old daughter of Ellen Brumfield. **Donnie Pfaster** steals some discarded hair from her bathroom wastebasket. ["Irresistible"]

BRUNDTLAND, TORK: Norwegian coaster captain who refuses to take Mulder and Scully to their desired coordinates, and acts as if he's afraid to go there. ["Dod Kalm"]

BRUNO: Teenage boy who dies under mysterious circumstances. ["Syzygy"]

BRUSKIN, PHIL: An older FBI agent who has traded in his cigarettes for nicotine gum, which he hates; present at the scene of **Tommy Philips**'s murder when **Jack Willis** reappears. Bruskin tracks Willis and Scully to **Lula Philips**'s apartment, only to discover all three missing, and follows the case to its end with Mulder. ["Lazarus"]

BRYLIN PSYCHIATRIC HOSPITAL: Where **Dr. Sheila Braun** counsels **Michelle**

Bishop, an eight-year-old girl with emotional problems. ["Born Again"]

BRYON, SEN. RICHARD: First-term senator who pulls the plug on the project designed to scan the sky for radio transmissions of an intelligent extraterrestrial origin. ["Little Green Men"]

BUCHANON, DR. HARVEY: A doctor who died in an arson fire at an abortion clinic in Teaneck, New Jersey. His name appears on a list of similar deaths e-mailed to Mulder by an anonymous source. Mulder is baffled upon learning that all three doctors, although apparently unrelated, were identical — and no body was recovered in any of the cases. ["Colony"]

BUDAHAS, ANITA: The wife of Col. Robert Budahas, who reports her husband's incarceration by the military as a kidnapping in the hope that the FBI might be able to secure his release. When her husband is finally returned to her and her children, she refuses to believe that it is actually him, but later — probably as a result of official pressure — accepts the situation and refuses to speak to the FBI. ["Deep Throat"]

BUDAHAS, COL. ROBERT: A test pilot at **Ellens Air Force**

Base in Idaho who is arrested by military police after allegedly violating base security by stealing a military vehicle. This, apparently, is related to a mysterious mental disorientation and a strange rash that affected him two years prior to this; Mulder believes these symptoms were caused by extreme stress induced by flying experimental, UFO-based aircraft at remarkable velocities. Budahas is returned to his family after a lengthy disappearance, but he is so changed that he seems a stranger to them; although he can remember facts as specific as the Green Bay Packers' lineup in the 1968 Super Bowl, he seems to have had all memories of his career as a pilot erased. In fact, Mulder believes this is exactly what happened to him. All told, a very sad fate for an officer who once received a presidential commendation. ["Deep Throat"]

BUFFALO MUTUAL LIFE BUILDING: Where **Leon Felder** works. ["Born Again"]

BUGGER, DR.: A professional bug exterminator in his fifties. He is somehow killed by the cockroaches he comes to exterminate. ["War of the Coprophages"]

BUNDESNACHRICHTEN-DIEST BUILDING: A government building in Pullach, Germany. A German official here phoned the **Cigarette-Smoking Man** to inform him that the **MJ documents** had been stolen, after being informed himself by a Japanese diplomat. The Cigarette-Smoking Man, of course, was already aware of this. ["Anasazi"]

BURKE: A crew member on board the Canadian fishing vessel *Lisette*, which finds Lifeboat 925 from the *Uss Argent* and rescues its survivors. ["Dod Kalm"]

BURK, CHUCK: The digital imaging expert Mulder asks to examine the photos taken of **Teddy Holvey** moments before his death. Burks extracts what appears to be a ghostly image from the photo, and later identifies the ash found in the Holvey home as vibuti, a Sanskrit term meaning "holy ash." ["The Calusari"]

BURST, FRANK: The FBI agent who captures **Robert Modell**, a.k.a. Pusher, only to have him escape when a semi hits his car. Burst survives this encounter and vows to capture Modell again. A bit over-wrought, Burst lets Modell talk him into a fatal heart attack over the phone. ["Pusher"]

BUSCH, SPECIAL AGENT: At FBI headquarters in Washington, he works in the latest fingerprint analysis lab. ["Irresistible"]

BUXTON, SARAH: **Kevin Kryder** shoots a spitball at her, which sticks to her hair. ["Revelations"]

BUXTON, STAN: The coroner of Johnston County, Oklahoma, where an unusually high incidence of death by lightning attracts the attention of Mulder and Scully. ["D.P.O."]

BYERS: One of the editors of the magazine *The Lone Gunman*. ["E.B.E." and "Blood"] He informs Mulder that the **Thinker** wants to meet him. ["Anasazi"] Mulder shows him a strange video trap device. He and Frohike determine that it sends another signal in along with the normal cable TV signal, which contains tachisto-scopic images designed to influence the person watching the program. ["Wetwired"]

[C]

CABLE MAN: He has been putting strange video traps on certain homes. These emit a signal that causes people to hallucinate and commit murder. The Cable Man is killed, along with **Dr. Stroman,** by **X.** ["Wetwired"]

CALCAGNI, PETE: Member of a witches' coven who commits suicide while under control of a demon. ["Die Hand Die Verletzt"]

CALECA, LINDA: A young agent right out of the FBI academy. Partnered with **Brian Fuller,** she helps guard **Walter Skinner** after he is shot. ["Apocrypha"]

CALIFORNIA INSTITUTE OF TECHNOLOGY: Home of the volcano observatory, in Pasadena. ["Firewalker"]

CALLAHAN, FRANCES: The wife of Gen. Thomas Callahan, killed by **"Rappo" Trimble** after he kills her son, Trevor. ["The Walk"]

CALLAHAN, GEN. THOMAS: Commanding officer of Fort Evanston, Maryland. He resists the FBI's investigation into the Stans case. Like **Lt. Col. Stans,** he is haunted by the ghostly image of a soldier. After his family is killed, he learns the identity of his tormentor from Stans, and confronts **"Rappo" Trimble** in his hospital room. He is saved from Trimble's psychic attack when Stans smothers Trimble. ["The Walk"]

CALLAHAN, TREVOR: Gen. Callahan's eight-year-old son. Fingerprints discovered after Trevor sees an intruder lead to the arrest of **"Roach" Freely,** but Trevor is killed by **"Rappo" Trimble**'s astral body after Freely's arrest. ["The Walk"]

CALTROP: Spikes left in the road to disable logging trucks. ["Darkness Falls"]

CALVERT STREET: The location of the office building where **Eugene Tooms** extracts the liver of Baltimore businessman **George Usher,** shortly before killing him. ["Squeeze"]

CALUSARI: In Romanian folk culture, elders responsible for the proper performance and observance of sacred rituals. A group of them are called in by **Charlie Holvey**'s grandmother **Golda** to perform a Ritual of Separation, but they encounter numerous obstacles before gaining Mulder as an unexpected ally. ["The Calusari"]

CAMOUFLAGE MAN: Apparent leader of the troop of commandos who burn out the boxcar where Mulder hides. ["Anasazi"] He pulls over Scully's car as she drives through the desert and retrieves the printouts of the secret files (Scully does not have the **MJ** files DAT). For some reason, he and his men do not harm Scully. ["The Blessing Way"]

CAMPBELL: One of the suicides at the **Arctic Ice Core Project.** ["Ice"]

CAMUS COUNTY: Where **Fairfield,** Idaho, is located. ["Fearful Symmetry"]

CANCER MAN: The nickname Mulder gives the **Cigarette-Smoking Man.**

CAPE COD, MASSACHUSETTS: Where Lord and Lady **Marsden** bring their family to avoid death threats. ["Fire"]

CARBOBOOST: An energy drink **Robert Modell** consumes in large quantities. Imposing his will on others drains his energy and leaves him exhausted. ["Pusher"]

CARDINAL, LUIS: One of **Alex Krycek**'s partners in skulduggery, involved in the inadvertent murder of **Melissa Scully.** ["The Blessing Way"] When **Walter Skinner** ignores threats to stay off the Melissa Scully murder case, the **Cigarette-Smoking Man** assigns Cardinal to shoot him. ["Piper Maru"] When Cardinal tries to finish off Skinner, Scully captures him. He tells her where to find Krycek in North Dakota, but is killed in his cell by associates of the Cigarette-Smoking Man, who make the death look like a suicide. ["Apocrypha"]

CARL: A twelve-year old boy, one of the children **Kevin**

Kryder tells a ghost story to at the Linley Temporary Home Shelter. When Kevin is kidnapped by **Owen Lee Jarvis,** Carl gives the police artist a good description of the man. ["Revelations"]

THE CAROLINIAN: A North Carolina newspaper that runs a fake article claiming **Liz Hawley** and **Jim Summers** have been rescued from their kidnapper. Mulder planted the article to trap **Luther Lee Boggs** in a lie, but the plan backfires. ["Beyond the Sea"]

CARPENTER, DR. ANN: Works in the Microbiology Department at Georgetown University. ["The Erlenmeyer Flask"]

CARVER, COMMANDER: Los Angeles Police Department officer overseeing the investigation into the murder of **Garrett Lorre.** ["3"]

CARYL COUNTY SHERIFF'S STATION: Where Scully interviews **Terri Roberts** and Mulder interviews **Margi Kleinjan.** The two teenage girls claim that **Jay DeBoom** was possessed and then killed by Satanic worshipers who were wearing hoods and carrying black candles. ["Syzygy"]

CASCADE VOLCANO RESEARCH TEAM: Using the robot named **Firewalker,**

it is exploring the volcano at Mount Avalon. ["Firewalker"]

CASH, JOSEPH: The warden of Central Prison in Raleigh, North Carolina. He refuses Scully's request to postpone **Luther Lee Boggs**'s execution. ["Beyond the Sea"]

CASSAL, JAY: **Walter Skinner**'s divorce lawyer. ["Avatar"]

CASTOR, NURSE: The young nurse assaulted by the ghost of **Michael Holvey** when she tries to give **Charlie Holvey** a shot. ["The Calusari"]

771 CATHERINE STREET: Location, in Washington, D.C., of the **Hotel Catherine,** where the FBI tracks **Marty** of the **Kindred** through credit card use. ["Genderbender"]

CDC: Centers for Disease Control, the federal agencies with jurisdiction over infectious diseases. May have been partly responsible for the destruction of the research base at Icy Cape, Alaska. ["Ice"] **Dr. Auerbach** and **Dr. Osborne** claim to be working for the CDC, but Osborne later reveals that they actually are working for **Pinck Pharmaceuticals.** ["F. Emasculata"]

CELLBLOCK Z: The cell in the **Whiting Institute** basement that holds the extremely dangerous **Eve Six,** as well as the

late **Dr. Sally Kendrick**'s two clones. ["Eve"]

CENTRAL PRISON: The state prison in Raleigh, North Carolina, where **Luther Lee Boggs** is imprisoned and executed. ["Beyond the Sea"]

CERULEAN HAULING: One of their trucks smashes the sheriff's car carrying **Robert Modell,** enabling him to escape. Modell had been talking about cerulean blue right before the impact, somehow hypnotizing the sheriff's deputy so he could not see the truck. ["Pusher"]

CHACO CHICKEN: The sole employer operating in **Dudley, Arkansas,** founded by **Walter "Chic" Chaco.** Bodies from local rituals are sometimes disposed of in the chicken feed grinder at the company's processing plant. ["Our Town"]

CHACO, WALTER "CHIC": Founder of **Chaco Chicken** and patron of **Dudley, Arkansas,** Chaco was born in 1902 and died in 1995 but looked like a man in his sixties at the time of his death. Chaco crashed in the Pacific during World War II and spent six months living among the Jalee tribe of New Guinea, where he apparently learned how to prolong human life through cannibalistic rituals. He founded

Chaco Chicken, as well as Dudley's bizarre version of a town picnic, upon his return from the war. Chaco loses his life when the townspeople turn against him, but his body is never found. ["Our Town"]

CHAMBLISS, DET.: Plainclothesman in Hollywood, investigating the murder of **Garrett Lorre.** ["3"]

CHANEY, SAM: An FBI agent who disappeared in 1942. He and his partner **Tim Ledbetter** were early experts on "stranger killings" (now known as serial killings). His body is found in a shallow grave in a vacant lot in 1995. ["Aubrey"]

CHAO, GLEN: A young Chinese-American detective with the San Francisco Police Department. Assigned to help Mulder and Scully investigate mysterious deaths in Chinatown, he is actually providing protection for a very sinister game. Working-class Chinese immigrants pay to enter a lottery to win a large jackpot; the catch is that they could wind up donating their own organs if they lose. Chao breaks up the game in disgust, discovers it was rigged, and rescues a participant, **Shuyang Hsin,** from having his heart removed. In retaliation, Chao

is burned alive. ["Hell Money"]

CHAPEL, AMBROSE: A CIA agent who approaches Mulder and explains that the identical doctors being killed in arson fires are the product of Soviet genetic experiments, planted in the United States to sabotage medical facilities in case of war, and that the Russians were killing them off with help from the U.S. government. He is actually the shape-shifting alien hit man known as the **Pilot.** ["Colony"]

CHAREZ, DANIEL: The court-appointed lawyer who represented **"Neech" Manley** eleven years before his execution. He felt he had been too young and inexperienced to defend Manley competently. He is smothered to death, the fourth victim of Manley's revenge from beyond the grave. ["The List"]

CHARLIE: The plant engineer at the Newark County sewage processing plant. ["The Host"]

CHARLOTTE'S DINER: A roadside restaurant in Craiger, Maryland, where Mulder and Scully meet **Walter Skinner** after their narrow escape from covert government forces at the **Strughold Mine.** They argue over turning over the DATs in order to save their

lives; Scully and Skinner win the argument. ["Paper Clip"]

CHARTERS, MICHELLE: A nurse at the **Excelsis Dei Convalescent Home** who is raped by an unseen force in one of the rooms. ["Excelsis Dei"]

CHARYN, DR. PENELOPE: Works at the **Grissom** Sleep Disorder Center in Stamford, Connecticut. ["Sleepless"]

CHECKPOINT ALPHA: The checkpoint where Mulder bypasses military security, enters a secured crash site in Wisconsin, and observes the remains of an alien spacecraft. ["Fallen Angel"]

CHESAPEAKE LOUNGE: The bar in the Ambassador Hotel in Washington, D.C., where **Walter Skinner** picks up a woman, takes her to his room, and wakes up the next morning to find her lying dead next to him. ["Avatar"]

CHICK: She and her friend **Stoner** witness the cockroach attack on **Dude.** ["War of the Coprophages"] She and Stoner turn up at **Heuvelmans Lake** in time to see **Snorkel Dude** get pulled underwater by a mysterious creature. ["Quagmire"]

CHOC-O-SAURUS: A chocolate treat, shaped like a dinosaur, favored by the unwilling psychic **Clyde Bruckman.**

["Clyde Bruckman's Final Repose"]

CHUNG, JOSE: Author of the novels *The Lonely Buddha* and *The Caligarian Candidate.* His publisher has assigned him the task of writing a nonfiction work about alien abduction. Chung calls it "nonfiction science fiction." He spent three months in Klass County, Washington, investigating an alien abduction case and everyone he spoke to had a different interpretation of what happened. He interviews Scully because she investigated the case (see also **Diana Lesky** and **Reynard Muldrake**). ["Jose Chung's *From Outer Space*"]

CHURCH OF THE RED MUSEUM: A strange religious cult in Delta Glen, Wisconsin. Their leader, **Richard Odin,** came to Wisconsin from California and bought a cattle ranch. They are all vegetarians and have made the five hundred head of cattle their pets. They believe that those who slaughter flesh also slaughter their own souls. They dress in white muslin and look like Sikhs, except that their turbans are red. ["Red Museum"]

CIA: One of the people who interrogate **Chrissy Giorgio.** At first she remembers him as looking like a Gray Alien.

["Jose Chung's *From Outer Space*"]

CIGARETTE-SMOKING MAN: Mulder calls him "Cancer Man." A government insider who does not approve of the X-Files because of the secrets they get close to, even going so far as to hide away evidence of the existence of UFOs [pilot episode]. He apparently pulls **Alex Krycek**'s strings throughout the **Duane Barry** incident, but his motives remain unclear. ["Ascension"] Tries to set up and discredit Mulder in the *F. Emasculata* outbreak, although he claims no knowledge of the disease. If Mulder had gone public with the information on the disease, he would have had no corroboration. ["F. Emasculata"] He is probably behind the contamination of the soft water tanks in Mulder's apartment building, an insidious plan to drive Mulder insane that doesn't work out as planned. He informs **William Mulder** that Fox is in trouble but claims he was "protecting" Fox and later denies any involvement with William's death — but this is a man whose main policy in life is "deny everything." He tells Fox that William had approved "the project," erroneously assuming that William had told Fox the truth before he died,

and tracks Fox to the Navajo reservation through his cellular phone. There he orders the destruction of **"the merchandise."** ["Anasazi"] He orders troops to set fire to the boxcar where Mulder discovers the alien corpses and presumes that Mulder has died in the fire. Unwilling to admit failure to the **Elders,** he tells them that the **MJ** files DAT tape has been recovered, an error in judgment that probably causes him more than a few sleepless nights. ["The Blessing Way"] Krycek's murder of **Melissa Scully** puts him in serious hot water with the Elders. He later claims that the DAT tape was destroyed in the car bomb explosions that "killed" Krycek, even though he knows Krycek is very much alive and has the tape in his possession. Skinner gets the upper hand over him with the help of **Albert Hosteen.** ["Paper Clip"] He retrieves the tape from an alien-possessed Krycek and then has the man sealed in a missile silo with an alien aircraft. ["Apocrypha"] **Mrs. Mulder** (Fox's mother) used to associate with CSM socially at the time that her husband, William, worked for the government, but she hates him now. When he comes to her to try to secure information she still has, she becomes violently angry, and moments after he leaves she suffers a severe and debilitating stroke. Only because **X** had been secretly observing her and made an anonymous call to 911 did she receive immediate paramedic assistance. When X shows Fox photos of CSM visiting Mrs. Mulder, Fox becomes incensed and comes close to killing him. He appears to be working closely with aliens on earth, who are perhaps mapping out colonization of the earth. ["Talitha Cumi"]

CLINE, ANDREA: One of the four teens who uses an occult book that summons a demon. ["Die Hand Die Verletzt"]

CLINE, DET.: One of the police detectives investigating a string of murders whose victims are all professional (or semi-pro) psychics of one sort or another. Cline calls in the Stupendous **Yappi** to help with the case. ["Clyde Bruckman's Final Repose"]

CLUB TEPES: Named after Vlad Tepes — a.k.a. Vlad the Impaler — of fifteenth-century Romania. Most of the people in the after-sunset club are pale-skinned and wear black. ["3"]

CLYDE: A security guard in the Eurisko Building. ["Ghost in the Machine"]

COCKROACH: An insect that is thought to have originated 350 million years ago, in the Silurian period. There are 4,000 known species. Mulder and Scully go up against roaches with artificial intelligence. ["War of the Coprophages"]

COCOON: Used by the prehistoric wood mites to imprison and kill those who disturb a certain area of the forest in the Pacific Northwest. ["Darkness Falls"]

COKELY, HARRY: A seventy-seven-year-old ex-con who went to prison in 1945 for rape and attempted murder. He carved the word "sister" on the chest of his victim, **Ruby Thibodeaux.** His weapon of choice was a strap razor. He served his time in the McCallister Penitentiary until he was released December 5, 1993. He was actually the Slash Killer but couldn't be connected to those crimes at the time. He now lives in Nebraska and needs a portable oxygen tank to get around. ["Aubrey"]

COLE, AUGUSTUS: One of the experimental subjects of **Dr. Saul Grissom**'s Vietnam-era experiments in sleep deprivation, assigned to Special Force and Recon Squad J-7. Of the thirteen original squad members, he is one of only two sur-

vivors. Cole and **Henry Willig** had four thousand confirmed kills while in Vietnam: the highest kill ratio in the Marine Corps. Cole has developed strange powers and kills Grissom with them to exact revenge. Twenty-four years after Phu Bai, the massacre of three hundred children by Recon Squad J-7, Cole decides to avenge the atrocities by murdering those he blames for creating the out-of-control killing machines. ["Sleepless"]

COLLINS: FBI agent on agent **Frank Burst**'s team. **Robert Modell** wills him to set himself on fire, but Scully douses the flames before he can be killed. ["Pusher"]

COLLINS, DR. RICHARD: A witness at the sanity hearing of **Eugene Tooms** in Baltimore. He comments favorably on the mental health of Tooms and claims he was the victim of false arrest by the FBI. ["Tooms"]

COLTON, TOM: FBI agent who trained at Quantico when Scully did. An ambitious rising star in the FBI's violent-crimes section. Asks Scully for help with a series of violent, locked-room murders in Baltimore, possibly because he's too embarrassed to ask "Spooky" Mulder for help directly. Interferes with Mulder's pursuit of the case and is reassigned to the white-collar crimes division in South Dakota. ["Squeeze"]

COMITY: A city of 38,825 which has been experiencing a rash of strange deaths. The town's motto is "The Perfect Harmony City." Astrologically speaking, Comity is in a geological vortex, sort of a cosmic G-spot. All of this culminates on January 12, when the planets come into perfect alignment. ["Syzygy"]

COMMERCIAL TRUST BUILDING: The site of a massacre committed by **Gary Taber** in Franklin, Pennsylvania. ["Blood"]

COMOX, SPECIAL AGENT: A forensics specialist who examines the piece of metal found in **Duane Barry**'s abdomen. He finds inexplicable microscopic etchings on it, resembling a bar code; it triggers a bizarre response when Scully runs it over a supermarket checkout scanner. ["Duane Barry"]

CONDUCTOR: On a train to West Virginia, Mulder gives the Conductor a gun to try to capture **Dr. Zama.** When the red-haired man (see **Malcolm Gerlach**) tries to chase down and kill the Conductor, he is just able to slam a train car door in the assassin's face,

thereby locking him in with Mulder in a car that has a bomb planted in it. ["731"]

CONNERVILLE, OKLA-HOMA: A small town where lightning strikes more people than is statistically feasible. This might be due to the proximity of the **Astadourian Lightning Observatory,** or it might have something to do with an unusual teenager named **Darin Peter Oswald.** ["D.P.O."]

THE CONUNDRUM: A circus freak living in Gibsonton, Florida, who has a jigsaw design tattooed on his entire body. He is a "geek," meaning he can eat anything: rocks, corkscrews, live crickets. Ultimately he eats **Leonard,** the misguided Siamese twin. ["Humbug"]

COOLEY, NURSE: On duty at the VA Medical Center when **Augustus Cole** somehow escapes. She claims **Dr. Pilsson** signed the order for Cole's release, which Pilsson denies. ["Sleepless"]

COUNTY ROAD A7: The main highway running past **Dudley, Arkansas.** Not a good place to stop for a picnic. ["Our Town"]

COUNTY ROAD D7: Location of the fire caused by the UFO crash near **Townsend, Wisconsin,** two miles west of the road's intersection with

Canyon Ridge. ["Fallen Angel"]

CRANDALL, JOE: A prisoner at **Tashmoo Federal Correctional Facility** who befriended **John Barnett.** Crandall was the sole beneficiary of Barnett's will. He confirms to Mulder that Barnett did not have heart problems, and discloses the operation he saw **Dr. Joe Ridley** performing on Barnett. ["Young at Heart"]

CRAZY BEDBUG MOTEL: Where the motel manager dies mysteriously and his body is found covered by cockroaches. ["War of the Coprophages"]

CREUTZFELDT-JAKOB DIS-EASE: A rare disease that eats holes in its victims' brains, reducing them to the consistency of sponges. It can be passed along by eating infected tissue, which leads to an unfortunate turn of events for the people of **Dudley, Arkansas:** twenty-seven citizens contract fatal cases, thanks to their cannibal barbecues. ["Our Town"]

CREW-CUT MAN: A government assassin who is killed by the father of a boy he kills in "Red Museum." Crew-Cut Man killed **Deep Throat** in "The Erlenmeyer Flask" and Mulder wanted to take him alive, but to no avail.

CRIKENSON, ROKY: A blue-collar utility worker in his fifties who is checking on a mysterious power outage in **Klass County, Washington.** Two black-clad men in a black Cadillac drive into his garage and spout anti-UFO gibberish. Crikenson believes they do this because he has written a manuscript called *The Truth About Aliens* in which he claims an alien he calls Lord **Kinbote** is not from outer space at all, but from the Earth's core. He quits his job with the power company and relocates to El Cajon, California, to preach to the converted. ["Jose Chung's *From Outer Space*"]

CROCKETT, ROGER: A homeless man dismembered by the **Jersey Devil.** ["The Jersey Devil"]

CROSS, DET. ALAN: A twenty-five-year veteran of the Cleveland Police Department's homicide squad who calls Mulder and Scully in on the murder of **Lauren Mackalvey.** A bit old-fashioned, he at first does not register Scully as an equal, but is soon content to let her work with her partner when he witnesses their intuitive chemistry. He is fatally slimed by **Virgil Incanto** while canvassing suspects. ["2Shy"]

CRYSTAL CITY, VIRGINIA: Headquarters of the Eurisko Corporation. ["Ghost in the Machine"]

CULVER CITY PLASMA CENTER: Los Angeles–area blood bank investigated by Mulder in his search for the people in the **Trinity** gang of vampiric killers. ["3"]

CUMBERLAND STATE CORRECTIONAL FACILITY: Virginia state prison where **Pinck Pharmaceuticals** and an unknown government agency conduct a controlled outbreak of a newly discovered disease that goes haywire when two infected prisoners escape. ["F. Emasculata"]

CURATOR: An elderly man who has a facial deformity and is in charge of the **Odditorium,** a museum of curiosa in **Gibsonton, Florida.** It's a musty place resembling an antique store. Admission is free to freaks. Among the exhibits are photos of circus freaks from years past. ["Humbug"]

[D]

DALTON, LAURA: Television reporter who covers the evacuation of **Townsend, Wisconsin,** and accepts the government's cover story about a toxic cargo spill. ["Fallen Angel"]

DALY, DR.: Intensive care doctor in charge of Scully at the Northeast Georgetown Medical Center in Washington, D.C. ["One Breath"]

DANIELS, LILLIAN: Wheelchair-bound wife of **Sheriff Maurice Daniels.** He believes **Samuel Hartley** is a fake and won't allow her to go to him to be healed. ["Miracle Man"]

DANIELS, OFFICER: Rookie cop who refuses to let **Jack Willis** enter the scene of **Tommy Philips**'s murder without his ID badge, until Scully identifies him. ["Lazarus"]

DANIELS, SHERIFF MAURICE: He believes the **Rev. Hartley** and his **Miracle Ministry** are running a scam. He ultimately has **Samuel Hartley** beaten to death. ["Miracle Man"]

DARK MATTER: Theoretical subatomic particle whose existence is proved, somewhat disastrously, by **Chester Ray Banton,** whose shadow becomes dark matter after a laboratory mishap. Thereafter, his shadow can reduce human matter into pure energy and absorb it like a black hole — fatal for anyone who touches the shadow. Banton is harmless only in the dark or in even, shadowless soft light. ["Soft Light"]

DARNELL, DET. JOE: Of the Aubrey, Missouri, police. He is the assistant of **Lt. Brian Tillman.** ["Aubrey"]

DA SILVA, DR. NANCY: Attractive but uptight civilian toxicologist who accompanies Mulder and Scully to investigate the **Arctic Ice Core Project** disaster. She is infected by the ice worm but survives after Scully and **Dr. Hodge** determine how to destroy the infection by introducing a second worm into the body. Unfortunately, this happens too late to save **Dr. Denny Murphy,** whom she killed while infected. ["Ice"]

DAT: Digital Audio Tape containing encrypted files of government conspiracy regarding UFOs. ["Paper Clip"]

DAVEY, DR. CHRISTOPHER: **Chester Ray Banton**'s business partner at **Polarity Magnetics.** He closes down the company after Banton's accident. He witnesses Banton's murder of **Det. Kelly Ryan,** and locks Banton in the accelerator chamber where the accident first occurred, intending to hand him over to the government. He is murdered by **X,** who disintegrates Davey's body in the accelerator chamber to make Mulder think Banton is dead. ["Soft Light"]

DAVIS CORRECTIONAL TREATMENT CENTER: The mental hospital in Marion, Virginia, where **Duane Barry** is held until his escape in 1994. He stabs a guard with a fountain pen, steals his gun, and takes **Dr. Del Hakkie** hostage. ["Duane Barry"]

DAWSON, SHARON: Administrator of the **Excelsis Dei Convalescent Home.** ["Excelsis Dei"]

D.C. CORRECTIONAL COMPLEX: Located in Lorton, Virginia. **John Mostow** is taken there after he's arrested for a series of murders. ["Grotesque"]

DEADHORSE, ALASKA: Mulder catches a military plane from Tacoma, Washington, to Deadhorse in his quest to catch up with the **Pilot.** ["End Game"]

DeBOOM, JAY "BOOM": Quarterback of his high school football team in Comity. A friend of **Bruno,** the boy who died under mysterious circumstances. It is believed Bruno was kidnapped and murdered by some unknown Satanic cult. Then the same thing happens to Jay: he is found in the woods, hanging from a rope. Although the verdict is suicide, some suspect foul play because Jay's is the third death of a high school boy in three months. He has actually been killed by **Margi Kleinjan** and **Terri Roberts.** At his funeral his coffin mysteriously catches on fire. When his corpse is examined, there is an image on the chest that some think resembles a horned beast. ["Syzygy"]

DEEP THROAT: Mulder's secret government contact, a

well-placed official who takes an interest in Mulder and the X-Files. When Mulder decides to investigate **Ellens Air Force Base,** Deep Throat reveals himself to warn Mulder off the case. ["Deep Throat"] Advises Mulder on the whereabouts of Eurisko Corporation founder **Brad Wilczek.** ["Ghost in the Machine"] Informs Mulder that a military operation to retrieve a crashed alien vehicle is under way in and around **Townsend, Wisconsin;** countermands FBI section chief **McGrath**'s decision to oust Mulder from the FBI following his insubordination in this case. ["Fallen Angel"] Clues Mulder in to the **Litchfield** cloning experiments and the location of **Eve Six** in the Whiting Institute. ["Eve"] Explains to Mulder that murderer **John Barnett** was negotiating with the federal government for the sale of **Dr. Joe Ridley**'s research, and that the government had known all along that Barnett was at large. ["Young at Heart"] He always tells Mulder, "Trust no one." He appears to Mulder in a vision while Mulder is undergoing the **Blessing Way** ceremony. ["The Blessing Way"] He was probably the third man who interviewed a *Zeus Faber*

crewman with **William Mulder** and the **Cigarette-Smoking Man** in 1953. ["Apocrypha"] After **Jeremiah Smith** is taken to a maximum security prison where he is interrogated by the Cigarette-Smoking Man, he gets into an argument with him and at one point Smith casually alters his appearance so that he looks like the by then deceased informant Mulder knew only as Deep Throat. ["Talitha Cumi"]

DELTA GLEN, WISCONSIN: Home of the **Church of the Red Museum,** a harmless religious cult being unfairly blamed for sinister activity. Incidents being investigated in Delta Glen by Mulder and Scully include a peeping Tom, kidnappings of teenagers, a plane crash, murder, and cattle being injected with alien DNA. ["Red Museum"]

DEN OF THE GREAT UNKNOWN: A special room of the **Odditorium.** Inside is a box that Scully opens to find — nothing! She was humbugged into paying five dollars to see what was in this room. ["Humbug"]

DEPRANIL: An enzyme-inhibiting drug used by **Dr. John Grago** to increase acetylcholine in the brains of his

Alzheimer's patients. ["Excelsis Dei"]

DEPARTMENT OF AGRICULTURE: An installation supposedly operated by this government agency is conducting experiments in Miller's Grove, Massachusetts, to determine what cockroaches respond to in order to better determine how to eliminate them. ["War of the Coprophages"]

DESMOND ARMS RESIDENT HOTEL: The sleazy dive near Washington, D.C., where **Jack Willis** kills **Tommy Philips.** Covering up his identity problems, Willis then shows up at the crime scene and misplaces the fingerprints that would have revealed him as the killer. ["Lazarus"]

DIAMOND, DR. ROGER: Scully's anthropology professor at the University of Maryland, who assists her and Mulder in the pursuit of the female **Jersey Devil.** ["The Jersey Devil"]

DICKENS, DR. JAMES: The fourth identical doctor, whose picture is e-mailed to Scully. He worked in Washington, D.C. He jumps out a second-story window in Germantown, Maryland, when he sees CIA agent **Chapel,** who then assumes his true identity as the **Pilot** and kills Dickens in an alley. Dickens's body is never found, although Scully ruins a pair of new shoes by stepping in the green residue left behind by his disintegration. ["Colony"]

DIE HAND DIE VERLETZT: "His hand is the hand that wounds." ["Die Hand Die Verletzt"]

DINWIDDIE COUNTY, VIRGINIA: Where Mulder tracks the escaped convict **Paul** by tracing the last call from a pay phone near **Angelo Garza**'s gas station. ["F. Emasculata"]

DINWIDDIE COUNTY HOSPITAL: **Paul**'s girlfriend **Elizabeth** is held here after her arrest because of her infection by the parasite that inhabits the insect *F. Emasculata*. ["F. Emasculata"]

DIXON, SGT. AL: A veteran of the Scranton, Pennsylvania, police force who arrests the **Rev. Calvin Sistrunk** as a suspect in the murder of **Dr. Landon Prince,** but the charges won't stick. ["Colony"]

DMITRI: Young Russian seaman who is trying to remove the blockage from inside a ship's sewage tank when he is attacked by a creature that pulls him into the water of the tank, where he disappears. The crew then flush the tanks, emptying them into the ocean. ["The Host"]

DOANE, JOSEPHINE: Administrator at the Washington, D.C., offices of the Navajo Nation who confirm that the documents in Scully's possession are in Navajo, and points out two words: "merchandise" and "vaccination," both modern additions to the Navajo language. She helps Scully contact **Albert Hosteen.** ["Anasazi"]

DOLE, LISA: FBI handwriting expert at the headquarters in Seattle, Washington. ["Roland"]

DOLL COLLECTOR: A victim of the serial killer known as the **Puppet,** who targets psychics. He left her eyes and intestines on the table in her living room, which is filled to the brim with her doll collection. Detectives at first can't see the link between this and the other murders until Mulder notices a cup with tea leaves in it and points out that she practiced tasseography. **Yappi,** a commercial psychic, claims the killer raped her before murdering her; **Clyde Bruckman** says she instigated the sex. ["Clyde Bruckman's Final Repose"]

DOMINION TOBACCO: A North Carolina tobacco company located in the Raleigh–Durham area. One of their executives, **Patrick**

Newirth, is reduced to a stain on a carpet after **Chester Ray Banton** knocks on his hotel room door by mistake. ["Soft Light"]

DORLAND, ROBERT: **Howard Graves**'s partner in HTG Industrial Technologies, he set up the company's illegal arms dealings with an Iranian extremist group. When Graves protested, Dorland had him murdered in a way that made it look like suicide. His subsequent attempts to silence **Lauren Kyte** aren't quite as successful. Dorland is eventually indicted for Graves's murder and a large number of federal charges. ["Shadows"]

DOUGHERTY, MRS.: **Michelle Bishop**'s latest nanny, who is mysteriously locked in the wine cellar when Michelle disappears from the house. ["Born Again"]

DRAKE, BENJAMIN: CEO of the Eurisko Corporation, mysteriously murdered by an electrical booby trap in the bathroom of his office. ["Ghost in the Machine"]

DRAPER, CAPT. JANET: Army officer at Fort Evanston, Maryland, who advises Mulder and Scully to drop the **Stans** case at the request of **Gen. Callahan.** She is drowned in a swimming pool by **"Rappo" Trimble.** Scully finds bruises on her neck, indicating a struggle. ["The Walk"]

DRUID HILL SANITARIUM: In Baltimore. **Eugene Tooms** had been housed here until a sanity hearing allowed him to be released. ["Tooms"]

DUDE: A drug user who sees a cockroach burrow into his arm through an open wound. He uses a razor blade to try to get it out and accidentally severs an artery, dying as a result. ["War of the Coprophages"]

DUDLEY, ARKANSAS: Home of **Chaco Chicken,** the town is practically ruled by **Walter Chaco,** who is as much its spiritual as economic leader. The river running through Dudley yields at least nine skeletons, including that of **George Kearns.** All are missing their skulls, and all appear to have been cooked by boiling. At least eighty-seven people disappeared near Dudley between 1944 and 1995. ["Our Town"]

DUKENFIELD, CLAUDE: The late owner of Uranus Unlimited, and a firm believer in astrology. He is killed by the **Puppet** and dumped in the woods around Shove Park, where Mulder and Scully find him with the assistance of **Clyde Bruckman** . . . who had sold him an insurance policy a few months before his death. ["Clyde Bruckman's Final Repose"]

DUNAWAY'S PUB: A tavern in Washington, D.C., where Mulder often goes. The informant known as **Deep Throat** first approaches Mulder in the men's room here in order to warn him against investigating events at **Ellens Air Force Base** in Idaho. ["Deep Throat"]

DUNHAM, PVT. HARRY: A friend of **Pvt. John McAlpin.** He reveals that **Col. Jacob Wharton** ordered the beating of inmates at the Haitian refugee center. He's later found murdered, and it emerges that he was filing a complaint against Wharton just prior to his death. ["Fresh Bones"]

DUPRE, WARREN JAMES: Born in Klamath Falls, Oregon, Dupre, age thirty, worked as a prison guard until his affair with **Lula Philips** led him to a life of crime. Their bank robberies are marked by extreme violence and seven deaths, including that of a sixty-five-year-old female teller at **Annapolis Savings and Loan.** Dupre shoots **Jack Willis** but is killed by Scully during his last robbery at the Maryland Marine Bank. Dupre has a dragon tattooed on his forearm. If one believes Willis's apparent delusion to be true, Dupre's spirit took over Willis's body and used it to be reunited with his true love, Lula. ["Lazarus"]

DURAN, DAVE: One of the four teens who uses an occult book that summons a demon. He checked out the book, *Witch Hunt: A History of the Occult in America.* ["Die Hand Die Verletzt"]

DWIGHT: Night watchman at the Skyland Mountain tram when Mulder and **Krycek** arrive there in pursuit of **Duane Barry.** He tells the agents that the tram is closed for the summer, but Mulder persuades him to start it up; Krycek disposes of Dwight while Mulder is riding the tram up the mountain. ["Ascension"]

DYER: One of a group of loggers in the Pacific Northwest who cut into an old tree and unleash ancient wood mites that attack out of self-preservation, becoming active only after sunset and before dawn. ["Darkness Falls"]

[E]

EASTON, WASHINGTON: When the thirteen-year-old **Lucy Householder** escaped from **Carl Wade** after being his prisoner for five years, she was found wandering near this town. This area is also where a tow truck driver has a strange encounter with Wade shortly after the kidnapping of **Amy Jacobs.** When the FBI suddenly arrives on Main Street, by chance Wade is there to see them pull up, and he guesses they are on to him. ["Oubliette"]

EASTPOINT STATE PENITENTIARY: In Florida. **Napoleon "Neech" Manley** is executed there for murder. His death is followed by six others. ["The List"]

E.B.E.: Extraterrestrial biological entity, essentially any creature not originally from Earth. ["E.B.E."]

ECCLESIASTES 3:19: "A man has no preeminence above a beast; for all is vanity." Biblical quote Mulder and Scully see on the marquee of a church following the end of a case involving animals that may be having their fetuses harvested by aliens in order to preserve the species. ["Fearful Symmetry"]

ECKBOM'S SYNDROME: A psychotic disorder suffered by some drug users that causes them to imagine their skin is infested with insects. ["War of the Coprophages"]

ECKERLE, DR. JEFF: President and chief science officer of **Alt.-Fuels Inc.** He

hires **Dr. Bugger** to exterminate cockroaches in his house. He witnesses the strange death of Dr. Bugger. ["War of the Coprophages"]

3243 EDMONTON STREET: The location of the industrial building in Germantown, Maryland, where **Dr. James Dickens** conducted his experiments in merging human and alien DNA. Scully finds the address on Dickens's medical bag and investigates, only to discover CIA agent **Chapel** demolishing the lab. Later investigation reveals the existence of hybrid fetuses there. ["Colony"]

EDWARDS TERMINAL: At this train station in Queensgate, Ohio, the red-haired man (see **Malcolm Gerlach**) who assassinated **Kazuo Takeo** turns up just as **Dr. Ishimaru** arrives. ["Nisei"]

EHMAN, JERRY: In August 1977 this astronomer found a transmission of apparent extraterrestrial origin on a printout and called it a "wow" signal. ["Little Green Men"]

EISENHOWER FIELD: An Air Force base in Siquannke, Alaska; Mulder is taken to the military hospital there for treatment after being found half-frozen on the icefields. ["Colony"] Doctors there treat

him for extreme hypothermia until Scully arrives and convinces them to keep his body cold; this, combined with several transfusions, clears the alien virus from his body. ["End Game"]

THE ELDERS: A group of elderly, powerful men who guard more than a few dark secrets and control the conspiracy that continues to affect the lives of Mulder and Scully. They convene at an office high above 46th Street in New York when the **Thinker** steals the **MJ** data and gives it to Mulder. The **Cigarette-Smoking Man** is apparently one of them, but he is obviously answerable to higher-ranking members such as the **Well-Manicured Man.** ["The Blessing Way"] They are not pleased when the French obtain information about a sensitive site in the North Pacific. Mulder gets the phone number of their office from a package in **Krycek**'s locker, but the number is disconnected after his brief conversation with the Well-Manicured Man. ["Apocrypha"]

ELDRIDGE, USS: U.S. Navy vessel involved in the alleged **Philadelphia Experiment** in 1944. ["Dod Kalm"]

ELIZABETH: Girlfriend of the escaped convict **Paul** (and

mother of his child). She is infected by *F. Emasculata* by Paul's fellow escapee **Steve.** She is arrested by U.S. **marshal Deke Tapia** while Paul is out and remains silent until Mulder convinces her to reveal Paul's destination by explaining the public health risk involved. ["F. Emasculata"]

ELLEN: Scully's best friend, a housewife and mother who tries to set Scully up with a divorced acquaintance, Rob. ["The Jersey Devil"]

ELLENS AIR FORCE BASE: In southwest Idaho. Mulder believes the government has developed top-secret aircraft there that utilize alien UFO flight technology salvaged from the 1947 Roswell crash. This base is so classified, it does not even appear on the U.S. Geographical Survey map of Idaho. Six pilots have been reported missing in action there since 1963. Mulder and Scully investigate the apparent disappearance of test pilot **Robert Budahas** here but encounter serious opposition from the military. Mulder believes he witnessed something incriminating here, but cannot recall anything after his brief incarceration by the military; he suspects they somehow "erased" his memories. Scully's primary recollection of

this investigation is of the extreme measures she resorted to in order to secure Mulder's release. The informant known only as **Deep Throat** first approaches Mulder in relation to this unresolved case. ["Deep Throat"]

ELLICOTT, REGGIE: A member of Parliament who may or may not have been blown up with a car bomb triggered by a car stereo; referred to in a practical joke played on Mulder by his former Oxford classmate, **Phoebe Green.** ["Fire"]

ELLIS, JAMES: The father of Ellis & Sons clothiers. A Memphis murder victim of the vampiric **Trinity.** ["3"]

EMBASSY ROW: In Washington, D.C., where a limo driver picks up **Kazuo Takeo,** the Japanese diplomat Mulder had captured at the scene of a murder. It is a trap: Takeo is murdered in the limo by a red-haired man (see **Malcolm Gerlach**) to cover up Takeo's sloppy work in **Allentown.** ["Nisei"]

EMIL: Teenage boy who sneaks onto **Ellens Air Force Base** to watch mysterious lights in the sky; he and his girlfriend Zoe help Mulder infiltrate the base. ["Deep Throat"]

ERIKSON: Chief seismologist of the **Cascade Volcano**

Research Team, whose body is found by the robot nicknamed **Firewalker.** ["Firewalker"]

ESCALANTE: One of the human–alien hybrids, who escapes execution at the **Hansen's Research Center Compound.** He is found by Scully while she is searching the place. ["731"]

EUBANKS, WALTER: FBI agent from the Seattle office who is investigating the kidnapping of **Amy Jacobs.** ["Oubliette"]

EURISKO BUILDING: Headquarters of the Eurisko Corporation. The building is run by a central operating system (COS) that creator **Brad Wilczek** secretly provided with a prototype artificial intelligence program that develops a mind of its own. ["Ghost in the Machine"]

EVE SIX: An extremely intelligent, psychotic, and dangerous product of the **Litchfield Project,** imprisoned in **Cellblock Z** of the **Whiting Institute** since 1983. She reveals that all the Adams and Eves are dead except her and two others, Eves Seven and Eight, who escaped years earlier. ["Eve"]

EVE EIGHT: The last surviving **Litchfield Project** child at large, she escaped imprisonment in 1985 and has since assumed the identify of a doctor with high military security, **Dr. Alicia Hughes.** ["Eve"]

EXCELSIS DEI CONVALES-CENT HOME: In Worcester, Massachusetts. The site of attacks by invisible entities. ["Excelsis Dei"]

66 EXETER STREET: The site of **Eugene Tooms**'s hideout in Baltimore. Tooms has used Apartment 103 in this building at least since 1903, according to the census; the first victim to fit Tooms's murder MO lived in Apartment 203, according to the X-File on this pattern of murders. Mulder and Scully find a strange, slimy nest festooned with Tooms's trophies there. ["Squeeze"]

EXOSKELETON: Mulder finds a cockroach exoskeleton and accidentally crushes it in his hand, which bleeds because the exoskeleton is made out of some kind of metal. ["War of the Coprophages"]

[F]

FACIPHAGA EMASCULATA: An insect of tropical origin, discovered by **Dr. Robert Torrence** in the jungles of Costa Rica. **Pinck Pharmaceuticals** is interested in it because it secretes a dilating enzyme, but the company is unaware that the bug is also

host to a parasite that attacks the human immune system. To further complicate matters, *F. Emasculata* has a complicated reproductive cycle. Its larvae grow in human boils, and spread from host to host after the boils explode when the victim dies. A total of eighteen people, mostly prisoners, died in an outbreak of this unnamed disease, which is covered up by Pinck with government assistance. ["F. Emasculata"]

FAIRFAX MERCY HOSPITAL: The hospital in Washington where **Robert Modell** obtains his prescription for **Tegretol.** ["Pusher"]

FAIRFIELD COUNTY SOCIAL SERVICES HOSTEL: **Teena Simmons** is housed here temporarily after the bizarre death of her father. ["Eve"]

FAIRFIELD, IDAHO: The site of the Fairfield Zoo, where many strange things have been happening. After an elephant escapes and a federal construction worker is killed by an unseen presence, Mulder and Scully are sent to investigate. ["Fearful Symmetry"]

FAIRFIELD ZOO: Ganesha the elephant escapes from here and then dies from exhaustion. Mulder and Scully learn that no animal at this zoo has ever had a successful pregnancy.

There have been other strange escapes and disappearances of animals from the zoo. ["Fearful Symmetry"]

FAIRLY, JUDY: Employee of **Lorraine Kelleher** at an escort service in the Georgetown area of the District of Columbia. When her boss is murdered, Fairly helps Mulder trap the man who did it. ["Avatar"]

FALLEN ANGEL: The code used by **Col. Henderson** to denote a downed alien craft and/or its occupant. ["Fallen Angel"]

FARMINGTON, NEW MEXICO: Where Scully takes Mulder after shooting him, en route to meet **Albert Hosteen.** ["Anasazi"]

FARRADAY, DR. PAUL: A biologist working in Striker's Cove on **Heuvelmans Lake.** He is concerned about the dwindling population of a rare kind of frog. ["Quagmire"]

FAST-FOOD RESTAURANT: Where **Lucy Householder** is working as a trainee when she suffers a strange nosebleed the instant **Amy Jacobs** is kidnapped by **Carl Wade.** ["Oubliette"]

THE FATHER: An older man, one of the vampiric trio of killers. He is killed by **Kristen Kilar,** who then burns his body. ["3"]

FAULKNER, BLAINE: A sci-fi buff in his late twenties, who wears a *Space: Above and Beyond* T-shirt to indicate that he's a real loser. He tells Chung that he wants to be abducted by aliens because he is so bored with life. He describes those who investigated the missing teenagers and their story. He's actually talking about Mulder and Scully, and his description of them is quite bizarre. He says Mulder looked like a "mandroid." He finds a dead alien in a field, who is actually a man wearing a Gray Alien costume. ["Jose Chung's *From Outer Space*"]

FEEJEE MERMAID: The half-man, half-fish creature in an old drawing done by **Hepcat Helm.** The creature is a "genuine fake" P. T. Barnum once exhibited, consisting of a mummified monkey sewn onto the tail of a fish. ["Humbug"]

FELDER, LEON: A thirty-seven-year-old insurance salesman who involves **Tony Fiore** and **Rudy Barbala** in illegal activity. Felder and Barbala kill police officer **Charlie Morris.** Felder is strangled by his scarf when **Michelle Bishop** uses her psychic powers to trap it in the door of a moving bus. ["Born Again"]

FENIG, MAX: A UFO enthusiast Mulder meets while imprisoned by the military during **Operation Falcon.** A member of NICAP (the National Investigative Committee of Aerial Phenomenon). Somewhat paranoid, Fenig is a crackpot version of Mulder who travels the country in an Airstream trailer fitted with all sorts of high-tech equipment. He provides Mulder with information about **Deputy Sheriff Jason Wright,** recorded from his radio scanners. Fenig has a small diamond-shaped scar behind his left ear and claims to have started having epileptic blackouts at the age of ten in South Dakota. Mulder believes that Fenig was a UFO abductee; Fenig himself professes no such belief. He is possibly reabducted by aliens in **Townsend, Wisconsin;** the military's claim that his body was found is probably false. ["Fallen Angel"]

FICICELLO FROZEN FOODS: Where **Donnie Pfaster** gets a job after being fired from the **Janelli-Heller Funeral Home.** He flirts with the receptionist there. ["Irresistible"]

FIEBLING, MR.: Teacher of the night school course "Intro to Mythology and Comparative Religion" that **Donnie Pfaster** attends. ["Irresistible"]

50 GREATEST CONSPIRACIES OF ALL TIME: A book about conspiracies by Vankin and Whelan, a favorite of the **Thinker.** ["Anasazi"]

FINGERS, DR.: A hypnotist who puts **Chrissy Giorgio** under to find out what really happened to her and **Harold Lamb** the night they disappeared for several hours. ["Jose Chung's *From Outer Space*"]

FINLEY, REV. PATRICK: As he is giving a sermon during a worship service, his hands bleed like the wounds of the crucifixion. Afterward he is murdered by the Millennium Man (**Simon Gates**). It is later discovered that the display of **stigmata** was faked. ["Revelations"]

FIORE, TONY: A police detective in his mid thirties who was the partner of **Charlie Morris.** He felt guilty over his connection to Morris's death and so he married Morris's widow. ["Born Again"]

FIORE, ANITA: Wife of Tony Fiore. She is the former wife of murdered policeman **Charlie Morris.** ["Born Again"]

FIREWALKER: A robot survey device invented by **Daniel Trepkos** for working inside a volcano. It looks like a large titanium bug. ["Firewalker"]

FIRST CHURCH OF THE REDEMPTION: In Waynesburg, Pennsylvania, where the **Rev. Finley** gives a sermon right before he's murdered by the Millennium Man. ["Revelations"]

FIRST ELDER: The syndicate leader previously seen in "The Blessing Way" and "Paper Clip." He interrogates Scully when she is captured at the **Hansen's Research Center Compound** in Perkey, West Virginia. In defending the work of **Dr. Ishimaru,** he states, "In a world of madmen, knowledge supersedes morality." He claims Ishimaru experimented on lepers, the homeless, and the insane, and that they were subjected to radiation tests and diseases. Scully believes him because Ishimaru did the same things during World War II. The Elder tells Scully that the man locked in the train car with Mulder has **hemorrhagic fever,** and isn't really a human–alien hybrid. ["731"]

FIRST X-FILE (1946): See **Richard Watkins.** ["Shapes"]

FLOYD, RAY: Construction worker in **Fairfield, Idaho,** who is knocked down and killed by an invisible force moving down the main street. His back is broken and there is an abrasion on his chest the size of an elephant's foot. ["Fearful Symmetry"]

FLUKEMAN: The half-human, half-fluke entity that finds its way to New Jersey from inside a Russian ship. He is cut in half in the climax, but we are led to believe that he may not have died, since the corpse opens its eyes in the final scene — or was that just a reflex muscle spasm? ["The Host"]

FLYING SAUCER DINER: A greasy spoon near **Ellens Air Force Base** in Idaho, which sells hamburgers that look vaguely like UFOs. The diner is owned and operated by a woman named **Ladonna,** who will sell you homemade UFO photos for a price. ["Deep Throat"]

FOLKSTONE INS PROCESSING CENTER: In North Carolina; 12,000 refugees, most of them Haitian, are housed here. It is little more than a collection of crude dormitories and tents. There has been unrest under the command of Marine **Col. Jacob Wharton,** and strange deaths are occurring in and around the town. ["Fresh Bones"]

FORAU: One of the Devil's disciples. This is the name **Simon Gates** uses when he rents a car. ["Revelations"]

FORNIER: A guard at **Eastpoint State Penitentiary** who is skeptical of **"Neech" Manley**'s claims that he'd be reincarnated. Fornier's severed head is discovered, writhing with maggots, inside an empty paint can by a prisoner on work detail. The rest of his body turns up in the office chair of warden **Leo Brodeur.** He is Manley's second victim. ["The List"]

FORT EVANSTON: U.S. Army base in Maryland commanded by **Gen. Thomas Callahan. Sgt. "Rappo" Trimble** is a patient in the base hospital.

FORT MARLENE HIGH CONTAINMENT FACILITY: Site of a secret cryo-lab where experiments with extraterrestrial viruses are conducted on human beings. ["The Erlenmeyer Flask"]

14th PRECINCT HOUSE: In Buffalo, New York. The site of the murder of police detective **Rudy Barbala.** ["Born Again"]

FOX FIRE: A folk legend from the Ozark Mountains. The phosphorescent glow caused by decaying wood was believed by many settlers (and modern-day Southerners) to be the spirits of massacred Indians. Mulder at first suspects such a phenomenon to be involved in a mysterious fire spotted near

Dudley, Arkansas, around the time of **George Kearns**'s disappearance. ["Our Town"]

FOYLE, CAPT.: Military coroner who finds a dog's corpse in the morgue drawer where **Pvt. John McAlpin**'s body is supposed to be. ["Fresh Bones"]

FRANKLIN, PENNSYLVANIA: The site of a spate of mysterious homicides. Seven killers have racked up twenty-two victims in six months by the time Mulder is called in. ["Blood"]

FRASER, LT.: An officer involved in **Operation Falcon,** under the command of **Col. Henderson.** The leader of the **Beta Team** strike force, Fraser is hospitalized with extreme burns, along with the surviving members of his team, after a deadly encounter with an invisible alien presence. ["Fallen Angel"]

FRASS, SHERIFF: Mulder encounters him in Massachusetts and learns from him that there have been an inexplicable series of "roach attacks," one of which the sheriff responds to while talking to Mulder. ["War of the Coprophages"]

FREDDIE: The leader of a group of people holding a UFO party after objects have been sighted two nights in a row. ["E.B.E."]

FREDDIES: Nickname given to employees of the U.S. Forest Service by ecoterrorists. ["Darkness Falls"]

FREDERICK COUNTY MORGUE: In Maryland. Mulder goes there to identify what the police say might be the body of Scully. It turns out not to be. ["Wetwired"]

FREDERICK, MARYLAND: Location of the U.S. Medical Research Institute of Infectious Diseases, where **Dr. Abel Gardner** discovers a mysterious virus in the body of FBI agent **Barrett Weiss.** ["End Game"]

FREELY, QUINTON "ROACH": An Army veteran who works in the mail room of the **Fort Evanston** hospital. He served in the Gulf War with Sgt. **"Rappo" Trimble.** After his fingerprints are found at **Gen. Callahan**'s home, he is arrested. Letters addressed to Trimble's victims are found in Freely's apartment. Freely dies in a locked cell, suffocated by a sheet stuffed down his throat. ["The Walk"]

FREE RADICALS: Chemicals that contain extra electrons and cause human DNA and proteins to oxidize, they are believed to be a primary factor in aging. Scully theorizes that the USS *Argent* and the meteor on the sea floor beneath it are acting as opposite poles of a gigantic magnetic field that is exciting the free radicals in its range, causing massive oxidizing of organic and inorganic matter — in other words, speeding up aging and corrosion. ["Dod Kalm"]

FREEDOM OF INFORMATION ACT: A law passed by Congress allowing American citizens access to formerly classified documents (suitably edited), which include Mulder's travel expenses. According to **Max Fenig,** Mulder's "fans" use these records to follow his activities. ["Fallen Angel"]

FROHIKE: On the staff of the magazine *The Lone Gunman.* He has a buzz cut and wears a Marine Corps watch. He thinks Scully is "hot." About him, Mulder observes, "It's men like you that give perversion a bad name." But his feelings include genuine respect as he goes to visit Scully at the hospital when she is in a coma in "One Breath." He also appears in "Blood," "Anasazi," and "E.B.E." He visits Scully, drunk, after he gets news of Mulder's apparent death, and shows her a newspaper clip about the death of the **Thinker.** ["The Blessing Way"] The last of the Lone Gunmen to see Mulder after his return, Frohike tells Scully of her sister's shooting. ["Paper Clip"] He is shown a strange video trap by Mulder. He and **Byers** determine that it sends another signal in along with the normal cable TV signal, a signal containing tachistoscopic images designed to influence the person watching the program. ["Wetwired"]

FULGURITE: Glass formed by the heat generated when lightning strikes sandy soil. One discovered near **Connerville, Oklahoma,** bears the imprint of a boot (size 8½). Scully also finds traces of antifreeze in the imprint, leading to auto shop employee **Darin Peter Oswald.** ["D.P.O."]

FULLER, AGENT: Head of the FBI's violent-crimes section, he stakes out the Calvert Street office building in the belief that the killer will return to the scene of the crime. Much to Mulder's surprise, **Eugene Tooms** does return, but only because his job with the Baltimore Animal Control Department brings him back to dispose of a dead cat in a ventilation duct. ["Squeeze"]

FULLER, BRIAN: FBI man in his forties who informs Scully that **Walter Skinner** has been shot. ["Apocrypha"]

FULLER, ROLAND: A mentally retarded janitor who works at the **Mahan Propulsion Laboratory.** His ID number is 315. He is actually the twin brother of the late **Arthur Grable.** They were separated at age three and Fuller grew up in an institute for the mentally retarded. After Grable is killed in a car accident and his head is preserved cryogenically, he's able to dominate Roland's mind and take control of his body. ["Roland"]

FUNSCH, ED: A fifty-two-year-old postal worker in Franklin, Pennsylvania, who is laid off due to budget cutbacks. He's a former Navy radio man whose wife died ten years ago. After he cuts himself on his machine, he starts to believe that he sees the machine he works on spelling out commands to "KILL 'EM ALL." It turns out that Funsch is afraid of blood. ["Blood"]

FYLFOT: Another term for the reverse swastika used as a protective charm by the **Calusari.** ["The Calusari"]

[G]

GAFFS: The name circus people give to phony freaks. ["Humbug"]

GALAXY GATEWAY: Mulder's motel in **Atlantic City** (Room 756). He lets **Jack** stay there instead of him. ["The Jersey Devil"]

GAMMADION: Another term for the reverse swastika used as a protective charm by the **Calusari.** ["The Calusari"]

GANESHA: The name of the twelve-year-old female Indian elephant that dies after apparently doing a lot of damage and killing a man in **Fairfield, Idaho.** The only problem is, the elephant was apparently invisible much of the time. ["Fearful Symmetry"]

GARDNER, DR. ABEL: Chief medical officer of the U.S. Medical Research Institute of Infectious Diseases. He discovers a mysterious retrovirus in the body of FBI agent **Barrett Weiss.** Scully had seen this virus before ["The Erlenmeyer Flask"] but is surprised when Gardner reveals that it goes dormant at low temperatures. ["End Game"]

GARNET: According to the **Lone Gunman** named **Byers,** the code name for the black ops (a secret government military outfit) unit dispatched to capture the **Thinker.** ["Anasazi"]

GARZA, ANGELO: A gas station employee who runs afoul of two infected prison escapees. He attempts to assist **Steve** when he finds him in the station's bathroom, but is assaulted by **Paul** for his trouble. Surviving that attack, he becomes infected by *F. Emasculata,* and is carried away via helicopter by **Pinck Pharmaceuticals'** minions. ["F. Emasculata"]

GATES, DAVID: The attorney representing **Jim Parker.** ["Shapes"]

GATES, SIMON: Also known as the Millennium Man. A businessman and CEO of a holding company based in Atlanta. Previous run-in with the law was an arrest on a DUI charge for an accident that paralyzed a young boy. Given a suspended sentence, he left the United States and traveled to Israel. He wears white patent-leather shoes. He exists to murder anyone he detects who has true spiritual power. He himself has supernatural power which he uses when he slays his victims, and leaves a burn mark on the neck of those he strangles. In three years he has murdered eleven people who seemed to be stigmatics, in case they might in fact be among the true twelve stigmatics (see also **stigmata**). ["Revelations"]

GAUTHIER: A French deep sea diver who locates a sunken World War II fighter plane in the Pacific Ocean. When he returns to the surface, he is possessed by an alien entity. By the time his ship, the *Piper Maru*, reaches San Diego, everyone aboard is suffering from extreme exposure to radiation — except him. The alien possessing him exits him in San Francisco and takes over his wife, Joan, leaving him with no memories of his time under its control. When Mulder locates him, Gauthier refuses to speak and demands to see the French consulate. ["Piper Maru"]

GAUTHIER, JOAN: The American wife of the Frenchman Gauthier. The alien that possessed him uses her body to travel to Hong Kong, abandoning her when it finds **Alex Krycek.** ["Piper Maru"] She is found, disoriented, in the men's room at the Hong Kong airport. ["Apocrypha"]

GAYHART, DR. DALE: A doctor who died in an arson fire at an abortion clinic in New York City. His name appears on a list of similar deaths e-mailed to Mulder by an anonymous source. Mulder is baffled upon learning that all three doctors, although apparently unrelated, were identical — and no body was recovered in any of the cases. ["Colony"]

GENERAL MUTUAL INSURANCE: The company where **Clyde Bruckman** was employed as a life insurance salesman. ["Clyde Bruckman's Final Repose"]

GENEROO, MICHELLE: A Mission Control communications commander for NASA in Houston who contacts the FBI when she receives evidence of sabotage from an aborted space shuttle mission. Concerned that the next launch — which her fiancé is flying on — is at risk, she helps Mulder and Scully figure out what is going on in the upper levels of NASA administration. The problem turns out to be **Lt. Col. Belt,** who is possessed by an alien entity of some sort. ["Space"]

GEORGETOWN MEDICAL CENTER: Hospital in Washington, D.C., where **Skinner** is treated after being shot by **Luis Cardinal.** ["Apocrypha"]

GEORGE WASHINGTON HOSPITAL: In Washington, D.C. A glassblower is taken here after he is attacked and his face is badly slashed. ["Grotesque"]

GEORGE WASHINGTON UNIVERSITY: In Washington, D.C. Art students there do sketches of a nude male model; shortly after class ends, the model is killed. One of the students is **John Mostow.** ["Grotesque"]

GERLACH, MALCOLM: The real name of the red-haired man. A professional assassin, his usual method of execution is with a garrote. He is ordered to eliminate **Dr. Zama.** After killing Zama, he attempts to kill Mulder. He claims he works for the National Security Agency. When he beats up Mulder and escapes from the **Quarantine Car,** he is shot and killed by **X.** ["731"]

GERMANTOWN, MARYLAND: A suburb of Washington, D.C., where Mulder investigates the mysterious death of a businessman; the victim entered his hotel room with a woman, but a man left, tying this in with other cases in Mulder's files. ["Genderbender"] Also where Mulder, Scully, and CIA agent **Chapel** locate **Dr. James Dickens.** Scully later hides out in a motel here as well. ["Colony"]

GIBSONTON, FLORIDA: Where circus freaks live during the winter. It was founded in the 1920s by members of the Barnum & Bailey circus. ["Humbug"]

GILDER, DR.: The doctor who pronounces **Rudy Barbala** dead. ["Born Again"]

GILLNITZ, JOHN: When Helene Riddock imagines she sees her husband, Victor, com-mitting adultery with the woman next door, she grabs a shotgun and kills Gillnitz, her neighbor, whom she mistakes for her husband. ["Wetwired"]

GIORGIO, CHRISSY: A beautiful teenage girl who with her date, **Harold Lamb,** is abducted by a UFO one night. When found the next morning she has no memory of what happened, and all of her clothes are on inside out or backward. Mulder believes she is suffering from post-abduction syndrome. ["Jose Chung's *From Outer Space*"]

GIRARDI, DR. FRANCIS: Worked with **Dr. Grissom** on the sleep eradication experiments on Parris Island in 1970. He performed the actual surgery. ["Sleepless"]

GLASS, DR. WILLIAM: Works at the Oregon State Psychiatric Hospital near Bellefleur. **Ray Soames** was his patient. [Pilot]

GLAZEBROOK, JERALD: He has reptilelike skin — hence his circus name, the Crocodile Man. He's married to the

bearded lady, and they have two young boys. He is killed by something that has killed forty-six other people in the previous eight years in Gibsonton, Florida. ["Humbug"]

GLENVIEW LAKE: The body of water where **Clyde Bruckman** correctly predicts the **Doll Collector**'s body would be found. ["Clyde Bruckman's Final Repose"]

GLOSSOLALIA: The religious phenomenon of speaking in tongues (that is, talking unintelligibly). **Lucy Householder** experiences it when **Amy**

Jacobs is kidnapped by **Carl Wade.** The words Lucy speaks are actually the same words spoken by Wade when he kidnapped Amy. ["Oubliette"]

GODFREY, DR. RICHARD: The town pediatrician. He's a cross-dresser. An old surgical bag of his is found buried in a yard with bones in it. It turns out they're animal bones from where someone buried their pet dog, a Mr. Tippy. ["Syzygy"]

GOLDA: The mother of **Maggie Holvey** and grandmother of **Teddy** and **Charlie Holvey.** A Romanian woman who did not approve of her daughter's marriage to an American, **Steve Holvey.** Highly superstitious, Golda brings a bizarre Old World element to the Holvey household when she comes to live there after the death of **Michael Holvey.** Highly superstitious, she performs strange rituals centered on Charlie that lead Scully to suspect her of **Munchausen by proxy.** Golda dies with her eyes pecked out by dead chickens. ["The Calusari"]

GOLDBAUM: A patient at the Bethesda Naval Hospital whose room **Jack Willis** hides in while escaping from the hospital after his near-death experience. ["Lazarus"]

GOODENSNAKE, GWEN: The sister of Joseph Goodensnake. She sees a werewolf kill **Jim Parker** and panics. Did she know that her brother was a shape-shifter? ["Shapes"]

GOODENSNAKE, JOSEPH: A werewolf killed by **Jim Parker.** The examination of his corpse reveals catlike fangs an inch long. His sister refuses to allow an autopsy, which might have revealed internal irregularities. ["Shapes"]

GORDON, MR. AND MRS.: A young couple who resist **Clyde Bruckman**'s pitch for life insurance because the husband would rather spend the money on a nice boat. Exasperated, Bruckman tells him how he will die in a head-on collision with a blue 1987 Mustang two years hence, leaving his wife and as-yet-unborn daughter bereft. ["Clyde Bruckman's Final Repose"]

GRABLE, DR. ARTHUR: An aeronautical scientist who worked at the **Mahan Propulsion Laboratory** until he was killed in a car accident in November 1993. His twin brother is **Roland Fuller,** but because Roland is retarded, the boys were separated at age three and Roland grew up in an institution. ["Roland"]

GRAGO, DR. JOHN: Works three days a week at the

Excelsis Dei Convalescent Home. He has been treating a group of Alzheimer's patients there for seven months. ["Excelsis Dei"]

GRAVENHURST HIGH SCHOOL: Where **Darin Peter Oswald** finishes his education (although not necessarily by completing it). It is here that he develops a serious crush on the remedial English teacher, **Sharon Kiveat.** ["D.P.O."]

GRAVES, HOWARD: Founder of **HTG Industrial Technologies.** When the company began to go under, Graves went along with his partner's plan to illegally sell parts to Iran. After a terrorist attack killed some American servicemen, however, he tried to back out, only to be killed for his trouble. His spirit lingers on for revenge, and to protect **Lauren Kyte,** whom he regarded as the daughter he once had. ["Shadows"]

GRAVES, SARAH LYNN: Howard Graves's daughter, who died at the age of three in a pool accident. Buried with Howard Graves. ["Shadows"]

GRAY, PAULA: A line worker at the **Chaco Chicken** processing plant in **Dudley, Arkansas,** she is the granddaughter of **Walter Chaco.** She flirts with USDA inspector

George Kearns in order to lure him to the community feast off County Road A7 — where he is destined to be the main course. She later attacks her supervisor, **Jess Harold,** with a knife, only to be shot by **Sheriff Tom Arens.** An autopsy reveals that she was suffering from **Creutzfeldt-Jakob disease.** Although born in 1948, she looked like she was only twenty or so when she died in 1995. ["Our Town"]

GREEN, ARLAN AND SUSAN: **Eugene Tooms** rents a room in the house owned by them. ["Tooms"]

GREEN "SAMANTHA": An alien clone in green hospital garb whom Mulder meets at the **Women's Health Services Center** in Rockville, Maryland. She reveals that the "return" of Mulder's sister has been a ruse to gain his assistance. She, along with the rest of the "Samantha" clones, is killed by the **Pilot.** ["End Game"]

GREEN, PHOEBE: A British classmate of Mulder's at Oxford University. They had an affair during their student days. A mover and shaker in Scotland Yard ten years later, she turns to Mulder for help in the **Cecil L'ively** case. Beautiful but prone to play

mind games, she has an affair with Lord **Marsden** while she assists Mulder in the apprehension of L'ively. ["Fire"]

GREENWICH, CONNECTICUT: Wealthy New York suburb where **Joel Simmons** is murdered by his daughter **Teena Simmons,** and Teena is abducted by **Dr. Sally Kendrick.** ["Eve"]

GREGOR: According to CIA agent **Chapel,** the code name for the identical doctors he claims are genetically engineered Soviet spies. In truth, they are alien colonists. Scully finds four more "Gregors" at the warehouse at 3243 **Edmonton Street** and places them in protective custody, but this is not enough to save them from being disposed of by the **Pilot** (see **"Samantha"**). ["Colony"]

GREINER, DEAN: A scientist at the **Astadourian Lightning Observatory** near **Connerville, Oklahoma.** ["D.P.O."]

GRIFFIN, LT.: Officer involved in **Operation Falcon** who reports the movement of the downed alien to **Col. Henderson.** ["Fallen Angel"]

GRISSOM, DR. SAUL: A pioneer in sleep disorders and founder of the Grissom Sleep Disorder Center. He was stationed on Parris Island, where

Marines receive basic training, from 1968 to 1971. In 1970 he conducted sleep eradication experiments there. His two greatest successes were **Willig** and **Cole.** He dies in his apartment when he believes he's trapped by a fire. Even though there is no fire, he suffers all the secondary physiological responses to having been burned, as if his body actually believed it was burning. ["Sleepless"]

GROVER CLEVELAND ALEXANDER HIGH SCHOOL: The school attended by the boys who are murdered by **Terri Roberts** and **Margi Kleinjan.** ["Syzygy"]

GUANACASTE RAIN FOREST: The jungle in Costa Rica where **Dr. Robert Torrence** discovers the insect named *Faciphaga Emasculata,* only to succumb to the parasite that lives in the insect. ["F. Emasculata"]

GUARDIANS OF THE DEAD: Two Indians, Bill and Tom, whose duty is to escort the deceased spirit to the next world as part of the funeral rites. ["Shapes"]

GUTIERREZ, PVT. MANUEL: A Marine who commits suicide. His body is stolen from its grave. ["Fresh Bones"]

[H]

HAGERSTOWN, MARYLAND: Small town where **Lula Philips** robs a drugstore of 200 units of insulin and a box of syringes for **Jack Willis.** ["Lazarus"]

HAGOPIAN, BETSY: Inside a **leather satchel** carried by a Japanese man who flees from a murder scene are high-resolution satellite photos and a list of Mutual UFO Network (MUFON) members in the **Allentown, Pennsylvania,** area. One name circled is Betsy Hagopian. When Scully visits Hagopian's house she finds a gathering in progress of people who claim that they were once abducted and taken to the **bright white place,** and that they recognize Scully as a fellow abductee. Hagopian is in the hospital, at the **Positron Emission Tomography Lab,** due to an undiagnosed cancerous condition. ["Nisei"]

HAKKARI, TURKEY: Where U.S. forces at a NATO surveillance station detect a UFO passing overhead after it is shot down. ["E.B.E."]

HAKKIE, DR. DEL: A psychiatrist at the **Davis Correctional Treatment Center. Duane Barry** takes him hostage, intending to transport him to the site where Barry was once abducted by an alien spacecraft and hand Hakkie over to the aliens. ["Duane Barry"]

HALE, GEORGE: Cover name used by Mulder when he phones Scully at the FBI academy at Quantico. ["Sleepless"]

HALOPERIDOL: An antipsychotic drug given to **Michael Kryder** at the mental hospital where he is imprisoned. ["Revelations"]

HALVORSON: Twenty-one-year-old Norwegian first mate of **Henry Trondheim**'s boat the *Zeal.* He is killed by the pirate whaler **Olafssen** on the USS *Argent.* ["Dod Kalm"]

HAMILTON, SHERIFF: The sheriff of **Gibsonton, Florida.** In 1933 he was a feral child discovered in a forest in Albania. He was exhibited in a Barnum circus as Jim-Jim, the Dog-Faced Boy. He finally escaped to begin a normal life outside the circus. ["Humbug"]

HAMMOND, JACK: A classic small-town character, a former high school football star whose career after graduation never went higher than pizza delivery. His attempt to bully **Darin Peter Oswald** away from his beloved Virtua Fighter 2 leads to his death by electrocution: he is fried to a crisp in his 1968 Oldsmobile 442. ["D.P.O."]

HAND, DR.: One of the people who interrogate **Chrissy Giorgio.** At first she remembers him as looking like a Gray Alien. ["Jose Chung's *From Outer Space*"]

1223 HANOVER STREET: The Georgetown address of the escort service **Carina Sayles** worked for. ["Avatar"]

HANSEN'S RESEARCH CENTER COMPOUND: In Perkey, West Virginia. A group of soldiers arrive there and herd the human–alien hybrids into the forest and shoot them all, Nazi fashion. Only one escapes to bear witness to the crime, although four others also survive the massacre. Scully traces **Dr. Zama** there while trying to track down the manufacturer of the computer chip she finds implanted in her neck. Hansen's disease is the scientific name for leprosy. ["731"]

HARBORMASTER: Visited by Mulder in Newport News, Virginia, when he's searching for the *Talapus.* ["Nisei"]

HAROLD, JESS: The floor manager of the **Chaco Chicken** processing plant in **Dudley, Arkansas.** He is attacked by **Paula Gray** when she succumbs to the effects of **Creutzfeldt-Jakob disease.**

One of the main townspeople to turn against **Walter Chaco,** he is trampled by a panicked crowd after Mulder shoots **Sheriff Tom Arens.** ["Our Town"]

HARPER, LT. RICHARD: A survivor of the USS *Argent* who leads the mutiny of eighteen men, abandoning the *Argent* in Lifeboat 925 over **Capt. Barclay**'s objections. Harper was the last mutineer to die; Scully sees him briefly at Bethesda Naval Hospital, and is stunned to note that he looks ninety years old. He is actually twenty-nine. ["Dod Kalm"]

HARTLEY, REV. CALVIN: The guardian of Samuel, the boy who can raise the dead. Now the owner of the Miracle Ministry, he was once a poor pastor who preached from a soapbox and collected dollar bills in a coffee can. ["Miracle Man"]

HARTLEY, SAMUEL: The adopted son of the Rev. Calvin Hartley. He has the power to bring the recently deceased back to life. In 1983, at the age of eight, he did this at the scene of a horrific car accident. But as an adult of eighteen, he kills people with a touch instead of healing them. He claims his "gift has been corrupted." ["Miracle Man"]

HARVEY MUDD: The college attended by **Dr. Nollette** in the 1970s. His quantum physics professor failed him one semester because he didn't agree with one of Nollette's theories. ["Roland"]

HAVEZ, DET.: The partner of **Det. Cline,** working on the **Puppet** serial killings. A serious chain smoker, he is relieved when **Clyde Bruckman** assures him he won't die of lung cancer. The **Puppet** stabs Havez to death minutes later. ["Clyde Bruckman's Final Repose"]

HAWLEY, LIZ: A nineteen-year-old student at Jackson University in North Carolina. She and her boyfriend **Jim Summers** are kidnapped and tortured by **Lucas Jackson Henry;** Hawley is rescued first, at **Lake Jordan.** ["Beyond the Sea"]

HELL MONEY: Paper currency burned by the Chinese to provide wealth to spirits in the afterlife. ["Hell Money"]

HELM, HEPCAT: A fifty-year-old artist who has lived in **Gibsonton, Florida,** for many years. He is also a mechanic and a carnival operator. He is killed by **Leonard,** the evil Siamese twin. ["Humbug"]

HEMORRHAGIC FEVER: The man imprisoned in **Quarantine Car** has this ail-

ment, and if the bomb in the car detonates, the disease — a deadly, leprosy-like ailment — will be spread to thousands of people nearby. ["731"]

HENDERSON, COL. CALVIN: Air Force officer in charge of **Operation Falcon.** Once assigned to preventing downed U.S. spy planes from falling into enemy hands, he now works in the field of UFO crash retrieval. Advises his prisoner Mulder to forget what he saw near **Townsend, Wisconsin.** ["Fallen Angel"]

HENDERSON, HEATHER: A brilliant FBI lab technician in her late thirties, and a friend of Mulder's. She matches **John Barnett**'s old handwriting to new notes with a 95 percent probability. She seems to have a thing for Mulder. ["Young at Heart"]

HENRY: Halfway house resident who helps **Lucy Householder.** ["Oubliette"]

HENRY, LUCAS JACKSON: A small-time crook, age twenty-eight, with a history of sexual assault and narcotics charges. He kidnaps and tortures **Liz Hawley** and **Jim Summers** in a psychotic attempt to work out his mental problems. An identical kidnapping one year earlier resulted in the deaths of his victims; Hawley and Summers are rescued. Henry may have aided **Luther Lee Boggs** in his last five murders, but this has never been proved. Henry falls to his death in the **Blue Devil Brewery** while fleeing the FBI. ["Beyond the Sea"]

HERITAGE HALFWAY HOUSE: The home of **Roland Fuller.** ["Roland"]

HEUVELMANS LAKE: Located in the Blue Ridge Mountains of Georgia, it has forty-eight miles of coastline. A mysterious creature known as **Big Blue** lives in this lake. ["Quagmire"]

HIGH-RESOLUTION MICROWAVE SURVEY: The project designed to scan the sky for radio transmissions of an intelligent extraterrestrial origin. A radio telescope in this survey is located at **Arecibo,** Puerto Rico. ["Little Green Men"]

HINDT, SHERIFF LANCE: He is investigating the disappearances and deaths at **Heuvelmans Lake** but thinks the deaths are ordinary accidents. ["Quagmire"]

HIRSH, JUDGE: One of the Maryland judges at the sanity hearing for **Eugene Tooms.** ["Tooms"]

HODGE, DR. LAWRENCE: A physician who accompanies Mulder and Scully to investigate the **Arctic Ice Core**

Project disaster. Arrogant and suspicious, Hodge erroneously believes that the FBI agents know more than they're letting on. He thinks Mulder is **Murphy**'s murderer until **Nancy Da Silva** is revealed as the real culprit. Hodge and Scully discover a way to defeat the ice worm infestation. ["Ice"]

HOHMAN, MARGARET: A sick woman who goes to be healed at the **Miracle Ministry** tent. When **Samuel Hartley** touches her, however, she dies instead of being healed. But an autopsy reveals that she was poisoned, not killed by Samuel. ["Miracle Man"]

HOLLOWAY, LOTTIE: A Mutual UFO Network (MUFON) member living in the **Allentown, Pennsylvania**, area. She is visited by Scully and is shocked to recognize her, claiming Scully is a fellow abductee. ["Nisei"]

HOLLY: An FBI research librarian, injured in a mugging. Some time after that, **Robert Modell** uses his persuasive powers to get her to provide him information about Mulder. When **Skinner** challenges Modell's presence in the FBI building, Modell makes her think Skinner was the man who mugged her. He escapes when Holly sprays the

Assistant Director with Mace. ["Pusher"]

HOLLYWOOD BLOOD BANK: A Los Angeles–area blood bank investigated by Mulder in his search for the people in the **Trinity** gang of vampiric killers. He hits pay dirt: **The Son** is working here as a night watchman and Mulder catches him raiding the blood bank. ["3"]

HOLTZMAN, VICTOR: An agent of the National Security Agency who investigates when Mulder faxes some of **Kevin Morris**'s binary scribblings to an FBI cryptologist. The fax includes top-secret military information, but the rest of Kevin's papers involve nothing classified. Holtzman's handling of the case is less than subtle, and results in the ransacking of the Morris residence. ["Conduit"]

HOLVEY, CHARLIE: The eight-year-old son of Maggie and Steve Holvey, he is a twin whose identical brother Michael died at birth. His grandmother **Golda** has spent years trying to protect him from the spirit of his twin, but these actions have been perceived as destructive superstition by his parents. Charlie knows of Michael's existence even though his parents have never told him about it. ["The Calusari"]

HOLVEY, TEDDY: The two-year-old son of Maggie and Steve Holvey, he is killed when he follows a drifting balloon onto the tracks of the miniature train ride at Lincoln Park in Murray, Virginia. Photo analysis reveals what appears to be a shadowy figure pulling the balloon, prompting Mulder's initial suspicion of poltergeist activity centering around Teddy's older brother Charlie. ["The Calusari"]

HOLVEY, MAGGIE: A Romanian woman who married Steve Holvey, an American diplomat, in 1984. They had three children: Michael, Charlie, and Teddy. Only Charlie has survived. Maggie saw her move to America as a chance to escape from the superstitions of her upbringing, but the events surrounding the untimely deaths of her husband, mother, and son Teddy lead her to reconsider the validity of Romanian folk beliefs. ["The Calusari"]

HOLVEY, MICHAEL: Charlie Holvey's twin brother, who died at birth. His spirit follows Charlie until it is exorcised by a Ritual of Separation; however, the **Calusari** hint that this may not have been Michael's spirit but a more malevolent

demonic force that took his form. This force notices Mulder during the ritual. ["The Calusari"]

HOLVEY, STEVE: An employee of the State Department whose son Teddy dies under unusual circumstances; Holvey's position leads to a routine FBI investigation of the death, which turns out to be anything but routine. Steve Holvey is killed when his necktie is caught in the drive train of an electric garage door opener he is trying to fix, causing death by strangulation while his son Charlie watches. ["The Calusari"]

HOMETOWN TRUST: The bank **Ed Funsch** uses in Franklin, Pennsylvania. The ATM monitor tries to tell Funsch to take the security guard's gun. ["Blood"]

HORNING, CRAIG: A researcher at the Boston Museum of Natural History, murdered by mysterious forces while working on the **Amaru** Urn. ["Teso dos Bichos"]

HORTON, DET. BILL: The investigating officer on the case of the death of **Dr. Saul Grissom.** ["Sleepless"]

HOSTEEN (ALBERT'S SON): Eric Hosteen's father, first name unknown. He takes part in Mulder's **Blessing Way**

ceremony. ["The Blessing Way"]

HOSTEEN, ALBERT: A Navajo code walker who helps translate the original **MJ documents** into Navajo, and later helps Mulder and Scully translate them back. He tells his grandson Eric to take the alien corpse back where he found it. ["Anasazi"] Hosteen and his family are brutalized by the troops controlled by the **Cigarette-Smoking Man,** but do not tell them anything. When Mulder's unconscious body is found in the desert, he conducts the Blessing Way healing ceremony but is unsuccessful. ["The Blessing Way"] By memorizing the information on the MJ files DAT (already encoded in Navajo) and passing it along orally to other members of his tribe, he helps **Skinner** to thwart the Smoking Man's plans for Mulder and Scully. ["Paper Clip"]

HOSTEEN, ERIC: Albert Hosteen's grandson, a Navajo teen who collects rattlesnake skins. He discovers a buried railway refrigeration car in the desert on the Navajo reservation after an earthquake reveals its location, and brings an alien corpse back into town. When Mulder comes to the reservation, Eric drives him to the site on his motocross bike. ["Anasazi"] After the **Cigarette-Smoking Man** interrogates Eric, he is brought back to the Hosteen home. Later, he takes part in Mulder's **Blessing Way** ceremony. ["The Blessing Way"]

HOTEL CATHERINE: The Washington, D.C., hotel where Mulder and Scully track **Marty** of the **Kindred.** They are unable to arrest him/her because he is captured by his own people, who then vanish. ["Genderbender"]

HOTEL GEORGE MASON: The plush Richmond, Virginia, hotel where **Patrick Newirth** is disintegrated. ["Soft Light"]

HOUSEHOLDER, LUCY: A thirty-year-old trainee working in an unnamed **fast-food restaurant.** She has short, dark hair and a pale face with haunted eyes. One night at work she suddenly gets a bloody nose, but this isn't an ordinary bloody nose. It is later determined that the bloodstains on her clothes are of two different types, O-positive and B-positive. Lucy is O-positive and **Amy Jacob**'s blood type is B-positive. When Lucy was eight years old she was kidnapped by an unidentified man (actually **Carl Wade**) and remained his prisoner for five years. When Amy is kid-

napped, Lucy experiences the trauma Amy is feeling. This happens at 10:05 P.M., at the exact moment Amy is kidnapped. Lucy has a variety of lingering emotional problems, including an aversion to being touched. When shown a photo of Wade, she identifies him as the man who kidnapped her years ago. But when the FBI determines that the blood on Lucy's clothes is an exact DNA match for Amy's, they come to arrest Lucy for complicity in the kidnapping. She disappears, only to be found in the basement of Wade's cabin, which she realizes is where she had been held those five years. ["Oubliette"]

HSIN, KIM: A young Chinese woman suffering from leukemia. Her father takes part in a dangerous game to help pay her medical bills. ["Hell Money"]

HSIN, SHUYANG: A carpet layer by trade, he gambles his own organs in an attempt to win money to pay for his daughter Kim's expensive leukemia treatment. He loses an eye in the process, but is rescued by **Glen Chao** before his heart can be removed. ["Hell Money"]

HTG INDUSTRIAL TECHNOLOGIES: A small defense subcontractor in Philadelphia

that becomes the focus of forces from beyond the grave after its founder, **Howard Graves,** is killed. Graves just can't stand to leave any unfinished business behind. ["Shadows"]

HUGHES, DR. ALICIA: The identity assumed by **Eve Eight** after her escape. Hughes has high-level Pentagon clearance. She visits **Teena Simmons** and **Cindy Reardon** after they are incarcerated at the **Whiting Institute.** ["Eve"]

HUMAN GENOME PROJECT: Experiments conducted on human beings with extraterrestrial viruses — the injection of alien DNA into humans. ["The Erlenmeyer Flask"]

HUMPHREYS, STEVE: Head of security for the **Schiff-Immergut Lumber Company.** He accompanies Mulder, Scully, and **Larry Moore.** He's caught inside his pickup truck at night and encased in a **cocoon** by the prehistoric wood mites. ["Darkness Falls"]

HUNSAKER, GEORGE: His son receives an anonymous call from someone who says he knows where a mass grave is located. ["Syzygy"]

HYMAN RICKOVER NAVAL HOSPITAL: In Seattle. Mulder, Scully, and **Larry**

Moore are taken here to be treated after they are cocooned by prehistoric wood mites. Unlike the other victims, they are found and rescued in time. ["Darkness Falls"]

HYNEK, SGT.: He comes to claim the body of Air Force Maj. **Robert Vallee.** His name is an inside joke: Dr. Allen J. Hynek is a UFO investigator who invented the term "close encounters." ["Jose Chung's *From Outer Space*"]

HYPOKALEMIA: A condition in which the blood contains unusually high levels of sodium and a commensurate decrease in potassium. Medical records from the hospital where **Darin Peter Oswald** was treated after being struck by lightning show that he suffered from this condition at the time, prompting Mulder to hypothesize that this unusual concentration of electrolytes enabled Darin to produce electricity with his body. Tests taken after Darin's arrest show no signs of hypokalemia. ["D.P.O."]

[I]

ICARUS PROJECT: The next generation of jet design, capable of doubling current supersonic speeds using half the fuel. Its goal is an engine that can achieve Mach 15 (fifteen

times the speed of sound). ["Roland"]

ICE WORM: An alien parasite brought to Earth by a meteor a quarter of a million years ago that lay dormant under two miles of ice until it is brought to the surface by the **Arctic Ice Core Project.** In its dormant state, it appears to be an ammonia-based microorganism; when it enters the bloodstream of a victim, the single-celled larva develops into a worm approximately one foot long and attaches itself to the hypothalamus gland. At this point it increases that gland's production of acetylcholine, which induces violent behavior in the victim. Removal of the worm by surgical means results in the death of the victim. Introduction of another live worm into the victim, however, causes both worms to kill each other, releasing the victim from the control of the ice worm. ["Ice"]

ICY CAPE, ALASKA: The location of the **Arctic Ice Core Project,** 250 miles north of the Arctic Circle. ["Ice"]

INCANTO, VIRGIL: A man with a rare disease: he has no fatty tissue and must ingest it from others. His body produces a highly acidic slime that allows him to dissolve people's skin.

At first he uses personals ads to find victims, but later moves onto the Internet. His favored victims are lonely, overweight women, but he resorts to prostitutes in a pinch. A scholar of sixteenth-century Italian poetry, he seems able to seduce women with ease. One of his intended victims, **Ellen Kaminski,** kills him with Scully's service revolver. His name was probably a pseudonym drawn from Dante. He killed at least forty-seven women. ["2Shy"]

INDIGO DELTA NINER: The military code used by **Col. Calvin Henderson** to initiate **Operation Falcon.** ["Fallen Angel"]

IONESCO: A crew member on board the Canadian fishing vessel *Lisette* who throws a line to Lifeboat 925 from the USS **Argent.** ["Dod Kalm"]

ISH: An old Indian man with one blind eye and shoulder-length gray hair. He wears a necklace made of animal claws and teeth. He has a scar down his face and was at Wounded Knee in 1973. His son is an Indian manitou, who attacks a rancher. His profession is mechanic. ["Shapes"]

ISHIMARU, DR.: Japanese scientist in his late sixties, with a silver streak in his hair. He is part of a mysterious experiment conducted in a train car. He has supposedly been dead since 1965, but he is still alive in the 1990s. He was in charge of a Japanese medical unit that experimented on living human beings. This included performing vivisections without anesthesia, testing frostbite tolerance levels on babies, and deliberately exposing people to diseases to chart their progress. Mulder believes Ishimaru has been trying to create a human–alien hybrid. Scully recognizes him as having been a part of whatever happened to her during the time she was missing after her abduction (see also **Dr. Zama**). ["Nisei"]

I-10: The interstate highway that runs through **Dudley, Arkansas.** A passing motorist sees a mysterious fire in a field off this highway the night USDA poultry inspector **George Kearns** disappears. ["Our Town"]

IVANOV, DR. ALEXANDER: An artificial-intelligence researcher who designs robots that look like insects. ["War of the Coprophages"]

[J]

JACK: A homeless man in his thirties who gives Mulder information about the activities of the **Jersey Devil** and the **Atlantic City** police. Mulder swaps his motel room for Jack's cardboard box in an alley, which he uses as a look-out point. ["The Jersey Devil"]

JACKSON: A member of **Operation Falcon**'s **Beta Team.** ["Fallen Angel"]

JACKSON: **Capt. Foyle**'s assistant. ["Fresh Bones"]

JACKSON UNIVERSITY: A college in Raleigh, North Carolina, where **Lucas Jackson Henry** kidnapped **Liz Hawley** and **Jim Summers.** ["Beyond the Sea"]

JACOBS, AGENT: She is following Scully when Scully goes to the Miami airport to catch a flight to Puerto Rico to search for Mulder. ["Little Green Men"]

JACOBS, AMY: Fifteen-year-old student at Valley Woods High in Seattle. At 10:05 P.M. one night she is kidnapped from her home by **Carl Wade.** As she is being carried out of her window by Wade, he puts his hand over her mouth and causes a nosebleed (see **Lucy Householder**). Wade keeps her locked up in the basement of his cabin, where there is no light, except for when Wade takes flash pictures of her. At one point she escapes, but Wade recaptures her. ["Oubliette"]

JACOBS, DAPHNE: The mother of Amy Jacobs. ["Oubliette"]

JACOBS, DR.: The Los Angeles Police Department's forensic dentist. ["3"]

JACOBS, SADIE: The five-year-old sister of Amy Jacobs. She shares a bedroom with Amy and witnesses her abduction, but all she sees is the back of the man who is carrying Amy out the open window. ["Oubliette"]

JALEE: Headhunting tribe of New Guinea long suspected of cannibalistic practices, which they taught to **Walter Chaco** when he was shot down near their Pacific island during World War II. ["Our Town"]

JANADI, SADOUN: Iraqi jet pilot who encounters a UFO and is attacked. ["E.B.E."]

JANELLI-HELLER FUNERAL HOME: Where **Donnie Pfaster** works until he is caught desecrating the corpse of a young woman. ["Irresistible"]

JANUS: FBI agent with medical training who goes into the **Travel Time Travel Agency** to assist the wounded hostage, **Bob Riley.** ["Duane Barry"]

JARVIS, OWEN LEE: Hired by **Susan Kryder** to do yard work after her husband is institutionalized, he is the defender of her son Kevin against the Forces of Darkness. When accused of kidnapping Kevin, Jarvis leaps out a second-story window, breaks free of the handcuffs on his wrists, and runs away. He successfully defends Kevin and dies doing so, killed by the Millennium Man (**Simon Gates**). After death his body doesn't decompose and emits the smell of flowers. ["Revelations"]

J.A.S.D. BEEF PACKING PLANT: In **Delta Glen, Wisconsin.** The "beef" it processes turns out to be human. ["Red Museum"]

JASON: The twelve-year-old boy unlucky enough to be headed to Toronto on the same bus as the escaped convict **Paul,** who takes him hostage until Mulder convinces Paul to let him go. ["F. Emasculata"]

J. EDGAR HOOVER BUILD-ING: The FBI's national head-quarters in Washington, named after the Bureau's orig-inal director.

JEFFERSON MEMORIAL HOSPITAL: In Richmond, Virginia. **Duane Barry** is hos-pitalized here after being shot by an FBI marksman at the **Travel Time Travel Agency.** ["Duane Barry"]

JENKINS: Maryland state's attorney at the sanity hearing held for **Eugene Tooms.** ["Tooms"]

JENSEN, DIANE: Secretary to **Assistant Director Walter S. Skinner** of the FBI. ["The Host"]

JERSEY DEVIL: The East Coast version of Bigfoot or the Abominable Snowman, it proves to be more than a leg-end when Mulder meets one face to face. In this case, it is a female, its mate apparently having died six months earlier, according to park ranger **Peter Boulle.** She is killed by the **Atlantic City** police, but her child survives in the wilds. ["The Jersey Devil"]

JERUSALEM, OHIO: Site of the **Twenty-First Century Recycling Plant,** owned by the holding company of which **Simon Gates** is CEO. ["Revelations"]

JERUSALEM SYNDROME: Affects some people who visit the Holy Land of Israel, lead-ing from religious delusions to irrational religious fanaticism. ["Revelations"]

JIM-JIM, THE DOG-FACED BOY: An exhibit in the 1930s circus of P. T. Barnum. He fled the circus and became **Sheriff Hamilton** in **Gibsonton, Florida.** ["Humbug"]

JIMMY DOOLITTLE AIR-FIELD: A small airstrip in Nome, Alaska, where Mulder and Scully meet **Drs. Denny Murphy, Nancy Da Silva,** and **Lawrence Hodge** on their way to the **Arctic Ice Core Project** base. The pilot known as **Bear** flies them from here. ["Ice"]

JOAN: Sen. Richard Matheson's secretary, who threatens to call security when Mulder, deranged by drugs in his drinking water, barges into Matheson's office. ["Anasazi"]

JOHANSEN, COMMANDER CHRISTOPHER: During World War II, Johansen served as the executive officer on the submarine **Zeus Faber.** He locked the alien-possessed **Capt. Kyle Sanford** below decks with the sick crewman when he realized the captain was a threat. Johansen was one of the seven men who survived the mission without radiation sickness. Later in his career he was a friend of **William Scully,** Dana's father. He tells Dana the true story of the **Zeus Faber**'s mission. ["Piper Maru"]

JOHN 52:54: The Biblical verse that reads "He who eats my flesh and drinks my blood has eternal life, and I will raise him up on the last day." The citation is found written in blood on the wall next to the body of **Garrett Lorre.** ["3"]

JOHNSON, DET.: A Baltimore cop at the scene of the

Werner murder. Johnson later informs Mulder that **Tooms** is missing from work. ["Squeeze"]

JOHNSON, VERNA: A murder victim. She was a teacher of high school drama. ["Aubrey"]

JOHNSTON COUNTY, OKLAHOMA: Location of the town of **Connerville,** site of unusual electrical activity centered on one **Darin Peter Oswald.** ["D.P.O."]

JONES, CREIGHTON: A mental patient who had an unknown traumatic experience in or near **Dudley, Arkansas**, between May 17 and May 20, 1961. He lost an arm as well as his mind, and was later filmed ranting about fire demons hungry for flesh. This film gave Mulder nightmares in college, causing him to remember it vividly when the **George Kearns** case brings him and Scully to Dudley. ["Our Town"]

JORGE: The frightened Puerto Rican man Mulder finds hiding in the bathroom inside the radio telescope building at **Arecibo,** Puerto Rico. The old man, who speaks no English, draws a crude but unmistakable image of an alien with large eyes and a triangular head. Mulder later finds the old man, who apparently died of fright. ["Little Green Men"]

JOSEPHS, DR.: Works at the hospital in Browning, Montana. He finds that **Lyle Parker** has ingested some of his father's blood, which could only have happened had Lyle eaten some of his father's flesh. ["Shapes"]

JOSH: A student and the lab partner of **Shannon Asbury.** ["Die Hand Die Verletzt"]

JTT0111471: Fox Mulder's FBI badge number. ["F. Emasculata"]

[K]

KALLENCHUK, JERALDINE: Operator of a salvage company in San Francisco. When she travels to Hong Kong to buy government secrets from **Alex Krycek,** she is killed by agents of the **Cigarette-Smoking Man.** ["Piper Maru"]

KALLENCHUK SALVAGE BROKERS: The salvage company operated by Jeraldine Kallenchuk. Mulder mistakenly assumes there is a Mr. Kallenchuk. ["Piper Maru"]

KAMINSKI, ELLEN: An intended victim of **Virgil Incanto,** she stands him up on their first date but later gives him a second chance that turns fatal not for her, but for him. She kills Incanto with Scully's gun after he has slimed her and is going after Scully. ["2Shy"]

KANE, BETH: A forty-year-old worker at the **J.A.S.D. Beef Packing Plant** in Wisconsin. She and her family have been the targets of a peeping Tom for several years. ["Red Museum"]

KANE, GARY: The sixteen-year-old son of Beth Kane. First string on the varsity football team and member of the 4-H club. He disappears one night and the next morning is found with the words "HE IS ONE" written on his back in black magic marker. He doesn't remember what happened to him, but he thinks a spirit entered him. ["Red Museum"]

KANE, STEVIE: The nine-year-old son of Beth Kane. ["Red Museum"]

KANN, JUDGE: Maryland state judge who presides over the sanity hearing for **Eugene Tooms.** ["Tooms"]

KARETZKY, DR.: A witness at the sanity hearing held for **Eugene Tooms** in Baltimore. She examined him for any physiological dysfunction and couldn't find anything. ["Tooms"]

KAUTZ: FBI ballistics expert who tests Mulder's gun for Scully when she needs to make certain that Mulder didn't shoot his own father. ["Anasazi"]

KAZANJIAN, DAN: A young agent who works in the FBI's computer crime section. He restores **Virgil Incanto**'s computer files and provides Scully and Mulder with a list of the killer's past and intended victims. ["2Shy"]

KAZDIN, LUCY: FBI agent in charge of hostage negotiations with **Duane Barry.** At first skeptical about Mulder, she later tells him about the strange metal objects discovered in Barry's body. ["Duane Barry"]

KEARNS, DORIS: The widow of George Kearns. She knew of her husband's fate but was promised protection by **Walter Chaco** — protection he was unable to provide to her. She became part of the community the **Dudley** way, by ingestion. ["Our Town"]

KEARNS, GEORGE: USDA poultry inspector stationed in **Dudley, Arkansas,** who displayed odd mental problems prior to his disappearance. Sent to investigate the disappearance of this federal employee, Mulder and Scully find his headless skeleton when the local river is dragged, and discover that he had been eaten by the locals. Unfortunately for the citizens of Dudley, Kearns's mental problems had been caused by **Creutzfeldt-Jakob disease,** which was passed along to them when they ingested his brain tissue. ["Our Town"]

KEATS: An aeronautical scientist who works at the **Mahan Propulsion Laboratory.** ["Roland"]

KELLEHER, LORRAINE: A woman in her late sixties who runs an escort service in Washington, D.C. She says **Walter Skinner** paid for the services of **Carina Sayles** the night Sayles died. Kelleher is later found dead, a supposed suicide, but her demise conveniently occurs just as Mulder is coming to interview her about who might be trying to frame Skinner. ["Avatar"]

KELLY, LAURA: The daughter of Stan Phillips. He has been living at the **Excelsis Dei Convalescent Home** and doesn't want to leave there to move in with her. ["Excelsis Dei"]

KELLY, LUCY: A woman with cancer who dies after **Samuel Hartley** fails to heal her. ["Miracle Man"]

KELOID SCAR: The surgical scar found on the back of the neck of the subjects in **Dr. Grissom**'s sleep eradication experiments. The operation involves cutting part of the brain stem in the midpontine region. ["Sleepless"]

KENDRICK, DR. SALLY: A product of the **Litchfield Project.** First in her class at Yale Medical School, this biogenetics specialist interned at the **Luther Stapes Center** until she was suspected of tampering with genetic material. In fact, she was implanting her own clones in fertility patients. She disappeared for years after her dismissal. Her clones **Cindy Reardon** and **Teena Simmons** murder her with a lethal dose of digitalis in a cup of soda. Kendrick was Eve Seven. ["Eve"]

KENNEDY: An FBI agent who staked out **Eugene Tooms**'s Exeter Street apartment for Mulder until Agent **Colton** called him off, resulting in unnecessary danger for Scully and Mulder. ["Squeeze"]

KENNEDY CENTER: A performing-arts complex in Washington, D.C.; Mulder meets **X** here and drags him away from a performance of Wagner's "Ring" cycle in order to find out more about the **Pilot.** X reveals where the Pilot's craft is located. ["End Game"]

KENWOOD, TENNESSEE: In 1983, **Samuel Hartley** brings a man back from the dead there at the scene of a horrible accident where the man had burned to death. The local

sheriff believes that the **Rev. Hartley** and his adopted son Samuel are running a scam. ["Miracle Man"]

KERBER, SCOTT: The Loudon County sheriff's deputy killed when a semi hits his car, freeing **Robert Modell** and injuring FBI agent **Frank Burst.** ["Pusher"]

KILAR, KRISTEN: The woman Mulder meets in the **Club Tepes,** where she orders Jordeen — red wine. The vampire trio are hunting her because she was once associated with the **Son.** She is ultimately responsible for the destruction of the Trinity. ["3"]

KINBOTE, LORD: A.k.a. the **Behemoth** from the Planet Harryhausen. A real alien who kidnaps **Harold Lamb** and **Chrissy Giorgio,** along with two military men disguised as aliens (**Lt. Jack Sheaffer** and **Maj. Robert Vallee**). This is the name given the alien in a manuscript written by **Roky Crikenson** called *The Truth About Aliens.* Crikenson claims Lord Kinbote is an alien from the Earth's core. ["Jose Chung's *From Outer Space*"]

THE KINDRED: An Amish-like isolationist religious group that have lived near **Steveston, Massachusetts,** for generations and are known for their distinctive white clay pottery.

The gender-shifting killer known as **Marty** runs away from them but is eventually taken back. The Kindred welcome Mulder and Scully into their community, but only after taking their guns. They seem to have some strange regenerative abilities, but the nature of them is unclear. The entire Kindred community disappears overnight, leaving behind a mysterious crop circle. ["Genderbender"]

KINKERY, MR.: The teacher who is replaced by **Phyllis Paddock.** ["Die Hand Die Verletzt"]

KIP: A biker with a UFO tattoo whom Mulder meets at the **Boar's Head** tavern in Sioux City, Iowa; Kip hints there are strange things out at **Lake Okobogee** at night. Mulder later encounters a biker gang that probably included Kip as one of its members. ["Conduit"]

KISSELL, COL. BLAIN: The director of communications at **Ellens Air Force Base** in Idaho. He refuses to talk to Mulder and Scully when they investigate the case of **Col. Robert Budahas.** ["Deep Throat"]

KITTEL, PVT.: **Col. Wharton**'s assistant. Mulder reveals to him that **Dunham** and **Gutierrez** had both filed complaints against Wharton just prior to their mysterious deaths. ["Fresh Bones"]

KIVEAT AUTO BODY: Where **Darin Peter Oswald** was employed. ["D.P.O."]

KIVEAT, FRANK: Proprietor of Kiveat Auto Body, and husband of Sharon Kiveat. In an attempt to impress Sharon, **Darin Peter Oswald** causes Frank to undergo cardiac arrest, interferes with the paramedics' equipment, and "saves" Frank with his own remarkable electrical powers. ["D.P.O."]

KIVEAT, SHARON: She teaches the remedial reading class at **Gravenhurst High School,** where **Darin Peter Oswald** develops a crush on her. Frightened by Darin's powers, she nevertheless risks her own safety to draw him away from others. ["D.P.O."]

KLAMATH FALLS, OREGON: Birthplace of bank robber and murderer **Warren James Dupre.** ["Lazarus"]

KLASS COUNTY, WASHINGTON: Site of a close encounter of the third kind that is investigated by Mulder and Scully. "Klass County" is an inside joke: Philip Klass is a UFO debunker. ["Jose Chung's *From Outer Space*"]

KLEINJAN, MARGI: A friend of **Bruno,** a boy who dies under

mysterious circumstances. She and her best friend, **Terri Roberts,** together have strange powers due to a peculiar alignment of the planets. She's a senior at Grover Cleveland Alexander High School in **Comity.** She has a grade point average of 3.75, and she's on the cheerleading squad with Terri. Astrologically speaking, Comity is in a geological vortex. On January 12 the planets come into perfect alignment. Since January 12 is Margi and Terri's birthday, and they were born in 1979, this gives them a Jupiter–Uranus opposition, which creates a grand square where the planets are aligned in a cross. This causes all the energy of the cosmos to be focused on them. ["Syzygy"]

KLEMPER, VICTOR: A Nazi scientist who escaped punishment at Nuremberg through **Operation Paper Clip.** The **Lone Gunmen** recognize him in the picture that Mulder finds of his father and other associates (including **Deep Throat,** the **Cigarette-Smoking Man,** and the **Well-Manicured Man**). Mulder and Scully track him down, still alive at American taxpayer expense, tending his orchids. He refuses to tell them anything but where the photo was

taken: the **Strughold** Mining Company in West Virginia, and a clue to the entry code. His taunting call to the Well-Manicured Man tips off the **Elders** that Mulder and Scully are headed to the mine. He dies soon after, perhaps of a real heart attack, perhaps of one staged by his former associates. ["Paper Clip"]

KNOXVILLE, TENNESSEE: Site where a mysterious train car is detached from a passenger train. The car is marked on top with the numbers 82594, and there is a satellite dish on the roof. ["Nisei"]

KORETZ, CREW CHIEF KAREN: One of the military personnel at the U.S. Space Surveillance Center who tracks a UFO to **Townsend, Wisconsin. Col. Henderson** orders her to report the object as a meteor despite all evidence to the contrary. She spots another, larger craft several days later in the same area. ["Fallen Angel"]

KOSSEFF, KAREN E.: An FBI social worker assigned to file a report on the Holvey family. Arriving at the home slightly before Mulder and Scully, she witnesses a strange ritual performed by the **Calusari** and finds what she thinks is **Charlie Holvey** having an unexplained seizure. When she questions Charlie at her office, however, he claims she had seen Michael — the dead twin brother his parents never told him about. ["The Calusari"] Scully goes to her for counseling because she is disturbed by aspects of the case she's working on involving a fetishist and grave desecrations. ["Irresistible"]

KOTCHIK, MISS: A patron of the **Provincetown Pub** who witnesses **Cecil L'ively** burst into flames. She experiences burns on both her hands from the ensuing bar fire, but is otherwise unhurt; she helps a police artist create a composite sketch of L'ively. ["Fire"]

KRAMER: FBI agent involved in the initial capture of **Eugene Tooms.** He is assigned by Mulder to stake out **Exeter Street** but is called off by Agent **Colton.** ["Squeeze"]

KRESKI: One of the FBI agents searching for **Carl Wade** and his kidnap victim, **Amy Jacobs.** He is with **Lucy Householder** when she starts having a strange attack. ["Oubliette"]

KREUTZER, LEO: A resident at the **Excelsis Dei Convalescent Home.** During the 1930s he was an artist who worked for the WPA. In the rest home he does some drawings, one of which is of a

woman with figures floating above her. ["Excelsis Dei"]

KRYCEK, ALEX: FBI agent assigned to work with Mulder. Mulder comes to trust him, but actually the man is trying to undermine Mulder's credibility. He is secretly reporting to the **Cigarette-Smoking Man.** ["Sleepless"] Krycek accompanies Mulder to the **Duane Barry** hostage situation but does little beyond getting coffee for Agent **Lucy Kazdin.** ["Duane Barry"] Subsequent events reveal the depth of his involvement: He may have provided Barry with Scully's address. Acting under the Smoking Man's orders, he stalls Mulder by stopping the tram up the mountain, and may have poisoned Barry and tried to frame Mulder for his death. A surprisingly inept operative, he doesn't seem to pull off his treachery as effectively as his superiors might have wanted him to. After the Duane Barry case ends, Krycek mysteriously disappears from view, his work apparently completed. ["Ascension"] Krycek crawls back out of the woodwork and murders **William Mulder** after the **MJ documents** are stolen. He may also have been involved in the poisoning of Fox Mulder's water supply with the mind-

altering drug that produced Mulder's psychotic behavior. Krycek then makes several attempts on Mulder's life, one of which almost kills Scully, and another that results in Mulder beating the living daylights out of him. He would probably be dead by now if Scully hadn't shot Mulder in the shoulder; it seems as if Krycek's superiors were setting up Mulder to kill Krycek with Krycek's gun, which would have conveniently framed Mulder for the murder of his own father as well. ["Anasazi"] Assigned to kill Scully by the Smoking Man, Krycek botches the job and kills her sister Melissa instead. ["The Blessing Way"] With his accomplices the **Suited Man** and **Luis Cardinal,** he assaults **Walter Skinner** and steals back the **MJ** files' DAT. He narrowly escapes being killed by his cohorts when they blow up his car; he flees with the tape and makes a threatening call to the Smoking Man. ["Paper Clip"] Escaping to Hong Kong, Krycek manages to break the code of the MJ files on the DAT and begins a lucrative career peddling government secrets. He sells the French the location where a UFO has been recovered, and is about to sell more secrets to

Jeraldine Kallenchuk when he is recaptured by Mulder. Before leaving Hong Kong he is possessed by the alien entity that occupied **Joan Gauthier.** ["Piper Maru"] Back in the USA, he escapes from Mulder and returns the DAT to the Smoking Man. In return, the Smoking Man takes Krycek and the alien to the decommissioned **Black Crow missile complex** in North Dakota, where the aliens' craft is stored. When Krycek regains control of his body, he discovers himself trapped in an abandoned missile silo with the UFO. ["Apocrypha"]

KRYDER, KEVIN: A ten-year-old student in the fifth-grade class of Mrs. Tynes at Ridgeway Elementary School in Loveland, Ohio. While writing on the blackboard in class, his palms start to bleed. He had been temporarily removed from his parents' custody a year before when he bled from his hands and feet. His mother was given custody after his father was arrested and institutionalized after a standoff with the police during which he claimed Kevin was the son of God (see also **stigmata.**) ["Revelations"]

KRYDER, MICHAEL: The father of Kevin Kryder. He knows his son is in danger from the Forces of Darkness who want to bring about Armageddon prematurely. ["Revelations"]

KRYDER, SUSAN: The mother of Kevin Kryder. She is angry at the suggestion that her son be placed in a shelter until the mystery of his bleeding palms can be investigated. She is later killed in a car accident while trying to protect her son from **Simon Gates.** ["Revelations"]

KYTE, LAUREN: **Howard Graves**'s secretary at **HTG Industrial Technologies**. After Graves dies, Kyte decides to leave Philadelphia, frightened that her life is in danger — a fear confirmed after two men attempt to kill her at her ATM machine. She knows why Graves was killed, and by whom, but remains silent out of fear. With a little help from Mulder and Scully — and a lot from the late Mr. Graves — she turns the tables on the treacherous **Robert Dorland.** ["Shadows"]

[L]

LABERGE, DR: He is caring for **Mrs. Mulder** in the hospital and tells Fox that her stroke was serious and she may never regain consciousness. ["Talitha Cumi"]

LACERIO, CAPT. ROY: The police officer in charge of the search for the fugitive who has escaped after an intense chase. The fugitive was shot and has left drops of green blood behind. ["The Erlenmeyer Flask"]

LADONNA: A robust woman in her fifties who runs the **Flying Saucer Diner** near **Ellens Air Force Base.** Claims to have seen UFOs and has a picture to prove it: a grainy shot of a triangular craft nearly identical to the one that allegedly crashed near Roswell, New Mexico, in 1947. She sells Mulder the photo for twenty dollars and draws a map to the air base on a napkin. ["Deep Throat"]

LAKE JORDAN: In North Carolina. Acting on information from **Luther Lee Boggs,** the FBI rescues **Liz Hawley** from **Lucas Jackson Henry** there. Henry shoots Mulder with a shotgun and escapes by boat with **Jim Summers** still his prisoner. ["Beyond the Sea"]

LAKE OKOBOGEE: Near Sioux City, Iowa. Known for its trout fishing and high incidence of UFO sightings, including one in 1967 by **Darlene Morris** and her Girl Scout troop. **Ruby Morris** disappears while camping here. ["Conduit"]

LAKEVIEW CABINS: On Flicker Road near **Heuvelmans Lake** in Georgia. Mulder and Scully stay here when they come to investigate some mysterious disappearances. ["Quagmire"]

LAMANA, JERRY: Mulder's former partner in the violent-crimes division. His career has not been exemplary since they split up, but rather marked by a number of high-profile foulups. Turning to Mulder for help with the murder of Eurisko CEO **Benjamin Drake,** Lamana steals Mulder's notes to make himself look better to their superiors, realizing Mulder was always the brains of their partnership. Killed in a mysterious elevator "malfunction." ["Ghost in the Machine"]

LAMB, HAROLD: A teenage boy who is abducted with his date, **Chrissy Giorgio,** by a UFO one night. ["Jose Chung's *From Outer Space*"]

LAMBERT, GAIL ANNE: A scientist employed at **Polarity Magnetics** who is the first of several unexplainable disappearances in the Richmond, Virginia, area. Her death is caused by a visit from **Chester Ray Banton,** who has yet to realize how deadly his shadow is. ["Soft Light"]

LANDIS, JESSE: Monica Landis's blind twelve-year-old daughter. She realizes that **Virgil Incanto** has done something bad to her mother when she smells Monica's perfume in his apartment. She makes the 911 call that leads Mulder and Scully to Incanto's home. ["2Shy"]

LANDIS, MONICA: **Virgil Incanto**'s landlady, and a would-be poet. She is interested in him, but he is oblivious to her. A slender woman, she's not his type. He kills her only after she discovers Det. **Alan Cross**'s body in his bathtub. ["2Shy"]

LANG, KYLE: An animal rights activist in his late forties, with the W.A.O. (Wild Again Organization). He goes to the **Fairfield Zoo** late one night and is killed by **Ed Meecham.** ["Fearful Symmetry"]

LANGE, MS.: **Lauren Kyte**'s new boss at the Monroe Mutual Insurance Company in Omaha, Nebraska, who doesn't know how lucky she is that **Howard Graves**'s spirit is finally at rest . . . if it really is. ["Shadows"]

LANGLY: The member of the Lone Gunmen who wears glasses with thick lenses. He tells Mulder that the **Thinker**'s real name might be Kenneth Soona. ["Anasazi"]

Helps identify one person in Mulder's mysterious photo of his father and associates: **Victor Klemper.** ["Paper Clip"] He also appears in "Blood" and "E.B.E."

LANNY: A circus freak in his fifties. He has a twin, **Leonard,** whose conjoining body is attached to his stomach. Unbeknownst to everyone else, Lanny's twin can separate himself from his body, and he wants to conjoin with a new brother. ["Humbug"]

LARAMIE TOBACCO: The company that employed **Margaret Wysnecki** until her retirement. The similarity between her disappearance and that of Dominion Tobacco executive **Patrick Newirth** leads Mulder to briefly consider a link based on their professional environment. ["Soft Light"]

LARKEN SCHOLASTIC: The photography company that took the student pictures at **Valley Woods High School.** ["Oubliette"]

LARSON, DR. JERROLD: When he's killed in a plane crash near **Delta Glen, Wisconsin,** it is revealed that he's been injecting local children with a strange substance and then tracking them over the years. The doctor claimed he was giving the children vitamin shots. He was carrying a briefcase filled with hundred-dollar bills. ["Red Museum"]

LASKOS, DR.: The physician in charge of the **Bethesda Naval Hospital**'s intensive care unit when **Lt. Richard Harper** is admitted. Laskos kicks Scully out of the ICU for having an invalid clearance code. She later saves Scully's and Mulder's lives, using Scully's field notes. ["Dod Kalm"]

LAZARD, DET. SHARON: A twenty-eight-year-old police detective who works at the **14th Precinct** in Buffalo, New York. She finds a lost eight-year-old girl named **Michelle Bishop** and takes her back to the police station. ["Born Again"]

LEADER: One of the phony Gray Aliens, who interrogate people they abduct. ["Jose Chung's *From Outer Space*"]

LEATHER SATCHEL: Found at the scene of a murder in the possession of **Kazuo Takeo.** Inside the bag are high-resolution satellite photos and a list of Mutual UFO Network (MUFON) members in the **Allentown** area. One name circled is **Betsy Hagopian.** ["Nisei"]

LEDBETTER, TIM: The partner in 1940 of FBI agent **Sam Chaney.** They were early experts on "stranger killings"

(now called serial killings), and both of them disappeared in 1942. Ledbetter's body is found in 1995 beneath a house **Harry Cokely** had rented in 1942. ["Aubrey"]

LEE, MR.: The manager of the apartment building where **Eugene Tooms** claims to live in 1993. Mulder and Scully find no signs of habitation there; Tooms was using it as a front address, preferring his nest in Apartment 103 of 66 **Exeter Street,** Baltimore. ["Squeeze"]

LEONARD: The name **Lanny** gave his Siamese twin. This twin is sentient, and it can separate itself from Lanny's body. ["Humbug"]

LESKY, DIANA: The pseudonym given to Scully in **Jose Chung's** book titled *From Outer Space.* ["Jose Chung's *From Outer Space*"]

LEWIN: One of the agents who has Mulder's residence under surveillance, and who confronts Scully when she goes there. ["Little Green Men"]

LEWTON, DR. JERROLD: Curator of the Boston Museum of Natural History. He is killed shortly after the disappearance of **Craig Horning.** ["Teso dos Bichos"]

LIFEBOAT 925: The lifeboat commandeered by **Lt. Richard Harper** and seven-

teen other mutineers when they defy Capt. **Phillip Barclay** and abandon the USS *Argent* in the Norwegian Sea. ["Dod Kalm"]

LIGHTHOUSE BUNGALOWS MOTEL: North of San Francisco. **Dr. Sally Kendrick** takes **Cindy Reardon** and **Teena Simmons** there. The manager tips off the FBI to their presence, but not soon enough to keep the two young clones from murdering Kendrick. ["Eve"]

LIMO DRIVER: On Embassy Row in Washington, D.C., he picks up **Kazuo Takeo,** the Japanese diplomat whom Mulder had captured at the scene of a murder. It is a trap, and Takeo is murdered in the limo to cover up his sloppy work in **Allentown.** ["Nisei"]

LINCOLN PARK: The amusement park in Murray, Virginia, where **Teddy Holvey** escapes from his baby harness, wanders out of a public bathroom, and is killed by a miniature train. ["The Calusari"]

LINHART, HARRY: FBI composite artist. ["Born Again"]

LINLEY TEMPORARY HOME SHELTER: **Kevin Kryder** is temporarily placed here. ["Revelations"]

LIQUID: One of the phony Gray Aliens, who interrogate people they abduct. ["Jose Chung's *From Outer Space*"]

LIQUORI, BART "ZERO": **Darin Peter Oswald**'s only friend. Zero dispenses change at the local video arcade in **Connerville, Oklahoma.** Believing that Zero has told Mulder and Scully about his powers, Darin kills him with a powerful electric discharge. ["D.P.O."]

LISETTE: The Canadian fishing vessel (ID number CV233) that rescues the mutineers who escape from the USS **Argent.** ["Dod Kalm"]

LITCHFIELD PROJECT: A highly classified eugenics experiment, sponsored by the U.S. government, in which identical, genetically engineered children are raised in a controlled environment in a town called Litchfield. The boys are called Adam, the girls Eve; all are assigned numbers. These children have fifty-six chromosomes instead of the usual forty-six; this allows them to develop superhuman attributes, including enhanced strength, intelligence, and extrasensory abilities. They also suffer from extreme psychosis. Many commit suicide. **Eve Six** has been incarcerated for years; **Eve Eight** is still at large. Eve Seven, a.k.a. **Dr. Sally Kendrick,** has created

clones of herself (**Cindy Reardon** and **Teena Simmons**) who eventually kill her with a poisoned soda. ["Eve"]

L'IVELY, CECIL: A Briton with pyrokinetic, or fire-starting powers. His normal body temperature is 111 degrees. He was employed on the estates of several British aristocrats who died by fire. The name L'ively may be a pseudonym: Lively is the name of a child murdered by a cult in 1963 *and* a solid British citizen who died in 1971. Cecil L'ively murders and replaces the caretaker at the Cape Cod residence where the **Marsden** family has sought refuge, then stages a rescue of their children in order to gain their confidence. Stopped before he can kill again, L'ively, known in the U.S. as **Bob,** suffers severe burns but heals remarkably fast. Finally incarcerated in a high-security federal medical facility, he is confined to a hyperbaric chamber to prevent fires. ["Fire"]

LLOYD P. WHARTON COUNTY BUILDING: The county administrative building of Johnston County, Oklahoma, located in the town of **Connerville.** Scully autopsies **Jack Hammond**'s body in the

postmortem facilities here. ["D.P.O."]

LO, JOHNNY: A Chinese man whose charred body is found in the crematorium at the Bayside Funeral Home. He has been burned alive. ["Hell Money"]

LOCKER 101356: The locker in an airport near Washington, D.C., where **John Barnett** places **Dr. Joe Ridley**'s research. ["Young at Heart"]

LOFOTEN BASIN: Norwegian ships are forbidden to sail beyond this point unless they are classified as ice class vessels. **Henry Trondheim** doesn't have a problem with this: his fifty-ton trawler, the *Zeal*, is completely seaworthy, until it reaches 58° N, 8° E. ["Dod Kalm"]

LONE GUNMAN: A magazine specializing in conspiracy theories. The April 1994 edition has an article on the CCDTH7321 fiberoptic lens micro video camera used by the CIA. ["Blood" and "E.B.E."]

LONE GUNMEN: A group of fringe conspiracy buffs whom Mulder consults on occasion. Three of them come to Mulder's apartment after the **Thinker,** a.k.a. Kenneth Soona, steals the **MJ documents.** A woman in Mulder's apartment building apparently goes crazy and shoots her husband while they are there. ["Anasazi"] They help Mulder locate **Krycek**'s locker, but the **MJ** files DAT is missing. ["Apocrypha"]

LONE GUNMEN'S OFFICE: Mulder goes there to show some high-resolution satellite photos to the guys to see what they can make of them. **Langly** tells Mulder that one of them is of a ship named the *Talapus*. **Byers** states that he believes the photo is from a Japanese surveillance satellite. **Frohike** states that he believes the Japanese launched it from a secret site in South America. ["Nisei"]

LORRE, GARRETT: A forty-eight-year-old, gray-haired businessman who is killed by a vampiric triumvirate. On the wall near his body, written in his blood, is **"JOHN 52:54."** ["3"]

LORTON, VIRGINIA: Location of the D.C. Correctional Complex. ["Grotesque"]

LOS ALAMOS, NEW MEXICO: The closest city to the Navajo reservation where Mulder is presumed dead by the **Cigarette-Smoking Man** but is rescued by **Albert Hosteen** and his family. ["Anasazi"; "The Blessing Way"] Also where the Manhattan Project scientists tested the first atomic bomb. What other as yet uncovered secret projects has the U.S. government undertaken here?

LOVELAND, OHIO: Location of Ridgeway Elementary School, where **Kevin Kryder** attends fifth grade. ["Revelations"]

LOWE, MRS.: **Clyde Bruckman**'s elderly neighbor. He foresees her death when he takes out her trash for her. Due to the lack of dog food in her apartment, Mrs. Lowe's remains were subjected to certain indignities by her small dog. ["Clyde Bruckman's Final Repose"]

LUDER, M. F.: A pseudonym used by Mulder when he published an article on the Gulf Breeze Sightings in *Omni* magazine. According to **Max Fenig**, UFOlogists following Mulder's career had no problem unscrambling the anagram. ["Fallen Angel"]

LUDWIG, JASON: Robotics engineer for the descent team on the **Cascade Volcano Research Project.** He's killed by **Trepkos** with a flare gun. ["Firewalker"]

LUTHER STAPES CENTER FOR REPRODUCTIVE MEDICINE: A fertility clinic in San Francisco where **Dr. Sally Kendrick** had her residency in 1985. The **Simmons** family and the **Reardon** family both came here while trying to conceive, only to have clones of Kendrick, a.k.a. Eve Seven, implanted instead. ["Eve"]

LYNN ACRES RETIREMENT HOME: A residence for the elderly that is not in very good repair. **Frank Briggs,** a police detective who once hunted **Tooms,** now lives here. ["Tooms"]

LYSERGIC DIMETHRIN: The substance similar in structure and effect to LSD. It is found in the bodies of the killers who went on a rampage in **Franklin, Pennsylvania.** It reacts with adrenaline to cause the person to become psychotic. A secret, experimental insecticide, it is sprayed on plants to cause a fear response in insects that touch them. ["Blood"]

[M]

McALPIN, JOHN "JACK": A twenty-three-year-old U.S. Marine private who dies when his car hits a tree near his home. A strange symbol is painted on the tree. Later his body vanishes and he's found alive. ["Fresh Bones"]

McALPIN, LUKE: Eighteen-month-old son of Robin and Jack. ["Fresh Bones"]

McALPIN, ROBIN: Wife of Pvt. John McAlpin. ["Fresh Bones"]

McCALL, DOROTHY: A resident at the **Excelsis Dei Convalescent Home.** She's able to see the disembodied spirits of the old men who are taking the secret drug. ["Excelsis Dei"]

McCALLISTER, DOREEN: A member of the Girl Scout troop that witnessed and photographed a UFO near **Lake Okobogee** in 1967. ["Conduit"]

McCALLISTER PENITENTIARY: Where **Harry Cokely** served his prison time from 1945 to 1993 for the rape and attempted murder of **Linda Thibodeaux.** ["Aubrey"]

McCLENNEN, JIM: A test pilot at **Ellens Air Force Base** who suffers from a stress-related syndrome called stereotypy (Scully's diagnosis). Disoriented and prone to compulsive, repetitive behavior like picking at his hair, he probably underwent the same stresses that affected **Col. Robert Budahas.** ["Deep Throat"]

McCLENNEN, VERLA: The wife of Jim McClennen. She accepts her husband's problems more readily than **Anita Budahas** accepts hers. ["Deep Throat"]

McGRATH, JOSEPH: FBI section chief who wants Mulder expelled from the Bureau and the X-Files unit disbanded. He almost gets his wish after certain events in **Townsend, Wisconsin,** but **Deep Throat** overrides his decision. ["Fallen Angel"]

MACKALVEY, LAUREN: A lonely, overweight woman whose bizarre murder brings Mulder and Scully to Cleveland, Ohio. Her skin and fatty tissue have been dissolved by a slimelike substance that reduces her body to mere bones a few hours later. She was killed by **Virgil Incanto.** ["2Shy"]

McNALLY, HARRY: **Ed Funsch**'s supervisor at the post office in **Franklin, Pennsylvania.** ["Blood"]

McROBERTS, BONNIE: She goes to pick up her Volvo at the garage in **Franklin, Pennsylvania,** where it's being worked on. The engine analyzer monitor starts telling her that the mechanic is lying to her, then tells her to kill him, which she does, with an oil can spout. When Mulder and Sheriff Spencer go to question her, she attacks Mulder with a knife and is shot and killed by Spencer. Her autopsy reveals that her adrenaline levels were two hundred times the norm. Also, an unknown chemical — later identified as lysergic dimethrin — found in her body has properties that would cause it to react with adrenaline to produce a substance similar in structure and effect to LSD. ["Blood"]

MADISON: A street in **Hagerstown, Maryland. Lula Philips** robs a drugstore at the intersection of Madison and Forge Road. ["Lazarus"]

MAHAN PROPULSION LABORATORY: Located at the Washington Institute of Technology in Colson, Washington, where **Roland Fuller** commits a series of murders. ["Roland"]

MAIN STREET: In Easton, Washington, where the FBI arrive to search for kidnapping suspect **Carl Wade.** ["Oubliette"]

MAJESTIC: The name of a top-secret report that **Deep Throat** gives Mulder. ["E.B.E."]

MALAWI: The African nation from which **Willa Ambrose** rescued **Sophie** the gorilla. The government there wants the gorilla back. ["Fearful Symmetry"]

MALLARD, DENNIS: A classmate of **Amy Jacob**'s at Valley Woods High in Seattle. ["Oubliette"]

MANDAS, MARILYN: She works for **Ficicello Frozen Foods,** which is where **Donnie Pfaster** gets a job after he's fired by the **Janelli-Heller Funeral Home.** ["Irresistible"]

MANDROID: A male android. An artificial person. **Blaine Faulkner** claims this is what he thinks Mulder is. ["Jose Chung's *From Outer Space*"]

MAN IN BLACK #1: He and his partner drive their silent black Cadillac into the garage of **Roky Crikenson** and spout strange anti-UFO gibberish. They try to convince Crikenson that he didn't see a UFO at all, just the planet Venus. ["Jose Chung's *From Outer Space*"]

MAN IN BLACK #2: A.k.a. Alex Trebek. ["Jose Chung's *From Outer Space*"]

MANITOU: An evil spirit that can change a man into a beast. One attacked **Richard Watkins** and began his shape-shifting and murders. ["Shapes"]

MANLEY, DANIELLE: The wife of "Neech" Manley. She has frequent dreams that her husband survived the electric chair. Believing that his soul has passed into the body of her lover, the prison guard **Parmelly,** she shoots him. ["The List"]

MANLEY, NAPOLEON ("NEECH"): A prisoner executed at **Eastpoint State Penitentiary** for a double homicide. Manley did not actually kill anyone, but as the driver of the getaway car he was charged with murder. He vows to be reincarnated and to avenge himself by killing five men. Two days after the execution, a guard is found dead of suffocation in Neech's empty cell. ["The List"]

MANNERS, DET.: He interviews **Harold Lamb,** who is believed guilty of date rape. Lamb's alien abduction story is found a bit preposterous by this hard-bitten detective. He speaks in sentences laced with expletives, but instead of the expletive we hear the words "bleeped" and "blankety-blank." ["Jose Chung's *From Outer Space*"]

MARIO: A new employee at the **Culver City Plasma Center.** Mulder considers him a possible suspect, but he's not the right one. ["3"]

MARION, VIRGINIA: Location of the **Davis Correctional Treatment Center,** where **Duane Barry** is held until his final escape in 1994. ["Duane Barry"]

MARSDEN, LADY: The wife of Lord Malcolm Marsden, she becomes the object of **Cecil L'ively**'s warm attentions; he sends her deranged love letters prior to his attempt on her children's lives. ["Fire"]

MARSDEN, LORD MALCOLM: **Cecil L'ively**'s intended victim, Marsden escaped death by fire in his garage in England and came to the United States for safety. L'ively's attention then shifts from this Member of Parliament to his children. Marsden avoids L'ively's deadly intentions but is unable to resist the more agreeable charms of Scotland Yard investigator **Phoebe Green.** ["Fire"]

MARSDEN, JIMMIE AND MICHAEL: The young sons of Lord and Lady Marsden. ["Fire"]

MARTINGALE: A tie-down chain that pulls an elephant's tusk to the ground. This forces the elephant to its knees, hobbling it. ["Fearful Symmetry"]

MARTY: Formerly Brother Martin of the **Kindred,** he ventures into the outside world to pursue sex with what he refers to as "human men and women." He can change genders at will. Death is an unfortunate side effect of sex with a Kindred, due to the incredibly high amount of **pheromones** they possess. Marty is taken away by the Kindred the night they seemingly disappeared from the face of the Earth. ["Genderbender"]

MARYLAND MARINE BANK: Site of the last robbery committed by **Warren James Dupre** and **Lula Philips.** The FBI is there, thanks to an anonymous tip; Dupre shoots agent **Jack Willis,** but is killed by Scully. Philips, the getaway driver, escapes. ["Lazarus"]

MASSACHUSETTS INSTI-TUTE OF ROBOTICS: Where an artificial-intelligence researcher designs robots that look like insects. ["War of the Coprophages"]

MATHESON, SEN. RICHARD: One of Mulder's occasional friends in high places, Matheson drops out of the picture when the going gets tough. **X** hints that the government has some incriminating information it uses to keep Matheson in line. ["Ascension"] Matheson takes a convenient vacation to the Caribbean after the **MJ documents** are stolen. ["Anasazi"; see also "Little Green Men"] Mulder goes to see him after a Japanese murder suspect is found dead and Mulder's apartment is ransacked by people trying to locate a briefcase Mulder appropriated from the murder suspect. Matheson advises Mulder to return the

satellite photos, which Mulder is reluctant to do. The senator gives Mulder the names of the four scientists who were murdered during an alien autopsy. ["Nisei"]

MATOLA, SALVATORE: A previously unknown survivor of **Dr. Grissom**'s sleep deprivation experiments at Parris Island. He is located at 2 Jay's Diner, Roslyn, New York. ["Sleepless"]

MAXWELL, MR.: Janitor at the **Hollywood Blood Bank.** ["3"]

MAYWALD, CARINA: A Social Services worker who comes to investigate when **Kevin Kryder** suffers from bleeding palms at school. ["Revelations"]

MAZEROSKI, RICK: The sixteen-year-old son of the sheriff of **Delta Glen, Wisconsin.** He is kidnapped and found with the words "HE IS ONE" written on his back. But he has also been murdered, shot in the head. ["Red Museum"]

MEECHAM, ED: Chief of operations for the **Fairfield Zoo** in Idaho. He has no explanation for how the elephant, **Ganesha,** escaped from her locked cage. He isn't asked whether Ganesha knew how to become invisible or not. The Wild Again Organization believe that Meecham has

been mistreating animals at the zoo, including elephants. ["Fearful Symmetry"]

MEN IN BLACK: Two men in dark suits, present during **Duane Barry**'s 1985 alien abduction ["Duane Barry"] and briefly present with **Alex Krycek** after Barry's capture at Skyland Mountain. ["Ascension"]

"THE MERCHANDISE": A veiled, perhaps coded, reference to the bodies Mulder found in a railroad car buried on the Navajo reservation near **Farmington, New Mexico. William Mulder** uses this term, which also appears in **MJ documents** about experiments conducted by Axis Powers scientists working for the U.S. government after World War II. It is unclear whether these bodies are human, alien, or some sort of hybrid, but Mulder notices smallpox vaccination scars on some of them before they are destroyed. ["Anasazi"]

MERCY MISSION: The soup kitchen in **Atlantic City** where Mulder meets the homeless man named **Jack,** who assists him with his investigation. ["The Jersey Devil"]

METHANE RESEARCH FACILITY: Run by **Alt.-Fuels Inc.** Their motto is "Waste is a terrible thing to waste." It gets blown up when **Dr. Eckerle** goes crazy and starts shooting at cockroaches in the plant. ["War of the Coprophages"]

MICHAEL: A man picked up by the female Marty who narrowly escapes death when the police mistake Marty for a prostitute and try to intervene. He describes Marty to Mulder, who convinces him to reveal that Marty seemed to be changing into a man when she escaped from the police. ["Genderbender"]

MIDNIGHT INQUISITOR: A tacky tabloid newspaper purchased by **Clyde Bruckman** at a liquor store shortly before his first encounter with the **Puppet.** The Stupendous **Yappi** offers celebrity predictions in the issue in question, including a romantic liaison between Madonna and Kato Kaelin. ["Clyde Bruckman's Final Repose"]

MIHAI: A Romanian form of the name Michael, used by **Golda** during the performance of an unsuccessful Ritual of Separation. ["The Calusari"]

MILES, BILLY: A friend of the victims of the mysterious killings in Bellefleur, Oregon, who were members of the high school class of '89. He was in an auto accident with **Peggy O'Dell** and became comatose — except during those times

when he is controlled by a mysterious outside force. [Pilot]

MILES, DET.: The father of Billy Miles. He doesn't want Mulder and Scully talking to his son. [Pilot]

MILFORD HAVEN, NEW HAMPSHIRE: Town where "Die Hand Die Verletzt" takes place.

MILLENNIUM MAN: See **Simon Gates.** ["Revelations"]

MILLER'S GROVE, MASSA-CHUSETTS: The site of some strange "roach attacks." ["War of the Coprophages"]

MINETTE, ETHAN: Scully's boyfriend in the pilot episode. She has to cancel a long-planned vacation with him in order to go to Oregon with Mulder on their first mission together. [Pilot]

MINNEAPOLIS COUNTY MORGUE: Where Scully does the autopsy on **Satin.** ["Irresistible"]

MIRACLE MINISTRY: Run by the **Rev. Hartley** and his son, **Samuel Hartley,** who once brought a man back from the dead. ["Miracle Man"]

MIRAMAR NAVY AIR BASE: North of San Diego, former home of the Top Gun fighter training program. Scully goes there to visit **Commander Christopher Johansen,** an old friend of her father's who

served on the submarine *Zeus Faber.* ["Piper Maru"]

MIRISKOVIC, LLADOSLAV: A Bosnian war criminal. **Joseph Patnik** believed that each of the five people he killed was Miriskovic. When Patnik is incarcerated in the Frederick County Psychiatric Hospital, he is watching TV and sees a news report about Miriskovic, whereupon Patnik becomes hysterical with fear and terror and has to be restrained. ["Wetwired"]

MR. X: See **X.**

M.J.: The roommate of **Michelle Charters.** ["Excelsis Dei"]

MJ DOCUMENTS: The complete Defense Department files on every UFO case from Roswell and after, stolen by the hacker called the **Thinker** and passed along to Mulder. These top-secret files are encoded in Navajo and contain many facts that have yet to be fully translated, including an explanation of Scully's disappearance, the truth about **Duane Barry,** and the story of **William Mulder**'s involvement in certain undisclosed government projects. ["Anasazi"]

MKULTRA: Pronounced M-K-Ultra. Refers to the CIA's mind-control experiments conducted in the 1950s. ["Jose Chung's *From Outer Space*"]

MODELL, ROBERT: A killer with psychic powers of persuasion, whose hits were all written off as suicides until he called up FBI agent **Frank Burst** and bragged about them. He allows himself to be captured twice. The second time, he gets off scot free because the murders have already been ruled suicides — and because he uses his willpower on the judge. Scully discovers that Modell had applied to the FBI for a job but was turned down. An all-too-average guy who never excelled at anything, Modell knows his powers are a direct result of a brain tumor. His condition is treatable, but he prefers to risk death and keep the powers that make him superior to other people for the first time in his life. ["Pusher"]

MOLITCH, HARVEY: When the son of **George Hunsaker** receives an anonymous call from someone who says he knows where a mass grave is located, **Bob Spitz** shows up with a backhoe wanting to dig up Molitch's yard. ["Syzygy"]

MONITORING CHIP: After Scully finds and removes this tiny chip from her neck in "Nisei," she takes it to FBI agent **Pendrell,** who scans it and discovers that it records memories to the degree that whoever monitors the chip could even monitor a person's thoughts. He discovers that it was manufactured in Japan. It is traced to a **Dr. Shiro Zama** at a facility in Perkey, West Virginia. ["731"]

MONKEY WRENCHERS: Radical environmentalists who drive spikes into trees and sabotage logging equipment. ["Darkness Falls"]

MONROE, KIMBERLY: An employee of the **Travel Time Travel Agency** taken hostage by **Duane Barry.** Mulder persuades Barry to set Monroe and Gwen Norris free. She tells Barry that she believes his alien abduction story. ["Duane Barry"]

MONTE, DR. AARON: The doctor in charge of **Eugene Tooms** at the **Druid Hill Sanitarium** in Baltimore. After Tooms is released, Monte is supposed to supervise him. Tooms later kills him and eats his liver. ["Tooms"]

MONTIFIORE CEMETERY: In Minneapolis. A fresh grave there is desecrated and some of the hair and fingernails are cut from the corpse of Catherine Ann Terle. ["Irresistible"]

MOORE, LARRY: A U.S. Forest Service employee. He goes with Mulder, Scully, and Humphreys to search for thirty missing loggers. ["Darkness Falls"]

MORGAN, WAYNE: A Navy investigator who accompanies Mulder and Scully when they take a look at the *Piper Maru.* ["Piper Maru"]

MORLEYS CIGARETTES: The brand smoked by the **Cigarette-Smoking Man.** ["One Breath"]

MORRIS, AGENT: He is following Scully when she goes to the Miami airport to catch a flight to Puerto Rico to search for Mulder. ["Little Green Men"]

MORRIS, CHARLIE: Police officer who worked narcotics in the 27th Precinct. He was killed gangland style in Chinatown. When he possesses eight-year-old **Michelle Bishop,** he displays his origami skills. ["Born Again"]

MORRIS, DARLENE: In 1967, she and members of her Girl Scout troop witnessed and photographed a UFO over **Lake Okobogee,** Iowa. In 1993, her daughter Ruby is abducted by a UFO at the same lake. At first cooperative, Darlene refuses to help Mulder and Scully after NSA agents ransack her home; when her daughter is returned, she denies anything unusual ever happened to either of her children (see **Kevin Morris**). ["Conduit"]

MORRIS, JANE: A secretary at **HTG Industrial Technologies** who comforts **Lauren Kyte** after **Howard Graves**'s apparent suicide. ["Shadows"]

MORRIS, KEVIN: The eight-year-old son of **Darlene Morris,** present when his sister Ruby is abducted. Kevin's own exposure to an alien presence enables him to somehow pick up binary transmissions that include some top-secret military satellite information, which he scribbles on pieces of paper. A valuable lead for Mulder, until Darlene blocks all access to her family. ["Conduit"]

MORRIS, RUBY: The sixteen-year-old daughter of **Darlene Morris.** Some believe she spent the month of her disappearance partying with a motorcycle gang, but Mulder suspects otherwise: she exhibits the same physical symptoms experienced by astronauts after prolonged weightlessness. Unfortunately, Darlene will not allow Mulder to talk to either of her children after the incidents around **Lake Okobogee.** ["Conduit"]

MORRISVILLE: A town in Virginia, location of the **Blue Devil Brewery** where **Jim**

Summers is rescued. ["Beyond the Sea"]

MORROW, DET. B. J.: Of the Aubrey, Missouri, police. Her father was also a policeman. She is having an affair with Lt. Brian Tillman and becomes pregnant. She goes to the **Motel Black** and later awakens from a trance to discover that she has uncovered a grave in a vacant field. In the grave is an old FBI badge. She is actually the granddaughter of **Harry Cokely.** Her father was the child **Ruby Thibodeaux** gave up for adoption in 1946. She has become a murderer just like her grandfather was. ["Aubrey"]

MORROW, RAYMOND: The father of B. J. Morrow, he is the son of **Harry Cokely** as a result of his rape of **Ruby Thibodeaux** in 1945. ["Aubrey"]

MOSIER, GARY: The man the tow-truck driver is looking for when he stops to talk to **Carl Wade.** ["Oubliette"]

MOSSBERG, BULLPUP: The variety of shotgun with which a soldier strikes Mulder when he intrudes on **Operation Falcon.** ["Fallen Angel"]

MOSSINGER, PAUL: A military agent masquerading as a local journalist, he tries to divert Mulder and Scully from investigating **Ellens Air Force Base** by directing them to local crackpots — not realizing Mulder will turn up a real lead or two that way. When things get serious, "Mossinger" tries to overpower Scully, but she turns the tables and uses him as a hostage to secure Mulder's release from the air base. ["Deep Throat"]

MOSTOW, JOHN: An art student and unemployed house painter, divorced, no children. Emigrated to the U.S. from Uzbekistan, where he'd spent much of his life confined in an insane asylum. In class, the model, Peter, is a nude man, but the drawing he makes is of a gargoyle. He is arrested for the murder of Peter, and is suspected of the serial murders of six other men over three years. The victims were all males ages seventeen to twenty-five. He claims he was possessed by a demon during the times he committed the murders. In his home is a secret room containing the bodies of more murdered men, but they have been covered with clay and made to appear to be statues of gargoyles. ["Grotesque"]

MOTEL BLACK: Where **B. J. Morrow** goes to meet **Brian Tillman** to talk after she tells him she's pregnant. ["Aubrey"]

MOTEL MANAGER: At the 2400 Motel he and Mulder are shot at by Scully. ["Wetwired"]

MOUNT AVALON: Where Mulder and Scully are flown to investigate the **Cascade Volcano Research Project,** which has encountered a serious problem. ["Firewalker"]

MOUNT FOODMORE SUPERMARKET: Site of **Robert Modell**'s premeditated apprehension by FBI agent **Frank Burst.** ["Pusher"]

MOUNTAIN HOME AIR BASE: The **Lone Gunmen** claim that this is a major hotspot in Idaho for UFO activity. ["Fearful Symmetry"]

MOUNTAIN RAVINE: Where the **Quarantine Car** is uncoupled from the train that had been pulling it. ["731"]

MTA OFFICER: He reveals to Mulder that a car has suddenly appeared on the surveillance video of track 17. ["Sleepless"]

MUGWORT: A ceremonial herb used by the **Calusari** while performing the Ritual of Separation on **Charlie Holvey.** ["The Calusari"]

MULDER, FOX: Oxford-educated psychologist who wrote a monograph on serial killers and the occult which assisted in the capture of Monte Propps (a serial killer) in 1988. Considered the violent-crime section's finest analyst. Worked three years for the FBI's behavioral science unit, profiling serial killers. Nickname "Spooky." Developed an intense fear of fire when a childhood friend's house burned down ["Fire"] While open to unusual and bizarre ideas, he refuses to believe

Luther Lee Boggs's claim of psychic abilities. ["Beyond the Sea"] Suffers simultaneously from exposure to extreme cold and a deadly alien virus during a private mission to the Arctic. ["Colony," "End Game"] Experiences accelerated aging, later reversed, on a mission in the North Atlantic. ["Dod Kalm"] Suffers temporary psychosis when the water supply in his apartment building is drugged; is shot in the shoulder by Scully to prevent him from murdering **Alex Krycek.** ["Anasazi"] Trapped in a boxcar filled with alien bodies, Mulder escapes death by fire by crawling through a narrow tunnel dug decades before by the doomed aliens and is nursed back to health by local Navajo healer **Albert Hosteen.** Mulder is originally suspected of killing his own father but later cleared. When he returns to his father's house, he finds an old photo of his father, **Deep Throat,** the **Cigarette-Smoking Man,** and the **Well-Manicured Man** (whom he does not know yet). ["The Blessing Way"] According to an offhand comment by psychic **Clyde Bruckman,** Mulder will die by autoerotic asphyxiation. ["Clyde Bruckman's Final Repose"] The fact that Mulder is red–green colorblind makes him immune to a signal from a TV broadcasting tachistoscopic images designed to influence the person who is watching the program. ["Wetwired"]

MULDER, MRS.: Fox Mulder's mother. She and her husband, William, were divorced by the time Fox was an adult. She is the first person to see her son alive after his disappearance. ["The Blessing Way"] When he confronts her with a photo of his father with **Deep Throat** and other, more sinister associates, she refuses to deal with the memories it awakens. In complete denial about her family's past, she cannot even recall the associates' names. ["The Blessing Way"] She admits to Fox that her husband asked her to choose which of their children should be taken away by aliens, but that she couldn't choose. When William Mulder made his choice, it destroyed their marriage forever. ["Paper Clip"] She used to associate with the **Cigarette-Smoking Man** socially at the time William worked for the government, but she hates him now. When he comes to her to try to secure information from her, she becomes violently angry, and moments after he leaves she suffers a severe and debilitating stroke. Only

because **X** has been secretly observing her and calls 911 does she receive immediate paramedic assistance. When X shows Fox photos of CSM visiting Mrs. Mulder, Fox becomes incensed and comes close to killing CSM. Mrs. Mulder gives Fox a clue to something she had hidden in her cottage at the lake, and Mulder finds the kind of personal weapon needed to kill aliens. ["Talitha Cumi"]

MULDER, SAMANTHA: The sister of Fox Mulder. She disappeared November 27, 1973, when she was eight years old, the apparent victim of alien abduction. According to Scully, Fox told her there was a bright light and a presence in the room when it happened — a classic UFO abduction story that explains Fox's lifelong obsession with cosmic mysteries of all sorts. Under hypnotic regression, Fox recalls that a voice in his head told him not to be afraid: that Samantha would not be harmed, and that some day she would return. ["Conduit"] First mentioned in the episode "Miracle Man." Also mentioned in "Little Green Men" (see also **"Samantha,"** whose true identity is still in question).

MULDER SUMMER HOME: Located on a lake at

Quonochontaug, Rhode Island. ["Talitha Cumi"]

MULDER, WILLIAM: Fox Mulder's father, a distant man who was not close to his son. He calls Fox at the FBI when his daughter Samantha appears to have returned after twenty-two years. ["Colony"] He becomes very angry with Fox when he receives the news that Samantha is lost again; this is before Fox learns that "Samantha" was really an alien clone. He also gave Fox a note from the false Samantha, which led to the abortion clinic at 1235 91st Street, Rockville, Maryland. ["End Game"] William Mulder is somehow associated with past UFO cover-ups, along with the **Cigarette-Smoking Man,** who advises him to deny his past to Fox. William instead decides to tell his son everything, but is murdered by **Alex Krycek** before he can do so, leaving Fox with nothing more than a tantalizing reference to **"the merchandise."** His name appears in the encoded **MJ documents.** ["Anasazi"] He worked on a secret government project years before, and he is assassinated by an agency concerned that he might reveal what he knows to his son. He appears to Fox in a vision during the **Blessing Way** ceremony. ["The Blessing Way"] According to the **Well-Manicured Man,** in the 1950s William Mulder was involved in collecting genetic samples from the general population — the files Fox found at the **Strughold Mine.** When William Mulder realized the true purpose of this activity, he threatened to expose it — so one of his own children was abducted as insurance. He was forced to choose which one. ["Paper Clip"] In 1953 he interviewed one of the surviving sailors who had been exposed to radiation on the submarine *Zeus Faber.* ["Apocrypha"]

MULDRAKE, REYNARD: The pseudonym given to Fox Mulder in Jose Chung's book titled *From Outer Space.* ["Jose Chung's *From Outer Space*"]

MULTREVICH: The manager of the apartment building where **Lula Philips** moves after the death of **Warren Dupre.** He calls the FBI to turn her in for a $10,000 reward, but his call is answered by **Jack Willis** and Scully, with unusual results. ["Lazarus"]

MUNCHAUSEN BY PROXY: A form of child abuse in which a parent or caretaker induces medical symptoms in a child in order to enhance his or her

status as the child's "protector." **Teddy** and **Charlie Holvey** both suffered from frequent and inexplicable childhood maladies, which leads Scully to suspect their grandmother **Golda** was committing Munchausen by proxy. **Steve Holvey** had already suspected as much, but had feared to admit this to his wife. ["The Calusari"]

MUNTZ, GALEN: A disturbed man who starts shooting people in a fast-food restaurant. But when he is shot by the police, **Jeremiah Smith** heals the gunman and the victims of all their wounds with just the touch of his hands. ["Talitha Cumi"]

MURPHY, DR. DENNY: A professor of geology at the University of California, San Diego. He accompanies Mulder and Scully to investigate the **Arctic Ice Core Project** disaster. A devoted football fan who listens to audiotapes of old playoff games. He is murdered at the Ice Core Project camp by **Dr. Nancy Da Silva** while she is under the influence of the alien **ice worm,** making him indirectly its seventh casualty. ["Ice"]

MURRAY, VIRGINIA: The location of **Lincoln Park,** where

Teddy Holvey dies. ["The Calusari"]

[N]

NAPIER'S CONSTANT: The numerical base (27828) for all natural logarithms. **Victor Klemper** mentions it to Mulder and Scully; it turns out to be the entry code to the secret information repository at the **Strughold Mine.** ["Paper Clip"]

NATIONAL COMET: The tabloid paper in which Mulder learns of the abduction of **Ruby Morris.** ["Conduit"]

NATIONAL SECURITY AGENCY: The red-haired man (**Malcolm Gerlach**) claims he works for the NSA. ["731"]

NAVAJO CODE TALKERS: During World War II, the U.S. military used Navajo servicemen to relay sensitive messages in their native language, which was impervious to Japanese code-breaking techniques. The top-secret UFO documents passed on to Mulder by the **Thinker** are encoded in this fashion. ["Anasazi"]

NEARY, LT.: A member of the San Francisco Police Department's homicide squad who investigates the premature cremation of several Chinese men. ["Hell Money"]

NEIL, MARTY: An overzealous classmate of Scully's at Quantico, nicknamed "J. Edgar Junior" by other agents. Mentioned in passing by agent **Tom Colton.** ["Squeeze"]

NELSON: The attorney representing **Eugene Tooms** at his sanity hearing. ["Tooms"]

NEMHAUSER, AGENT GREG: Arrests **John Mostow** for the murder of Peter, an artist's model. He is bitten by Mostow during the arrest. ["Grotesque"]

NEMMAN, THERESA: Daughter of the county medical examiner in **Bellefleur, Oregon.** Fearing for her life, she comes to Mulder for help. She was friends with the other members of the class of '89 who have died. [Pilot]

NEMMAN, DR. JAY: County medical examiner in **Bellefleur, Oregon.** [Pilot]

NETTLES, DET.: Plainclothes detective in Hollywood, California, investigating the murder of **Garrett Lorre.** ["3"]

NEW AGE: The time that will come after **Kevin Kryder** is killed, or so says the Millennium Man (**Simon Gates**). ["Revelations"]

NEWIRTH, PATRICK: An executive of the **Morley Tobacco** company who goes missing from Room 606 of the Hotel George Mason in Richmond, Virginia, leaving behind his luggage, a half-finished glass of Scotch, and a mysterious burn mark on the carpet. Mulder suspects spontaneous human combustion, but the truth is far stranger. ["Soft Light"]

NEWPORT NEWS, VIRGINIA: At the **harbormaster**'s office here, Mulder inquires after the salvage ship **Talapus.** ["Nisei"]

NEWTON, DR. RICK: Medical examiner for Miller's Grove, Massachusetts. ["War of the Coprophages"] He had an article published in the *Journal of Forensic Sciences.* In the FBI Sci-Crime lab Mulder has him test an air bag to see whether the pattern of a face can be picked up from it. The bag is from **Walter Skinner**'s car, which someone borrowed to frame Skinner for attempted murder. ["Avatar"]

THE NIAGARA: An old bar in Raleigh, North Carolina, with a neon sign of a waterfall. This fits a description given by **Luther Lee Boggs,** and leads Scully to find a nearby warehouse where **Lucas Henry** has hidden his victims **Liz Hawley** and **Jim Summers.** This may have been set up by Boggs, unless he really possesses psychic powers. ["Beyond the Sea"]

NICAP: The National Investigative Committee of Aerial Phenomena, a UFO fringe group. **Max Fenig** is a member. ["Fallen Angel"]

NIH: The National Institutes of Health. **Dr. Joe Ridley** worked there on progeria research in the 1970s, until his dismissal for unethical practices. ["Young at Heart"]

"NOBODY'S GOING TO SPOIL US": The words spoken by **Carl Wade** when he kidnaps **Amy Jacobs.** ["Oubliette"]

NOLLETTE, FRANK: A scientist who works at the **Mahan Propulsion Laboratory.** ["Roland"]

NORMAN, DET.: Policeman at the crime scene in Newark, New Jersey, when Mulder arrives. He hands Mulder a pair of yellow boots to put on because the crime scene is inside a sewer. ["The Host"]

NORRIS, GWEN: An employee of the **Travel Time Travel Agency** taken hostage by **Duane Barry.** Mulder persuaded Barry to set her and **Kimberly Monroe** free. ["Duane Barry"]

NORTHEAST GEORGETOWN MEDICAL CENTER: The Washington, D.C., hospital where Scully is brought to the intensive care unit, but no one knows who admitted her.

["One Breath"] Scully is there to recover from the effects of the strange video trap which had caused her to hallucinate that Mulder, the **motel manager,** and even the police were out to kill her. ["Wetwired"]

NORTHERN, PENNY: A Mutual UFO Network (MUFON) member in the **Allentown** area. She claims Scully is a fellow abductee and talks to her about her experience. She reveals to Scully that there is a mark on the back of her neck, which Scully hadn't been aware of before. ["Nisei"]

NUTT, MR.: A midget motel manager in his sixties, in **Gibsonton, Florida.** He owns a pet dog. ["Humbug"]

[O]

OAKES, SHERIFF JOHN: He investigates the murder of sixteen-year-old **Jerry Stevens,** who has been killed by a demon, his heart and eyes cut out. His body is displayed according to the rites of Azazel. ["Die Hand Die Verletzt"]

OATES: The counsel of the governor of Florida. He advises **Daniel Charez** there's little hope that the governor will extend clemency to **"Neech" Manley.** ["The List"]

ODDITORIUM: A museum of curiosa in **Gibsonton, Florida.** It's musty and resembles an antiques store. Admission is free to freaks. Among the exhibits are photos of circus freaks from years past. ["Humbug"]

O'DELL, PEGGY: A friend of the victims of the mysterious killings in **Bellefleur, Oregon,** who were members of the high school class of '89. She was in an auto accident with **Billy Miles.** Confined to a wheelchair in the state hospital for four years, she disappears from there one night and is found dead on the highway. She ran out of the woods and into the path of a truck. [Pilot]

ODIN, RICHARD: The leader of the **Church of the Red Museum** in **Delta Glen, Wisconsin.** Real name Doug Herman. Left the American Medical Association in 1986 over an ethics issue. ["Red Museum"]

OLAFSSEN: A pirate whaler who is rescued by the USS *Argent* when his ship sinks, Olaffsen avoids aging after he discovers that the recycled sewage water on the ship is uncontaminated. He is stranded on the rusting *Argent* when his crew steals **Trondheim**'s boat, the *Zeal.* After he reveals his survival secret to

Trondheim, Olafssen disappears; Trondheim claims he has escaped, but it is more likely that Trondheim has killed him. ["Dod Kalm"]

O'NEIL, JESSE: Member of the **Cascade Volcano Research Team.** She's infected with the silicon-based life form and dies. **Trepkos** takes her body deep into the volcano with him, as they had been lovers. ["Firewalker"]

OPERATION FALCON: Top-secret military mission with the objective of recovering a downed alien craft and any surviving crew. Corollary objectives include evacuating nearby civilians and conducting an intensive disinformation campaign. Mulder walks right into the middle of all this, which is not appreciated by the military. ["Fallen Angel"]

OPERATION PAPER CLIP: A program under which the United States protected Nazi scientists in exchange for their expertise. Werner von Braun and **Victor Klemper** were both beneficiaries of this operation. ["Paper Clip"]

OPPENHEIM, DR. JEFFREY: A physician on duty at the county hospital in **Townsend, Wisconsin,** the night **Jason Wright** is admitted. Angry about the government cover-up, he tells Mulder the truth about Wright, and enlists Scully's aid when soldiers from **Beta Team** are admitted with severe burns, over **Col. Henderson**'s objections. ["Fallen Angel"]

OPTIONS HALFWAY HOUSE: Where **Lucy Householder** lives. ["Oubliette"]

ORIGINAL "SAMANTHA": The original alien visitor from whom many more were cloned, including the one who pretended to be Mulder's lost sister. When Mulder, angry at the trick, refuses to help her and her clones, she claims to have information about the real Samantha, but it is too late: by this time, the **Pilot** has arrived to murder all the clones. It is presumed that he also kills the original "Samantha." ["End Game"]

OSBORNE, DR.: One of the doctors involved in **Pinck Pharmaceuticals'** unethical test of a newly discovered disease at the **Cumberland State Correctional Facility.** Osborne falsely claims to be working for the **Centers for Disease Control,** but reveals to Scully that ten out of fourteen infected prisoners are already dead. Osborne is infected by pus from the body of **Bobby Torrence,** and confides the truth to Scully before he dies: the entire situation is

the work of the Pinck Pharmaceuticals company. His body is incinerated. ["F. Emasculata"]

OSWALD, DARIN PETER: Nineteen years old, barely literate, romantically obsessed with his high school English teacher (who flunked him), Darin would be just another small-town loser in **Connerville, Oklahoma,** if not for his ability to channel powerful electrical currents. This apparently began after he survived being struck by lightning. Several people who annoyed him die of electrocution before his capture, as well as an undetermined number of cattle. He also causes Mulder's cellular phone to melt. After Darin attempts to kidnap **Sharon Kiveat** and kills **Sheriff Teller,** he is held in a special room at the Oklahoma State Psychiatric Hospital. ["D.P.O."]

OSWALD, MRS.: The overweight, TV-addicted mother of the electrified teenager Darin Peter Oswald. ["D.P.O."]

OWENS, G.: An intensive care nurse who watches over Scully, but about whom no one at the hospital knows anything. ["One Breath"]

[P]

PADDOCK, PHYLLIS: The demon who is accidentally summoned by **Jerry Stevens.** She looks like an ordinary fifty-two-year-old schoolteacher, except that she keeps Jerry's eyes and heart in her desk drawer. No one at the school in Milford Haven, New Hampshire, remembers hiring her. ["Die Hand Die Verletzt"]

PALM: The word **Mrs. Mulder** scratches out on a piece of paper. Because of the stroke she has suffered, she scrambles the letters: Fox Mulder later figures out that she had wanted to write the word LAMP. Inside a lamp he finds hidden a device that has a button on it which releases a thin pointed blade, the kind of weapon used to kill alien clones. ["Talitha Cumi"]

PALOMAR OBSERVATORY: Located just north of San Diego; built in 1948 by George Ellery Hale. Mulder claims Hale got the idea from an "elf" that climbed in his window. ["Little Green Men"]

PARKER, JIM: A rancher in his late fifties in Montana who is embroiled in a border dispute with the Trego Indian reservation. One night he shoots and kills an animal that turns out to be an Indian werewolf. Later

Parker is killed by another werewolf. ["Shapes"]

PARKER, LYLE: Jim Parker's son. He's bitten by a werewolf and then becomes one. He kills his father and later is killed by Sheriff **Charley Tskany.** ["Shapes"]

PARMELLY: A prison guard present at the execution of **"Neech" Manley.** He takes Scully aside and tells her that the prisoner named **Roque** has a list of Manley's intended victims. Parmelly is romantically involved with Manley's wife Danielle, making him a suspect. Danielle shoots him because she comes to the conclusion that he is possessed by her husband's spirit. ["The List"]

PATNIK, JOSEPH: A secret TV signal has caused him to hallucinate that everyone he sees is a Bosnian war criminal named **Lladoslav Miriskovic.** He even mistakes his wife for the man and kills her. He also kills four other people before the police arrest him. He is taken to the Frederick County Psychiatric Hospital in Braddock Heights, Maryland. While there, he sees a TV news report about Miriskovic, whereupon he becomes hysterical with terror and has to be restrained. ["Wetwired"]

PATTERSON, BILL: Mulder's former mentor, an FBI agent in his fifties, who runs the investigative support unit at Quantico. He accompanies agent **Greg Nemhauser** when **John Mostow** is arrested for murder. He finds the murder weapon, a bloodstained carpet knife. Patterson becomes possessed by a demon and in gargoyle form is shot and killed by Scully. ["Grotesque"]

PAUL: One of two prisoners at the **Cumberland State Correctional Facility** who use the confusion surrounding the death of **Bobby Torrence** to escape in a laundry cart. He attempts to flee to Toronto by bus, but is tracked down by Mulder, who is on the verge of persuading him to surrender when Paul is shot by unknown government forces covering up the *F. Emasculata* outbreak. With Paul dead, Mulder and Scully are the only witnesses left. ["F. Emasculata"]

PENDRELL: The agent to whom Scully takes the metal implant after she has it removed from her neck. It is just like one she previously came across in "The Blessing Way." Pendrell states that the implant is some kind of microprocessor. ["Nisei"]

PERKEY, WEST VIRGINIA: Site of the **Hansen's Disease**

Research Facility. A mass execution is conducted there. It is also where **Dr. Shiro Zama** (a.k.a. **Dr. Ishimaru**) conducts secret experiments. ["731"]

PERKINS: A logger in the Pacific Northwest, one of a group who cut into an ancient tree and unleash prehistoric wood mites that attack out of self-preservation, becoming active only after sunset and before dawn. He and **Dyer** become imprisoned in **cocoons** by the teeming wood mites. ["Darkness Falls"]

PERKINS: A detective at Buffalo's **14th Precinct.** ["Born Again"]

PERRY, SIMON: The executioner who pulled the switch on **"Neech" Manley.** Mulder and Scully find him tied to a chair in his attic, his body swarming with maggots. He is Manley's third victim. ["The List"]

PETER: An artist's model. He is killed by **John Mostow,** a man possessed by a demon. ["Grotesque"]

PETERSON, CLAUDE: An undercover government agent, probably with the Department of Defense, who infiltrates the Eurisko Corporation as the systems engineer for the building. His real mission is to crack the artificial-intelligence program used in the building security system designed by **Brad Wilczek.** ["Ghost in the Machine"]

PFASTER, DONNIE: Employee of the Janelli-Heller Funeral Home. A fetishist who collects the hair and fingernails of dead young women, he is fired when he's caught cutting off some of the hair of one of the bodies. ["Irresistible"]

PHEROMONES: Hormonal sexual attractants secreted by various animals. Human pheromone production is so minimal that scientists are unsure whether humans actually possess them or not; if **Marty** of the **Kindred** is any indication, his people produce several hundred times more pheromones than any other creature known in nature, raising the question of whether they are actually human. ["Genderbender"]

PHILADELPHIA EXPERIMENT: A top-secret U.S. military project, perhaps mythical, conducted at the Philadelphia Navy Yard on July 8, 1944. The experiment resulted in the disappearance of a battleship, which reappeared hundreds of miles away near Norfolk, Virginia, in a matter of minutes. Mulder suspects that the experiment involved wormholes, and at first believes that

the disappearance of the USS *Argent* has been caused by something similar. ["Dod Kalm"]

PHILIPS, LULA: A career criminal, age twenty-five, she did time at the Maryland Women's Correctional Facility for manslaughter. While there she had a clandestine affair with prison guard **Warren James Dupre;** he was fired when this was discovered. They marry and embark on a short-lived but intense crime career after her release on May 2, 1993, specializing in violent bank robberies. She sets up Dupre by tipping off the FBI to their final bank robbery. When **Jack Willis** claims to be Dupre, she plays along until she can get an advantage by withholding insulin from the diabetic Willis, then demands $1 million from the FBI for the return of the kidnapped Scully. Willis kills Lula shortly before the FBI storms her hideout. ["Lazarus"]

PHILIPS, TOMMY: Lula Philips's brother, a small-time crook so addicted to television that he'll even watch it if the sound isn't working. Killed by **Jack Willis** for finking on **Warren Dupre** and Lula, although Tommy was not actually responsible. ["Lazarus"]

PHILLIPS, DR.: A physician at the University of Pennsylvania Hospital's Bone and Tissue Bank. He confirms that five of **Howard Graves**'s organs were used in transplant surgery shortly after his death, and provides tissue samples which Scully uses to prove that Graves is really dead. ["Shadows"]

PHILLIPS, STAN: A resident at the **Excelsis Dei Convalescent Home.** He's lived there three years and doesn't want to leave. ["Excelsis Dei"]

PIEDMONT, VIRGINIA: Location of **Yaloff Psychiatric Hospital,** where **Chester Ray Banton**'s shadow kills two government operatives out to kidnap him. ["Soft Light"]

PIERCE, ADAM: Member of the **Cascade Volcano Research Team** working at the California Institute of Technology in Pasadena. He accompanies Mulder and Scully to **Mount Avalon** and is killed by **Trepkos** shortly after arrival. ["Firewalker"]

THE PILOT: An alien bounty hunter, according to one of the false Samantha invaders, sent to Earth with a mandate to assassinate the alien colonists involved in human–alien DNA experimentation. He can assume any form at will, and

can be killed only by piercing the base of his skull. If shot, he emits a toxic green gas from his wounds, apparently containing an airborne alien virus that kills humans by causing their blood to coagulate. (This same virus was encountered in "The Erlenmeyer Flask.") The virus can be rendered dormant with low temperatures. Although a ruthless assassin, the Pilot seems unwilling to kill humans unless it is absolutely necessary, as is seen in his final confrontation with Mulder on the icebound USS **Allegiance.** In light of this, it is unclear whether he actually killed the crew of the *Allegiance* (as he told Mulder while impersonating Navy Lt. Terry Wilmer) or whether their deaths were caused by other means. The Pilot is last seen taking the *Allegiance* to the location of his own craft. His final words to Mulder are that the real Samantha is still alive. ["Colony," "End Game"]

PILSSON, DR. ERIK: The physician who has been monitoring the condition of **Augustus Cole** for the last twelve years. Cole is kept in an isolation ward because he disrupted the sleep of the other patients. ["Sleepless"]

PINCK PHARMACEUTICALS: One of the largest manufacturers of drugs in the United States, based in Wichita, Kansas. This company was behind the outbreak of contagion at the **Cumberland State Correctional Facility,** apparently during an experiment to test possible treatments of *F. Emasculata*. ["F. Emasculata"]

PIPER MARU: The salvage vessel that takes a group of French scientists, including **Gauthier,** to locate a World War II fighter plane (call numbers JTTO 111470) that contained an alien entity. Its crew, with one exception, later suffered severe radiation burns. When Mulder examines the ship, he detects no radiation, but he does find a videotape of the plane at the bottom of the sea. ["Piper Maru"]

PLAIN-CLOTHED MAN: He meets with Mulder in Washington, D.C., and tells him about **Joseph Patnik** and the five people he killed in **Braddock Heights, Maryland.** He won't say who sent him to give Mulder this information, but apparently it was **X.** ["Wetwired"]

PLITH, DR.: Forensic anthropologist who examines the body found in cement at the **Ruxton chemical plant.** He finds gnawing marks near the ribs. ["Tooms"]

POLARITY MAGNETICS: The company where **Chester Ray Banton** worked prior to his accident. Mulder learns the company name from a patch seen on Banton's jacket in a train station security video. The company's main focus is magnetic levitation design for bullet trains and similar applications, but Banton was pursuing more esoteric research involving subatomic particles. Polarity Magnetics was shut down after the accident. ["Soft Light"]

POMERANTZ, DR. MARK: A psychiatrist who hypnotizes Scully and helps her remember events related to her abduction. She bolts from the procedure, overwhelmed, before anything substantial can be recovered. ["The Blessing Way"]

POSITRON EMISSION TOMOGRAPHY LAB: Where **Betsy Hagopian** is taken due to her undiagnosed cancerous condition. Her body is full of tumors. Scully is told by **Lottie Holloway** that all of the abductees will eventually end up in that condition because of what was done to them when they were abducted. Hagopian, now in her forties, has been abducted many times since she was in her teens. ["Nisei"]

POWERTECH: The facility where an E.B.E. (extraterrestrial biological entity) is being held, and which Mulder and Scully manage to penetrate using phony identification. ["E.B.E."]

POWHATTAN MILL KILLINGS: The 1933 crime spree during which **Eugene Tooms** killed five people and cut out their livers. Only four

of those victims were found; Tooms hid the fifth. ["Tooms"]

PRIEST: After she saves the life of **Kevin Kryder,** a true stigmatic, Scully goes to a Catholic church and inside a confessional she talks to a priest, something she has not done in six years. The priest casually makes a remark that echoes something said to her during this case, about things coming "full circle." Scully has seen things she cannot explain, and that she cannot share with Mulder. ["Revelations"]

PRINCE, DR. LANDON: A physician who died in an arson fire at an abortion clinic in Scranton, Pennsylvania. His name appears in a list of similar deaths e-mailed to Mulder by an anonymous source. Mulder is baffled upon learning that all three doctors, although apparently unrelated, were identical — and no body was recovered in any of the cases. ["Colony"]

PROGERIA: A rare disease that accelerates aging. Some victims may survive to early adulthood, but most die at seven or eight years of age, looking like midget ninety-year-olds. Death is generally due to cardiac arrest or loss of circulation in the brain. **Dr. Joe Ridley** saw progeria as a possible key to slowing or reversing the aging

process, but his methods were too extreme for the National Institutes of Health. ["Young at Heart"]

PROVINCETOWN PUB: A bar burned down by **Cecil L'ively,** probably to taunt the authorities trying to solve his crimes. ["Fire"]

PULASKI, VIRGINIA: Small town where **Duane Barry** lived alone at the time of his alien abduction on June 3, 1985. This was not his first abduction, but it was the one during which he saw humans — government agents — cooperating with the aliens. ["Duane Barry"]

THE PUPPET: A serial killer whose victims are all professional psychics of some sort: astrologers, palm readers, tarot readers, even a tea leaf reader. He possesses a certain limited psychic skill himself, getting glimpses of his crimes before he commits them. He feels as if he has no control over his actions (like a puppet) and hopes that his victims can explain them to him. **Clyde Bruckman** helps clarify matters by pointing out that the Puppet is a homicidal maniac. ["Clyde Bruckman's Final Repose"]

PURDUE, REGGIE: A black FBI agent in his fifties, a widower, who works in the violent-crimes division in Washington, D.C., and is writing a mystery novel in his spare time. He was Mulder's superior on the **John Barnett** case in 1989 and calls his friend Mulder in when evidence suggests that the allegedly dead Barnett is somehow responsible for a new crime. Purdue is killed by Barnett as a warning to Mulder. ["Young at Heart"]

PUSHER: The alias used by **Robert Modell,** the hit man who wills his victims to kill themselves. ["Pusher"]

[Q]

QUANTICO, VIRGINIA: Location of the FBI academy, which is often referred to only as "Quantico" by those who have passed through there.

QUARANTINE CAR: The train car Mulder believes is transporting a human–alien hybrid (see also **Hansen's Research Center Compound**). ["731"]

QUEENSGATE, OHIO: Where **Dr. Shiro Zama** boarded a train that also picked up the inaccessible **Quarantine Car.** (see also **Dr. Ishimaru**) ["731"]

QUEEQUEG: Scully's little dog. Originally the pet of **Clyde Bruckman**'s elderly neighbor **Mrs. Lowe.** When Mrs. Lowe died, the dog had no food and apparently ate part of its deceased mistress to survive. Bruckman retrieves the dog shortly before his suicide, and suggests that Scully take it. She names it after a character in *Moby Dick,* since she and her father had nicknamed each other after that book's Starbuck and Ahab. ["Clyde Bruckman's Final Repose"] The poor dog meets its end when it's eaten by an alligator. ["Quagmire"]

QUINNIMONT, WEST VIRGINIA: Where Mulder finds a train that he's been looking for, the one with the car where the alien autopsy was interrupted by gunfire that killed four Japanese scientists. He sees some men board the train, including someone in a radiation suit who appears to be an alien. ["Nisei"]

QUONOCHONTAUG, RHODE ISLAND: Where the Mulders have a lakefront house. Mrs. Mulder is met there by the **Cigarette-Smoking Man;** they have an argument. ["Talitha Cumi"]

[R]

RADIO SHACK: A national electronics chain store operated by the Tandy Company. Mulder buys a laser pointer at one of their outlets for $49.95. ["Soft Light"]

RANA SPENOCEPHALA: A type of rare frog on the verge of extinction. It is found in Striker's Cove on **Heuvelmans Lake** in Georgia. The population there of this type of frog has dropped to less than 200. ["Quagmire"]

RAND: One of the agents who has Mulder's residence under surveillance, and who confronts Scully when she goes there. ["Little Green Men"]

RANDALL, GREG: A young man who tended bar at the **Boar's Head** tavern in Sioux City, Iowa, and vanishes around the same time as **Ruby Morris,** but is cleared of any suspicion when he is found dead in a shallow grave near **Lake Okobogee** by Mulder and Scully. He was killed by **Tessa Sears,** who was pregnant with his child. ["Conduit"]

RANDOLPH, DR. VANCE: The staff doctor at the **Chaco Chicken** processing plant who treats **Jess Harold**'s neck wound after he is attacked by **Paula Gray.** ["Our Town"]

RANFORD, CHRISTINE: The wife of Frank Ranford. She discovers that her toilet is blocked and is unaware that **Eugene Tooms** is using the sewer pipe to gain entrance to her house. ["Tooms"]

RANFORD, FRANK: A man in his mid-thirties who is stalked by **Eugene Tooms.** ["Tooms"]

RANHEIM: A truck driver whose vehicle loses power when a UFO comes down nearby. He shoots at what he thinks is an alien, then gets a rash on his face and hands. Scully learns that his real name is Frank Druse and his truck is transporting something secret — possibly an alien or the wreckage of a UFO. ["E.B.E."]

RAT-TAIL PRODUCTIONS: The name of the small company in **Allentown, Pennsylvania,** that sells copies of the **alien autopsy** video. It is located in a private residence, a boarded-up house that appears to be abandoned. Upon entering the house, Mulder and Scully find the still-warm corpse of a man, and Mulder chases a Japanese man, who is carrying a **leather satchel,** and finally catches him. ["Nisei"]

RAVEN: An overweight prostitute attacked and killed by **Virgil Incanto** after a struggle. Scraps of his skin under her fingernails provide an important clue in the case. ["2Shy"]

REARDON, CINDY: An eight-year-old girl, one of **Dr. Sally Kendrick**'s clones. She plot-ted with **Teena Simmons** to murder their fathers, apparently through a cross-country psychic connection. They later murder Kendricks together, try to divert Mulder's attention, and finally attempt to poison Mulder and Scully when they grow suspicious. ["Eve"]

REARDON, DOUG: A resident of Marin County killed at the exact same time as **Joel Simmons,** in the exact same fashion, right down to the swing. Father of Cindy Reardon. ["Eve"]

REARDON, ELLEN: Wife of Doug and mother of Cindy Reardon. Tells Mulder that Cindy was conceived through in vitro fertilization at the **Luther Stapes Center.** She disowns Cindy after the truth is revealed about the nature of her conception. ["Eve"]

RECYCLING PLANT: Where the Millennium Man (**Simon Gates**) takes ten-year-old **Kevin Kryder** to kill him (see also **Twenty-First Century Recycling.**) ["Revelations"]

RED-HAIRED MAN: See **Malcolm Gerlach.**

RED HEAD: A member of the W.A.O. (Wild Again Organization), he watches with quiet belligerence as Mulder and Scully interrogate **Kyle Lang.** Scully follows him one night when he breaks into the Fairfield Zoo. He is observing a tiger in its cage when it seemingly disappears, then an invisible presence attacks him outside the cage, mauling him to death. ["Fearful Symmetry"]

RED ROCK QUARRY: Location of the buried boxcar containing piles of alien bodies, where Mulder narrowly escapes death. ["The Blessing Way"]

REGAN, LT.: One of the firefighters who finds the dead body of **Dr. Grissom** in his apartment. ["Sleepless"]

REHOBOTH, DELAWARE: The community where the **Thinker,** possibly a.k.a. Kenneth Soona, lived until the authorities' discovery of his access to sensitive government files obliged him to flee. ["Anasazi"]

RETICULANS: Alien beings whom Scully facetiously accuses of being possibly responsible for an experiment involving induced paranoia that seems to be taking place in **Franklin, Pennsylvania.** ["Blood"]

RICH: FBI agent in charge of the complete operation surrounding the **Duane Barry** hostage situation. ["Duane Barry"]

RICHMOND, DR. JANICE: Physician on call when **Eugene Tooms** is brought in to the emergency room. ["Tooms"]

RICHMOND TRAIN STATION: **Chester Ray Banton** spends most of his days and nights here after his accident, depending on the waiting room's diffused fluorescent light to keep his shadow from showing. He unintentionally kills two Richmond policemen in an alley outside the station. ["Soft Light"]

RICHTER, JOHN: A top geophysicist, head of **Arctic Ice Core Project.** A week after retrieving an ice core sample a quarter-million years old, Richter and other members of his team began to show signs of extreme mental disturbance. His last transmission, on November 5, 1993, includes the cryptic words "We're not who we are," and ends when he and his teammate Campbell commit suicide simultaneously. The other three members of the team were already dead. ["Ice"]

RIDDOCK, HELENE: Imagining that she sees her husband, Victor, committing adultery with the woman next door, she grabs a shotgun and kills her neighbor, John Gillnitz, whom she mistakes for her husband. ["Wetwired"]

RIDGEWAY ELEMENTARY SCHOOL: In Loveland, Ohio, where **Kevin Kryder** attends the fifth grade. ["Revelations"]

RIDLEY, DR. JOE: Performed experiments on prisoners at **Tashmoo Federal Correctional Facility** in his efforts to reverse the aging process. Previously he worked at the National Institutes of Health, where he was investigating the disease **progeria** until, in violation of NIH policy, he began unapproved human trials. Colleagues secretly nicknamed him "Dr. Mengele" for his Naziesque disregard of his patients as anything but test subjects. The state of Maryland revoked his medical license in 1979 for research malpractice and misuse of government grant money. After leaving Tashmoo, he disappeared from sight, working in Mexico, Belize, and other Central American countries until **John Barnett** stole his research. Ridley has reversed his own aging, but suffers from cataracts because his "cure" for aging does not work on the eyes for some reason; he has a cerebral vascular disease. ["Young at Heart"]

RIGDON, GEORGIA: Mulder drives on County Road 33 through here on his way to **Heuvelmans Lake** to investigate the disappearance of a U.S. Forest Service official. ["Quagmire"]

RILEY, BOB: Middle-aged, balding employee of the **Travel Time Travel Agency** taken hostage by **Duane Barry,** who unintentionally shoots Riley during a mysterious blackout. Barry lets him go for medical treatment in exchange for Mulder. ["Duane Barry"]

"RING THE BELLS": A song by the band James, this was the last piece of music heard by **Jack Hammond** before his untimely demise at the age of twenty-one. ["D.P.O."]

RITUAL OF SEPARATION: A Romanian ritual intended to separate the soul of a living child from the soul of a dead twin. When one of her twin sons died at birth, **Maggie Holvey** refused to let her mother **Golda** perform the rite, which led to nothing but trouble for her family. When Mulder helps the **Calusari** finally perform the ritual, he becomes known to the demonic entity that had taken the place of the dead twin's soul; according to the Calusari, this is the Devil himself. ["The Calusari"]

RIVERS, POLICE CHIEF: Investigates **Ranheim**'s shooting of what may have been a mountain lion. He doesn't want the FBI investigating it. ["E.B.E."]

ROB: A divorced father who dated Scully once after a mutual friend set them up, but Scully was too involved in her career to see him again. ["The Jersey Devil"]

ROBERTO: A young Latino janitor working at the Idaho Mutual Insurance Trust in **Fairfield, Idaho,** when some invisible force causes the windows at the front of the bank to shatter. ["Fearful Symmetry"]

ROBERTS, TERRI: A friend of **Bruno,** a boy who dies under mysterious circumstances. She and her best friend, **Margi Kleinjan,** together have strange powers due to a peculiar alignment of the planets. A senior at Grover Cleveland Alexander High School in Comity, she has a grade point average of 3.98 and is on the cheerleading squad with Margi. Astrologically speaking, Comity is in a geological vortex. On January 12 the planets come into perfect alignment. Since January 12 is her birthday as well as Margi's, and they were born in 1979, this gives them a Jupiter–Uranus opposition, which creates a grand square where the planets are aligned in a cross. This causes all the energy of the cosmos to be focused on them. ["Syzygy"]

ROCKVILLE, MARYLAND: Location of the Women's Health Services Center, where Mulder meets more alien clones. ["End Game"]

ROOSEVELT, DR. CARL: A respected American archaeologist in his sixties, who disappears from an archaeological site in Ecuador shortly after the discovery of the **Amaru** Urn. ["Teso dos Bichos"]

ROQUE, SAMMON: A prisoner at **Eastpoint State Penitentiary** who taunts **"Neech" Manley** on his way to the electric chair. He supposedly has the list of Manley's intended victims, and tries to get transferred out of Eastpoint. Instead, he is beaten to death by prison guards commanded by warden **Leo Brodeur.** ["The List"]

ROSEN, TRACY: A mentally retarded friend of **Roland Fuller**'s. ["Roland"]

ROSSLYN, VIRGINIA: Location of **Gen. Thomas Callahan**'s family home. ["The Walk"]

ROSWELL, NEW MEXICO: Area where it's believed that a UFO crashed in 1947. The source of much lore on the subject.

ROUTE 44: A highway near the **Kindred** community in Massachusetts, where Brothers Andrew and Martin find the magazines that interest Martin

in the outside world. ["Genderbender"]

ROUTE 229: A highway passing through Rixeyville, Virginia, where a highway patrol officer pulls over **Duane Barry** in Scully's car, only to be shot. The officer's car-mounted video camera records the entire incident, and reveals that Scully is in the trunk of the stolen vehicle. ["Ascension"]

RUBES: A term used by circus people to describe outsiders. ["Humbug"]

RUXTON CHEMICAL PLANT: Located in Baltimore. It is where **Eugene Tooms** hid one of his victims in 1933 in the concrete of a then newly poured foundation. In 1994, modern technology is able to locate where the body is entombed. ["Tooms"]

RYAN, DET. KELLY: Newly promoted in the Richmond, Virginia, police force, this former student of Scully's calls in Scully and Mulder for assistance in her first assignment as detective, a missing-persons case that started when **Patrick Newirth** vanished, but she shuts the FBI agents out of the case after two Richmond police officers die and the goings get weird. She dies as a result of contact with **Chester Ray Banton**'s shadow, the only person Banton killed on purpose. ["Soft Light"]

[S]

SAI BABA: An Indian guru whom **Chuck Burk** claims to have witnessed creating an entire feast out of thin air in 1979, a feat accompanied by the production of the holy ash called vibuti. ["The Calusari"]

SAINT IGNATIUS: According to Catholic tradition, he could be in two places at once by creating an illusionary double of himself. **Kevin Kryder** is able to do this. ["Revelations"]

SAINT MATTHEW'S MEDICAL CENTER: Where **Charlie Holvey** is taken after being removed from his family home by FBI social worker **Karen Kosseff.** Mulder and the **Calusari** perform the Ritual of Separation on Charlie there. ["The Calusari"]

SAL: A waitress at a café in **Gibsonton, Florida.** She is half-man, half-woman. ["Humbug"]

SALINGER, BEATRICE: The night nurse on duty at the Siloam County Hospital. She claims she saw **Samuel Hartley** get up and walk out on his own, and his body is missing. ["Miracle Man"]

"SAMANTHA": An alien clone claiming to be Mulder's sister Samantha, she appears at **William Mulder**'s house during the **Gregor** case. She knows plenty about Fox and his sister, right down to their fondness for the game Stratego, and claims to have been returned to Earth and raised by aliens passing for humans. ["Colony"] According to her, the identical aliens were clones of the two original "visitors" who arrived on Earth in the late 1940s (possibly at Roswell, although she doesn't say). Because their identical appearances made it necessary to disperse across the world, the clones were experimenting to meld alien and human DNA in order to diversify their appearance and increase their numbers. These experiments were unsanctioned, resulting in the arrival of the **Pilot,** whose mission is to destroy the colony. This Samantha is abducted by the Pilot; when her body is recovered, it disintegrates into a green liquid, revealing her to be one of the alien clones. ["End Game"]

SANFORD, CAPT. KYLE: Commander of the submarine ***Zeus Faber*** during World War II. He was possessed by an alien entity found at the site of a downed UFO. ["Piper Maru"]

SATIN: A hooker in Minneapolis whom **Donnie Pfaster** picks up and kills. Then he washes her hair. She is his first victim. ["Irresistible"]

SAUNDERS: CIA agent who turns to Mulder and Scully for help when his case, involving illegal arms trading, turns up a potential X-File connection. ["Shadows"]

SAWMILL: The location where everyone meets at the end and there is a question as to who will survive. ["Talitha Cumi"]

SAYLES, CARINA: A former secretary for a Washington, D.C., law firm, she was fired because she was moonlighting for an escort service. Her nude, lifeless body is found in bed with **Walter Skinner,** who remembers picking her up in the Chesapeake Lounge downstairs in the Ambassador Hotel but not how she died. Scully determines that the cause of death was a crushed spinal cord and the cervical vertebrae were fractured. Scully also finds an odd residual phosphorescence covering the dead woman's nose and mouth. ["Avatar"]

SCHIFF-IMMERGUT LUMBER COMPANY: A logging outfit in the Pacific Northwest. Thirty of their loggers have disappeared from a single area virtually overnight. Ecoterrorists are suspected. ["Darkness Falls"]

SCHNABLEGGER, DR.
GLENNA: County pathologist
at Atlantic City, she allows
Mulder and Scully to observe
the examination of a dead
homeless man brutally murdered and maimed by human
teeth. ["The Jersey Devil"]

SCHOOL NURSE: She treats
Kevin Kryder after his palms
begin to bleed in school, spraying Bactine on the wound.
When she takes his temperature, the thermometer in the
boy's mouth rises quickly and
then pops. ["Revelations"]

SCHUMANN RESONANCE:
The radio wave frequency
emitted by lightning flashes:
eight cycles per second.
["D.P.O."]

SCOPOLAMINE: A drug used
for motion sickness, but which
in large quantities is an anes-
thetic with hallucinogenic
qualities used to drug those
who are to become "victims" of
the cult. ["Red Museum"]

SCULLY, BILL JR.: Dana's
older brother. ["One Breath"]

SCULLY, CHARLES: Dana's
younger brother. ["One
Breath"]

SCULLY, DANA: Born February
23, 1960, the daughter of a
U.S. Navy captain. She spent
part of her childhood living on
Miramar Naval Air Base, north
of San Diego. ["Apocrypha"]
She did her undergraduate

work in physics (her thesis was
"Einstein's Twin Paradox: A
New Interpretation") and took
her medical degree at the
University of Maryland, but
then disappointed her parents
by joining the FBI. She is
assigned by section chief **Scott
Blevins** to work with agent
Fox Mulder on the X-Files and
write field reports and evalua-
tions of their activities.
Personal ID number
X197735VW3. Her gun is a
Smith & Wesson 1056. Initially
assigned by her superiors with
the intent to debunk Mulder's
X-Files investigations, she
instead becomes Mulder's
greatest ally. Placed on manda-
tory leave and forced to surrender her badge and weapon
in the aftermath of Mulder's
disappearance, she is obliged
to go through the metal detector at the front of FBI headquarters, whereupon she
discovers a small piece of
metal, resembling a computer
chip, implanted in her neck.
["The Blessing Way"]
Disarmed by **Virgil Incanto,**
she is saved when **Ellen
Kaminski** kills him with
Scully's gun. ["2Shy"] Scully
captures **Luis Cardinal,** the
man who killed her sister and
shot **Skinner.** ["Apocrypha"]
For six years she has been
something of a lapsed Catholic,

even though she still wears a
crucifix on a chain around her
neck. But following the events
she witnesses and experiences
in "Revelations," she goes to
see a **priest** to discuss her concerns and misgivings. For a
time she has a little dog named
Queequeg, which is eaten by
an alligator in "Quagmire."

SCULLY, MARGARET: Dana
Scully's mother, fifty-eight at
the time of her husband's
death in 1993. She had four
children: Bill Jr., Melissa,
Dana, and Charles. ["Beyond
the Sea"] She comes to Dana's
apartment after **Duane Barry**
kidnaps Dana; she had
dreamed that someone had
taken Dana away, but was
embarrassed to tell her about
it. Margaret tells Mulder to
keep Dana's crucifix necklace
until he can give it back to her.
["Ascension"; see also "One
Breath"] Dana visits her after
Mulder's apparent death.
["The Blessing Way"] When
Dana begins to hallucinate that
everyone is out to get her, she
goes to see her mother.
["Wetwired"]

SCULLY, MELISSA: Dana's
older sister. She is apparently
psychic, but Margaret doesn't
approve of such talk. Melissa
says she can feel the emotions
of the comatose Dana. ["One
Breath"] She tries to comfort

Dana after Mulder's apparent death, and convinces her to undergo hypnosis in order to remember events concerning her own disappearance the previous year. Melissa is erroneously shot in Dana's place by **Krycek** and his associates. ["The Blessing Way"] She dies in a coma after unsuccessful cranial surgery some time later. ["Paper Clip"] Dana becomes consumed with finding her sister's killers.

SCULLY, WILLIAM: Dana Scully's father, a retired Navy captain. He would have been happier if his daughter had stuck with medicine instead of joining the FBI. He dies of a massive coronary at age sixty-three, during the Christmas season in 1993. ["Beyond the Sea"] After his death, he appears to Dana when she is in a coma. ["One Breath"]

SEARS, TESSA: A teenage acquaintance of **Ruby Morris,** who tells Mulder and Scully that Ruby got pregnant by her boyfriend **Greg Randall** and ran away with him. This is a lie: Tessa is pregnant by Greg, but killed him by **Lake Okobogee** because she was jealous of his involvement with Ruby. ["Conduit"]

SEATTLE FBI REGIONAL FIELD OFFICE: Where Mulder and Scully meet with Agent Eubanks to discuss the status of the case of the kidnapping of **Amy Jacobs.** ["Oubliette"]

SECARE, DR. WILLIAM: The fugitive who has escaped from a government facility involved in alien/human experiments. He has green blood and can breathe underwater. ["The Erlenmeyer Flask"]

SECONA: A tribe that lives in the mountains of Ecuador and still practices ancient shamanistic rituals centered around jaguar worship. ["Teso dos Bichos"]

SEIZER, DR.: Physician at the naval hospital in San Diego who treated the French seamen from the *Piper Maru* for radiation burns. ["Piper Maru"]

SETH COUNTY, ARKANSAS: Location of **Dudley,** home of **Chaco Chicken.** When Mulder and Scully go to the county courthouse to confirm that **Paula Gray** was born in 1948, they discover that all the county records have been burned to ashes. ["Our Town"]

SHAMROCK WOMEN'S PRISON FACILITY: Where **B. J. Morrow** is sent to the psychiatric ward. ["Aubrey"]

SHEAFFER, LT. JACK: Phony Gray Alien #2. He is planning to abduct and interrogate **Harold Lamb** and **Chrissy Giorgio** when all of them are abducted by real aliens from space. Mulder finds Sheaffer wandering naked down a road saying "This is not happening!" Sheaffer says he has flown a flying saucer and observes, "Afterwards sex seems trite." **Sgt. Hynek** takes him into custody, and shortly thereafter Sheaffer's body is found in a crashed Air Force jet. ["Jose Chung's *From Outer Space*"]

SHEHERLIE, SARAH: An agent in the FBI Sci-Crime Lab. ["Grotesque"]

SHERMAN CRATER: Part of the volcano at **Mount Avalon.** ["Firewalker"]

SHOVE PARK: The wooded region near Minneapolis where **Claude Dukenfield**'s body is dumped. ["Clyde Bruckman's Final Repose"]

SILICON-BASED LIFE FORM: Previously unknown, it is discovered inside the **Mount Avalon** volcano. The robot probe **Firewalker** brings the new life-form to the surface, where it proceeds to infect the research team. ["Firewalker"]

SILOAM COUNTY HOSPITAL: Where the body of **Samuel Hartley** is being kept until it disappears. The night nurse, Beatrice Salinger, claims she saw Samuel walk out under his own power. ["Miracle Man"]

SILOAM COUNTY JAIL
HOUSE: Where **Samuel Hartley** is beaten to death in a cell while Deputy Tyson looks on approvingly. ["Miracle Man"]

SIMMONS, JENNIFER: A young woman with long, blond hair who has recently died. Her body is at the **Janelli-Heller Funeral Home** and **Donnie Pfaster** is caught cutting off some of her hair. ["Irresistible"]

SIMMONS, JOEL: Father of Teena Simmons. He dies of hypovolemia: 75 percent of his blood has been drained from his body. His lips have also been surgically removed. Mulder at first thinks this is linked to cattle mutilations. ["Eve"]

SIMMONS, SCOTT: A basketball player at Grover Cleveland Alexander High School in Comity. He's described by **Terri Roberts** as "babe-alicious in overtime." His girlfriend, **Brenda Jaycee Summerfield,** is killed purposely by **Margi Kleinjan** and Terri, and then Scott is killed accidentally by the same blonde duo. ["Syzygy"]

SIMMONS, TEENA: Eight-year-old girl orphaned when her father is killed; her mother died of ovarian cancer some years earlier. Psychic in some fashion, Teena plays in to Mulder's desire to link the murder with aliens, but actually committed the crime herself. In fact, she is a clone of **Dr. Sally Kendrick,** who abducts her. ["Eve"]

SIMPSON, HOMER J.: A yellow-skinned resident of Springfield, Illinois, who is mowing his lawn on the screen saver on the computer in the **Thinker**'s office when the black ops unit break in looking for the **MJ documents.** ["Anasazi"]

SIQUANNKE, ALASKA: Location of Eisenhower Field, where Mulder is taken for medical treatment after his encounter with the **Pilot.** ["Colony," "End Game"]

SISTER ABBY: The member of the **Kindred** who acts as their main spokesperson when Mulder and Scully visit them in Massachusetts. ["Genderbender"]

SISTRUNK, REV. CALVIN: A right-wing fundamentalist originally suspected in the arson fires at several abortion clinics in the eastern United States. He was arrested in Scranton, Pennsylvania, carrying a copy of the newspaper ad with **Dr. Landon Prince**'s picture, but was released when he provided an alibi for the other arsons out of state. ["Colony"]

SIOUX CITY PUBLIC
LIBRARY: Mulder and Scully receive a note directing them here, where they receive misinformation from a teenage girl later revealed to be **Tessa Sears** about the disappearance of **Ruby Morris.** ["Conduit"]

65TH PARALLEL: The meteor or alien object that caused the USS **Argent**'s accelerated corrosion was located along this parallel, 8 degrees east longitude, in the North Atlantic. Other ships that vanished there are listed in the X-Files, including a British battleship in 1949 and an entire fleet of six Soviet mine sweepers in 1963. Mulder plots this location by overlapping his X-Files notes with the *Argent*'s course. ["Dod Kalm"]

SKEPTICAL: One of the phony Gray Aliens, who interrogate people they abduct. ["Jose Chung's *From Outer Space*"]

SKINNER, SHARON: Walter Skinner's soon-to-be ex-wife. She visits him one night and shortly thereafter someone runs her off the road; Walter is the prime suspect. Actually someone "borrowed" his car to frame him. She is seriously injured in the accident, but recovers. Her husband takes a leave of absence from the FBI to spend some time with her. ["Avatar"]

SKINNER, ASSISTANT DIRECTOR WALTER S.: Introduced in "Little Green Men." Mulder's immediate superior in the FBI, he is sympathetic to Mulder but walks a fine line between helping him and obeying those superiors who want Mulder out of the picture permanently. After Agent **Krycek** disappears in the wake of the **Duane Barry** incident, Skinner is angry enough to defy his superiors and reopen the X-Files. ["Ascension"] Notifies Mulder that Agent **Weiss** is dead and terminates Mulder's investigation of the abortion clinic murders. Also informs Mulder that there is a family emergency. ["Colony"] Helps Mulder organize a rescue team to free Scully from the **Pilot.** Skinner at first refuses to help Scully find Mulder, but later confronts **X** and extracts the information. ["End Game"] Advises Mulder to forget about the *F. Emasculata* outbreak, and hints that Mulder's enemies are about to speed up their efforts to discredit or destroy him. ["F. Emasculata"] Skinner finds his patience pushed to the limit when Mulder physically attacks him, not realizing that Mulder has been poisoned by the forces out to discredit him.

["Anasazi"] Skinner secretly assists Scully by taking the DAT tape into his own custody, while publicly joining in the FBI's censure of her. When he admits this to Scully, she has a hard time accepting his sincerity. ["The Blessing Way"] He refuses to give up the tape when Mulder reappears, as uncertain as Mulder about who to trust. Krycek and his accomplices (including **Luis Cardinal**) later take the tape from Skinner by force. ["Paper Clip"] Personally intervenes to free **Kazuo Takeo** after Mulder arrests the Japanese man at the scene of a murder in **Allentown, Pennsylvania.** Skinner states that Takeo is a high-ranking diplomat, and it is obvious that someone is pulling Skinner's strings on this one. ["Nisei"] Skinner contests the decision to drop the investigation into **Melissa Scully**'s murder, only to be shot by Cardinal while dining at his favorite coffee shop. ["Piper Maru"] He wakes up next to the nude, lifeless body of a woman he picked up in a bar the previous night, and becomes the chief suspect in her murder. He had been experiencing a recurring dream in which he's confronted by an old woman, but now he is starting to see her when

he is awake as well. She is the same apparition he saw once before, when he was the only survivor of an attack on his unit in Vietnam. Sharon Skinner, Walter's estranged wife, visits him one night and shortly thereafter someone runs her off the road; Walter is the prime suspect. Actually someone "borrowed" his car to frame him. He is cleared and takes a leave of absence to spend some time with his wife and try to put his marriage back together. ["Avatar"]

SKYLAND GRILL: The restaurant, closed for the summer, at Skyland Mountain, used as an interrogation room and holding cell after the apprehension of **Duane Barry. Alex Krycek** may have poisoned Barry there. ["Ascension"]

SKYLAND MOUNTAIN: A tourist attraction near Rixeyville, Virginia, off the Blue Ridge Parkway. Mulder tracks **Duane Barry** to this location, where, Barry claims, he experienced his first abduction by aliens. Mulder does not locate Scully there, but he does find her car and her gold crucifix necklace, and witnesses what may have been an alien craft departing. Agent **Alex Krycek** was last officially seen here. ["Ascension"]

SLASH KILLER: Serial killer in the early 1940s whose three victims were young women between twenty-five and thirty; he carved the word "sister" on their chests. His name was **Harry Cokely.** ["Aubrey"]

SLAUGHTER, DR. RUTH: Navy pathologist who performs the autopsy on **Duane Barry.** Her report does not address Mulder's suspicion that Barry may have been poisoned by **Alex Krycek,** part of a military cover-up. ["Ascension"]

SMALLPOX: An infectious disease that was the focus of an extensive inoculation campaign in the U.S. during the 1950s and 1960s. According to the **Well-Manicured Man,** this was a front to collect genetic materials from the general populace, to be used in alien–human hybridization experiments. ["Paper Clip"]

SMITH, JEREMIAH: A mysterious man (an alien clone?) living in Suitland, Virginia, who can heal people with his touch. He is able to slip away from the scene by changing his appearance in the blink of an eye. He is imprisoned and interrogated by the **Cigarette-Smoking Man,** until Smith tells him that he has cancer. Smith is one of several identical clones all named Jeremiah Smith. ["Talitha Cumi"]

SNORKEL DUDE: At **Heuvelmans Lake** he gets pulled underwater by a mysterious creature while **Chick** and **Stoner** look on dumbfounded. All that floats to the surface is Snorkle Dude's head. ["Quagmire"]

SOAMES, RAY: Third victim of the mysterious killer in **Bellefleur, Oregon.** Upon exhuming his grave, Mulder and Scully find a small, nonhuman corpse, which is later stolen from the coroner's office. [Pilot]

SOCIAL SECURITY OFFICES: Where **Jeremiah Smith** works. ["Talitha Cumi"]

SODIUM CHLORIDE: Ordinary salt. Blood tests conducted aboard the USS *Argent* reveal that Mulder, Scully, and **Trondheim** have impossibly concentrated levels of salt in their bloodstream, causing serious cellular damage. ["Dod Kalm"]

THE SON: One of the vampiric trio of killers known as the Trinity. He is a violent sociopath who firmly believes that he is one of the undead who will live forever so long as he drinks human blood. He has bloodshot eyes, unwashed hair, and cuts and scratches on his face and arms. (One wonders how he ever got hired as a security guard.) When he is

exposed to sunlight in his jail cell, he shrivels up and dies horribly from severe epidermal burns. But later he turns up alive in the final confrontation with the Trinity. His real name is John, and **Kristen Kilar** originally met him in Chicago. When she left him, John and the other members of the Trinity began searching for her, committing murders along the way. ["3"]

SOONA, KENNETH: This may have been the real name of the hacker known as the **Thinker,** who stole the **MJ documents.** ["Anasazi"]

SOPHIE: A lowland gorilla at the **Fairfield Zoo** in Idaho. **Willa Ambrose** is fighting a lawsuit with the **Malawi** government, which wants the gorilla back. Ambrose rescued Sophie from a North American customs house ten years earlier and raised the ape herself, teaching her sign language. Sophie can "speak" six hundred words in sign language and understands a thousand. ["Fearful Symmetry"]

658 SOUTH HUDSON AVENUE #23: The Cleveland address of **Ellen Kaminski,** where **Virgil Incanto** meets his fate. ["2Shy"]

SPENCER, JIM: Venango County sheriff investigating the sudden spate of homicides in **Franklin, Pennsylvania.** ["Blood"]

SPERANZA, JOHN: A prisoner at **Eastpoint State Penitentiary.** He believes **"Neech" Manley** was reincarnated, and claims to have seen him after his death. ["The List"]

SPILLER, NANCY: A forensics instructor at the FBI academy, secretly nicknamed "The Iron Maiden" by her students. Organizes the team to investigate the murder of **Benjamin Drake,** which includes the ill-fated special agent **Jerry Lamana.** ["Ghost in the Machine"]

SPINNEY, DOUG: A "monkey wrencher," a radical environmentalist who drives spikes into trees and sabotages logging equipment. ["Darkness Falls"]

SPITZ, BOB: The high school principal in Comity. He shows up at the funeral of **Jay DeBoom** ranting and raving about how they all have to put a stop to these Satanic murders. ["Syzygy"]

SPITZ, DR. JOEL: Hypnotist who regresses **Michelle Bishop.** ["Born Again"]

SPONTANEOUS HUMAN COMBUSTION: A rare phenomenon in which a human body is quickly oxidized without any heat, leaving a pile of ashes without burning anything else in the vicinity. Mulder has a dozen or more case files on this phenomenon, but has never encountered an instance of it himself, although he considers it a possibility in the case of **Patrick Newirth.** ["Soft Light"]

SPREE KILLING: The type of murder committed in a public place in which the killer has a complete disregard for personal safety or anonymity. A number of such killings occur in a short period of time in **Franklin, Pennsylvania.** ["Blood"]

51 STANHOPE: FBI agent **Jack Willis**'s address in Washington, D.C. ["Lazarus"]

STANS, LT. COL. VICTOR: A veteran of recent wars with an exemplary record who tries repeatedly to kill himself in order to escape the psychic torment inflicted on him by **Sgt. "Rappo" Trimble.** He almost succeeds by scalding himself to death in an overheated hydrotherapy tub. Although horribly burned, he later manages to kill Trimble in his hospital bed. ["The Walk"]

STARBUCK: **William Scully**'s pet name for his daughter Dana, taken from a character in Herman Melville's *Moby Dick.*

STATE FORENSIC LABORATORY, HAMILTON COUNTY, OHIO: When **Owen Lee Jarvis** is murdered, the burn marks on his neck are in the form of a hand, and fingerprints are lifted from that mark here. The fingerprints are of **Simon Gates.** ["Revelations"]

STEFFEN, JOANNE: A friend and neighbor of **Ellen Kaminski**'s who advises her not to go out with her Internet pen pal after she receives an FBI alert on her computer screen. ["2Shy"]

STEFOFF: One of the phony names used by Mulder and Scully to get inside a complex where an E.B.E. (extraterrestrial biological entity) is apparently being held. ["E.B.E."]

STEVE: One of two prisoners at the **Cumberland State Correctional Facility** who use the confusion surrounding the death of **Bobby Torrence** to escape in a laundry cart. They hijack a family's motorhome to make their getaway, killing the father in the process. Steve dies of *F. Emasculata* infection at the home of his cellmate **Paul**'s girlfriend, **Elizabeth,** but not before infecting her as well. ["F. Emasculata"]

STEVENS, JERRY: One of the four teens who uses an occult book that summons a demon,

Azazel, which kills him and cuts his heart and eyes out. His body is displayed according to the rites of Azazel. ["Die Hand Die Verletzt"]

STEVESTON, MASSACHU-SETTS: Mulder traces the first of a series of murders here, where a labor organizer is found dead. The case leads him to investigate a religious group called the **Kindred** who live nearby. ["Genderbender"]

STIGMATA: Bleeding wounds that mimic those of Christ when his hands and feet were nailed to the cross, considered a sign from God bestowed upon the righteous. The **Rev. Finley** displays stigmata shortly before he is murdered, but in his case they were fake. According to Christian mythology, there are twelve true stigmatics in the world at any one time, representing the original twelve apostles. ["Revelations"]

STODIE, MRS.: The social worker who runs the Heritage Halfway House for the mentally retarded where **Roland Fuller** lives. ["Roland"]

STONER: He and his friend **Chick** witness the cockroach attack on **Dude**. ["War of the Coprophages"] He and Chick also turn up at **Heuvelmans Lake** in time to see the man called **Snorkel Dude** get pulled underwater by a myste-

rious creature. All Stoner wanted to do was find the kind of toad that produces a hallucinogen that you can lick off its back. ["Quagmire"]

STRIKER'S COVE: In **Heuvelmans Lake.** ["Quagmire"]

STROMAN, DR. HENRY: A psychiatrist called down from the District of Columbia to observe the case of **Joseph Patnik** at the Frederick County Psychiatric Hospital in **Braddock Heights, Maryland.** He's actually part of the conspiracy that is causing people to act insanely. Mulder traces Stroman to a local house, where he finds him and the Cable Man dead — killed by **X.** It turns out that the name the man was using isn't his own, as the real Dr. Henry Stroman died in 1978 in Falls Church, Virginia. ["Wetwired"]

STRUGHOLD MINE: The location of ultra-secret government files dealing with alien experiments. The files for 1964 include one for Dana Katherine Scully, complete with a recent tissue sample. The file for **Samantha Mulder** was originally in Fox Mulder's name, but his name has been covered by a label bearing hers. Aliens inhabit some areas of this vast under-

ground complex, but may have been evacuated by the UFO Mulder sighted there. The files may have been relocated since Mulder and Scully visited there. ["Paper Clip"]

SUCCUBUS: A female spirit that visits men in the night, sometimes in the form of an old woman. **Walter Skinner** has been experiencing a recurring dream in which he's confronted by an old woman. ["Avatar"]

SUITED MAN: One of **Alex Krycek**'s accomplices, seen lurking around **Melissa Scully**'s hospital room. ["Paper Clip"]

SUITLAND, VIRGINIA: Where **Jeremiah Smith** lives. ["Talitha Cumi"]

SULLIVAN, JUDGE: One of the judges at the sanity hearing for **Eugene Tooms.** ["Tooms"]

SUMMERFIELD, BRENDA JAYCEE: A student at Grover Cleveland Alexander High School in Comity and the girlfriend of **Scott Simmons.** At the birthday party for **Terri Roberts** and **Margi Kleinjan,** she is killed by flying glass from a broken mirror. ["Syzygy"]

SUMMERS, JIM: A nineteen-year-old student at Jackson University in North Carolina. He and his girlfriend **Liz Hawley** are kidnapped and tortured by **Lucas Jackson**

Henry. Summers is rescued by the FBI at the **Blue Devil Brewery.** ["Beyond the Sea"]

SUN, LINDA: A Memphis murder victim of the vampiric Trinity. The fact that her name is Sun (a soundalike for "son") helps to link her murder to the Trinity killers. ["3"]

SURNOW, RONALD: Aeronautical scientist who works at the **Mahan Propulsion Laboratory.** For four years he's been working on a project to crack Mach 15. He is killed when **Roland Fuller** locks him in a wind tunnel and turns on the jet engine inside it, the second scientist on the project to die within six months. ["Roland"]

SWAIM, JEFFREY: The real name of **Dr. Blockhead.** ["Humbug"]

SWASTIKA: An ancient symbol of great power used by many cultures, including China and India, before it became associated with the Nazis in this century. **Golda** and the **Calusari** use a reverse swastika with four dots between its arms as a protective talisman when dealing with the possession of **Charlie Holvey.** ["The Calusari"]

SWENSON, KAREN: A victim of the mysterious killings in **Bellefleur, Oregon,** which have targeted certain members of the high school class of '89. [Pilot]

[T]

TABER, GARY: A forty-two-year-old real estate agent who is inside an elevator when he believes that its digital display is telling him there is no air. Finally the digital display says, "KILL 'EM ALL," so he kills four people who are in the elevator with him, and then a security guard kills him. Mulder finds a greenish-yellow residue under Taber's fingernail. ["Blood"]

TABERNACLE OF TERROR: **Hepcat Helm**'s description of the funhouse he operates. ["Humbug"]

TACOMA, WASHINGTON: Mulder takes a commercial flight there en route to **Deadhorse, Alaska.** ["End Game"]

TAKEO, KAZUO: Supposedly a high-ranking Japanese diplomat whom Mulder catches at the scene of a murder. He is assassinated in Washington, D.C., along Embassy Row by a red-haired man (see **Malcolm Gerlach**). Takeo's body is found floating in the C&O Canal (see also **"Rat-Tail Productions"**). ["Nisei"]

TALAPUS: A ship photographed by a satellite. The picture is found by Mulder in the leather satchel taken from a Japanese man who attempts to flee a murder scene. The *Talapus* is a salvage ship from San Diego that had been searching for a sunken World War II Japanese submarine. The sub was supposedly carrying a cargo of gold bullion. The satellite photos track the ship through the Panama Canal to the naval shipyard at Newport News, Virginia, where the name has been obliterated and it has been hidden in plain sight at dockside. Mulder sneaks aboard, only to see cars with black-suited soldiers arrive outside; they begin to board the ship. Mulder has to leap off the ship before he has a chance to search it. But in a nearby warehouse he discovers what appears to be a crashed UFO, which is what he thinks the *Talapus* recovered. ["Nisei"]

TALBOT, DET.: He brings **Eugene Tooms** to the emergency room after finding him beaten up and unconscious out on the street somewhere. Tooms tells Talbot that Mulder was his assailant. ["Tooms"]

TANAKA, PETER: Systems analyst on the **Cascade Volcano Research Team.** He is infected with a subterranean organism, which manifests as a six-inch spike bursting from his throat, followed by sand spilling from the wound. ["Firewalker"]

TAPIA, DONALD "DEKE": The U.S. marshal in charge of the pursuit of the two prisoners who have escaped from the **Cumberland State Correctional Facility.** He grudgingly accepts Mulder's assistance in the case, but suspects him when mysterious decontamination-suited men carry away a key witness. ["F. Emasculata"]

TAROT DEALER: A male professional psychic murdered by the **Puppet.** In his rush to meet **Clyde Bruckman,** the killer neglects to remove this victim's eyes (although he does leave a salad fork in his left eye). ["Clyde Bruckman's Final Repose"]

TASHMOO FEDERAL CORRECTIONAL FACILITY: In Pennsylvania. **John Barnett** was a prisoner here, as is **Joe Crandall; Dr. Joe Ridley** served as a prison physician there until 1989, when he vanished to continue his research in Mexico and Belize. ["Young at Heart"]

TASSEOGRAPHY: The art of divining the future by reading tea leaves. Practiced by the **Doll Collector.** ["Clyde Bruckman's Final Repose"]

TAYLOR, CORP. BRYCE: The officer stationed at the U.S. Space Surveillance Center who alerts **Col. Henderson** to a UFO sighting. He orders **Karen Koretz** to file a report but is countermanded by Henderson. ["Fallen Angel"]

TAYLOR RECITAL HALL: In Washington, D.C., where a friend of Scully's has a cello recital. **John Barnett** finds out about it from Scully's answering machine and disguises himself as a piano tuner in order to kill Scully there, unaware that the FBI knows he is there. ["Young at Heart"]

TEAGUE, STEVEN: A "monkey wrencher," a radical environmentalist who drives spikes into trees and sabotages logging equipment. He is an early victim of the ancient wood mites that are released by loggers who illegally cut down an old-growth tree. ["Darkness Falls"]

TED'S BAIT & TACKLE: Mulder and Scully stop here upon arrival at **Heuvelmans Lake,** where Mulder suspects that **Big Blue,** the Southern Serpent, may be responsible for some human disappearances. The owner of this shop, **Ted Bertram,** is a huge Big Blue fan, although he's never actually seen it. ["Quagmire"]

TEE-TOTALLERS: A golf driving range with a too-cute name, where **Robert Modell** leads Mulder and Scully. When Agent **Collins** apprehends him there, Modell wills the agent to douse himself with gasoline and light it. ["Pusher"]

TEGRETOL: A prescription drug that prevents seizures caused by epilepsy. Scully finds a bottle in **Robert Modell**'s medicine cabinet. ["Pusher"]

TELLER, JOHN: An officer of the Johnston County, Oklahoma, sheriff's office. He insists that nothing unusual is happening in **Connerville.** Mulder's suggestion that **Darin Peter Oswald** has murdered people by creating lightning is the craziest thing Teller has ever heard in his life. This skepticism does nothing to protect him from being killed by Darin's wrath, although his death is ruled accidental. ["D.P.O."]

TEPES, VLAD: Also known as Vlad the Impaler of fifteenth-century Romania. This historical figure inspired Bram Stoker to create the character he called Dracula. The **Club Tepes** in Los Angeles is named after Vlad. Most of the people who frequent the after-sunset club are pale-skinned and wear black. ["3"]

TERLE, CATHERINE ANN: Her body is desecrated by **Donnie Pfaster** at the Montifiore Cemetery in Minneapolis. ["Irresistible"]

TERREL, LISA: A member of the Girl Scout troop that witnessed and photographed a UFO near Lake **Okobogee** in 1967. ["Conduit"]

THIBODEAUX, RUBY: She was raped by **Harry Cokely** in 1945 in Terrence, Nebraska (a one-hour drive from Aubrey, Missouri). He carved the word "sister" on her chest, but she survived and he was sent to prison. As a result of the rape, she bore a child she gave up for adoption. He grew up to become the father of **B. J. Morrow.** Thibodeaux now lives in Edmond, Nebraska. She has a scar on her face from where Cokely slashed her. ["Aubrey"]

THE THINKER: A new member of the **Lone Gunmen.** He's not seen because he's agoraphobic and will only communicate with people via computer. ["One Breath"] A radical anarchist and hacker, he has set up a random access code program to break in to Defense Department files, little suspecting he would ever succeed. Fearing for his life, he arranges to pass a tape of the **MJ documents** on to

Mulder, and is later captured by a black ops unit. His real name may have been Kenneth Soona. ["Anasazi"]

THOMAS: An FBI agent, first name unknown, present when **Liz Hawley** identifies **Lucas Henry**'s photograph. ["Beyond the Sea"]

THOMAS, GERD: The peeping Tom. He formerly ran a day care center. He knew about **Dr. Larson**'s tests and believed that Larson had turned the children into monsters. Larson was also using Thomas to inoculate cattle with alien DNA. ["Red Museum"]

THOMPSON, MIKE: The detective in charge of investigating the Atlantic City murders of several homeless men. He resents the FBI's intrusion, but with good reason: he knows what's behind the murders, and is out to cover it up in order to protect local tourism. ["The Jersey Devil"]

TIERNAN, MERV: An orderly at the **Excelsis Dei Convalescent Home.** He is lured up to the roof and when he leans out a window is pushed and falls to his death. Traces of ibotenic acid, a powerful hallucinogen, are found in his body. ["Excelsis Dei"]

TILDESKAN: A port town in Norway; Mulder and Scully

meet **Capt. Henry Trondheim** in a bar there and convince him to take them to find the USS **Argent.** ["Dod Kalm"]

TILESTON, VIRGINIA: Scully takes the four remaining **Gregors** to the federal stockade here for protection, but they are killed by the **Pilot** posing as a federal marshal. ["Colony"]

TILLMAN, LT. BRIAN: Of the Aubrey, Missouri, police. He is having an affair with Det. **B. J. Morrow.** ["Aubrey"]

TIPPY, MR.: The pet dog whose bones are found in an old medical bag buried in a back yard. There is nothing sinister about this, as it turns out (see **Dr. Richard Godfrey**). ["Syzygy"]

TOEWS, JACKSON: **Donnie Pfaster**'s supervisor at the **Janelli-Heller Funeral Home.** ["Irresistible"]

TOOMS, EUGENE VICTOR: Although he appears to be in his early thirties, he is some sort of genetic mutant who has lived a great deal longer; the first known record of him is in the 1903 census. He lives at 66 **Exeter Street,** and records show a Eugene Tooms has lived at that address since 1903. A serial killer who has committed five homicides in Baltimore every thirty years beginning in 1903, Tooms cuts out the liver from his victim and consumes it. He also takes a small trophy from each victim. He can elongate and contort his body into inhuman proportions in order to crawl through seemingly impossibly small spaces. Eleven-inch-long fingerprints were found at seven of the nineteen crime scenes. In modern times he has worked for the Baltimore County Animal Shelter. After making his fifth present-day kill, he builds a nest for his thirty-year hibernation underneath the escalator at the new mall built at 66 Exeter. Mulder finds the nest and Tooms attacks and tries to kill him, but Mulder escapes and turns on the escalator, which catches Tooms and pulls him into its gears, crushing him to death. ["Squeeze"; "Tooms"] While investigating the locked-room disappearance of businessman **Patrick Newirth,** Mulder checks a heat vent, obviously thinking of Tooms or someone like him as a possible suspect. ["Soft Light"]

TORONTO, CANADA: The ultimate destination of the escaped convict **Paul.** He never gets there. ["F. Emasculata"]

TORRENCE, BOBBY: A prisoner at the **Cumberland State Correctional Facility** in Virginia who receives a package originally addressed to **Dr. Robert Torrence.** It contains a pig's leg, wrapped in a Spanish-language newspaper, that is infected with larvae of the *F. Emasculata* insect. Bobby Torrence is infected as a result, and dies some time thereafter; his body is incinerated. ["F. Emasculata"]

TORRENCE, DR. ROBERT: A scientist involved in the **Biodiversity Project** who, while in the field, succumbs to the parasite that lives in the insect *Faciphaga Emasculata.* ["F. Emasculata"]

TOWNSEND, WISCONSIN: A small town whose twelve thousand inhabitants are evacuated when an alien spacecraft crashes into the woods nearby. The government explains this action with a fictional toxic train spill, even though there is no railway nearby. When Scully uses her clearance to get to the truth, she discovers that a Libyan jet with a nuclear warhead is the real cause for the crisis — but this is just another level of misinformation. The military is unable to capture the invisible alien pilot, whose own mission is centered on **Max Fenig.** ["Fallen Angel"]

TOWNSEND YMCA: The federal government commandeers this building to use as a relief center for evacuees during **Operation Falcon.** ["Fallen Angel"]

TOW-TRUCK DRIVER: He is looking for Gary Mosier when he stops to talk to **Carl Wade,** whose car has broken down by the side of the road. But Wade becomes irate and warns the driver to leave him alone. ["Oubliette"]

TRAIN CAR: The site of a mysterious experiment. In an operating theater inside it, a body is operated on by four Japanese doctors, who draw a green fluid out of it. In the middle of the procedure, black-garbed soldiers burst in and shoot the doctors. Then they put the gray alien corpse into a body bag (see also **Knoxville, Tennessee**). ["Nisei"]

TRAVEL TIME TRAVEL AGENCY: In Richmond, Virginia. Because he could not remember where he was abducted, **Duane Barry** stops here with his hostage, **Dr. Hakkie,** in order to get directions, only to take three employees hostage as well. ["Duane Barry"]

TREGO INDIAN RESERVATION: In Browning, Montana. They are having a property line fight with rancher **Jim**

Parker, plus a nagging problem with werewolves. ["Shapes"]

TREPKOS, DANIEL: Volcanologist who invented the robot named **Firewalker.** His intent was to find out how the Earth was created by exploring the fire where it all began. ["Firewalker"]

TRIMBLE, SGT. LEONARD "RAPPO": A quadruple amputee at the **Fort Evanston** military hospital, wounded by friendly fire during the Gulf War. A bitter young man who blames his fellow soldiers and their commanding officers for his condition, he uses his powers of astral projection to take vengeance on them. He is smothered to death by **Lt. Col. Victor Stans** while his spirit is out of his body. ["The Walk"]

TRINITY KILLERS: X-File number X256933VW. A trio of vampiric killers who call themselves the **Father,** the **Son,** and the **Unholy Spirit.** They have committed murders across the United States. ["3"]

TROITSKY, DR. KIP: Astronomer who works at the U.S. Naval Observatory in Washington, D.C. ["Little Green Men"]

TRONDHEIM, HENRY: American sea captain who relocated to Norway, presumably his ancestral home, to pursue a fishing career. He tells Mulder and Scully of the ancient Norse legends about a stone from the sky falling into the sea. Trapped on the USS *Argent* when his boat, the *Zeal,* is stolen, Trondheim becomes so desperate to survive that he is willing to sacrifice the lives of Scully and Mulder. He drowns when the *Argent*'s outer hull is breached and flooded with freezing sea water. ["Dod Kalm"]

TRUITT, JOHN: County coroner in **Bellefleur, Oregon**. [Pilot]

TRUMAN, MATT: FBI photo analysis specialist. ["Roland"]

TRUSTNO1: The secret password Mulder uses on the files in his personal computer at home. ["Little Green Men"]

THE TRUTH ABOUT ALIENS: Title of a manuscript written by **Roky Crikenson** in screenplay format. ["Jose Chung's *From Outer Space*"]

TSKANY, CHARLEY: The sheriff in Browning, Montana. He supports the Indians and their beliefs, since he is the Native American tribal law for the **Trego Indian reservation.** He calls Mulder "Running Fox" and "Sneaky Fox." ["Shapes"]

TURBELLARIA: A flatworm, or fluke. During an autopsy Scully removes a twelve-inch fluke from the body of a man found in a sewer in Newark, New Jersey. It had attached itself to the bile duct and was feeding off the liver. It attaches itself with a scolex, a suckerlike mouth with four hooking spikes. A carnivorous scavenger, some species depend on using more than one host to complete their life cycle. ["The Host"]

TWENTY-FIRST CENTURY RECYCLING PLANT: In Jerusalem, Ohio. **Simon Gates** takes **Kevin Kryder** here to kill him. ["Revelations"]

2400 MOTEL: In **Braddock Heights, Maryland.** Mulder and Scully stay here when investigating a series of inexplicable murders committed by ordinary people. ["Wetwired"]

TWO GREY HILLS, NEW MEXICO: Home of **Albert** and **Eric Hosteen,** on the Navajo reservation in New Mexico. Eric finds an alien corpse nearby after an earthquake reveals its hiding place. ["Anasazi"]

TWO MEDICINE RANCH: **Jim Parker**'s ranch in Browning, Montana. ["Shapes"]

2SHY: The on-line alias **Virgil Incanto** uses to lure lonely women into his murderous trap. ["2Shy"]

TYNES, MRS.: Kevin Kryder's fifth-grade teacher at Ridgeway Elementary School in Loveland, Ohio. ["Revelations"]

TYSON: Sheriff Daniels's deputy. He comes to arrest Daniels for being involved in the death of **Samuel Hartley.** ["Miracle Man"]

TYVEK: A company that manufactures decontamination suits. ["F. Emasculata"]

[U]

ULLRICH, DR. JIM: The Florida state medical examiner who conducts an autopsy on the prison guard **Fornier** and finds Fornier's lungs filled with the larvae of the green bottle fly. ["The List"]

UNHOLY SPIRIT: One of the vampiric trio of killers. She is impaled on a large nail on a garage wall. Her body is destroyed when the house and garage are burned down. ["3"]

UNIT 53: A firefighter unit that suffers casualties when it encounters the alien crash near **Townsend, Wisconsin.** ["Fallen Angel"]

UNIVERSITY OF MARYLAND: Where Scully earned her medical degree, prior to her FBI training at Quantico. ["The Jersey Devil"] She and Mulder discuss near-death experiences with Dr. Raymond Varnes of UM's biology department. ["Lazarus"]

UNIVERSITY OF WASHINGTON MEDICAL CENTER: The Seattle hospital where **Lucy Householder** is taken when she suffers a spontaneous nosebleed. Mulder arrives there at 10:31 the morning after the kidnapping of **Amy Jacobs.** ["Oubliette"]

UPSHAW, DON: An orderly at the **Excelsis Dei Convalescent Home.** He disappears and his body is found in the basement, buried in a mushroom patch. ["Excelsis Dei"]

URANUS UNLIMITED: An investment firm that based its marketing plans on astrological forecasts. Owned by **Claude Dukenfield,** a victim of the **Puppet.** ["Clyde Bruckman's Final Repose"]

U.S. COAST GUARD HEAD-QUARTERS: Mulder goes there to inquire about the salvage ship **Talapus.** The Coast Guard had gone out to search it but were called back by the DEA. ["Nisei"]

USHER, GEORGE: A Baltimore businessman found murdered in his locked office. **Tooms**'s third victim in 1993 and the one that leads Mulder and Scully to the trail of the flexible killer. ["Squeeze"]

U.S. MEDICAL RESEARCH INSTITUTE OF INFECTIOUS DISEASES: When the pathologists who conduct the original autopsy on FBI agent **Barrett Weiss** become ill, the body is brought here for further examination in a secure, sterile environment. ["End Game"]

U.S. SPACE SURVEILLANCE CENTER: A top-secret military installation at Cheyenne Mountain, Colorado. Its monitors detected a possible alien craft entering Earth's atmosphere off the Connecticut coast and tracked it to the area of **Townsend, Wisconsin.** ["Fallen Angel"]

[V]

VACATION VILLAGE MOTORLODGE: Motel in Germantown, Maryland, where Scully hides out when she realizes that CIA agent **Chapel** is a threat. Chapel, a.k.a. the **Pilot,** follows her there disguised as Mulder and takes her hostage. ["Colony"]

VALADEO, DANNY: He tracks down the son of **Ruby Thibodeaux** for Scully and reveals that the child's adopted name was Raymond Morrow. ["Aubrey"]

VALLEE, MAJ. ROBERT: Phony Gray Alien #1. He is planning to abduct and interrogate **Harold Lamb** and **Chrissy Giorgio** when all of them are abducted by real space aliens. Vallee is later found and he dies from an abdominal wound. ["Jose Chung's *From Outer Space*"]

VALLEY WOODS HIGH SCHOOL: Where fifteen-year-

old **Amy Jacobs** is a student in Seattle. ["Oubliette"]

VANCE, LEONARD: The man **Samuel Hartley** raised from the dead in 1983. He then went to work for the **Rev. Hartley**'s **Miracle Ministry.** He hates how deformed he is and so to get revenge he starts killing people who come to be healed by Samuel. After Samuel is beaten to death in his jail cell, he appears to Vance and confronts him about the crimes. He forgives Vance, who then commits suicide by taking poison. ["Miracle Man"]

VANKIN: Co-author, with Whelan, of *50 Greatest Conspiracies of All Time,* a book read by the **Thinker.** ["Anasazi"]

VARNES, DR. RAYMOND: Chairman of the biology department at the **University of Maryland;** Mulder and Scully consult him about near-death experiences. ["Lazarus"]

VENABLE PLAZA HOTEL: In Boston. A party is being held there in honor of Lord and Lady **Marsden** when fire breaks out on the fourteenth floor where their children are sleeping. Their caretaker **Bob (Cecil L'ively)** rescues them. ["Fire"]

VENANGO COUNTY: The location of **Franklin, Pennsylvania,** the site of sev-

eral unexplained homicides. ["Blood"]

VIBUTI: A Sanskrit term meaning "holy ash," a mysterious substance that contains neither organic or inorganic material. According to **Chuck Burk,** it is produced when spirit beings are present, or when a person's psychic energy is transported from one place to another. It is found on several occasions at the **Holvey** home, always after an inexplicable occurrence or **Calusari** ritual. ["The Calusari"]

VIRTUA FIGHTER 2: The arcade game favored by **Darin Peter Oswald.** ["D.P.O."]

VITARIS, PAUL: Thirty-five-year-old black member of a witches' coven. He is killed by **Calgagni** while under the control of the demon. ["Die Hand Die Verletzt"]

VOSBERG: Member of the **Cascade Volcano Research Team** working at the California Institute of Technology in Pasadena. ["Firewalker"]

VOYAGER: The two spacecraft launched August 20 and September 5, 1977. The satellites contained messages which it was hoped could be interpreted by any extraterrestrial intelligence that might encounter them. These messages included recordings, the first of which is the *Brandenburg Concerto No. 2 in F* by Bach. ["Little Green Men"]

[W]

WADE, CARL: The assistant to the school photographer for Valley Woods High in Seattle. He is fired the day after the photo shoot. When he sees fifteen-year-old **Amy Jacobs** he is immediately attracted to her, in an unhealthy way. He has a darkroom in the small, windowless basement of his cabin near Easton, Washington. He creates a photo montage of himself and Amy, then he goes out and kidnaps the girl. He previously kidnapped an eight-year-old girl named **Lucy Householder** and kept her prisoner in his basement dungeon, or oubliette, for five years, until she escaped. He was never captured for that crime, but did later spend fifteen years in a mental institution due to a bipolar condition. He was released not long before he kidnapped Amy. By the time the FBI tracks him to his home, he has already fled with Amy. He is hunted down and shot to death by Mulder. ["Oubliette"]

WALDHEIM, KURT: UN Secretary General whose recorded voice was carried aboard the Voyager spacecraft. ["Little Green Men"]

WALK-INS: People who believe that other spirits can temporarily take possession of their bodies. ["Red Museum"]

WALLACE, CAROL: An ailing woman who dies minutes after **Samuel Hartley** tries to heal her with a laying on of hands. ["Miracle Man"]

WALLACE, FATHER THOMAS: A priest and a murder victim of the vampiric **Trinity.** The fact that he is a "father" helps to link him as a victim of the Trinity murders. ["3"]

WALLENBERG, STEVE: The FBI agent killed during the apprehension of **John Barnett** in 1989, he left behind a wife and two children. Mulder blamed himself for his death. ["Young at Heart"]

WALSH, CLAYTON: The fourth **Dudley, Arkansas,** resident to contract **Creutzfeldt-Jakob disease,** after **George Kearns, Paula Gray,** and an unknown truck driver. ["Our Town"]

WALTOS, DET.: He is investigating the murder of a nude woman found in **Walter Skinner**'s Washington, D.C., hotel room. He considers Skinner a suspect. ["Avatar"]

W.A.O.: The Wild Again Organization, an animal rights group opposed to keeping animals locked up in zoos. ["Fearful Symmetry"]

WASHINGTON COUNTY REGIONAL AIRPORT: A small-craft airport near **Lula Philips**'s hideout. Background noise of an airplane on her ransom phone call helps the FBI locate her general vicinity. ["Lazarus"]

WASHINGTON INSTITUTE OF TECHNOLOGY: Where the **Mahan Propulsion Laboratory** is located. ["Roland"]

WATERGATE HOTEL & OFFICE COMPLEX: Scully and Mulder meet secretly in the underground parking lot of this famous Washington, D.C., building. ["Little Green Men"]

WATERS, BERNADETTE: A woman listed in Mulder's files, who bore a small diamond-shaped scar behind her left ear, as did **Max Fenig.** Mulder believes her claim to be an abductee. ["Fallen Angel"]

WATKINS, DONNA: While jogging with her husband, Ted, this Greenwich, Connecticut, resident discovers **Teena Simmons** and the corpse of her father **Joel Simmons.** ["Eve"]

WATKINS, GINA: A clerk at the county hospital in **Townsend, Wisconsin.** She is unable to find any record that deputy sheriff **Jason Wright** had ever been a patient there. ["Fallen Angel"]

WATKINS, RICHARD: Part of the first X-file case in 1946. In the Pacific Northwest and in Browning, Montana, people were killed and ripped apart. When the killer was trapped and shot in Glacier National Park, the body of Watkins was found instead of the body of the animal they had cornered. It was believed that this wave of crimes had ended, but the mysterious murders erupted again in 1959, '64, '78, and '94. ["Shapes"]

WATKINS, TED: With his wife, Donna, finds the body of his neighbor **Joel Simmons,** sitting in a swing, drained of blood, with its lips cut off. ["Eve"]

WAYNESBURG, PENNSYLVANIA: Location of First Church of the Redemption, where the **Rev. Patrick Finley** is murdered by the Millennium Man **(Simon Gates).** ["Revelations"]

WEBSTER: CIA agent teamed up with CIA agent **Saunders** to investigate **HTG Industrial Technologies.** ["Shadows"]

WEISS, BARRETT: FBI special agent stationed in Syracuse, New York, who checks out **Dr. Aaron Baker** for Mulder but is killed by the **Pilot,** his body locked in the trunk of his car. The Pilot impersonates him when Mulder and Scully arrive on the scene. No cause of death could be found; when Scully reads Weiss's autopsy report, however, she learns that his blood was unnaturally clotted. ["Colony"] Further examinations at the **U.S. Medical Research Institute of Infectious Diseases** reveal an alien virus in his blood. ["End Game"]

WELL-MANICURED MAN: An older, high-ranking member of the **Elders,** who is suspicious of the **Cigarette-Smoking Man**'s claims that the **MJ** files DAT has been recovered. Calm, serene, and utterly Machiavellian, he makes CSM look like a street punk. He approaches Scully at **William Mulder**'s funeral, admits his involvement in events surrounding the DAT, and advises her that her life is in danger. His motives are not benevolent: he merely feels that her death would draw attention to him and his associates. He and a younger **Deep Throat,** CSM, and William Mulder can be seen in an old picture, circa 1973, found by Fox Mulder. ["The Blessing Way"] He calls CSM on the carpet after **Krycek** kills **Melissa Scully.**

Fox Mulder meets him for the first time at the late **Victor Klemper**'s greenhouse, where he offers hints about William Mulder's activities as a member of the intelligence community and suggests that Nazi scientists were involved in creating human–alien hybrids using physical materials recovered from the Roswell UFO crash in 1947. ["Paper Clip"] He meets with Mulder in Central Park after Mulder finds his secret phone number, and confirms that a UFO was downed by American pilots during the final days of World War II. ["Apocrypha"]

WELLS, MS.: An employee of the Fairfield County Social Services Hostel in Greenwich, Connecticut who takes care of **Teena Simmons** after her father's death. ["Eve"]

WERBER, DR. HEITZ: At the Oregon State Psychiatric Hospital, he examines **Billy Miles,** who confesses to having been abducted and controlled by a mysterious light. [Pilot] He conducted hypnotic regression therapy sessions with Mulder in 1989, heard by Scully on tapes in the X-File on the disappearance of **Samantha Mulder.** ["Conduit"]

WERNER: **Eugene Tooms**'s fourth victim in 1993, eviscerated and killed (in that order) in his suburban Baltimore home. ["Squeeze"]

WEST TISBURY, MASSACHU-SETTS: A town on Martha's Vineyard, where Mulder's father lives. ["Colony"]

WESTIN: FBI agent who takes part in the raid on **Lula Philips**'s hideout, disguised as a phone worker for cover. ["Lazarus"]

WHARTON, COL. JACOB: The Marine in command at the **Folkstone INS Processing Center,** in charge of supervising 12,000 refugees. He's killed by **Pierce Bauvais** but awakens in his coffin — buried alive. ["Fresh Bones"]

WHELAN: Co-author, with Vankin, of *50 Greatest Conspiracies of All Time,* a book read by the **Thinker.** ["Anasazi"]

WHITE, DET. ANGELA: She is investigating the strange deaths in Comity and tells Mulder and Scully what she knows. It is believed that the deaths are connected to a Satanic cult, but there is no hard evidence of this. ["Syzygy"]

WHITE, KATE: One of the four teens who use an occult book that summons a demon. ["Die Hand Die Verletzt"]

WHITE "SAMANTHA": An alien clone in a white lab coat

whom Mulder meets at the **Women's Health Services Center** in Rockville, Maryland. This clone introduces Mulder to the **original "Samantha"** alien from whom she and the others were cloned; they trick Mulder into helping them in the hope he would protect the original. White "Samantha" is killed by the **Pilot,** along with the rest of the "Samantha" clones. ["End Game"]

WHITING INSTITUTE: A highly secure medical facility that houses **Eve Six. Teena Simmons** and **Cindy Reardon** are taken there after Mulder apprehends them for the murders of their "fathers" and **Dr. Sally Kendrick.** ["Eve"]

WICCA: The religion of modern witches. They are occult, but they do not practice black magic. ["Die Hand Die Verletzt"]

WICHITA, KANSAS: Scully traces the package that infected **Bobby Torrence** to the address of **Pinck Pharmaceuticals** in this city. ["F. Emasculata"]

WILCZEK, BRAD: Visionary founder of the Eurisko Corporation. A computer genius in the Steve Wozniak rather than the Bill Gates vein. Forced out by CEO **Benjamin**

Drake (with a hefty payoff of about $400 million). Idealistic, precocious, and manipulative, he was opposed to any use of Eurisko's software in military or governmental applications. He falsely confesses to murdering Drake and FBI agent **Jerry Lamana** in order to protect the artificial intelligence of the COS (central operating system) in the **Eurisko Building.** Later helps Mulder destroy the system, but is "disappeared" by the government. According to **Deep Throat,** Wilczek is being "persuaded" to yield his AI knowledge to the military. ["Ghost in the Machine"]

WILKINS: An intensive care nurse for Scully at the Northeast Georgetown Medical Center. ["One Breath"]

WILLIG, HENRY: One of the experimental subjects of **Dr. Saul Grissom**'s Vietnam-era experiments in sleep deprivation. He was in the Marines in 1970 and was assigned to Special Force and Recon Squad J-7. Of the thirteen original squad members, he is one of only two survivors. He is killed by one of **Augustus Cole**'s unusual hallucinations, but Willig welcomes death after twenty-four years without sleep. ["Sleepless"]

WILLIS, JACK: An older, diabetic FBI agent, born in 1955, who was one of Scully's instructors at the FBI academy and shares her birthday, February 23. Willis and Scully dated for about a year, but she broke it off because he was too intense about his work. Assigned to a series of bank robberies by the violent-crimes section, Willis becomes almost obsessed with his subjects and he is furious at the relationship between **Warren Dupre** and **Lula Philips,** even expressing jealousy at their fatalistically romantic relationship. After Dupre shoots him during the **Maryland Marine Bank** robbery, Willis is technically dead for thirteen minutes before being revived. After this he begins to display erratic behavior that includes chopping three fingers off Dupre's corpse, becoming left-handed, kidnapping Scully, declaring his love for Lula Philips, and forgetting such details as his own birthday and the fact that he is diabetic. One explanation is that the shock of his experience, combined with his obsession with Dupre and Philips, caused him to believe Dupre's spirit is now living in his body. (Mulder is inclined to believe that this is not a delusion.) Willis dies of apparent hyperglycemia (too much blood sugar) after killing Philips. ["Lazarus"]

WILMER, LT. TERRY: The sole survivor of a U.S. Navy submarine (presumably the USS *Allegiance*) stranded in Arctic ice. He claims to have hidden from the **Pilot** by concealing himself under the body of a dead chief petty officer. After Mulder handcuffs Wilmer to himself, Wilmer reveals that he is really the **Pilot** in disguise. ["End Game"]

WILMORE, CRAIG: A student at Grover Cleveland Alexander High School in Comity. He's mentioned in passing by **Terri Roberts.** ["Syzygy"]

WINDLESHAM, ENGLAND: Site of Sir Arthur Conan Doyle's tomb. Mulder had a tryst with **Phoebe Green** there, apparently on the tomb itself, when they were students at Oxford. ["Fire"]

WINN, MS.: **Robert Dorland**'s assistant. When she gives **Lauren Kyte** a hard time, a mysterious force causes her hot coffee to spill into her lap. ["Shadows"]

WINSTON: The guard at the **Cumberland State Correctional Facility** in Virginia who delivers **Bobby Torrence**'s last package to him. ["F. Emasculata"]

WINSTON, BONNIE: A member of the Girl Scout troop that witnessed and photographed a UFO near **Lake Okobogee** in 1967. ["Conduit"]

WINTER, LARRY: The supervisor for Venango County, Pennsylvania. ["Blood"]

WINTERS, DR.: The veterinarian who performs the autopsy on **Mona Wustner**'s dog. He determines that the dog has died of poisoning by eating a rat that had eaten strychnine. ["Teso dos Bichos"]

WITCH HUNT: A HISTORY OF THE OCCULT IN AMERICA: The book checked out by **Dave Duran.** Reading from it at a Black Mass altar in Milford Haven, New Hampshire, summons a demon. ["Die Hand Die Verletzt"]

WITCH'S PEGS: Three-pronged stakes driven into the ground to ward off evil spirits in the Ozarks, dismissed by **Sheriff Tom Arens** as a leftover superstition. ["Our Town"]

WITHERS, JACK: Deputy sheriff of Sioux City, Iowa, who favors a mundane explanation for **Ruby Morris**'s disappearance, and considers her mother to be a flake. Investigates the murder of **Greg Randall.** ["Conduit"]

WOLF INDUSTRIES: A company that supplies the CIA with surveillance equipment. **Max Fenig** owns a Wolf's Ear 2000, a sort of souped-up police scanner that can pick up over a hundred channels per second. ["Fallen Angel"]

WOMEN'S CARE FAMILY SERVICES AND CLINIC: The abortion clinic where **Dr. Landon Prince** was killed. The authorities initially suspected right-wing religious extremists in the case, not realizing it was the work of an extraterrestrial assassin. ["Colony"]

WOMEN'S HEALTH SERVICES CENTER: The abortion clinic in Rockville, Maryland, where Mulder encounters more "Samantha" clones and discovers that he has been used. Later burned to the ground by the **Pilot.** ["End Game"]

WONG, CHERYL: A woman listed in Mulder's files, who bore a small diamond-shaped scar behind her left ear, as did **Max Fenig.** Mulder believes her claim to be an abductee. ["Fallen Angel"]

WOOSLEY, SCOTT: A Boy Scout leader who disappeared at **Heuvelmans Lake** in Georgia. All that's ever found of him is his lower torso, which still has his wallet in the back

pocket. Did **Big Blue** chow down on a man whose motto was "Be prepared?" ["Quagmire"]

WORKMAN, JENNIFER: **Lauren Mackalvey**'s roommate. She reveals that Lauren met her final date over the Internet, and gives Mulder copies of **2Shy**'s letters. Quotations from rare sixteenth-century Italian poetry in the letters help locate the killer, who must be a scholar with access to exclusive academic libraries. ["2Shy"]

WORMHOLES: Theoretical portals where matter's interaction with time is radically sped up or slowed down. Mulder believes they were used in the **Philadelphia Experiment** in 1944, and erroneously thinks they might explain the disappearance of the USS **Argent** and the accelerated aging of **Lt. Richard Harper.** ["Dod Kalm"]

"WOW" SIGNAL: In August 1977, astronomer **Jerry Ehman** found a transmission of apparent extraterrestrial origin on a printout and called it a "wow" signal. This was a signal thirty times stronger than galactic background noise. It came through on a frequency not used by terrestrial satellites. ["Little Green Men"]

WRIGHT, JASON: A young sheriff's deputy in **Townsend, Wisconsin,** who is severely burned by a bright light while investigating what appeared to be a forest fire near the town. He dies of his injuries. ["Fallen Angel"]

WRIGHT, BELINDA: The widow of Jason Wright. The government refuses to release his body to her and threatens to cut off his pension if she protests. She has a three-year-old son. ["Fallen Angel"]

WUSTNER, MONA: A graduate student working with Ecuadoran artifacts at the Boston Museum of Natural History whose death is part of a series of unsolved murders revolving around the **Amaru** Urn. ["Teso dos Bichos"]

WYATT, MRS.: She is working at the blood drive table at a Franklin, Pennsylvania, department store. ["Blood"]

WYSNECKI, MARGARET: A sixty-six-year-old widow, retired from the **Laramie Tobacco** company, who disappears in Richmond, Virginia, presumably a victim of **Chester Ray Banton**'s shadow. ["Soft Light"]

[X]

X, MR.: A middle-aged black man, he first appears in "The

Host" as Mulder's new inside contact at the FBI, his new **Deep Throat.** He is a shadowy character who is working for the **Cigarette-Smoking Man** but is trying to undermine his activities. ["Wetwired"] Warns Mulder that he could not find out what he needed to know about the **Duane Barry** case. Mulder suspects that X knows Scully's whereabouts. ["Ascension"] Reveals that a U.S. Navy attack fleet is en route to destroy the **Pilot** and his spacecraft. Angered when Scully signals him at Mulder's apartment, he plays dumb and refuses to tell Scully where Mulder was going but reluctantly gives Assistant Director **Skinner** this information after a less than friendly discussion. ["End Game"] Denies all knowledge of **Chester Ray Banton** when Mulder turns to him for help, only to orchestrate an attempted abduction of Banton that leaves two of X's subordinates reduced to burn marks on the floor of Banton's hospital room. X later kills **Dr. Christopher Davey** at the **Polarity Magnetics** lab and delivers Banton to an unknown government agency for study. ["Soft Light"] X apparently did not respond to Mulder's signal — a taped X in his window lit

from within — during the events surrounding the theft of the **MJ documents.** ["Anasazi"]

[Y]

YAJE: Pronounced "YAH-hay." A vine used to prepare hallucinogenic potions by shamans in Ecuador. **Dr. Alonso Bilac** was taking large doses during a series of murders at the Boston Museum of Natural History, perhaps to open himself up to possession by a jaguar spirit. ["Teso dos Bichos"]

YALOFF PSYCHIATRIC HOSPITAL: In Piedmont, Virginia. Mulder and Scully take **Chester Ray Banton** there for safekeeping. Mulder is unwise enough to mention Banton's location to **X,** resulting in an ill-fated abduction attempt. ["Soft Light"]

YAMAGUCHI, DR.: The pathologist who does the autopsy on **Charlie Morris.** He notes that Morris was drowned in sea water. ["Born Again"]

YANI: The Greek janitor in **George Usher**'s office building. He doesn't clean Usher's office the night Usher is killed. ["Squeeze"]

YAPPI, THE STUPENDOUS: A publicity-hungry psychic whose abilities are dubious. He accuses Mulder of being a skeptic

who is sending out "negative energy" and insists that Mulder leave the scene of the **Doll Collector**'s murder. His predictions are very vague (the killer "is aged seventeen to thirty-four and may or may not have a beard"), but he does seem able to read a rude thought in Mulder's mind. Yappi's predictions are published in the *Midnight Inquisitor.* Those convinced of his abilities can make use of them, for a price, by calling 1-900-555-YAPP. ["Clyde Bruckman's Final Repose"] He is the narrator on part of the "alien autopsy" video. ["Jose Chung's *From Outer Space*"]

YUNG, DAVID: An acquaintance of **Kristen Kilar**'s. Mulder follows him but is knocked out and is thus unable to prevent him from being attacked and killed by the **Father** and the **Unholy Spirit.**

[Z]

ZAMA, DR. SHIRO: The name adopted by **Dr. Ishimaru.** He is traveling incognito on a train boarded by Mulder and is later killed in a restroom by the redhaired man (**Malcolm Gerlach).** Ishimaru was involved in experimenting on humans, and he is the one who put the monitoring chip implant in Scully's neck. Other people, who believed wrongly that they were abducted by aliens, have also been taken to train cars where Ishimaru conducted his experiments on them. ["731"]

ZEAL: **Henry Trondheim**'s boat, a fifty-ton trawler with double hulls. It is stolen by members of the pirate whaler **Olafssen**'s crew, leaving Mulder, Scully, Trondheim, and **Olafssen** stranded on the USS *Argent*. ["Dod Kalm"]

ZELMA, MADAME: A fake gypsy psychic and palm reader. The **Puppet** consults her, hoping to find out the reasons for his actions. Then he kills her, gouging her eyes out with the shards of her crystal ball. **Clyde Bruckman** finds her body in the Dumpster outside his apartment building. ["Clyde Bruckman's Final Repose"]

ZENZOLA, DR. JO: At the Middlesex County Hospital in Sayreville, New Jersey, she examines a sewer worker who was attacked and briefly pulled underwater by some unseen creature that left a vicious wound on his back. The worker claims he has a bad taste in his mouth. Later the man is in

his shower when a large fluke exits his body through his mouth. ["The Host"]

ZEUS FABER: A U.S. Navy submarine, active at the end of World War II. Mulder discovers its name written on a chart on the *Piper Maru*, prompting Scully to visit a former crewman of the *Zeus*. At the end of the war, the *Zeus* was assigned to locate a downed bomber carrying a third A-bomb headed for Japan. This was a cover story; the real mission was to protect a downed UFO. ["Piper Maru"] An alien entity from the UFO possessed the captain, **Kyle Sanford,** but abandoned him when the sub was attacked by a Japanese destroyer. It survived beneath the sea for fifty years before using **Alex Krycek** to return to its craft, now hidden by the U.S. government. ["Apocrypha"]

ZEUS STORAGE: Located at 1616 Pandora Street in Maryland. It contains a secret lab that has five bodies suspended in huge liquid-filled cylinders. Experiments with extraterrestrial viruses are being conducted on humans. ["The Erlenmeyer Flask"]

ZINNZSER, STEVEN: A Mutual UFO Network (MUFON) member living in the **Allentown** area. He was murdered by **Kazuo Takeo** because Zinnzser intercepted a satellite transmission of an alien autopsy and had been selling the videotape of it through magazine ads. He operated under the name **Rat-Tail Productions.** ["Nisei"]

ZIRINKA: An astrologer in the city of **Comity.** The sign on her business reads ASTROLOGY, NUMEROLOGY, RUNES, READINGS. She reveals that the Earth is entering a planetary alignment with Mars, Mercury, and Uranus and states that she believes this is behind the strange things going on in Comity. Mars, Mercury, and Uranus come into conjunction once every eighty-four years, but this time Uranus is in the House of Aquarius. ["Syzygy"]

ZOE: A teenage girl who sneaks onto **Ellens Air Force Base** to watch mysterious lights in the sky; she and her boyfriend Emil help Mulder infiltrate the base. ["Deep Throat"]